Integrated Sustainable Design

Jón Kristinsson

Edited by Andy van den Dobbelsteen

Integrated Sustainable Design

Author: Jón Kristinsson
Editor: Andy van den Dobbelsteen
Editor of the Dutch book that formed the basis of this one: Riet Kristinsson-Reitsema

All images (photos, figures, graphs and tables) are by Jón Kristinsson, Riet Kristinsson-Reitsema or Andy van den Dobbelsteen, unless indicated otherwise.

Keywords: sustainable development, sustainability, integrated sustainable design, integrated design, sustainable design, sustainable building, autonomous building, energy-neutral building, zero-energy building, dwelling without central heating, minimum-energy dwellings, solar cavity dwellings, Villa Flora

Cover illustration: Villa Flora, designed by Jón Kristinsson
Cover design by Craig Martin, based on a photo by Marco Vellinga.

2012, Delft/Deventer, 312 pages

ISBN 9789052694085
Nur code 648 Bouwkunst, Architectuur

Published and distributed by Delftdigitalpress
info@delftdigitalpress.com

© 2012. All rights reserved.
Downloads are permitted only for private, non-commercial use.
No part of this publication may be reproduced or stored by any electronic or mechanical means (including photocopying, recording, data storage, and retrieval) or in any other form or language for commercial use without the written permission from the Publisher.

Sustainable is everything future generations want to inherit, use and maintain

Jón Kristinsson

TABLE OF CONTENTS

01	PROLOGUE		9
	Preface by Jón Kristinsson		10
	Preface by Riet Kristinsson-Reitsema		12
	Introduction by the editor		14
02	ENVIRONMENTAL PHILOSOPHY		17
	02.01	Sustainable building within an ecological system	18
		02.01.01 Analysis of the environmental system	19
		02.01.02 Climate change	23
		02.01.03 The changing world from a distance	24
		02.01.04 Our ecological footprint – the time factor	25
	02.02	Sustainable technology: the New Necessity	29
		02.02.01 The factor of 20	29
		02.02.02 Backcasting the sustainable future	31
03	THEORY ON INTEGRATED DESIGN		33
	03.01	How architects think	34
	03.02	A bridge between architecture and nature	36
	03.03	Insolation	38
	03.04	Examples of integrated designs	40
	03.05	The right building on the right spot	42
	03.06	Themes of sustainable building and living	44
		03.07.01 Theme 1: indoor climate	44
		03.07.02 Theme 2: soil, insolation, green and surface water	45
		03.07.03 Theme 3: transport	46
		03.07.04 Theme 4: construction and building materials	49
		03.07.05 Theme 5: energy	50
		03.07.06 Theme 6: potable water	50
		03.07.07 Theme 7: food	51
		03.07.08 Theme 8: waste	51
		03.07.09 Theme 9: social aspects	52
	03.08	Instance of a sustainable house	53

04	SMART ENERGY TECHNOLOGY		53
	04.01 Basic introduction to energy		54
		04.01.01 Energy in and around the house	54
		04.01.02 Exergy next to energy	56
	04.02 Thermal insulation		57
		04.02.01 Wrapping up the building	57
		04.02.02 Thermally insulating shutters	61
		04.02.03 Energetic renovation of 448 tenement flats, Schiedam (1989)	67
	04.03 Ventilation with heat recovery		72
		04.03.01 The Slootweg Unit	72
		04.03.02 The fine-wire heat exchanger	73
		04.03.03 The Breathing Window	77
		04.03.04 The Air-Mover	85
	04.04 Light		87
		04.04.01 Daylight and roof lights	87
		04.04.02 Parabolic roof shells	89
		04.04.03 Artificial lighting	90
	04.05 Free-cooling roofs		91
		04.05.01 The physical principle	91
		04.05.02 Sports complex with innovative ice-skating rink, Deventer (1989)	94
		04.05.03 Free-cooling roofs in desert areas	96
	04.06 Smart Skin		96
		04.06.01 Introduction	96
		04.06.02 How to make a translucent Smart Skin	97
		04.06.03 Every innovation creates a problem	98
		04.06.04 Heat storage in the ground	98
		04.06.05 The design of an experimental Smart Skin building	100
		04.06.06 Conclusion and discussion	101
		04.06.07 Follow-up	102
	04.07 Soil energy		103
		04.07.01 Introduction	103
		04.07.02 Hollow heat-exchanging foundation piles	104
		04.07.03 Deventer fire station (1990)	106
		04.07.04 Sustainable fire station, Soest (1998)	108
		04.07.05 Greijdanus, school of fresh air, Meppel (1990)	113
	04.08 Interseasonal heat storage		114
		04.08.01 Working principle	1144
		04.08.02 Beijum, Groningen (1982)	116

05	**TOWARDS ZERO-ENERGY BUILDINGS**		119
	05.01 Minimum-Energy Dwellings		120
	05.01.01	Energy saving in social housing through limited investment	120
	05.01.02	The Dwelling without Central Heating, a giant leap forward (1981)	121
	05.01.03	Minimum-Energy Dwellings, Schiedam (1984)	127
	05.01.04	30 years ahead of the Energy Performance Code	135
	05.02 Solar Cavity Wall Dwellings		137
	05.02.01	Background of the solar cavity	137
	05.02.02	Background of the solar garden	138
	05.02.03	1st generation Solar Cavity Wall Dwellings: Leiderdorp (1983)	141
	05.02.04	2nd generation: Drachten (1992)	145
	05.02.05	3rd generation: Ede (1995)	148
06	**INFRASTRUCTURE**		149
	06.01 Introduction		150
	06.02 A different approach to infrastructure		152
	06.02.01	Terrain analysis, soil and green	152
	06.02.02	'De Kersentuin', Leidsche Rijn district, Utrecht (2003)	153
	06.03 Water		157
	06.03.01	Water at all scale levels	157
	06.03.02	Integrated water management	159
	06.03.03	Waste water treatment	163
	06.03.04	Morrapark, Drachten (1990)	164
	06.04 Building in nuisance zones		166
	06.04.01	Manifesto 50/50, Midden-IJsselmonde, Rotterdam (1995)	167
	06.04.02	Sustainable playgroups in a noise barrier, Amersfoort (1996)	170
	06.04.03	Study of noise barrier dwellings, Ede (1998)	172
	06.04.04	Railtrack-view dwellings, Elst (1998-2002)	175
	06.05 Transportation		177
	06.05.01	The necessity of a sustainable collective transport mode	177
	06.05.02	Future commuter traffic – individual/collective	180
	06.05.03	Sustainable individual/collective transport, Zwolle (2000)	181

07	NEW SUSTAINABLE URBANISM		183
	07.01	Introduction	184
	07.02	History	186
		07.02.01 Early civilisation	186
		07.02.02 Cities and energy	188
		07.02.03 Cities and water	189
		07.02.04 Monofunctionality of industrial and commercial districts	190
	07.03	The sustainable city	191
		07.03.01 The sustainable city, backcasted from 2048	191
		07.03.02 The two urban structures: water and roads	191
		07.03.03 Light Urbanism	192
		07.03.04 Drachten urban border vision(1994)	195
	07.04	Zonneterp, the Greenhouse Village (2006)	200
		07.04.01 The Energy-Producing Greenhouse	200
		07.04.02 Closed cycles	201
		07.04.03 The Solar Village	207
08	HOLISTIC ARCHITECTURE		209
	08.01	Autarchic town hall, Lelystad (1976)	210
		08.01.01 Background philosophy	211
		08.01.02 Functional description of the building	216
		08.01.03 Parabolic roof shells	216
		08.01.04 Interseasonal heat storage	217
		08.01.05 Daylight, roof lights, sunshading and insulating shutters	219
		08.01.06 Artificial illumination	220
		08.01.07 Balanced ventilation with heat recovery	221
		08.01.08 Wind energy	222
		08.01.09 Conclusion	223
	08.02	Intermediate projects 1976-2006	224
		08.02.01 Salland Water Board office, Raalte (1980)	224
		09.02.02 Economical office, The Hague (1994)	229
		09.02.03 Apartments for the elderly, Hengelo (1994-2001)	237
		09.02.04 Exergy Dwelling competition and realisation (1996-1997)	242
		09.02.05 Sustainable highrise, Dordrecht (2000)	245
		09.02.06 Housing for life, De Marsse, Nunspeet (2002)	246
	08.03	World Sustainability Campus, Afsluitdijk (2009-2010)	251
		08.03.01 The World Sustainability Campus	252
		08.03.02 The Lapwing's Egg	253
		08.03.03 The island	255
	08.04	'Boskantoor', forest office of Staatsbosbeheer, Ugchelen (2010-2011)	257
		08.04.01 Modest, small, yet beautiful	257
		08.04.02 Timber structure	258
		08.04.03 The energy system	259
		08.04.04 The Bird Hotel	262

09	MAGNUM OPUS: VILLA FLORA (2006-2012)		263
	09.01	Villa Flora, Venlo	264
		09.01.01 Background	264
		09.01.02 The complex indoor climate	266
		09.01.03 Requirements	268
	09.02	Integrated Sustainable Design	268
		09.02.01 Location	268
		09.02.02 Parabolic solar collectors	269
		09.02.03 Heat and cold storage	270
		09.02.04 Fine-wire heat exchangers	271
		09.02.05 Organic waste	271
	09.03	Indoor climate	272
		09.03.01 Air heating	272
		09.03.02 Ventilation	272
		09.03.03 Radiant heating	273
	09.04	The Holcon floor	273
	09.05	The process to delivery	275
		09.05.01 From design to construction	275
		09.05.02 Encountering Murphy's Law	276
		09.05.03 Delivery and further use	277
	09.06	Conclusion	278
10	ADDITIONAL IDEAS AND INVENTIONS		281
	10.01	The bookshelf ceiling (1966)	282
	10.02	Energy-saving cooking (1991)	284
	10.03	Meat safe of the cool façade (1984)	285
	10.04	The 'sund-pit' (early 1970s)	287
	10.05	Integrated street lanterns, Leerdam (1974)	288
	10.06	Tidal mills (1991)	290
	10.07	North Sea atolls (1980)	292
	10.08	Respect the tree	295
	10.09	Dying sustainably	296
	10.10	Lustrum books and Christmas cards	299
11	EPILOGUE		301
	Significance		302
	Acknowledgements		303
	References		304
	Abbreviations		307
	Synopsis: events, projects and awards		308
	Biography of Jón Kristinsson		310
	Biography of Riet Reitsema		311
	Biography of Andy van den Dobbelsteen		322

01

PROLOGUE

Preface by Jón Kristinsson

In the year 1954, on the 17th of June, 3:30 PM Central European Time I found myself in the following circumstances[1]:

> - My position was 51°59'30" North Latitude, 04°07'00" Eastern Longitude.
> - My altitude of observation was 10 m.
> - I had a straightforward course of 110°, with a speed of 12 knots (12 x 1,852 = 22.2 km/h) and with a speed of 10 knots over ground.
> - The sea water temperature was 288 K, the river water temperature 290 K.
> - The water contained floating sediment – heavy metals.
> - The wind was East by South-East by a force of 2 on the Beaufort scale (1.6 – 3.3 m/s).
> - Above the continent there was a high-pressure area of 1010 mBar, while above Iceland there was a deep depression.
> - The air temperature amounted to 301 K, radiation temperature was 298 K.
> - The relative humidity was 50%, so the concentration of moisture was 13.6 g/m³.
> - The noise level was 70 dB(A).
> - Per m³ the air contained 30 ☐g of N☐ and more than 10 ☐g of S☐.
> - The sky was clear blue, cloudless.
> - The direct solar radiation was 700 W/m², whereas the indirect radiation was 115 W/m², with reflections from water and glass in the surroundings.
> - There was a landscape park on starboard.
> - The eclipse factor of sunlight was 3.5.
> - The isotherms covered a vast area in central Western Europe.

One can say the same in different ways:
"The very first time I came to the Netherlands was a radiant summer afternoon, some fifty-five years ago, as a crew member of the motorship M/S Fjallfoss sailing from Iceland.
On the Nieuwe Waterweg ('new waterway') near Hoek van Holland (1) you could sniff the exhaust air from the oil refinery of Pernis. On the starboard side I saw the nature reserve De Beer ('the bear') and on port side the sunlight reflected upon the horticultural greenhouses of the Westland. What a country, what a flat country – a moment in my life that I still remember".

What is the moral to this story?
The summary is exact, without emotion, scientifically useful and controllable. The description below is short and emotional.
Every human being sees upon the built environment through his own glasses, from his own personal background. The architect mostly thinks in dimensions of shape, distance, area, space, light and colour, but not in temperature, radiation, differences in luminance, light pulses, air quality, weight, specific heat etcetera. Nevertheless, without integrated physical knowledge no fully sustainable building will evolve that can withstand the nick of time.

---

[1] This is a quote from my inaugural speech at the Delft University of Technology, May 14th 1993, entitled 'Integrated Design – or the New Necessity'.

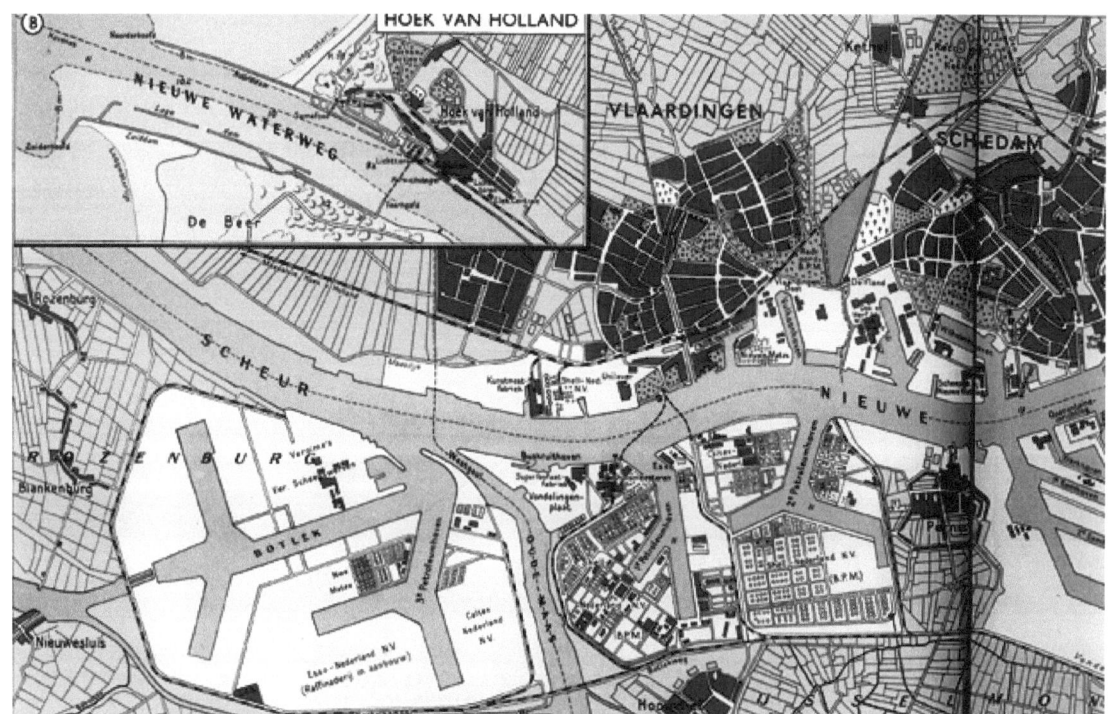

Figure 01.01: A map of the Rotterdam harbours around 1954, when Jón Kristinsson arrived in the Netherlands and stayed for good

This book is about integrated design. My definition of this is: "a holistic physical approach to ecological building". The essence of integrated design is the integration of emotion and ratio, of heart and brains. Good cooperation between the two human brain halves, the emotional right-hand side and the rational left-hand side, can be learned. Integrated design forms the bridge between architecture and nature; it starts with the sun and ends in the earth's magma.

Figure 01.02: Industrial activities in the Rotterdam harbour, 1954

Jón Kristinsson

Preface by Riet Kristinsson-Reitsema

Living in the Dutch town of Velsen-Noord, near the blast furnaces where my father worked as an engineer, I was an only child of a liberal married couple. I am proud of my parents who gave me so many chances to grow in freedom.
My societal engagement was clearly inherited from both sides. My mother's parents were liberal-socialist gentleman farmers from the remote province of Drenthe. My father's parents where humanistic teachers. After retirement in the year 1923 they had set up a small ecological paradise, with a latrine box for garden fertilisation, a kitchen garden, an orchard, a carp pond and bees. They also already had a bathroom and a dark room for the development of photographs.

Figure 01.03: Velsen-Noord nowadays, still home to Holland's large blast furnaces

In 1955 I went to study architecture in Delft, where my father had studied mechanical engineering. In that era, the DVSV ('Delft female students society') was a necessity for 60 girls among 6000 boys. I learned a lot there and organised many events on a small scale. In that period study was long and very intensive; everything was done on the drawing table.
In the year 1962 the annual excursion of Stylos, the faculty's study society, went to Egypt, which was very special. Four of the 32 students were girls of whom three eventually married a boy from the group. So did I: Jón Kristinsson was the Icelandic treasurer of Stylos. We were married in 1965, settled in the city of Deventer, yet also had an office in Iceland for several years, mainly in summer.

We got four children: two boys, in 1967 and 1969, and two twin girls in 1972. After having thoroughly refurbished a 1932 house, where which we added the cellar to the living room, we bought two terraced houses from 1889, which were needed after the additions to the family and for the accommodation of the steadily growing office. This way the contact with our children was arranged well, even though I always worked 100% and probably more. A firm family was raised without the mention of any problems.

The 1969 establishment and 1972 report of the Club of Rome ('Limits to Growth') made a big impression on me and has influenced my world of thoughts deeply. In our designs I used natural materials as much as possible, also at home: cotton, linen and woollen cloths, no make-up or perm. I was a colour advisor to Linoleum Krommenie for many years (linoleum is a natural product from jute and linseed oil).

For the office I have done a lot of work on the documentation of projects. It commenced in 1971, five years after starting, and thus our lustre books were born. In the year 2001 I said goodbye to the office with the seventh lustre book, at the age of 65½. I was happy to receive the Deventer Stadspenning ('city award') mainly thanks to my cultural activities for the city.

Figure 01.04: Reit Kristinsson-Reisema receives the Deventer Stadspenning, 2001

In the year 2002 I made the book from Jón's lecture notes, his inaugural and exit speeches, completed with sustainable designs by the office. It was called Integraal Ontwerpen – Vitale Architectuur ('integrated design – vital architecture') and this book before you is largely based on it. The book coincides with my efforts to complete a documentary film on Jón's range of ideas.

Riet Kristinsson-Reitsema

Introduction by the editor

The 2008 fire in the Architecture faculty building in Delft had many devastating effects. One of them was the loss of the last set of 'Integraal Ontwerpen – Vitale Architectuur', the Dutch book on Jón Kristinsson's sustainable building projects.

Demand for it had always been frequent, and many students used it for inspiration and reference since the grand master himself had retired from university. Apart from some international conference papers, Jón's work had never been translated in English, and many an enthusiastic listener to his speeches was sad to hear of their fate.

Figure 01.05: What remained of Andy van den Dobbelsteen's room after the TU Delft Faculty of Architecture fire, 13th of May 2008

Jón, his wife Riet and I often talked about having 'Integraal Ontwerpen' translated to English, which was complicated due to issues related to the publisher. After the Architecture fire however, we decided that I would completely re-edit and translate the book, involving Jón and Riet's latest projects. Hampered by my own busy life it took quite a while, but the upside to that was the complete inclusion of master pieces as the 'Lapwing's Egg', the 'Boskantoor' and Villa Flora, which became the focal point for the narrative, where in the past the never realised town hall of Lelystad had been.

Conveying the magic
More than a designer, Jón Kristinsson is an inventor and magician. One of the great pleasures of these is the inspiration and magic they can converse to others, as well as the virtually infinite conception of ideas. Digging into the myriad of projects and solutions conceived by Jón, one could easily swoon. And the line of thinking of an inventor or magician is different from, say, the analytical administrator. This lateral thinking, with both sides of the brain, can be learned but is not always comprehendible to 'normal' earthly creatures.

Luckily, having worked as a building physicist, Jón has always expounded on the fundamentals of his approach to sustainable building ('avant-la-lettre'), so his principles are clear. Riet Kristinsson-Reitsema has always documented their projects well, so also the outcome of Jón's integrated design process can be found in many places, predominantly in the Netherlands. I noticed however that many interested people are unable to directly connect the physical principles to eventual buildings. The process in-between is blurry and given mainly to the creator himself. How would you explain the conception of an insight?

This kept me busy since 'Integraal Ontwerpen' was an abundant collection of projects, technology and ideas, a work of inspiration to many yet also sometimes too overwhelming to some. I felt that if the narrative were restructured, the approach to integrated design would become clearer to most readers and more treasures of the work of Jón would be revealed.

Focal point
The core of this book is Jón Kristinsson's explicit examples of holistic architecture based on his integrated design approach. Until 2008 the best example of this had been his mourned design for the Lelystad town hall, the 1976 project in which Jón en Riet put all of their soul and belief but which was not selected for construction. I truly believe that the realisation of the Kristinsson design would have put sustainable building thirty years ahead. Not one project has equalled the expected performance of 'Lelystad' yet.

The master had to challenge his Lelystad himself and the result of was completed 35 years later. I am talking about Villa Flora, which in many respects resembles the Lelystad design but of course encompasses better modern technology. Closing every essential cycle (energy, water, material and their waste streams), Villa Flora goes beyond any other project so far. Therefore, Villa Flora became the focal point of this book and everything discussed works towards it.

Outline
This book commences with Jón Kristinsson's vision on the environment and the necessity of sustainability (chapter 02) and his theory of integrated design (chapter 03).
Following is a line of chapters (04 to 07) that discuss sustainable design, from the small scale of smart technology to the large scale of sustainable urbanism, illustrated by projects from the Kristinssons's office and Jón Kristinsson's chair at TU Delft.
The main part, as announced comes with chapter 08, where starting from the Lelystad townhall design of 1976 best examples of holistic architecture through integrated design are displayed, up until chapter 09, where Villa Flora, Jón Kristinsson's magnum opus, is discussed.
Chapter 10 is an intellectual dessert, a collection of other brilliant ideas and imaginations by the grand master, followed by an epilogue, reference list, synopsis of projects and biographies.

Jón Kristinsson often cites a philosopher who once said: "an image says more than one thousand words". Therefore we have included numerous images that will clarify ideas better than any text alongside.

I hope you will be awed, inspired and set to action. The world still needs it.

Andy van den Dobbelsteen

02

ENVIRONMENTAL PHILOSOPHY

02.01 Sustainable building within an ecological system

The demise of the living environment on earth has led to anxiety among an increasing number of people. Primary environmental problems are depletion, deterioration of eco-systems and deterioration of the human health, caused by mankind with its unlimited demand for consumable goods and commodities, thereby using non-sustainable resources and producing hazardous waste.

> The environment is the collection of conditions for life. Ecology is the part of biology that studies relationships between organisms and their environment.
>
> *Taeke de Jong*
> *TU Delft emeritus professor of Technical Ecology and Planning*

Rather than ourselves our children and grandchildren will be confronted with this decline and not just because of the harmful effects to their health. World-spanning problems are the amplified greenhouse effect and severe climate change, depletion of the ozone layer, disappearance of tropical rainforests, extinction of irreplaceable biotopes, limited access to potable water, production of waste and depletion of limited resources.

Additional to substantial financial efforts, behavioural changes will also be needed. In order to slow down and – if possible – neutralise the decline, knowledge, will and dedication is indispensible.
Living consciously in the environment, with all its facets, is necessary more than ever. A priority being the primary needs of life: food, clothing, shelter, work, recreation and mobility. Once environmentally conscious we can comprehend: disturbing the living environment as little as possible, or stated positively: improving the living environment.
It is therefore of the greatest importance that we gain insight into our ecological system. By visualising this interaction lines will become clear.

02.01.01 Analysis of the environmental system

To visualise the 'environment' and our relationship with it, we can best look at an illustration of W. Tomásek, in which all elements of the environment are gathered within technical components, biotic components and abiotic components.
- Technical components: everything made by human beings (buildings, roads, pipelines, canals, products)
- Biotic components: everything living (organisms: plants and animals)
- Abiotic components: the non-living elements (water, soil, air, heat, light, radiation)

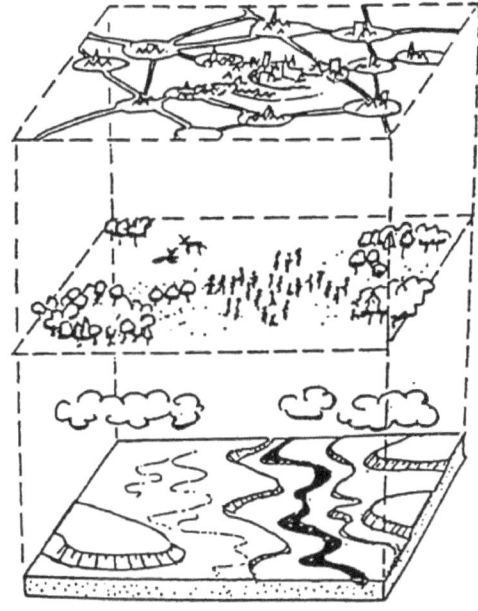

Fig. 02.01: Tomásek's system

The second illustration is an interpretation of H.T. Odum, who describes the relationship of the city with its environs. In this sketch the inter-exchange is given: what do you receive from the environment and what do you deliver to it. For every building, dwelling, factory, sailing yacht etc. a similar sketch can be produced.

Fig. 02.02: Odum's system

These extremely valuable and orderly illustrations can be combined into an image of the environmental system. It is obvious to split the abiotic component of Tomásek in two separate ones: the non-living earth as a static component and the versatile, endless physical shell of the earth as a dynamic fourth component. There are clear interactions between the components.

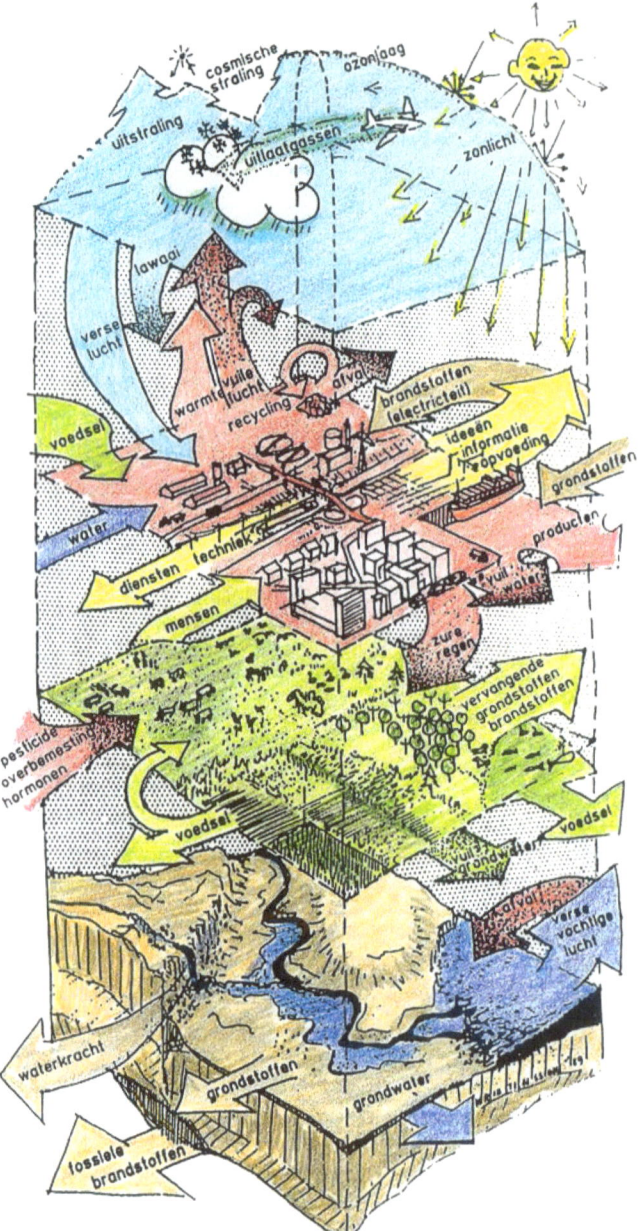

Fig. 02.03: Interactions in Kristinsson's system

When we commence from the bottom, in the abiotic component, we see the earth as an empty moon landscape, in which the resources, metals as well as fossil fuels, yet also water (saline seas, fresh water, flowing water in rivers and the water underground) are enclosed. Many building resources are in fact sediment from the rivers.

What we give back to this abiotic component is ground water polluted with pesticides and hardly or non-decomposable chemical and radioactive waste material, which we dump into the sea. The winning of ground water goes beyond any description.

Fig. 02.04:   The a-biotic component: Landmanurlaugar (Iceland) with black sky

The second primary component is the biotic one, or all living creatures, visible and invisible. Wood, for instance, also belongs to it as fuel or building material. Conspicuous is the influence of acid rain on forests and the addition of pesticides, hormones and fertilisers from industrial farming. The result of it all is obvious and disturbing.

Fig. 02.05:   The biotic component: agricultural monoculture

The third primary component is the technical, anthropogenic component; it includes all that has been conceived and produced by mankind, big and small, the entire built environment with all its infrastructure, yet also all commodities. Important in this respect is a far-reaching intention to re-use and a long functional lifespan.

Fig. 02.06:   The technical component

By means of our technology and long-lasting structures (sustainable and durable), ecological usage of resources and computers, this component 'in operation' can be improved. Buildings form an essential element of this component; hence the ceaseless flow of fossil fuels from the abiotic component to heat and cool these buildings. Cars and especially aeroplanes are big consumers of fossil fuel. Mechanised agriculture is totally dependent on fossil fuel.

Finally there is the fourth primary component, the invisible physical shell of the earth (air, light, heat, moist, sound, radiation, ozone layer etcetera). The atmosphere around the earth is different from what we think: it is relatively thin and vulnerable and proportionally not thicker than a plastic foil around a football.

Fig. 02.07:   The sky

Only a very small amount of solar energy reaches the earth, but this solar energy is many times more than what we need. Despite the relatively small energy intensity per square meter, this remains our (relatively) everlasting energy source. Due to the diurnal cycle of day and night, the availability has a phase difference in supply and demand. Summer and winter cause an even larger phase difference to bridge, which is difficult without fossil fuel. In the near future we should not forget that, beside wind energy, also sea tides, as a result of the gravitation force of the moon to the earth, should be made useful. There are optimists who assert that the sustainable solution is in sight through a quick deployment of cheap 'high-performance' photovoltaic (PV) cells for the generation of electricity. Producing these cells is not difficult: the slicing of siliceous sand grains is, simply said, sufficient. The efficiency of present-day PV cells is only 7 to 18%.
For the 3000 km race of the Solar Challenge (in Australia, bi-annual) very expensive PV cells are used with an efficiency of over 25%. Several versions of the ultra-lightweight solar NUNA car series achieved a speed exceeding 100 km/h in full sun.

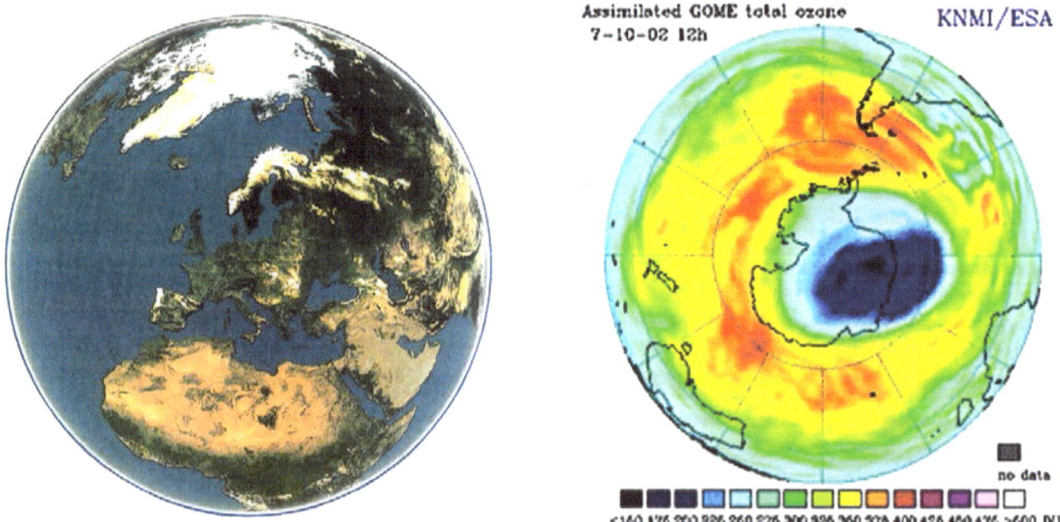

Fig. 02.08:   The Earth seen from a satellite (left) [source: Jorden, Globala förändringar] and the hole in the earth's ozon layer (right) [source: KNMI/ESA]

When we step into a plane, air hostesses demonstrate the use of an oxygen mask in case the pressure in the cabin fails. We then realise that the atmosphere in which we live is less than 10 km thick and that the temperature at this altitude is approximately -50°C. The atmosphere consists of different layers, among which the ozone layer that protects us against excessive ultraviolet radiation. In the 1990s holes in this layer were discovered around the South Pole, caused by (H)CFCs in volatile gases. This is harmful to flora and fauna.

02.01.02 Climate change

Climate change is nothing new. Once, the Rhine and Thames flew together across the North Sea plain. In the Miocene and Pliocene Europe was warmer and during the ice ages, of which the last one ended 12,000 years ago, considerably colder.
Climate change by human actions is a new phenomenon 'of nature'. Philosophers still do not agree completely on the extent to which this will occur. One claims no significant change is taking place while the other speaks of dramatic effects of the temperature rise resulting from an aggravated greenhouse effect (through CO_2 emissions mainly).
That nothing is happening is a euphemism, because temperature increase is evident; the Southern Arctic Sea has even become 2.5°C warmer since monitoring started. That climate change will mainly happen in the industrialised northern hemisphere (with more air pollution) is not entirely correct. Also the southern hemisphere is becoming warmer.
The most recent reports by the Intergovernmental Panel on Climate Change [IPCC, 2007], backed up by thousands of scientists, leave no doubt as to the sincerity of climate change. With the years evolving the margins of their predictions become smaller. We will have to endure a world that will be a few degrees hotter, locally worse. This seems bearable but a few degrees will have devastating effects to areas on the edge of climatic equilibrium, such as the ones within the Arctic Circle.

Let us take the Netherlands as another example, which together with Western Europe is warming up twice as fast as the rest of the world [KNMI, 2009].
Through backcasting (rather than forecasting), in 50 years the Netherlands can expect an average temperature increase by 1.5 to 2 degrees. Regarding the sea level rise, philosophers do not agree. Some say that the melting of glaciers will not lead to a 0.2 to 0.3 m rise, but instead 2 to 3 meters as a result of expansion of the cold water mass in the polar areas when its temperature increases to 4°C. Al Gore's figures [2006] mentioned 6 meter, based on the total melt of Greenland or Antarctica, or half of both. Some others assert that as a result of the temperature rise, more evaporation will occur, leading to more precipitation rather than sea level rise. The Dutch meteorological institute predicts a sea level rise between 0.35 to 0.85 m before 2100 [KNMI, 2009]. The IPCC foresees more dramatic figures as the melting of Greenland and Antarctica goes faster than expected.

From these differences in opinion we need to draw conclusions, and we will take a middle position between these extremes. If we assume that the Netherlands by 2050 is 1.5°C warmer and has taken the climate of central France. In summer, due to the urban heat island effect, the temperature in the city will be around an additional 9°C higher than the surrounding rural areas, comparable to the climate of Southern Spain. To many people this may seems tempting, were it not that our cities have not been designed for these temperatures and more people will simply die before their time, as empirical studies have revealed [e.g. Huynen et al. 2001].

The icecaps will surely be melting. The sea level will have risen by 1.5 meters and land subsidence by sagging, gas and water extraction will be approximately 50 cm.
This temperature rise will have an influence on the fauna and thereby on the agricultural business. Across the world river deltas are the place for a lot of agriculture, and these will be threatened by flooding. In chapter 10 we will present a solution to oppose this threat.

02.01.03   The changing world from a distance

If we look at earth from a space capsule at night, we will see that all places where humans live and work radiate light. The continents are distinguished mainly by urban concentrations. Now it turns out that human beings are the only species active 24 hours a day: the city never sleeps. In the picture we for instance see Europe with large patches of light in the triangle of Ruhrgebiet, Randstad and Belgian industry, around cities as London, Saint Petersburg and especially Moscow, as well as from the oil rigs in the North Sea.

Fig. 02.09:   The Earth at night [source: Jorden, Globala förändringar]

Above the northern arctic circle in winter time the sun does not shine and there is little daylight. The energy need in the dark cold winter months has a reversed phase of long-lasting sunlight in the summer months. Here we can store season-long energy usefully to enable use of flowing energy every time of the year. This part of the world is thinly populated, has a high standing of prosperity and has a lot of technical and spatial potential to produce energy, such as 'white coal' (hydro-power) in Norway and Sweden.

If we consider the world as a landscape model of extrapolated growth of population in the current century (presented in the year 1993), North and Western Europe will show a limited increase in population and Japan even a decrease. The United States, Mexico and South America will present a clear growth in birthrate following the Pope's visit to these regions in the 1990's. Extreme growth however will appear particularly in West Africa and Asia, to be seen by the stalactites in the picture. How this growth will lead to migrations using historical models is difficult to predict, just as we cannot predict which language or religion one will seek refuge.

Fig. 02.10:   Local growth on the Earth, depicted as enormous stalacmites; left: Europe and Africa in the middle; right: India seen from South-East Asia (photos taken in the Moderna Museet Spårvagnshallarna, Stockholm)

02.01.04 Our ecological footprint – the time factor

'Our Ecological Footprint', the book by Wackernagel & Rees [1996], led to new insights into the impact of our ways of living would affect the environment. The ecological footprint of a society is the area of land required to comply with the annual needs and the processing of waste. The world is a closed cycle system.

The five most significant causes of environmental damage are:
1. Food: fruit, vegetables, cereal, animal products
2. Accommodation: construction, maintenance, operation
3. Motorised transportation: private and public transport, goods
4. Consumption goods: packaging, clothes, furnishing, printing work, stimulants, recreation devices, other goods
5. Services: government, education, health care, social services, tourism, leisure, banking and insurances, other services.

The Netherlands is a country of food interbreeding with a high added value. After the USA it is the greatest food-exporting country in the world, with predominant export of poultry and pigs. The vegetable food for this industrialised bio-industry enters the country from all over the world but especially from developing regions. Thus Dutch agriculture uses 5 to 7 times their own space elsewhere. The vulnerability of Dutch agriculture therefore is evident, even if one considers new landscape parks. For urbanisation, food, agricultural products and forestry, the Netherlands (33,000 km^2) needs an area the size of France (450,000 km^2), 15 times larger. Figure 02.11 gives a distorted image of the world as it actually would be when countries were as large as the space on Earth they live from.

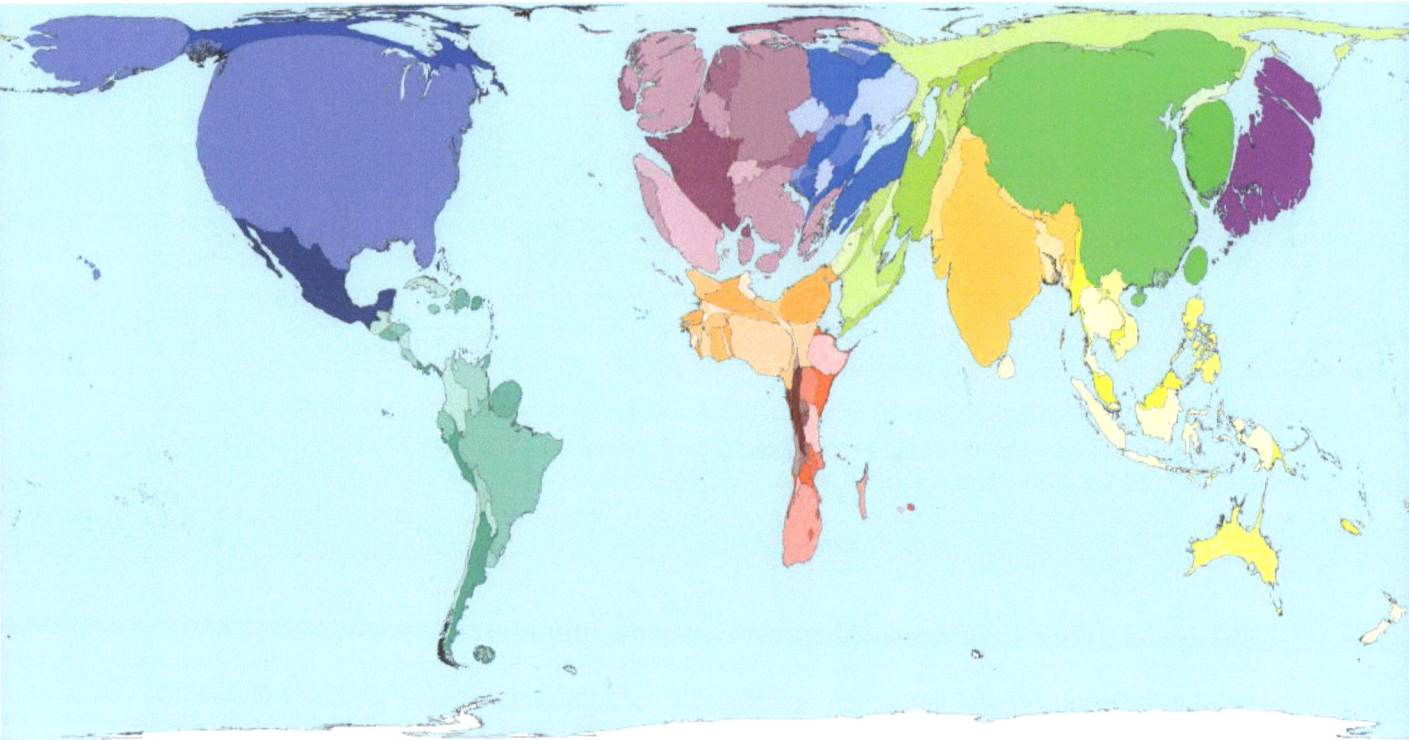

Fig. 02.11: Ecological footprint of all countries in the world, shown in actual size: the land area needed for food, water, energy and materials [Dorling et al., 2009, download www.worldmapper.org]

Ecological holism is a necessity. Human beings are a very special species of animal, according to Rees. Significant facts are known. From a biological perspective mankind is a macro consumer: it eats everything that lives. Human activity has become global. Human knowledge and technology develops. Human language is an expression of clenched culture. Whales are the biggest eaters, followed by humans. Half of all grass land is reserved for the feeding of one animal species: man. The threats of humans to the environment are enormous. Human entrepreneurship expels flora as well as fauna. Overcropping is being committed to irreplaceable natural riches. The human spirit works with visually oriented models. If we reconstruct our chimaeras, we will discover a Cartesian dualism. On the one hand sits economic growth, on the other a reducing habitat.

There is a clear relationship between energy sources and waste. The twenty richest peoples consume 60 to 100 times more than the poorest peoples. Even though we know better, we attribute fundamental value to economic growth. We can hardly imagine negative prosperity growth. Negative growth (positive shrinkage) however seems unavoidable in many countries, as we have experienced since 2008.

Water – energy – food

Half of the world population has a shortage of water and diurnally 5000 children die of thirst. In many countries the ground water table drops dramatically by the extraction of water for agriculture. Half of all oil is used for various kinds of pumps. There are 25 million environmental refugees!
In the Netherlands the permanent consumption of energy per household is around 6.4 kW. A human being produces 100 to 130 W of power, so every Dutch family has 50 'energy slaves' at work, day and night. Before Obama the American consumption of fossil fuel was four times as high as Europe.

Agriculture is more dependent on water than on temperature, even though crops can hardly resist temperatures above 32°C. Agriculture worldwide is mechanised and fully dependent on fossil fuel. The efficiency of solar energy for plant growth is 2% at the maximum. In Brazil a significant part of all vehicles is fuelled by organic alcohol.

The world population consumes 1.9 billion tons of grain. In the year 1978 the world had a grain reserve of 200 days; now this has been reduced to 40 days. In 1980 the cereal yield per area was the highest and catch from fisheries maximal.
We are beyond the peak of agricultural production and we are losing. There is ever less covered land and erosion is increasing. The fertility of the earth is decreasing. We have reached our limits!

The megacities

In 1950 New York had 10 million inhabitants. After 2015 23 cities will have more than 10 million and 44 cities more than 5 million inhabitants, 30 to 39 of which are in developing regions. The biggest growth will take place in these regions. This takes place against the background of an ever increasing world population that will have doubled within 27 years.
The growth of poor megacities is diffuse, explosive and unmanageable. These cities usually have only drinking water facilities for 75% of the population and sewage for 50%. When urbanites start to drift, they are an army destroying everything.
The extent of self-provision of these cities is of importance. During communism half of Moscow's meat was produced within the city borders. Good recycling of waste stands for hygiene in the city. Land-saving vertical gardens deserve attention. The need for innovative low-tech facilities is great.

Fossil energy

We often think that oil companies produce oil, but there are no oil-producing companies. There are only oil-extracting companies. Pumping up and winning oil is increasingly difficult. In the past one barrel of oil was necessary to win 50 barrels; now this ratio is 1:5.

The availability of energy per person is becoming a limiting factor. For crude oil one pays the market price, but what is the physical boundary of the oil flow? The break-even point between supply and demand, so-called 'peak oil', was passed in September 2008. Until that moment the demand for fuel kept increasing and the oil production by OPEC countries had grown, in contrast to non-OPEC countries. In September 2008 we reached the ceiling! We will have to approach the world differently and understand that we will face severe changes.

Uranium for nuclear energy is a finite resource. Its reserves are expected to last no more than 80 years, under the condition of current demands. Increasing the production of nuclear energy is rapidly bringing the limits closer, and if the whole world had to rely solely on nuclear energy, reserves would only be sufficient for 3-5 years maximum [Hoogakker, 2010].

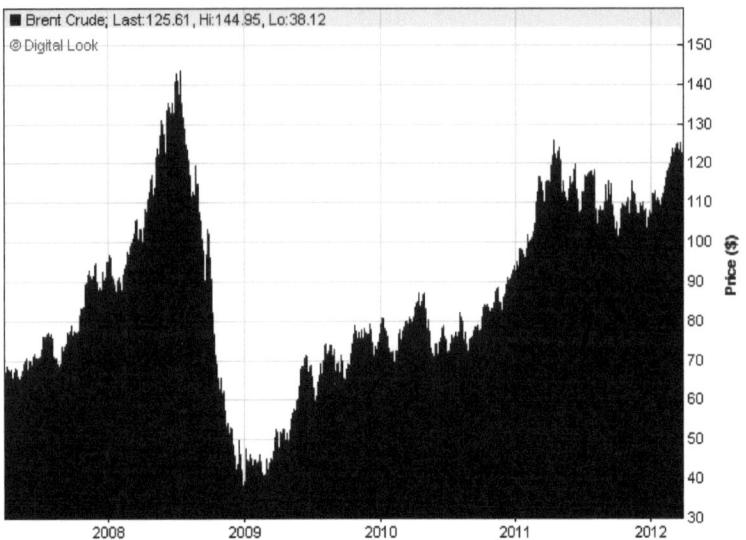

Fig. 02.12: Brent Crude: the price of a barrel of crude oil, between January 2007 and 2012 [source: Digital Look, www.digitallook.com]: we see the oil price reaching $ 145 per barrel mid 2008, an emerging energy crisis, 'saved' by the credit crunch, however to be followed by a repeated crescent to high levels again

Some facts are withheld as they are politically undesired or unsellable, even if we look for new energy sources.
There is a growing demand for energy and there is a predictable maximum supply of oil. This is the amount of crude oil that rock can maximally release.
The world's largest oil-consuming country, the USA, reached its own maximum level of oil winning back in 1984, now it is 60% dependent on oil imports. The World Watch Institute stated that 40% of all building material production, 35% of all energy consumption and 65% of the world's production pollution takes place in the US.

No matter how we estimate the remaining oil, gas and coal reserves, in due time, the period from around 1800 till 2100 will be considered as a very special, brief period in human history – let alone the earth's geographical history – where almost all of the fossil carbon hydrates developed during the Devone and Carbon era were depleted and converted back to carbon dioxide, by human activity alone. The Fossil Age will be considered a period of incredible industrial and technological prosperity and, regarding the use of natural resources, unresponsible societal decadence.

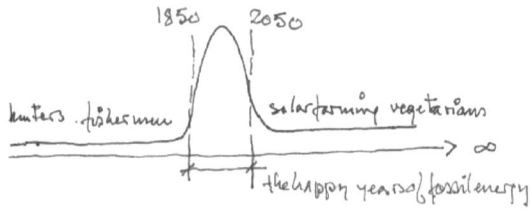

Fig. 02.13: The human period between pre- and post-industrialism is very short

How do you solve the energy problem?
A. We will go on with more demand than supply. Our century of prosperity will remain dependent on fossil energy and eventually collapse.
B. We will find replacing energy: nuclear energy, wood, other biomass, wind energy, solar energy, tidal energy...
C. We will reduce our consumption of energy drastically, for instance to one tenth or one twentieth (the famous factor of 20).

The conclusion is: the most desirable solution will be the development of a new sustainable life style as well as technologies that are suited to a situation of decreasing oil winning.

02.02   Sustainable technology: the New Necessity

02.02.01   The factor of 20

On the global scale, the environmental metabolism in relation to the population growth, prosperity and the environment in the following years is a source of concern to many people. Nevertheless, the predominant part of the world population hardly has any notion of this. What is desirable, possible and acceptable is deliberated in interaction with culture, social structures and technology. Sustainable technological development goes slowly.

The assignment to maintain and possibly improve the built-up world in an ecological sense, through a drastically reduced environmental load, we name: the New Necessity. This is a worldwide challenge for the current and next generation of architects, designers, technicians, public servants and decision-makers on every level. Decisive factors are: the deterioration of the environment, fast growth of the population and the need for an improving prosperity.
Increases in the deterioration of the environment should not only be prevented but at least be halved. Meanwhile it is probable that between 1990 and 2040 the world population will double and that we will not diminish our prosperity whilst developing regions should be offered an improvement of theirs.

$$PE = Pop \times Pr \times Env$$

PE = the pressure on the environment
Pop = world population
Pr = the average level of prosperity
Env = the environmental burden caused per capita, as a function of prosperity means, such as buildings and products =
the average environmental load = environmental metabolism

This approach of equilibrium by Barry Commoner [1971] set into a mathematic equation by economist Speth [1989] and ecologists Ehrlich & Ehrlich [1990], is the foundation for the argument below. From different scenarios we will choose a precautious position in the middle.

Environmental buffer – the factor of 20

Under sustainable development human activities should lead to a pressure on nature and the environment that does not exceed the available 'environmental buffer'. If the pressure is not bigger than the environmental buffer, nature and the environment have the potential to take this burden or to restore the damage. If the pressure is bigger, irreversible changes will occur: species will become extinct, natural reserves will deplete and natural cycles will be disturbed. The New Necessity is evident: restoration of the ozone layer and avoiding the aggravation of the greenhouse effect.

Welfare, which until the 1990s had been privileged to the western world and Japan, will in fifty years have reached China, India, the former Soviet Republic, South America and Africa. The total rate of prosperity will multiply fivefold. On the global scale the West mainly has luxury problems.

If we fill in the values of the Ehrlich & Ehrlich and Speth, we see a simple outcome:

	PE	=	Pop	x	Pr	x	Env
1990:	1	=	1	x	1	x	1
2040:	½	=	2	x	5	x	1/20

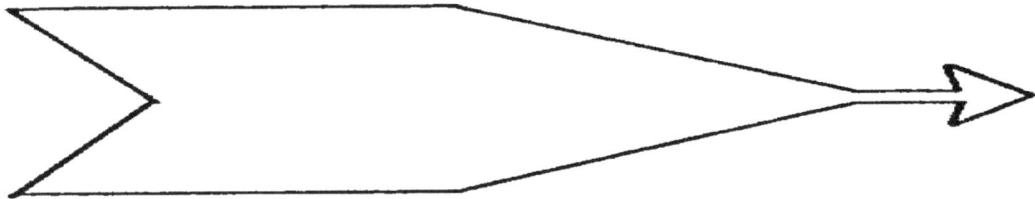

This implies that the environmental load of our products and commodities needs to be reduced to one twentieth, taking 1990 as the reference year. Time makes a luxury problem into a real-life problem.

Is this gigantic challenge realistic? Can we produce for more people with greater prosperity against on average 1/20 of the environmental buffer of 1990?

The New Necessity assumes we can; in most cases it will however require an entirely new way of designing – a trend cleavage.

Time can be reasonably overlooked. After peak oil we can expect structural supply and demand during an energy crisis. The New Necessity concept is a philosophy rather than an expression of architecture, introvert rather than extrovert and often of an invisible quality. It is also the art of omission and seeing things objectively without the burden of prejudice by tradition and official directives. It is the guts to stick ones neck out, willingness to undergo child's diseases and failure, however not to perish and behave like a centipede who is contemplating how to walk and thereby inapt to put another foot forward. It is doing with your hands and working with your head. From our architectural perspective we only experience the visible part of the environmental iceberg. Political and food aspects should also be given attention.

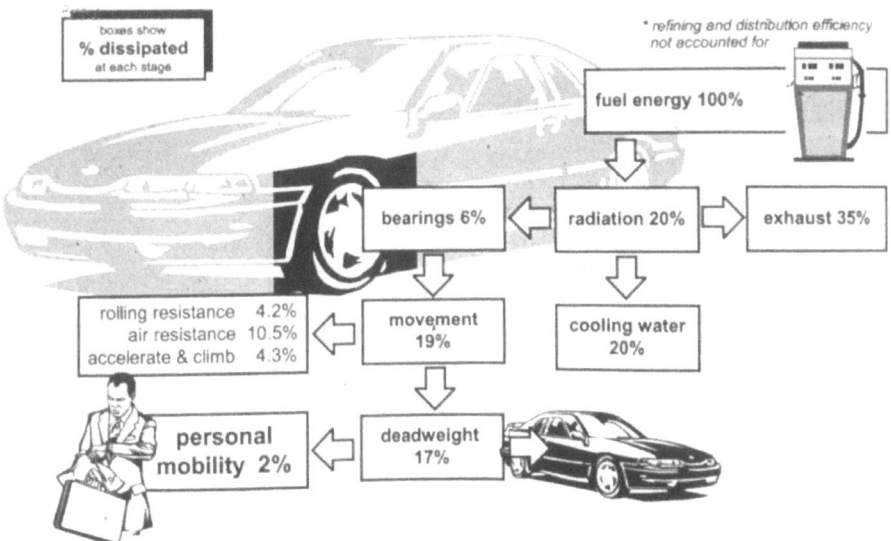

Fig. 02.14:   Car efficiency: only 19%, and when considering deadweight of the car: 2% only. This should be improveable…

02.02.02   Backcasting the sustainable future

Backcasting is the approach to describe a desired (sustainable) future state, based on primary human needs and constraints at the time, and translate this situation back to action needed now [Heel & Jansen, 1992].

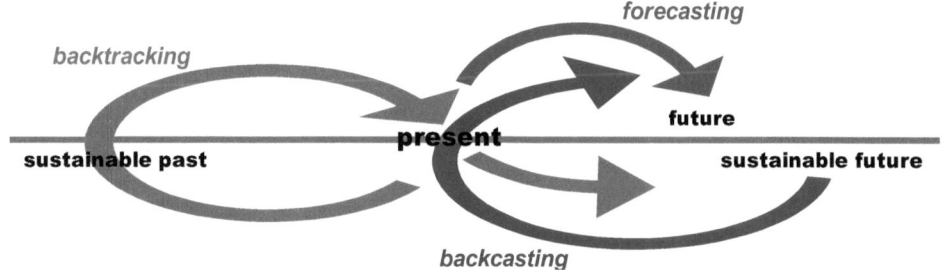

Fig. 02.15:   Three ways to approach a sustainable future: forecasting (extrapolating), backcasting (imagining the inevitable future and acting accordingly) and backtracking (learning from a sustainable past) [Dobbelsteen et al., 2006]

The predictable expected change of the built environment within the coming fifty years forms the background of the story about the sustainable city and infrastructure. How would our grandchildren want us to act so that their future is secured? "An integrated approach to the factors of culture, structure and technology is needed in order to establish sustainable innovation" [Jansen[2], in Kasteren, 1997].

---

[2] Prof.dr.ir. J.A. Jansen, emeritus professor at Delft University of Technology

We cannot backcast in steps of ten or twenty years as these periods are too short for cultural turn. Extrapolation of the current developments does not lead to the vision required for completely new (technological) concepts. The present analytical perception of environmental problems blocks new ideas. For the achievement of sustainable development a lateral approach[3] (along a lateral way) is necessary so as to release old, outdated concepts and welcome new, creative and sustainable solution.

The ancient interwoven relationship between living and working has almost disappeared. We have sleeping cities to live, an industrial site for work and a shopping centre with a supermarket for groceries. The relationship between seasons and food production has become more diffuse due to the replacement of local greengrocer and waste food collector (with horse and carriage) by the international supermarket that hardly knows of seasons. The greengrocer was the daily relation between city and countryside and one had summer or winter cooking on the table. The 'grey' economy of all kinds of allotments could restore the relationship with season-bound production of food and diminish the ever growing monofunctionality of the city[4].

It would also be desirable to allow backyard construction in zoning schemes, which could function as leisure time for, amongst others, people who are incapacitated for work. For example: a greenhouse, aviary, music room, oldtimer garage, guesthouse or maintenance workshop. Important too is extrascholastic care, together with retired craftsmen, because of whom youths could be at work and gain experience.
Working with hands and brains together is important yet not or hardly taught at school.

---

[3] Lateral thinking is a concept of Dr. Edward De Bono.
[4] See also: "From Cities to Living Machines", by Todd

03

THEORY ON INTEGRATED DESIGN

03.01   How architects think

An architect usually thinks and designs in squares and cubic metres, lines, areas, volumes, luminance differences and just to a little extent in money. For me, integrated sustainable design starts with the sun, at a distance of 149 million kilometres or 8.3 light minutes from the earth, and ends with the earthquake-prone geothermal heat, fed by the earth's magma. (Therefore, the scientific background of the ideal dean of a school of architecture needs to encompass astronomy and geophysics.)

Historically, architecture is bound to locations with climatic features. In Western Europe buildings used to be massive with small windows; at present it is the opposite. The range of buildings is usually light-weight with large surfaces of glass; they sit on very diverse grounds with different temperatures, water tables and bearing capacity. How can the modern architect bring these buildings to maturity without interest in and knowledge of wind, light and soil?

Which means of expression as design tools do we find in the suitcase of the architect?
According to Niels Prak, TU Delft professor of elementary design theory, there are five:
- Form: in plain or spatial
- Structure: smooth or rough
- Harmony, form similarity
- Contrast: light and dark
- Colour, a rainbow of possibilities

Deduced expressions are:
- Scale: large or small
- Number: proportions

The architect thinks in spatial images.

One observes by means of differences in luminance, so architecture needs light to be seen. In a cinema one does not experience shape; in the dark one has no observation of form except from echoes, but a cinema is acoustically dead.

Integrated design usually has a hidden, invisible, added value as quality.
If we add our five basic sensory observations - see, hear, feel, smell and taste - we can start to design with gravity as the only essential opponent.

The difference between spatial architecture and building design is: architecture needs to be seen but people should also be able to listen to the silence and sound of a building. One should be able to touch, sense, caress, sniffle, smell, bite into or eat from a building. Neither Newton's gravity, nor the buoyancy of Archimedes, including the understanding that pile-founded buildings in delta areas bob on floating layers of sand, form no part of the architect's standard toolkit. The power of Watt, kilowatt-hours as energy unit and even the natural gas equivalent from home ground commonly are no topic for discussion.

A normal professor only performs around 125 W continuously, so can only generate 1 kWh per working day. Expressed in electricity this is not more than 20 eurocents per day! Be unconcerned, however, for at the moment an average Dutch household needs 1.9 kW permanently (a powerful vacuum cleaner running all day, every day, or 3.5 kW including travel). This equals 35 professors as energy slaves in a treadmill, working a 10-hour day! We tend to live more with financial values rather than kilowatt-hours of energy…

Vitruvius' five books on architecture are highly regarded. In Jakarta, back in 1975, professor Bismo Suwondo Sutedjo managed to tell me who I am. The cultural background western people received in the cradle, European architects in particular, can be explained in a compact, clarifying and historical manner:

1. The logical thinking of the Greeks
2. The organisational skills of the Romans
3. The fighting belief of Israel

Saint Paul, the founder of the Christian church of Rome, is the exponent of these three properties. This definition of our background was a revelation. If we have a good design brief and use all laws of nature as obvious instruments to design good buildings with a healthy indoor climate by means of the indispensible building physics, then we will comply with all the necessary conditions to develop socially responsible buildings.

Nothing can go wrong?
No, according to environmental design we are not that far yet, for we miss a holistic triggering factor in our western actions: the factor of time. Time can be an instantaneous sample as a photo; however, sustainability is of a longer term. The difference between economy and ecology is time. The period of time the sun needs to make a trip around a building visualises the cycle of living - working - recreating: the long shadow in the cool morning, the sharp short shadow around noon and the warm afternoon sun that will not be obstructed by horizontal sunshading.

The human life is relatively short, so a building is made for the offspring. The material cycle does not reside under the responsibility of the designer, although this is about to change. Alongside with the building specifications belong the specifications for demountability.
The desired extreme indoor and outdoor climate is a given or should be given in the design brief. However, this is not the case by far and many projects of new construction decorating the sleeve of architecture magazines defy laws of nature. The minimum and maximum temperatures, as well as unwanted ventilation through draft, are never mentioned. The accuracy, diligence and objectivity of information are grossly low in architecture magazines. What is mentioned is the name of the photographer, but sporadically the time of day, the diaphragm, shutter time, brand and light sensitivity of the film.
One can study architecture and graduate on unrealistic, uninhabitable buildings, so long as they are beautiful or exciting.

03.02 A bridge between architecture and nature

Design parameters verbalised
In practice, integrated design is the combining of physical parameters for design with other knowledge and experience. The constant pursuit for high tech will often end in low tech. Nature is the apex of high tech.

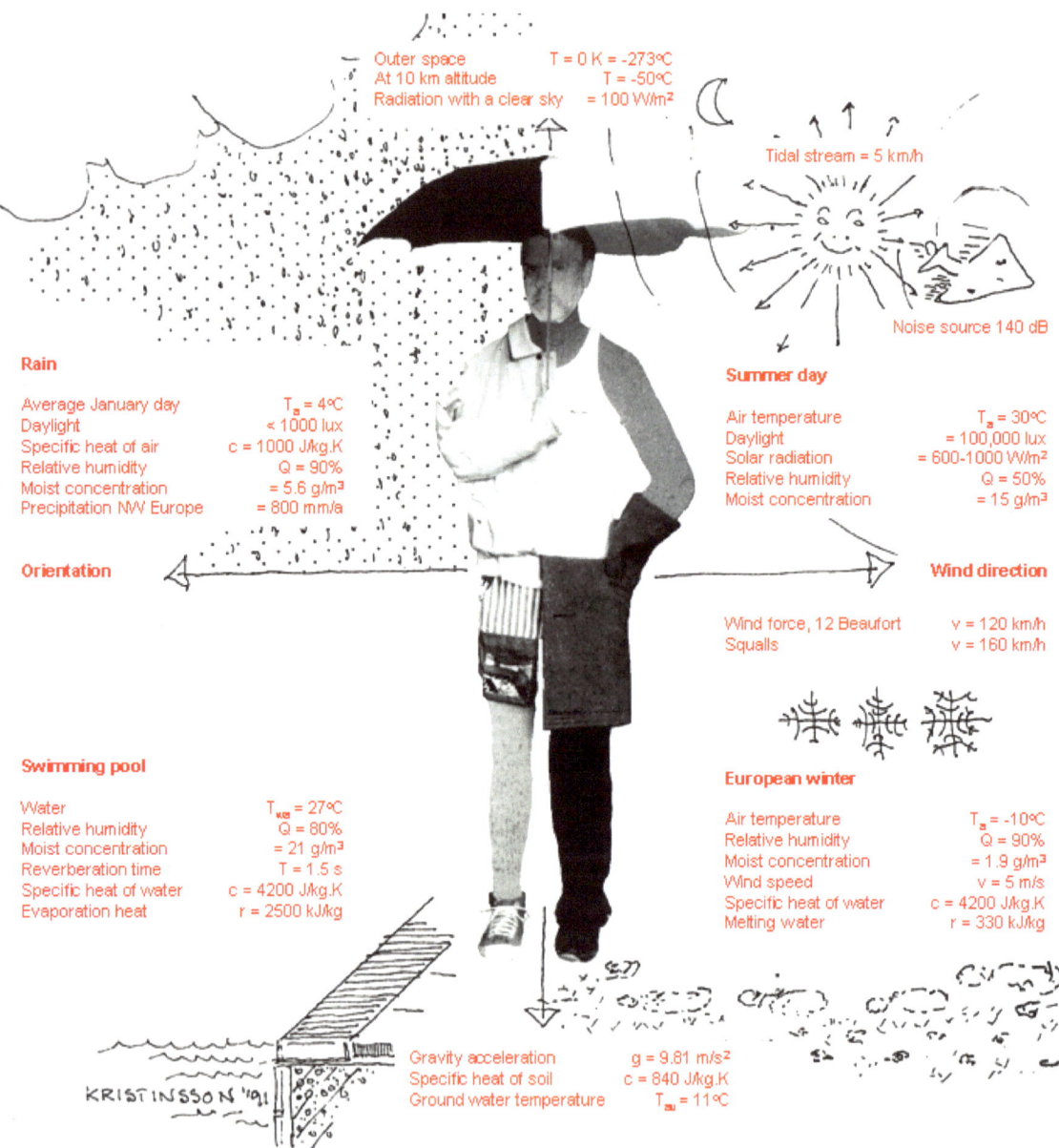

Fig. 03.01:   Design parameters, with man in the middle

We put the designer in the middle of the elements and give global physical dimensions to natural phenomena. Below we discuss physical parameters that need to play a significant role in sustainable architecture. Examples are given of phenomena, effects occurring, ubiquitous or local quantities and potentials for design

	phenomenon	Effects	ubiquitous quantities	local quantities	potentials
the clear sky	on a clear day or night heat radiates towards space, where the temperature is close to the absolute minimum	freezing rain on front and back windshield of cars at night condensation/ freezing rain on scaled roofing tiles	outer space temperature: 0 K = -273°C radiation: 50 – 200 W/m² day and night		dew and condense water for plants free-cooling roofs
sunshine	solar irradiation direct and diffuse sunlight, moonlight ultraviolet and infrared light solar energy, solar load light temperature luminance difference	light, glare heat, over-heating artificial lighting needed when not enough daylight	limit to human registration of colour: 2- 6 lux	solar power (in temperate climates: 500 – 2000 W/m2 in summer) daylight (in temperate climates:100,000 lux in summer and < 1,000 lux in winter)	play with the right orientation shadow, shading against direct sunlight photovoltaic (PV) technology for electricity flat solar collectors for hot water parabolic collectors for hot water, power and cooling sun concentrating mirrors light-controlling foils
wind	movement of air from high- to low-pressure areas (caused by the sun and rotation of the earth) wind directions wind speed and force gust of wind seasonal trade winds local microclimates	under- and over-pressure wind acceleration, lee, wind nuisance odour, stench, olfactory nuisance the sound of wind	12 Beaufort = 120 km/h = 33.3 m/s speed of windblasts: 160 km/h = 44.4 m/s	average wind speed (in Western Europe: 4 – 5 m/s) wind direction and frequency (in Western Europe: omni-directional, mostly SW to W, 15-20% of the time) predominant direction of dry or wet air and precipitation predominant direction of relatively cold or warm air	play with the compass rose and orientation to the wind using the chimney effect passive cooling and heating wind turbine
sound	- vibrations between specific frequencies can be heard as sound - audible versus intelligible sound - reverberation time	- background noise, birds singing, voice recognition - loudness, deafening noise, noise nuisance	- human beings can usually hear frequencies between 20 and 20,000 Hz - noise levels: whispering 30 dB(A), rock concert 110 dB(A), jet airplane passing 140 dB(A) - ear damage above 115 dB(A)		- the art of acoustics - playing with sound insulation, reflection and absorption - music

Jón Kristinsson   Integrated Sustainable Design

precipitation	- rain, hail, snow, fog - drizzle, steady rainfall, downpour, rainstorm, cloudburst - open water, water quality - ground water, age of ground water, water seepage	- storm water - waste water: black, brown, yellow, grey water - pesticides in open and ground water	- gravity: 9.81 m/s2 - relative humidity: between 0% (absolute dryness) and 100% (water) - specific heat capacity of water: 4,200 J/kg.K - heat from melting water: 330 kJ/kg - heat from evaporation: 2,500 kJ/kg	- average rainfall quantity and frequency (in Western Europe: 500-900 mm/a) - ground water table and store - relative humidity (in temperate climates: 50% in summer, 90% in freezing winter or during rainfall, 80% in a swimming pool) - moist content (in temperate climates: 15 g/m3 on a hot summer day, 1.9 g/m3 in freezing winter, 5.6 g/m3 on a cold rainy day, 21 g/m3 in a swimming pool)	- potable water, utilisation water, cooling water, swimming water - water storage, water infiltration
soil	- ground constitution, soil constitution - bearing capacity - water permeability, aquifers - geothermal heat		soil temperature beneath 1-2 m = the mean annual temperature!	- specific heat capacity (in the Netherlands: 840 J/kg.K) - evaporation - groundwater temperature - geothermal temperature	- creating frost-free spaces - soil exergy: passive cooling or heating - heat exchange with the soil: cooling and heating via collectors or heat pumps - water filled foundation piles - thermal couples - seasonal storage in aquifers or in fixed underground - geothermal energy

03.03 Insolation

According to us, the integrated design of a building commences with the sun at 149 million km distance, or at 8.3 light minutes from the earth. Because of the daily spinning and annual tilting of the earth around the sun we know full days and seasons. We can also calculate when it becomes dark and at which hour and day of the year which solar height is occurring. Due to the position of the earth in our solar system our environs usually receive solar power of 300 – 1000 W/m^2 in the form of short-wave rays of light.

Good usage of daylight in buildings is often thwarted by inconvenient reflection on computer monitors. For this something needs to be created. Our eyes can only see with light; without light architecture cannot be observed.
External solar shading, to keep out excessive solar heat, changes the frequency of these short-wave rays to infrared rays of heat. The wind needs to carry these off.
The winning of solar heat through glass is called 'passive', by means of a fan 'hybrid' and in the case of an installation of solar collectors 'active'.

To fence off the high sunlight in summer by means of big (roof) overhangs is a godsend for house owners. In humid countries in delta areas they also lead to dry gables on the side facing heavy wind and rainfall. The elevation most exposed to the climate should, from a sustainable point of view, be constructed of very durable or repairable material.

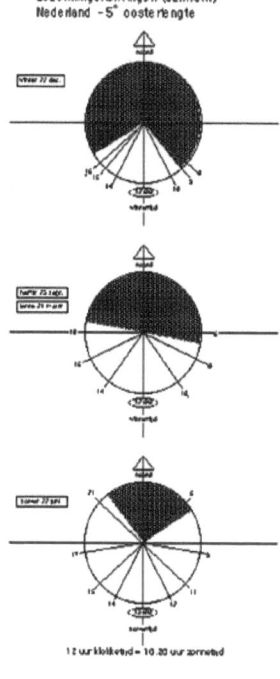

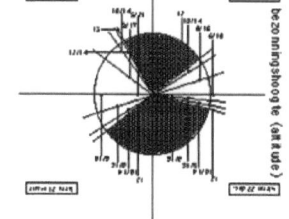

Fig. 03.02:   Solar diagrams

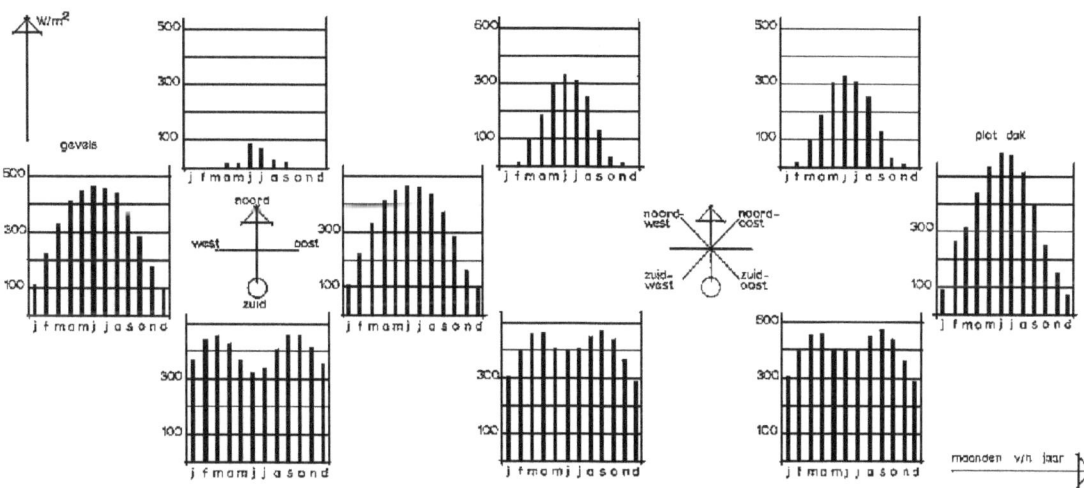

Fig. 03.03:   The sun at different elevations

Jón Kristinsson — Integrated Sustainable Design

03.04 Examples of integrated designs

Free-cooling roofs

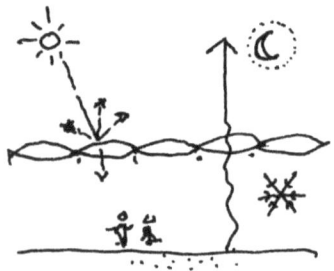

When we start at the top we see the phenomenon of thermal radiation to the clear sky. If we used this, we could establish free-cooling. Free-cooling roofs are inflated white poly-ethylene cushions that reflect sunlight but let through infrared rays, thus creating an artificial night during daytime. Apart from the pre-chilled ventilation air in commercial buildings, one would also desire this for all artificial ice rinks. In the tropics cheap, environmentally sound free-cooling roofs would be of great value. Further on in this book we will explain how the principle theoretically works and in which manner we can manufacture these roofs.

Fig. 03.04:   A roof of inflated polythene cushions that reflect sunlight yet let infrared radiation through – an artificial night during the day, suited for ice-skating rinks

Tidal mills
The gravitation force from the moon and the sun on the earth causes tidal currents four times a day. Electrical tidal plants making use of the great drop between low and high tide can be encountered near the river mouth of La Range in North-Western France. Less known or unknown are tidal plants that generate power from currents with a limited drop. One can imagine tidal mills as a bound fleet of sailing ships, which sail upside down around two anchor buoys in the marine current. Rounding the one buoy requires tacking, and the other buoy jibing.

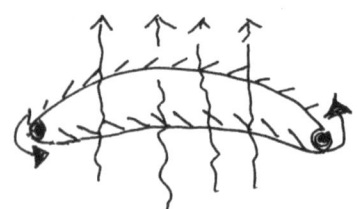

Slow is strong, we could say. The speed of tidal water is known, usually 5 km/h. Because of the low energy density a large harvesting area is primary.

Fig. 03.05:   A tidal mill can be imagined as a fleet of sailing boats tied upside-down in the see current, which sail around two anchor buoys. One has to gybe around the one buoy, and tack around the other.

Solar energy
Solar energy can be harvested for instance in a sun-oriented parabolic solar collector. The problem is: it is available for space heating in summer, when we do not need it. We could however use this energy if we buffered it in a seasonal storage for the winter. We will discuss the principle of seasonal storage further on.
In the dark months in the temperate climatic zone, with a shortened season of heating for well-insulated houses, the sun only shines 8% of the time. Through collection of solar heat in a conservatory (which in fact is a solar collector), with the related greenhouse effect, and venting this air in an anchorless (sound-insulating) cavity wall between two dwellings, the high solar temperature is converted to radiation temperature. The dwelling profits from this through the separating wall four or five hours later. We call this solar cavity heating.

Fig. 03.06: Solar energy is for instance collected in a sun-oriented parabolic solar collector and stored for winter in the soil underneath the building.

Wind energy

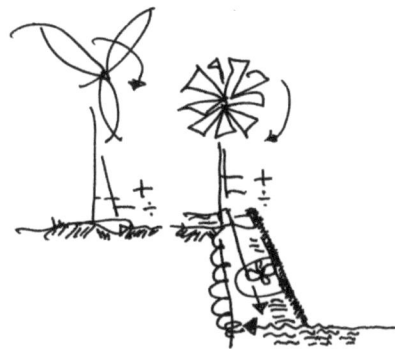

Wind energy is another clean type of energy that should be promoted. Wind speeds of 0 to 40 m/s are not so easily understood due to a lack of technological development. The science that a rotor diameter quadratically contributes to the generation of electricity, and that the wind speed does so to the power of three, marks out this area for connoisseurs.
A polder mill draining water is low tech in comparison with the tall slender turbines.

Fig. 03.07: A polder mill that drains water is low tech in comparison with the tall slender turbines with rotors.

Soil energy

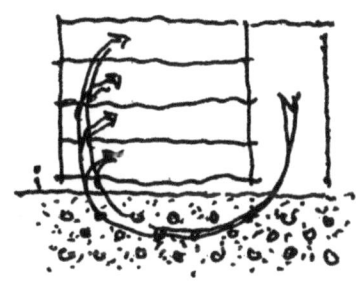

By using the stable groundwater temperature, normally equal to the mean annual temperature (in the Netherlands: 11°C), it is possible to cool a building in summertime and pre-heat it in winter. We can do this by means of a register of air ducts in the ground (e.g. polypropylene copolymer, diameter of 18 cm), without the need of a traditional heat exchanger or the common air-conditioning. The air is led through these ducts under the building and henceforth distributed by a ventilator.
Examples of this principle will be discussed further on.

Fig. 03.08: Air is led into pipes under a building, in or above the ground water table, and then distributed by a ventilator.

03.05   The right building on the right spot

The building industry is significantly responsible for ecological problems around the world. 50% of all materials are used for building and 50% of the total amount of waste comes from it[5]. In addition, the built environment uses 40% of all energy used in the world.

'Refraining from' (letting, not-doing, not-building) often is a great quality. From an optimal environmental viewpoint five aspects we want to bring to attention are:

1. To build or not to build
2. Where to build?
3. What to build?
4. How to build?
5. Integrated design: the right building on the right spot.

The first aspect: to build or not to build

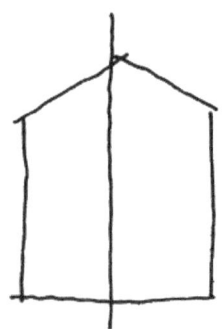

In general poor peoples treat the earth better than rich ones, but refraining from, not being able to pay we consider inequitable in this democratic era. We want to bring across the art of letting through better understanding. Nobody ever asks a municipality whether someone really needs a new building or not. You will be rewarded with a building permit if you pay the dues. Construction is an economic activity.
In contrast, the architect could suggest to the principal, after seeing the building brief: "can you not organise the company better, or merge with another company?" The architect is also a real estate consultant. Existing premises can be refurbished or improved. Sometimes reuse is compulsory!

The second aspect: where to build?

In terms of the low-exergy principle, we would build in climatic zones that reflect our desired comfort temperature, in order to reduce the amount of energy needed for heating or cooling. A little to the cooler side, as artificial cooling costs more energy than heating. Another expression of this aspect: building where transport is. We may consider this broadly. In most western countries the accessibility by public transport is primary. For instance think of theatres or hospitals next to a train or bus station. Nevertheless, our trust in and the use of personal cars has outweighed that of any mode of public transport.

---

[5] The Netherlands alone produce 18 million tonnes of construction and demolition waste annually. This equals the foundation for a six-lane motorway connecting the uttermost south with the highest northern point of the country. Every year…

The third aspect: what to build?

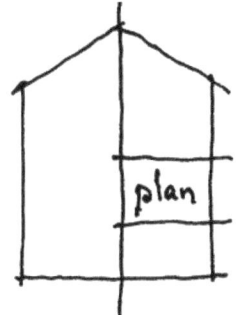

What should we build? Sustainable is what future generations desire to inherit, to use well and maintain. Many view-defining monuments were listed to be demolished because they were not functional. Later an appropriate function could be found.
A building needs to be flexible in structure, layout and use, and spacious in properties in order to accommodate new functions. An aesthetically pleasing building that people want to maintain will become a protected monument in time. Beauty is the first precondition for sustainability; in due time social acceptance is of importance as well.

Fourth aspect: how to build?

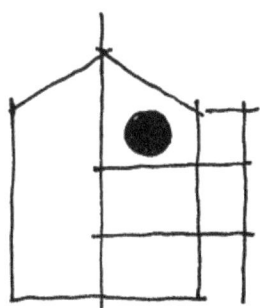

According to most, however durable one builds is the key of the matter. We know everything of constructing; various building schools and technical universities have contributed to its understanding. Various public institutions, public utilities etcetera engage in rules, levies and preparative work, execution, control and construction. The way health laws want us to fit out our living and working environment lacks all psychological incentives and is sensorially poor.
It is obvious that social housing, 15% more spacious than minimum properties, become twice as sustainable. At this moment ever taller growing youths walk with their aura in the steel reinforcement of the concrete floor above. Ceiling heights were once reduced to enforce a minimum height, this becoming the standard, for economic reasons, ever since. A ceiling height of at least 2.6 m will be elementary if we want to design for a long future.
Space for home working, books and a personal computer is still not common yet belongs to societal developments to be reckoned with.

Fifth aspect: integrated design

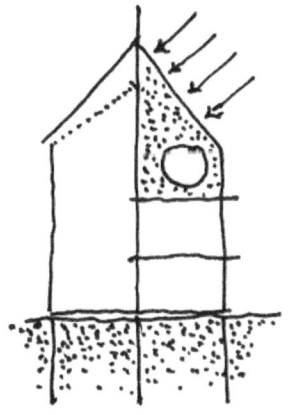

Integrated design equals the right building on the right spot in relationship to its surroundings. The added value of sustainability has not been described, yet to the non-initiated it is often an invisible ecological quality. Only the experienced camper puts his tent in the right place. According to integrated design a building starts with the sun and ends in the geothermal layers above the liquid magma of the earth.

03.06   Themes of sustainable building and living

The normal building brief is hardly a measure of sustainability. The European energy codes to some extent give an idea of the environmental soundness of a building, however, energy for cooling is hardly accounted for. Cooling by means of electricity costs five to six times more primary energy per degree Celsius than heating. Commuter distances are neither mentioned, just as the natural balance in the built environment. Which housing corporation does want bird's nests under the lowest roofing tiles, whereas birds are insectivores par excellence? A songbird eats approximately 25 kg of insects and larvae. Which project developer has ever recorded songbird's nests or grass roofs in the building brief, in order to make the urban climate more agreeable?

Operable windows (controlled by the users themselves) are important, as well as the usage of the structural mass for storage of heat and cold. For low-caloric (< $100^{\circ}C$) space heating solar heat is best used. The noble fossil fuels with combustion temperatures above $1000^{\circ}C$ (process temperature) should be used for different purposes and preserved for our grandchildren.

Furthermore, in the construction costs no account is made of expenses for demountability or waste processing in case the building becomes derelict.
The environmental assessment tool GreenCalc+ calculates the hidden environmental costs of buildings. As explained earlier, for the applied construction and finish materials the environmental effects need to be assessed for the different stages: initiative, site selection, design, operation and management, renovation and (possibly) demounting or demolition.
Simple products, but also cars, always have an instruction manual. With a house one never gets a user manual. For the usage as well as for (preventive) maintenance and the resolution of irregularities a manual with revision drawings is of paramount importance. It should have a place in the meter cupboard.

03.06.01   Theme 1: indoor climate

Designing the indoor climate is of great importance. This can be executed in different ways:

- Passive and active solar energy
- Roof overhangs for the south elevation
- (Vertical) sun-shading devices for the east and west elevation
- (Deciduous) trees
- Green facades, season-variable
- Evaporation

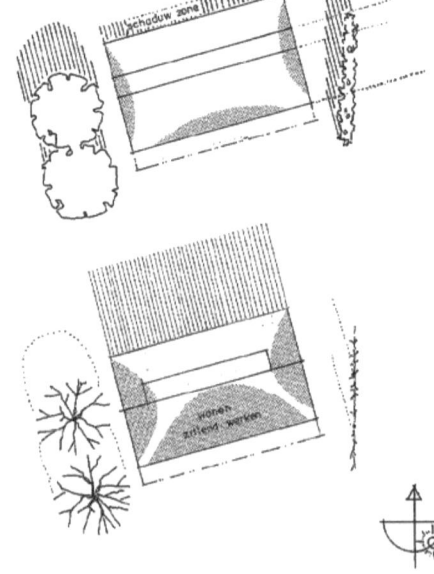

Fig. 03.09:   What makes a house comfortable: limited insolation in summer, a lot of low insolation in winter, a canopy and trees that loose their leaves in autumn; all defines the indoor climate

These measures together with the use of thermal mass in and around the building and cooling by cross-ventilation are generic solutions for warm climates. Cooling by evaporation is also a well-known phenomenon in arid regions with the use of courtyard fountains and water integrated wind-catchers towers.

Starting from childhood we assume that the sun is positioned in the south at 12 O'clock. This is not completely correct. This may sound strange but the building industry tends not to think about the actual direction of the north arrow. In the Dutch city of Delft, 4°7' eastern longitude, there is a 26° difference between 12 O'clock in summer and 12 O'clock in winter. Greenwich lies on 0° eastern longitude, at an hour difference from Delft. In Holland we use the solar time of Berlin, at 15° eastern longitude, implying a difference of 11° or 40 minutes. The Dutch summer time is the solar time of Saint Petersburg, corresponding with 26° beside the polar north. On the north arrow of a drawing in Delft the sun in summer does not cross the south at 12:00 h, but at 13:40 h. The Dutch live recklessly 1 hour and 40 minutes beside the solar time. And in Spain this is even worse!

Now we know this, we can design a more comfortable indoor climate. For, what makes a house comfortable is: limited solar irradiation in summer, abundant low solar irradiation in winter, a canopy and trees that lose their leaves in the fall.

The time factor with regard to building

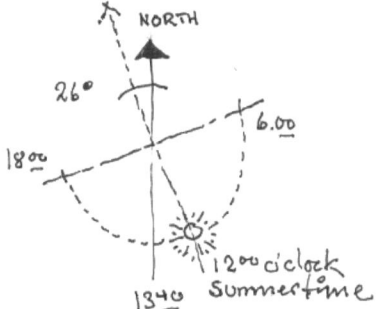

Some instants of time:
- A moment for instance is a photo of a building.
- A full day describes the journey of the sun around the building.
- Seasons define cold, warm, wet and dry periods.
- A year is demonstrated by deciduous trees.
- A century makes people humble; our lives are limited; eventually we always build for someone else.

Fig. 03.10: In spite of what many people think, at 12:00 hrs the sun is perfectly south only in few places of the world. In the Netherlands in summer it reaches south at 13:40 hrs CET: 40 minutes delay from Berlin, one hour extra for summertime.

To be sustainable, we build for the generations that follow. The approaches above signify all buildings should have a climate-directed orientation, with respect to the sun, wind, precipitation and also time. Architecture and nature should coincide.

03.06.02 Theme 2: soil, insolation, green and surface water

The ground on which we live has ecological and economic value. We strive for a natural fit out of the living environment with fewer pavements:
- A healthy living environment, a pleasant way of biding time
- Greening, trees and eco-zones, providing more habitats for plants and animals

- A good urban microclimate with more constant air temperatures, a higher relative humidity and less fine particles; sustainable cycles will evolve
- Slower run-off of rainwater, leading to more down-sinking surface water to the groundwater
- Greater commitment of dwellers and users with their direct environs
- Integration of public, semi-public and private green spaces, occupational and movement space, contact with slow traffic
- Noise prevention using all available innovative green technologies
- Roofs, facades and fences should also qualify for greening, making them less susceptible to graffiti and leading to season-variable buildings adapted to the climate.

In the early 2000s Germany awarded funding of € 37/m^2 for vegetation roofs to promote a better inner-city climate; asphalt can never contribute beneficially to this.

03.06.03   Theme 3: transport

Unorthodox action is needed in different areas of policy for transport:
- Reduction of car traffic by integration of a different means of transport, for instance the 'Icarus' individual and collective transport, a 24-hour low-tech solution[6]
- Reduction of mobility through interweaving of living, working and leisure
- In concurrence with theme 1: the reduction of pavement for cars and other motorised traffic
- Grouping parking lots and concentrating these near the main disclosures

Fig. 03.11:   Public bikes in Lyon. Over long distances we can travel collectively, individually by bike or taxi when we want to be dropped of at home. 'Whitecars', rickshaws, train, taxis and public bike systems are alternatives for the local bus.

- Free issue of bikes (as in Copenhagen 1996, being a cultural capital, as in the Dutch national park De Hoge Veluwe and during the SASBE2009 conference)
- Reducing infrastructure by free public transport[7] (as in the Belgian town of Hasselt, where the number of passengers increased eightfold), avoiding the necessity for new beltways and conserving this money for the general living environment.

---

[6] We can travel collectively over long distances and if we want to be delivered to the front door, we travel individually by bike or taxi. The Icarus system uses small individual cars that drive onto a collective carrier for long distances.
[7] Riksha, train taxi and 'white car' are alternatives to the local bus.

Fig. 03.12: Curitiba in Brazil has an urban structure strongly connected to public transport. Transport lines are the arteries of the city, attracting a lot of new high-density construction alongside them. The smart system of checking-in supports faster bus stop changes.

03.06.04 Theme 4: construction and building materials

Ecological building is more than energy-efficient building: the expected useful lifespan and maintenance should define how we construct. Constructing with bricks and in-situ concrete belongs to flexible buildings with a long expected service life. Building materials (and reuse of them) from the surroundings in principle are the least environmentally damaging. The building industry however knows no briefs for demounting.

Fig. 03.13: While Japan is the front-runner in (de)mountable building, making well-accessible structural connections where bending moments are zero (left), this way of constructing has proceeded little in half a century (right); here connections are still made at nodes, complicating mountage and demountage.

03.06.05 Theme 5: energy

The current mindless and large-scale consumption of fossil fuel is disadvantageous for the environment and economy: in the planning stage opportunities should be created for the limited use of energy during the production and operation stage of houses and other buildings.
This theme of energy will be discussed and elaborated much further in the following chapter and thereafter.

03.06.06 Theme 6: potable water

> *Worldwide the ground water table sags almost everywhere.*
> *The western world should quickly make a difference between drinking water, flushing water and washing water, as much as between surface water, ground water and desalinated sea water.*

Clean potable water in the world is a significant and ever-present problem.
- Unnecessary use of potable water should be restricted.
- The pollution of ground and surface water by agriculture should be prevented.
- Desiccation of the environment by a low groundwater table should be combated.
- Use of rainwater for toilet flushing, (car) washing and gardening should be promoted.

Regarding the last recommendation: the ground water table sinks almost everywhere around the world. The western world should quickly make a distinction between drinking water, flushing and washing water, as well as between surface water, groundwater and desalinated seawater.

Despite the world-wide perception, according to Saeijs[8] the Netherlands is not a watery country due to desiccation, water spilling and a devastating fluvial system. In the poor districts around megacities (e.g. the townships in South Africa and favelas in Brazil) disaster is imminent because of polluted water. In the USA one fears poisoned water sources.

03.06.07 Theme 7: food

Our present-day centrally organised food provision uses a lot of material and energy with packaging and transportation.
- Self-provision should be encouraged by allotment facilities in the living environment.
- The borderland between city and country should be leased per harvest.
- The processing of food can be more environmentally sound.
- Eating food from the concurring season is disappearing, as well as eating food grown locally.
- The contact between city and hinterland via markets has vanished.
- Compost from the city has no demand market from the (monocultural) agricultural farmland.
- Alas there is a global market for junk food.

Fig. 03.14: In China human faeces have been used as natural fertiliser in agriculture for centuries (picture taken in Suzhou, 1990)

03.06.08 Theme 8: waste

Growth of the waste problem should be slowed down by production and consumption of sustainable goods, by reuse of suitable materials and by the far-reaching separation of waste components. As a result of this the amount of waste will decrease, waste processing will become controllable and no valuable materials will be lost. The compost toilet also fits into this strategy. The concept of 'domestic waste' should be altered into 'material for reuse'.

---

[8] Source: Prof.ir. H.L.F. Saeijs, Erasmus University, Rotterdam, the Netherlands

Fig. 03.15:   Waste collectors, example from the Morrapark in Drachten

In housing areas 'material for reuse' can be addressed by:
- A quality fit out in public areas; consultations with occupants regarding cleaning and control.
- A well-deliberated selection of materials, as these eventually can be environmentally damaging as construction and demolition waste; this does not apply to unpainted timber.
- Rewarding occupants for the processing of well-separated waste, for which opportunities of recycling and composting should be present in the living environment; this waste should be bought.
- A good housing design with technical facilities for the reduction of waste production, and a design that stimulates appropriate behavioural patterns, such as creating extra space in the kitchen for waste separation.

Fig. 03.16:   The collection of waste in exchange for food and washing powder, in Curitiba, Brazil (left) and Jón Kristinsson meeting Jaime Lerner, mayor of Curitiba, who is personally accountable for the city's sustainable shift (right)

03.06.09   Theme 9: social aspects

The commitment of dwellers is essential for an optimal result. "Gross national happiness goes above gross national product" [Stevaert, 2001]
- Deciding together about the quality of the fit out of the living environment.
- Stimulating care and responsibility for each other and the surroundings.
- Promoting social security, child- and woman-friendly urban furnishing within the neighbourhood.

- Handing people something back for the effort: space, a good design, a lot of green and playing grounds etcetera.
- The influence of the shape and place of stairs on the constitution of a housing area has never been studied.

The figure depicts the probable influence of stairs on the demographic constitution of a neighbourhood. Poor stair design and location in plan can have a dramatic effect on mobility around the house, youngsters in particular want to have the freedom to come and go unseen.

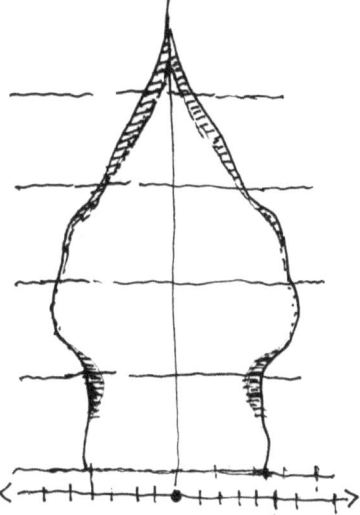

Fig. 03.17: Effect of the stairs to the demographic constitution of a living area.

03.07 Instance of a sustainable house

The image of figure 03.19 is exemplification of a sustainable house, incorporating the themes discussed previously. It will be discussed via four quarters, starting in the top left corner, clockwise.

Water
The water quarter contains the collection of precipitation: a 'high-water' tank for the short term and cool storage for the long term in pressureless water bags placed in the crawlspace. The crawlspace can be kept dry by slowing down evaporation by means of a (> 50 mm thick) layer of loose pearls of polystyrene. The hollow foundation piles contain a capacious tube in their core through which the water can circulate. A heat pump can be connected to this for heating and cooling.

Energy
The energy quarter utilises the energy of the sun. It can harvest passive solar energy through glass, hot water through a solar collector and electricity through PV cells. Heat-insulating shutters in front of the windows on the north elevation and a conservatory on the south are design elements that lead to a comfortable indoor climate.

Flora and fauna
The ground-bound life of flora and fauna forms the third quarter. Water purification by rush ponds and green algae is depicted as entirely safe in operation. Nevertheless a well was installed for inspection. A personal kitchen garden is also proposed. Washing machines of the

future will bind dirt and used soap together, this separation preventing their drainage into the sewage system.

Mobility
The quarter of individual and collective transport encompasses the infrastructure and neighbourhood-surpassing facilities of roads and pedestrian priority areas.

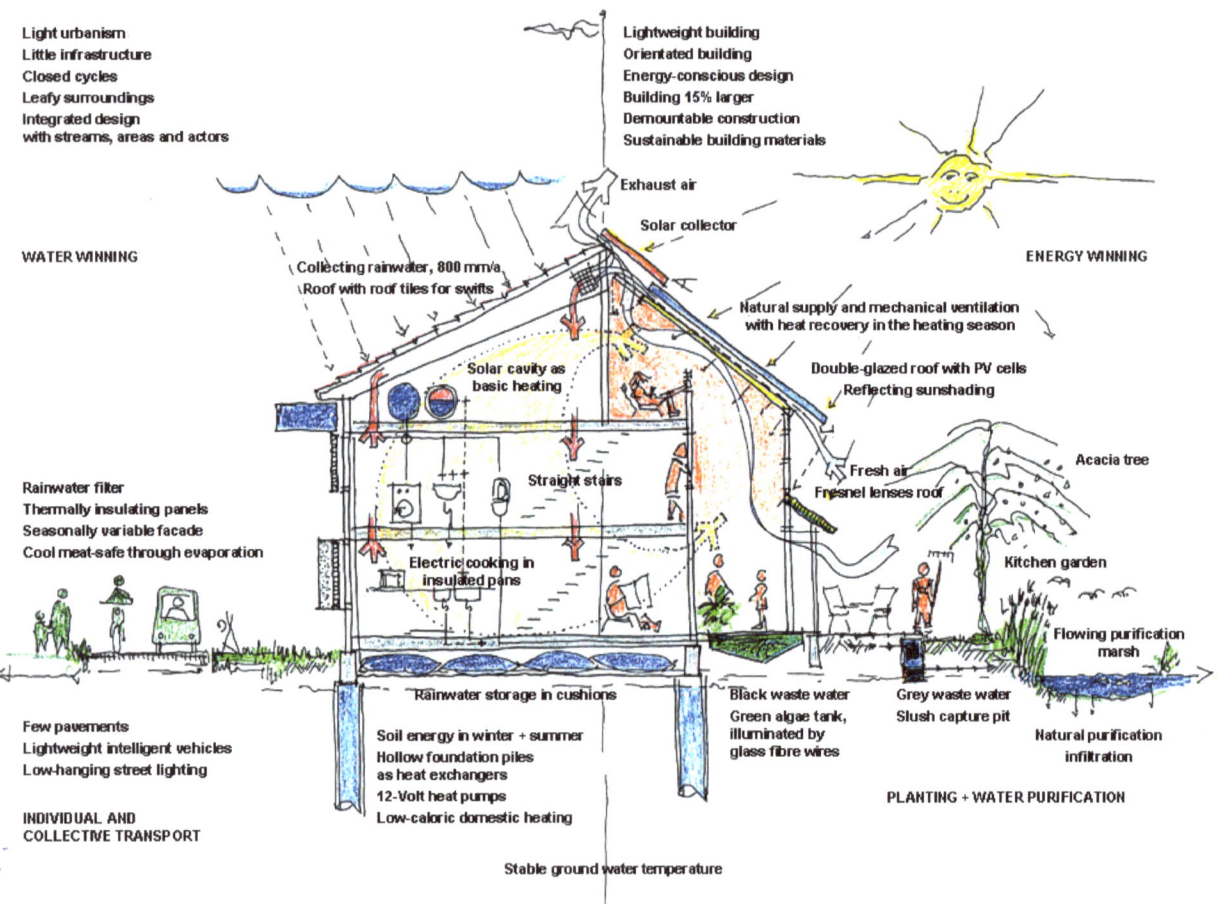

Fig. 03.18:   A sustainable house, with explanations

04

SMART ENERGY TECHNOLOGY

04.01 Basic introduction to energy

04.01.01 Energy in and around the house

Energy in the built environment in relationship to people is simultaneously complex and simple. It is complex because we deal with different forms of energy and conversion factors. Yet it is also simple because energy equals power times time. Therefore, we need to understand energy and its basic units. First, energy is the unit of Joule, J. One Joule is one Newton.metre (N.m, or $kg.m^2/s^2$). So energy is used when a force (accelerated mass) has moved something over a certain distance. Power is energy used by unit of time, Joule/second (J/s), or simply Watt (W).

Table 04.01: Energy and power units

kJ	kilojoule	10^3 J		kW	kilowatt	10^3 W
MJ	megajoule	10^6 J		MW	megawatt	10^6 W
GJ	gigajoule	10^9 J		GW	gigawatt	10^9 W
TJ	terajoule	10^{12} J		TW	terawatt	10^{12} W
PJ	petajoule	10^{15} J		PW	petawatt	10^{15} W
EJ	exajoule	10^{18} J		EW	exawatt	10^{18} W

Table 04.01 gives energy and power units.
Table 04.02 presents conversion values for energy and power.

Table 04.02: Energy and power conversion factors

1 kWh	kilowatt hour	3.6×10^6 J = 3.6 MJ
1 kWh	kilowatt hour	0.1022 m^3 nge[9]
1 kWh	kilowatt hour	864 kcal
1 m^3 nge	natural gas equivalent	35.2 MJ
1 m^3 nge	natural gas equivalent	9.78 kWh
1 m^3 nge	natural gas equivalent	7980 kcal
1 cal	(small) calorie	4.18 J
1 Cal or kcal	(large) calorie, food calorie	4.18 kJ
1 hp	Horsepower	0.736 kW
1 hph	horsepower hour	2.647 MJ
fir wood		10.5 MJ/m^3
domestic fuel oil		40 MJ/l (appr.)
diesel		36 MJ/l (appr.)
petrol		33 MJ/l (appr.)

---

[9] Natural gas equivalent. This only concerns the energetic content. In the generation of electricity losses occur. The efficiency of power generation is approximately 50% with gas-fired plants. This implies consumption of 0.205 m^3 of natural gas for 1 kWh of electricity.
The value mentioned for 1 m^3 of natural gas is high caloric value (HCV), so condensation of exhaust gases it is 35.1 MJ/m^3. At low caloric value it is 32 MJ/m^3.

All human activities cost energy. Table 04.03 gives an overview of the power of these activities. A human being typically performs 130 W x 24 h = 3 kWh per day. Table 04.03 also gives approximated values for power of domestic appliances.

Table 04.03: Human activities (left) and technology around us (right)

Sleeping	75 W	Lamp	25-100 W
Sitting	115 W	Computer	200-300 W
Walking	230 W	Television	100-120 W
Race walking	345 W	Vacuum cleaner	1200-1800 W
Cycling	475 W	Small car	75 kW
Swimming	550 W	Big car	80 kW
Running	670 W		
Judo	1150 W		

Let us take the Dutch as an average for Western European countries. By 2010 an average Dutch household used 3,500 kWh of electricity and 1,500 m^3 of natural gas. Together this is 65.4 GJ or 16.7 MWh. With an average distance of 20,000 km a year by a moderately efficient car, the energy used for transport is no less than 14 MWh, almost as much as normal living needs. And this does not include flying trips…

> An empty Boeing 747-400 weighs 180 tons. A typical arrangement of the aircraft with three classes transports 416 passengers [www.airliners.net]. With 50-65 tons of cargo and 170 tons of kerosene it weighs 400 tons.
> End of June 2012 the price of a gallon of kerosene was $ 4.00 [www.nyserda.org]; this equalled 4.00/3.8*1.25 = € 1.32/l of kerosene. Note that in the same period the price of petrol for cars in Northern Europe varied around € 1.75/l.
> It is a 13 hour flight from Amsterdam to Singapore. With an average occupancy of 85% our Boeing 747-400 will carry 354 people. Fuel consumption is around 12 tons of kerosene per hour (3.3 litre per second – some figures state a gallon per second, which would mean 3.8 l/s), so 156 tons of kerosene in total. 156.000/354= 441 l/passenger, or 882 l after returning. In total this costs € 1,164 per passenger. With European car fuel prices the expenses would have been € 1,544.
> Aviation does not pay excises on fuel so we can travel wherever we want…

Now, all of this energy used needs to be generated somewhere. At the moment, most of this is established through fossil energy resources, which will gradually deplete and have a serious impact on anthropogene climate change in the meantime. So we have to find sustainable alternatives, for which the New Stepped Strategy is helpful:
1. reduce the demand
2. reuse waste energy
3. generate energy from renewable sources (sun, wind, water, earth and life itself).

The following sections will explore in detail energy saving and sustainable generation, so let's first have a look at the human aspect to it: how to we keep ourselves supplied with energy?   By food and drinks, of course. Table 04.04 presents the energy we as human beings absorp, provided by food we eat and beverages we drink. These are approximate values.

Table 04.04: Energy in food and beverages

Sugar	one tea spoon	13 kcal	55 kJ
Ketchup	one portion	15 kcal	60 kJ
Broth	one cup	20 kcal	85 kJ
Knäckebröt	one piece	35 kcal	150 kJ
Jam	one soup spoon	44 kcal	185 kJ
Rye bread	one slice	55 kcal	230 kJ
Whole milk	one glass (¼ l)	69 kcal	290 kJ
Cola	one glass (¼ l)	80 kcal	335 kJ
Red wine	1 glass (120 ml)	85 kcal	355 kJ
Coffee garnish	one portion	90 kcal	380 kJ
Fries	50 g	130 kcal	550 kJ
Peanuts	20 nuts	140 kcal	590 kJ
Trout, cooked	one piece	150 kcal	630 kJ
Grape juice	one glass (¼ l)	160 kcal	670 kJ
Roast beef	one piece	175 kcal	735 kJ
Beer	one pint	182 kcal	761 kJ
Ice cream	one portion	200 kcal	840 kJ
Apple pie	one piece	300 kcal	1260 kJ
Creme pastry	one piece	400 kcal	1680 kJ
Farmer's sausage	125 g	515 kcal	2160 kJ
Chocolate	125 g	680 kcal	2850 kJ
Butter	100 g	750 kcal	3300 kJ

04.01.02 Exergy next to energy

In the building industry we should not use high-caloric energy to produce low-caloric heat at the end of the process.

> It is a problem that a gas heating flame of 1200-1500°C
> should keep our homes at a level of 20°C. 'Waste' heat is not used.

Energy companies and building utility manufacturers must come to their senses. It is inevitable that the essential temperature for heat demanded on one side, on an energetic base, must be aligned with the heat sources that are available on the other side.
This has far-reaching consequences for buildings that use low-caloric heating in floors and walls, especially when larger building surfaces are becoming more common.
A large variety in types of energy supply is needed.

There are two important reasons why we consume so much unnecessary process energy.
1. There are profits to be made by inefficient energy use, that is to say: fossil energy is too cheap.
2. We lack the knowledge and facilities to apply sustainable heating.

Let's assume that the last reason is the most important one. It is not hard to make a product fit for its circumstances (1 to 9) looking at the environmental conditions and composition (atmosphere, hydrosphere, lithosphere).

The definition of the exergy of a product (flow) is the maximum amount of labour that is available within this product (flow), per mass unit, based on the differences according to the environmental condition in terms of pressure, temperature and chemical composition.
For example, natural gas of 175 bar and 60°C (as in a reservoir) is not equal to the environmental circumstances, in all three exergetic parameters[10]:
- natural gas (CH_4) ≠ N_2, O_2, H_2O, CO_2
- 175 bar ≠ 1 bar
- 60°C ≠ 15°C

It appears that despite this definition energy and exergy can be easily confused.
When I look at my energy saving projects in the past, in which mainly exergy was applied for ventilation systems and heat exchange, the energy possibilities can be counted on 10 fingers.

Low-exergy design principles
- Small isolated core
- Bike-shed
- Rain water collector and storage (e.g. in bags)
- Combined solar boiler
- Heat exchanger in foundation piles
- Sequence of energy utilization: from electricity, process heat to low-caloric heat

04.02   Thermal insulation

04.02.01 Wrapping up the building

Insulating foundations
We were the first to introduce thermal insulation of foundations in the Netherlands and probably also one of the first elsewhere in the world. Today it seems logical but around 1980 it was far from common. Our work changed the direction of construction forever.

The idea was born with a simple calculation.
When foundation beams have the same temperature as the ground in winter (appr. 6°C), heat losses from a dwelling with a typical 38 m^2 of concrete beams will be approximately 500 kWh per heating season (corresponding to a consumption of around 80 m^3 of natural gas). To avoid these thermal bridges an interruption in the concrete can be made by for instance foam glass.

---

[10] Source: Prof. J. de Swaan Arons, TU Delft

Another option is covering the foundation beams with 100 mm thick polystyrene insulation panels (figure 04.01).

Fig. 04.01:   *Permanent polystyrene insulation underlayer for foundation beams (1982, left) and casting of the concrete inside the foundation insulation (2010, right)*

For ground floor insulation above the crawl space, polystyrene cushions can be placed between and under pre-stressed concrete beams (figure 05.02). These cushions function both as thermal insulation and as permanent formwork for the floor on top. The concrete finish floor then functions as a compression zone together with the pre-stressed concrete beams.

The permanent polystyrene insulation formwork for foundation beams was once innovative but has become standard since. Among others, this system is being recommended by labour inspection because the minimal weight of the product, leads to less worker back problems during installation. The concrete reinforcement cages are delivered on site prefabricated.

Fig. 04.02:   *Polystyrene cushions placed between pre-stressed concrete beams*

Insulating walls

Thermally insulated walls had become a habit already long before the insulated foundation. We built the very first Dutch house with thermal insulation in the roof and cavity of the gable in 1967. This soon became the standard after the oil crisis in 1973.

Fig. 04.03: The plasterers are working outside one of our well-insulated houses in the 1980s. Extra reinforcement was applied in fragile places at the edges of the window-frames. One had no experience, so everything was done as safe as possible.

In the 1980s we introduced PUR sealings between precast concrete wall elements to optimise the energy performance of buildings. This of course was combined with thick façade insulation and air-tight wooden Swiss window frames with triple glazing. These were sealed by intumescent strips. On the construction site, polyurethane (PUR) has become the preferred resolution for minor mistakes in detailing. Seams are usually sealed with polyurethane foam. PUR has various negative environmental properties, but since 1990 Freon as propellant is substituted by gases that do not damage the ozone layer.

Fig. 04.04: This is how the facade of the dwelllings eventually turned out.

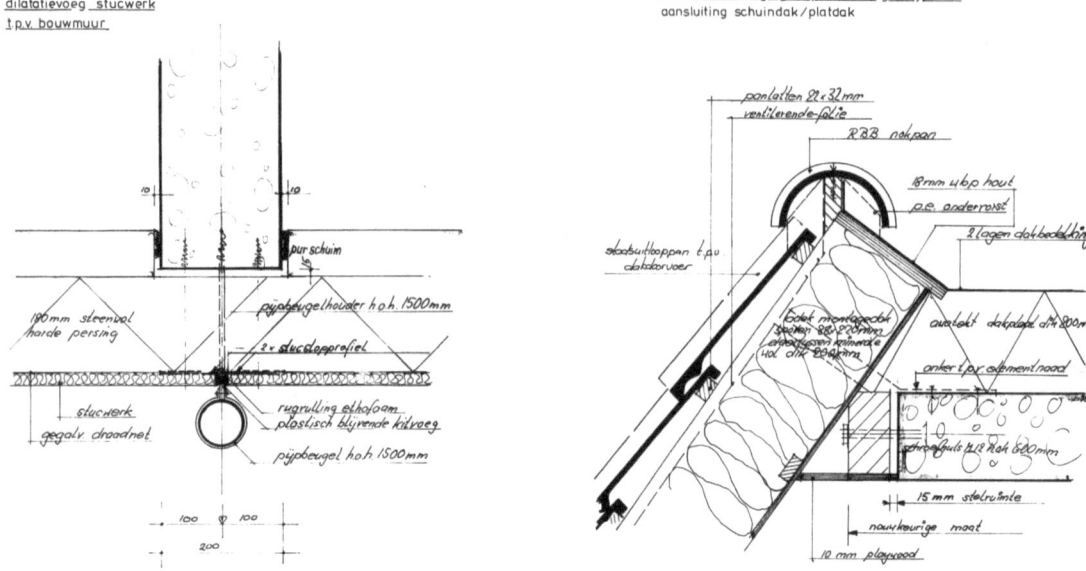

Fig. 04.05:   Old details of a well-insulated house: horizontal section of a plastered gable (left) and vertical section of the connection of a slanted roof to a flat roof part (right)

Insulating roofs

Another novelty to the building industry was the use of prefabricated rafter roof elements. In the earliest versions these had a 10 mm bottom multiplex board. A package of 200 mm of mineral wool lay between the rafters. Under the tile laths a man-bearing ventilating foil was placed. On top of it, ceramic or concrete roofing tiles finished the structure. Danish Velux windows were often placed in the roof elements during fabrication. These windows were chosen because of their uncomplicated use and maintenance.

Fig. 04.06:   The piled-up rafter roof elements with thermal insulation (left) and the roof with integrated Velux windows just before the roof tiling works

This was all done long before the introduction of the passive house principle, including a heat-recovery system to be discussed further on. According to measurements the average air-tightness of the dwellings was generally good. The system was not disturbed with the opening of windows during night-time.

04.02.02 Thermally insulating shutters

Introduction
The ability to minimise heat flows, into or out of the building according to the season, is an energetic factor of great significance. in a well-insulated dwelling with a façade that is adaptable to the seasons, we can win solar energy in winter and prevent its entry in summer:
- In the heating season thermally insulating shutters in front of windows, for the evening and at night.
- With the use of a narrow and wide window strip, shutters in front of the wide strip of bedroom window can stay closed in winter.
- Optimal daylight access: high and wide for maximum light admittance (possibly diffuse), adjustable in summer.
- Exterior sun protection, against over-heating in summer, preferably adjustable, transparent and storm proof.
- Deciduous climbing plants, not attached to the façade, or knotted lime trees.

In this way we can make a summer and winter house in one, but also a night and day house.

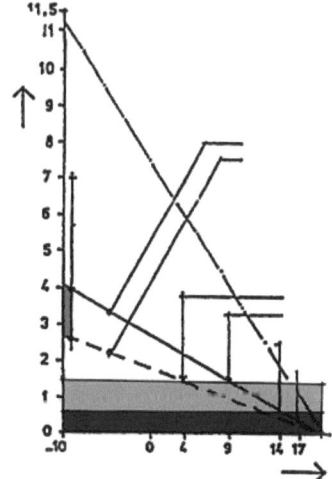

Fig. 04.07: Changes to the heating season as a result of the internal heat production, and the difference of having shutters or not. Vertical are heat losses in kW, horizontal the outside temperature in °C; the dark grey area is a house uninhabited, the light grey area inhabited. The crossing sloped lines depict at which temperature heating is required when they cross the light or dark barrier: the dashed line is with shutters closed, the full line with shutters open.

The winter house of Frank Lloyd Wright in Taliesin West, near Phoenix (figure 05.07), is a beautiful example of a winter house that was kept at temperature by a roof of milk glass. In summer this house was empty due to overheating. Yet the house is also used in summer months due to its architectural significance, made possible thanks to a large air conditioner as we see more often in "Gods own country".

Fig. 04.08:   Taliesin West, by Frank Lloyd Wright: meant as a winter palace, nowadays used as museum and air-conditioned all year round.

Insulating shutters are rarely seen on buildings. They do sometimes function as sun protection, as slats and for security. It is obvious to use thermally insulating shutters as elements that form the architectural image, but this happens sporadically.

Fig. 04.09:   The Danish 'zero'-energy house: simultaneous development of shutters at the Technical University of Copenhagen (above) and Hjortekjear, also in Copenhagen – dwellings with outside shutters that set the architectural scene (below)

In theory the thermally insulating shutters can be shut for two-thirds of the time in schools and offices, since they are closed during that time. For bedrooms and/or study rooms in dwellings the period of required daylight is equal to or less than in offices. For an average room (T_i = 21°C) the shutters reduce 30 m^3 nge/m^2/year with single-glazed windows and 10 m^3 nge/m^2/year with double-glazed windows.

Fig. 04.10: Test of thermally insulating shutters in the Beijum district of Groningen (left) and the ones applied in the neighbourhood of Woudhoek-Zuid in Schiedam (right)

Examples from practice insulated shutters

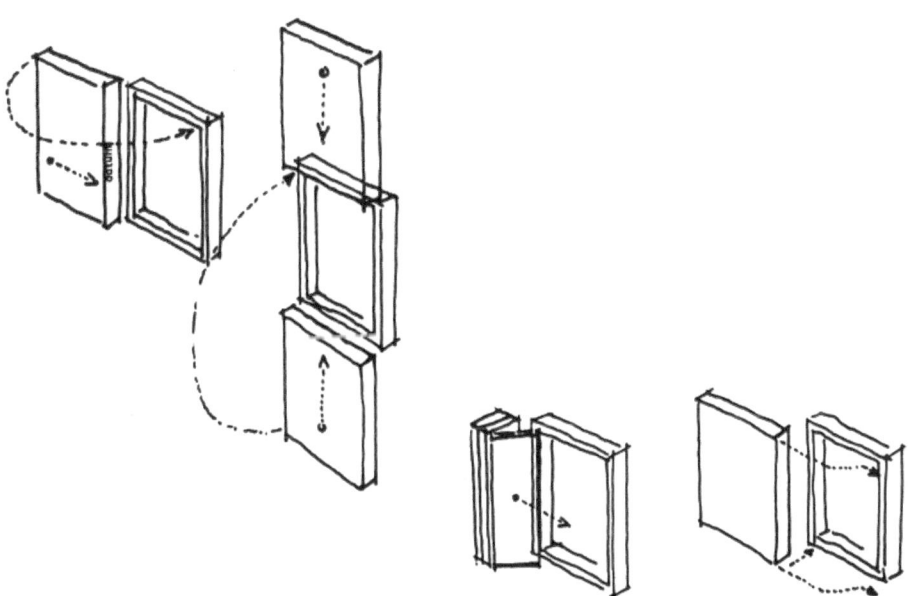

Fig. 04.11: Various examples of thermally insulating shutter principles

A thermally insulating shutter can (in principle) be operated in three different manners: sliding, rotating and folding. A reliable operating system for rotating shutters that can be opened and closed from the inside took 1.5 years to develop.

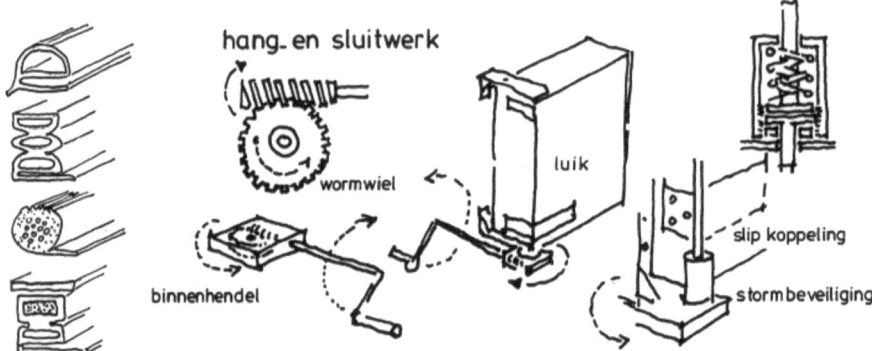

Fig. 04.12:   Examples of sealing rubber gaskets for insulating shutters (left) and the original sketches of worm wheel for operating shutters (right)

The combination of a worm wheel with a warranty (coming from sunscreens) with a steel spring to bear wind forces and to ensure a good sealing, appeared to work well for the Minimum-Energy Dwellings in Schiedam. The operating system had to be as easy as possible.

Later, in the working-class district of Klarendal in Arnhem, the small windows with rotating shutters were replaced by folding shutters after which the window had to be opened to adjust the shutters. Sliding insulated shutters of large dimensions (2 x 2 m) at ground level are adjustable by a rail and a hinge system, known from mini-vans. A sliding shutter on the outside of a façade is a very effective solution with a stark architectural expression.

Fig. 04.13:   Folding shutters, operable by hand, in the Klarendal district in Arnhem

For the internal orientation in a house it is important that part of a window, for example the operable part, is not completely closed by insulating shutters. If nine tenth of the window is covered, a large energetic effect will already be accomplished whilst ensuring daylight access.

Fig. 04:14:   Sliding shutters with the rail system of a van

Another option is the use translucent insulation materials in shutters: good for daylight inside and insulation in winter. In summer these shutters provide little cooling. This can be rectified by applying white reflecting material or colloidal foil that turns white at high temperatures on the translucent shutters. An option is a combination of insulating shutters and PV cells on the south as a new architectural element.

The implementation of interior shutters is less complicated. In most cases magnetic locking is used, also when the shutters swing open to a ceiling or 180° against an indoor wall. Condensation against the strongly cooled glass in winter is inevitable, but in the space between the shutter and the glass there is little air. Suppose 0.2 m^3 with a relative humidity of 50%. That is 1 m^2 x 0.2 m^1 x 50% x 17 gr/m^3 = 0.2 x 0.5 x17 = 0.17 gr of condensate. When the shutters are opened this condensate appears to be evaporated in 2 to 3 minutes. The shutters will have to be air-tight.

Fig. 04.15:   Translucent insulating shutters seen from the outside and inside

A sliding alternative, where insulation grains are captured between two layers of glass, is difficult to establish in the building industry, when a warranty of ten years cannot be given.

Are there more possible applications for insulated shutters? Yes, certainly. For low-rise buildings a wooden terrace in the form of the old portcullis, such as castles have, can also form a thermal insulation part of the façade. In the upright position it can function as a security system against burglary.

Fig. 04.16:   Pre-manufacturing an insulating shutter

Other useful applications of insulated shutters for example are not thermal, but acoustical, as noise insulation. For instance, for discos and youth societies at inner-city locations that do not close at 11 PM. Sound insulating shutters enable a double use of space. It also makes the city livelier when housing and recreation go hand in hand. These shutters can be fixed on the inside, with a hinge. They have a double rabbet and are made of heavy plated material filled with sound-absorbing filling. In case an even higher insulation is needed, an extra external shutter can be considered. The strength of the chain is determined by the weakest shackle.
Sound-tight ventilation cannot be forgotten.

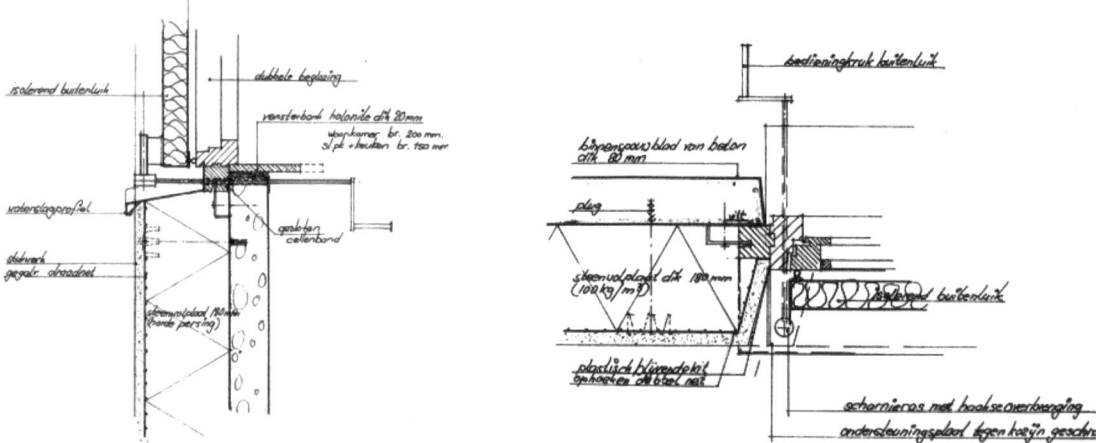

Fig. 04.17:   Detail of the sill at the parapet, with external shutter (left), and of a window-frame connection with external shutter controllable from the inside

Rough results for thermally insulating shutters by TNO in 1983
Accomplished measurements of thermally insulating shutters determined the following:
1. The practical heat resistance measured at panel shutters is 35 to 40% higher than the resistance of the best insulating window surfacing (reflecting roller-blinds).
2. The selection of cover and core material for the panel shutters is hardly of influence on the practical heat resistance. Wooden shutters are a fraction better than metal or synthetic ones.
3. The maximum practical heat resistance measured for the total façade element appears to be approximately 1.25 m^2K/W, i.e. a U value of 0.8 W/m^2K, with insulation glass.
4. Fastening or totally sealing off of the rubber strips does not lead to major improvements in heat resistance.
5. The window-frame onto which the shutter is fixed appears to be an important thermal bridge. An important heat resistance improvement of the total construction can only be realised with a totally separated internal and external window-frame, also interesting for the costs and benefits.
6. The operational system with a turning-arm instead of a turning-axis for wind control is recommended with external shutters, in which the wind control should better not contain cast-iron parts.
7. Load-bearing tests indicate that users need to be instructed not to operate the shutters at a wind force of 6 Beaufort or more.
8. Shutters with large dimensions should be avoided. Up to 1 m^2 a shutter can operate with normal driving-components and connection parts. For larger shutters the double folding shutter principle with guard bead, or sliding shutters should be applied.

Concluding remarks
Fortunately we can determine that the thermal quality of double-glazing has improved with large steps each time against little extra costs. The float glass technique where melted glass floats seamless on tables filled with tin, instead of the large rollers used in the past, is a revolution in the production process (of the first order). In this way glass has become relatively cheap and has had many possible functional applications. Glass is manufactured from material that is nearly unlimited and that can be recycled through a melting process.
The thermal improvement of 'cheap' glass prevented the expensive shutters from competing. Moreover, the window-frame has become the thermal bridge and not the glass pane, as around the time of the Schiedam Minimum-Energy Dwellings for example. The next energetic measure is to improve the window-frames. In second instance the insulating shutters can, as adjustable façade, have a great influence on the dimensions of the building heating and cooling services.

04.02.03   Energetic renovation of 448 tenement flats, Schiedam (1989)

448 tenement flats, spread over 15 blocks in the neighbourhood Nieuwland in Schiedam and dating from 1956, were due for renovation. After 32 years of intensive use this was (also in regards to comfort and the new energy reduction programme of the government) desperately needed. Our office got the honour to provide an answer. We started with one building block of 32 flats.

Fig. 04.18: Font side of the tenement flats in Schiedam after renovation

Old situation

The tenement flats each contain apartments with three or four rooms, divided over three or four storeys. The type is representative for many apartments from that period. The storage rooms are situated in the basement of the buildings. The size of the flats was originally derived from requirements and suggestions dating back to 1951; according to current criteria they are small, especially the kitchens. The balconies partly protruding from the building are small (1 x 1.85 m) and therefore limited in their usage.

The thermal bridges at the balconies caused moisture problems, condensation, mould, etcetera. There was of course no mechanical ventilation. The ventilation mainly occurred through chinks, by opening windows and via the ventilation shaft in-between shower and toilet.
In the beginning the flats had been heated by coal stoves. Later these were replaced by gas heaters put in the living room. Thermal comfort in these flats was poor. The disadvantage of stoves and gas heaters is an uneven distribution through dwellings without thermal insulation.

Fig. 04.19: Old kitchen

Deduced from measurements by TNO (a Dutch building investigation institute) the temperature gradient between floor and ceiling within one space turned out to be ΔT = 17°C (in the case of an outside temperature of -3°C). Especially the dwellings above the basement had very little comfort. Next to the stove at the floor in the living room the temperature was 14.5 °C, at the ceiling 31°C and next to the window respectively 11.5 °C and 29°C. In the unheated bedroom the temperature measured was 6.5°C. The average energy consumption, including all energy needed for cooking and hot water, was 1,830 m^3 of natural gas per year for upper and lower dwellings and around 1,130 m^3 of natural gas for the dwellings in-between.

Fig. 04.20:   Impression of the new balcony, removal of the balconies and a new one in place

Improvements
- Enlargement of the balcony at the front side and the application of extra sliding windows
- Enlargement of the kitchen and a new kitchen block
- A new façade surrounding the new balconies at the backside
- Reduction of the glass area at the shadow side
- Installing 150 mm thick thermal insulation on the outside
- Replacement of the wood windows and window frames
- Replacement of single glazing by double glazing
- Applying roof insulation and new roofing
- Heating the whole apartment instead of just the living room
- Insulating storage boxes in the basement to prevent heat loss from the lower dwellings
- Seamless all around finishes

New situation
The main goal was to improve the indoor climate. As a test-case one dwelling was renovated and the air-heating installation was tested. The residents were informed at an early stage. The façade placed around the balconies led to disappearance of thermal bridges and moisture.

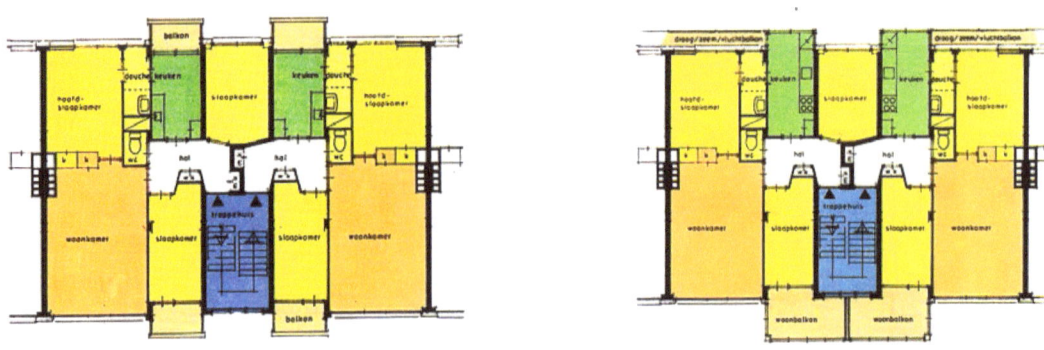

Fig. 04.21:   Floor plan, old (left) and new (right)

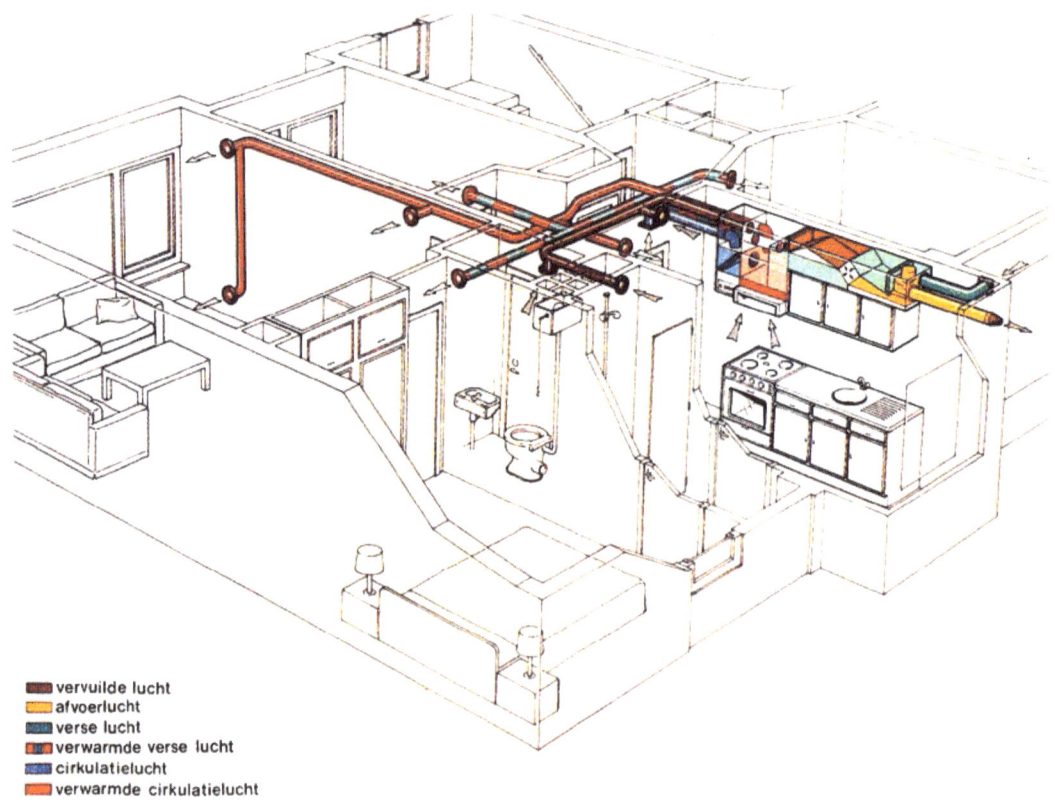

Fig. 04.22:   'Combiduct' installation of the energetic renovation in Schiedam

For the tenement flat renovation an efficient use of energy, a good living comfort and letability on the longer term were the main issues. Due to the adjustments to the dwellings a traditional central heating system would lead to increased energy costs in contrast to the low energy costs of the former gas stoves. This would come on top of the higher rent. That is why we developed something new.

The 'Combiduct' air-heating installation had been designed especially for apartments, where space is scarce. The Combiduct was placed in the kitchen above the cooking-stove. It bundles four functions in one machine: balanced ventilation, heating, hot tap water and heat exchange from flue gasses and exhaust air. The machine had an outlet-valve that when pulled out gave the ventilator extra acceleration. The heating of air and the ventilation system had two compartments: the bedrooms and the compartment of the living room, kitchen and shower. In the bedrooms only fresh air was added. The temperature in the main bedroom could be adjusted through a thermostat, independent from the living area. Living room, kitchen and shower received recirculated air and had their own thermostat.

Fig. 04.23:   Proposal of new facades, front (left) and back side (right)

Thanks to the balanced ventilation system it was possible to completely seal the apartment, without the risk of moisture problems. When the installation was set for summer operation, only the out-blowing ventilator functioned. The air inlet in that case needed to be through open windows.

Energy consumption and climate in the living area

Calculations indicated that the new energy consumption needed for the heating of an in-between apartment was approximately 400 m^3 nge/year, and about 570 m^3 nge/year for an upper or lower apartment. The extra use of electricity for the ventilators was 540 kWh/year. As a result of this a large part of the energy reduction would be lost. The consumption of natural gas for cooking and such was estimated at approximately 80 m^3 nge/year, and 250 m^3 nge/year for hot water. 100 m^3 nge/year could be reduced by a heat exchanger. The expectation was that 70% of the flats would not deviate from more than 20% this value.

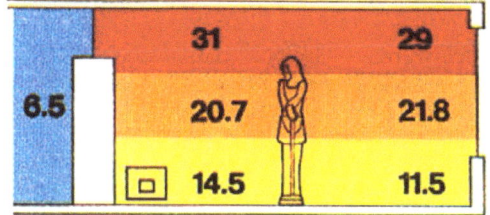 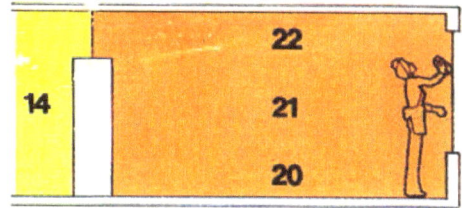

Fig. 04.24:   Temperature distribution before (left) and after renovation (right)

It has to be pointed out that the living comfort had improved enormously. These improvements become apparent when temperature differences in one space at the floor and ceiling are compared with each other (at an outdoor temperature of -3°C). Before the renovation it was impossible to keep your feet warm, with a floor temperature of 11 to 14°C, while the temperature at the ceiling was around 30°C. The spaces were apparently heated in favour of the neighbour above.

After the renovation the temperature difference between floor and ceiling did not exceed 2°C. Moreover, the entire apartment was heated, in contrast with one room in the old situation. The energetic renovation, the new heating system and the hot tap water facility led to a maximum increase of the rent of only € 20.42 (lowest storeys) or € 15.18 (middle storeys) per month per apartment, while this merited a monthly energy reduction of € 59.45.

It became one of the renowned projects of the National Renovation Prize of 1989, awarded by the Ministry of Economic Affairs.

The expenses for the improvement of the first 32 buildings were € 21,345 per dwelling excluding VAT: residents had a better apartment and the neighbourhood was preserved – the functional lifespan was prolonged. Later, with a subsidy of the European Community the other 416 buildings were renovated as well.

04.03   Ventilation with heat recovery

04.03.01   The Slootweg Unit

The 'Slootweg' heating and ventilation unit that was installed in the tenement flats of Schiedam has never been developed further than the 0-series. This is extremely regrettable because it had a simple operating system, was small and compact, with no electronic high-tech and easy to produce in quantity.
Nevertheless there were problems with the Fasto geyser boiler (not enough warm water and undesired lowering at night, set for energy savings by the Ministry of Economic Affairs). The connection of the Fasto geyser and the Slootweg unit eventually caused the designer/fitter, after whom the system was named and who was responsible for the total contract installation, to go bankrupt.

It is clear that the possibilities for architects to build 'Minimum-Energy Dwellings' was ever more reduced; the government and housing corporations speculated wrongly on cheap natural gas (as long as it is available!).
Nowadays, the development of the successful Fasto geyser and Nefit heating boilers could be traced back to the original 'Slootweg' unit, then without balanced ventilation with heat recovery and fresh air heating.
With the current energy performance requirement for small dwellings a simple air heating system would be much more appropriate. Apparently, one still considers the traditional radiator heating system – old-fashioned but familiar – the safest option. Meanwhile, the convectors needed for the bedrooms became unnecessary!

04.03.02 The fine-wire heat exchanger

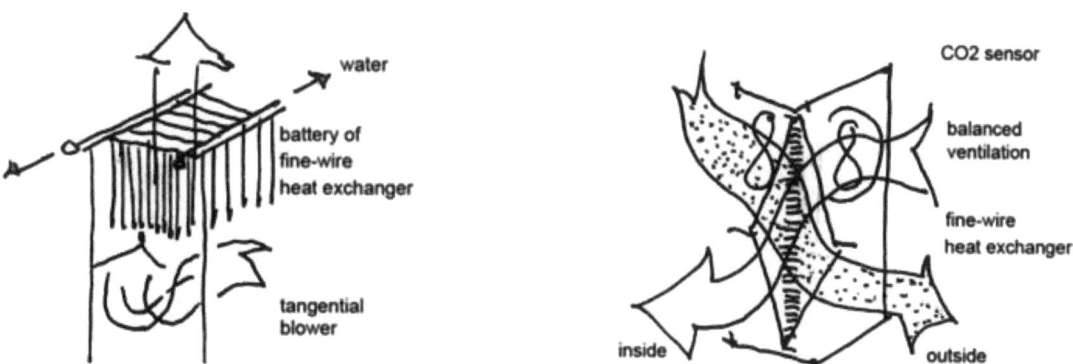

Fig. 04.25:   Water/air Fiwihex heating/cooling (left) and air/air Fiwihex balance ventilation (right)

Introduction
Why did it take such a long time to make the fine-wire heat exchanger suited to the market when the calculated output raised such high expectations? How air had to be led through or along the Fiwihex device was unknown, various prototypes were tested.
The knowledge of weaving textiles had disappeared to developing countries. A weaver had to be found who was willing to invest in an expensive, complicated loom that could weave 1/10 mm copper wire.

Why is greenhouse horticulture so slow in switching from natural gas to solar energy?

There are at least three reasons:
1. Natural gas is very cheap for market gardeners.
2. When burning natural gas, CO_2 arises, which the plants use as fertilizer (yielding 20% more output).
3. The unfavourable investment climate does not allow much innovation.

A foreseeable breakthrough and application is at hand. Seasonal heat and cold storage is generally situated at a depth of 20 to 50 m in an aquifer, a wet layer of sand enclosed between impervious layers of clay. These soil conditions are often found in the Rhine delta of The Netherlands. In brief: This new technology will be applied on a large scale, as it allows Dutch greenhouse horticulture to change from being a wholesale natural gas consumer into a solar energy supplier using seasonal storage in aquifers. The late eminent innovator Dr. Noor van Andel, a retired director of corporated research of Akzo Nobel, advanced experiments into fine-wire by acquiring the skills of Gerard ter Beek, the only skilled textile weaver and employer to be found in the eastern part of the Netherlands. Beek was willing to accept the challenge to develop a new loom capable of weaving copper wire.

How to make a fiwihex?
The Fiwihex devices for heating and cooling are woven with a warp of ø 1/10 mm tinned copper wire and a weft of ø 2 mm water-conducting tubes of 9,5 mm centre to centre (Figure 04.27). The dimensions of every heat-exchanging mat are: 2 mm thick, 150 mm wide and 300 mm high. Side by side with an in-between distance of 10 mm the mats are soldered to thicker pipes at top

and bottom. The final air-heating element measures 200 x 1050 mm. To this a tangential ventilator is added between the plant tables. This appears to function well in practice and the plants are not hindered by draught. When applied in factories and workshops the Fiwihex fans are mounted high. The shafts have become higher and at the lower end equipped with a streamlined outlet of water-absorbing material to catch possible condensation water collected during the cooling process. The soldered components are now glued (with hot melt glue) including the synthetic main tubes, shortening assembly time. These Fiwihex devices are tested in practice at max. 2 bar (20 m head of water).

 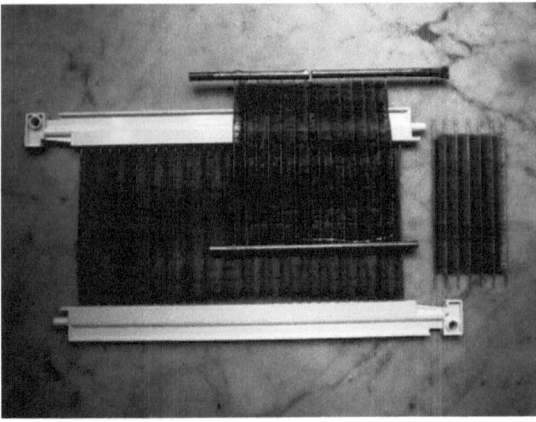

Fig. 04.26: Three steps of Fiwihex elements, showing the twinning machine for the ø 0.1 mm copper wire at the back, an air-to-air heat exchanging element at the front and an element with air conductors behind it (left) and three steps for an element with heat transmission from air to water or reverse, including interwoven thin water pipes (ø 2 mm) (right)[11]

Industrial ventilators have to be transformed for use in private houses. In this phase we go back to an approved very low temperature decentralized air-heating device on the ceiling. Inside a round woven fine wire heat exchanger of ø 0,6 m and 0,2 m high, slowly rotates a fan which keeps moving 1000 m3/h of air. This ceiling air heater has proved to operate free of dust. The first large-scale application will be the new Kramer-laboratory at TU Delft. Fresh outside air is led to the offices through fans in the lowered ceiling. Laboratories require highly controlled, extremely well ventilated spaces; therefore cheap heating is critical.

A combination of basic radiation heating and lower temperature air heating may be a better solution. We can postulate that when the demand for it arises. In the longer-term smaller and more silent running fine wire air heating elements are in the process of developement.
When this paper was written in January 2009, experiments were being carried out with small Fiwihex transparent convectors, driven by small LTV-tangential ventilators.

First application of the greenhouse technology of tomorrow
After many years of development the 'fine-wire heat exchanger' has now reached its first phase of application. In Dutch greenhouse horticulture studies has been presented that show that by using fine-wire heat exchangers greenhouse energy consumption can be reduced from

---

[11] Photos by Trudy Veldhof

approximately 50 m³ natural gas/m² per year to zero (though electricity is used to power the pumps).

Fig. 04.27:   Fiwihex hanging in a rose greenhouse for heating and cooling

Excess solar energy can be stored in an aquifer. On an annual basis at our latitude of 52° north, about 7 times more solar heat enters the greenhouse than leaves it due to transmission losses. It is clear that cooling is no less important than heating. It is customary to whitewash glass roofs to keep out the heat and to open skylights to outside fresh air. In the case of the energy-producing greenhouse such as the one described here, it is taken for granted that the greenhouse is kept closed all year round and in hot sunny weather is cooled by the same water/air heat exchanger which heats up the green-house during the night. Keeping greenhouses closed all the year round has three advantages. Firstly, the relative humidity inside the greenhouses can be kept at a steady level (for example 80%). Secondly, vermin is kept to a minimum. The third advantage is vegetation stimulation. In further developments of the energy-producing greenhouse all organic waste matter will be collected and anaerobically converted by means of biogas fermentators, the fuel to be used in micro turbines or diesel engines to generate electricity. The filtered CO_2 will be blown into the greenhouse to manure the plants. CO_2-neutral greenhouse horticulture arises when the CO_2 concentration of 500 ppm in open greenhouses is increased to 1,000 parts per million (ppm), resulting in a productivity increase of 20%.

Villa Flora, a greenhouse with a 25 m high landscaped office, located in The Horticulture world exhibition Venlo, The Netherlands, will be discussed in more detail in chapter 09.
The inside climate of Villa Flora's greenhouse, with 35,000 visitors on peak days, is mainly controlled by Fiwihex air cooling and heating. The fine wire heat-exchanger already works at very low temperatures. Insulation, concrete core activation (cooling floors with water), can also influence radiation heat. The perceptible temperature range for humans is the average temperature of air and radiation. There is a clear relation between the inside climate of the greenhouse and the heat and cold storage in the aquifer. A greenhouse of 2 ha (150 x 150 m) is large enough for seasonal heat storage (aquifer) to function with edge losses. The heat excess from the greenhouse can provide 8 ha. (i.e. a maximum of 200 passive houses) with heating and cooling. The cooling water from the diesel engine provides the houses with hot tap water. This new greenhouse technology will be introduced into dwellings and offices.

Fig. 04.28:   Fiwihex box in a factory

Greenhouse technology for private houses

The translation of greenhouse horticulture technology to private houses has not yet been realised. In some houses an aquifer cannot be installed. A minimum roof collector surface of 1 ha. is necessary, assuming that a simple version of a roof collector is twice as efficient than a closed greenhouse. Often there is also excess heat of 25 to 30°C in various forms e.g. cooling milk at a dairy farm. This is a new technology, a minimalist approach without the aid of heating pumps and fossil fuels.
The electricity consumption of pumps with little resistance can be reduced if the diameter of the pipes is wide enough and the conveying height small. The temperature level inside the house is bound to limits of comfort. Most Europeans find 17° to 23°C comfortable.

Now we have to consider radiation heating, air heating and the localised preferences of the building occupants. Low radiation heating in floors and walls is based on a constant temperature of 19°C in the living area/room, to which the option is added to use ΔT 3°C air heating to heat up or cool down the house individually/automatically. Heating and cooling follow the same procedures.

Is greenhouse air heating suitable for private houses? The air heating installation is too big, makes too much noise and the living room is not free of dust. There are two main types of fine-wire heat exchangers that can resolve these issues: the fine-wire water/air heat exchanger and the fine-wire air/air heat exchanger.

Breathing Window

When you as a university professor at the end of your professoriate unexpectedly receive the Royal/Shell Award in person, what do you do with the tax-free money? According to the chief author of this paper the ventilation in buildings is the weakest link in the building industry. Much money has been spent on this. The list of conditions did not require extrapolation, improving existing techniques, but devising from scratch an optimal ventilation system that is small, user-friendly, intelligent, with hygienic CO_2 control and inaudible. In the meantime, in the course of a parallel search for a smart effective decentralized room ventilation device, a new type of fine wire heat exchanger was developed, with the same partners as Fiwihex. We call it a "Breathing Window", and the technique will be discussed in the following section.

This air/air fine wire heat exchanger is not woven but wound with ø 1/10 mm copper wire on a big rotating drum. This new air/air heat exchanger measures 16 x 200 x 400 mm. Each heat exchanger consists of a warp of 15 km of ø 1/10 mm diameter copper wire weighing 500 gr. The weft is glued nylon thread with a centre-to-centre distance of 12.5 mm. Its small size making it easier to remove the heat exchanger from its casing for cleaning. The stacked wefts must be mutually airtight, forming 13 small air-channels of 2 x 220 mm, each having a width of 16 mm. Due to two counter-current flows evenly distributed by conical air ducts, the channels are alternately hot inside and cold outside.

04.03.03   The Breathing Window

Background

The annual Royal/Shell Prize for Science (new style) was awarded to me in 1998.
I was nominated for the award by The Dutch Society of Sciences and the Royal Dutch Academy of Sciences for a scientific break-through in technological innovation in the field of sustainable development and architecture. The prize ($fl.$ 200,000 ≈ € 90,000) provided me with financial and technological opportunities, as well as social obligations. Therefore I thought seriously where the gaps are in sustainable building knowledge. From my point of view the ventilation in buildings is the weakest link in the chain. Due to regulations the natural ventilation in houses is more and more mechanically controlled from a central point with heat recovery.

Fig. 04.29:   Certificate of the Royal Shell Prize for Science

What we had in mind is a decentralised high-tech breathing skin of buildings, a 'Breathing Window'. The ventilation system is often over- or under-dimensioned, mostly with an incomprehensible control system. The central ventilation ducts are hidden behind thermally insulating suspended ceilings, as a result of which the thermal mass of the floors contributes only very little to a balanced indoor climate.

The search for an optimal high-efficiency heat exchanger lasted for two years. It was finally descovered in a company named Fiwihex, located in Almelo, 40 km from Deventer where I live.

Fiwihex had a fine wire heat exchanger under development. Together with the inventor, Noor van Andel, and his son Eur, we set up a three-year research and development project for Breathing Windows, with additional financial support from Senter, part of the ministry of Economic Affairs.

The aim is to create a healthy indoor climate in buildings, by ventilating every room through a Breathing Window, each according to its needs. Technically translated this meant a computer-controlled, compact and efficient system for air ventilation and heating.
Often it is extremely difficult to develop something simple. The development of the Breathing Window was a challenge with a high level of complexity.

Indoor-air quality

An investigation into the indoor-climate quality of private houses in the Netherlands has yielded some remarkable results. Research worker ir Evert Hasselaar attached to OTB of the Delft University of Technology investigated 500 houses in various categories. Two thirds of the housing stock had mechanical ventilation. Non-subsidized houses had balanced ventilation with heat recovery to reach a low EPC. After some years the ventilation capacity was halved, a reduction of some 10% per year due to dust. In additon, because of the excessive noise caused by the fan, sometimes the whole mechanical ventilation had been simply shut off. Another discovery was that in 4/5 of the houses with natural ventilation the occupants did not open their master bedroom windows, not even at night, due to traffic noise. This leading to adverse levels of CO_2 concentration, fine dust and house mites. The bathroom, which was used for showers three times a day, generally had too little ventilation to get dry resulting in black spots of mould. There was no significant difference between built-in bathrooms or bathrooms with a window in the outer wall.

Fig. 04.30: *Breathing Window fine-wire heat exchanger element: 7.5 km of 0.1 mm copper wires (400 g in total) run left to right; plastic partitions separate the canals where ingoing and outgoing air flows in turns exchange heat*

Present installations

Ventilation studies in house-building, commercial and industrial buildings in the Netherlands show a large disparity in results expected and those observed in practice. Factors are: concept, design, saving, execution, control, adjustment, use and maintenance. At every phase calculation errors may be concealed by over-dimensioning. Fig. 1. In the conceptual (draft) phase the architect should design the overall indoor-climate in a crosscut fashion, write his ideas down and explain them to the principal and the installation consultants. In practice it usually does not work out this way. The help of experts is called upon. Without affecting the layout, all heating, ventilation and air-conditioning systems are drafted by consultants and usually concealed in lowered ceilings. The internal thermal mass of the building is for the greater part put out of action. Lowered ceilings conceal air ducts claiming 15% building volume.

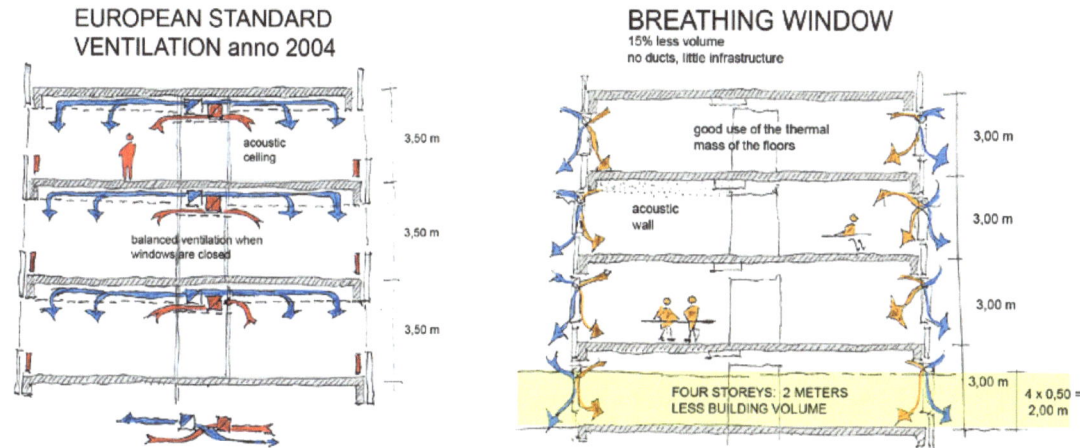

Fig. 04.31:   Standard ventilation system – cross-section of lowered ceilings = 0.6 m (left) and ventilation in the skin of building –15% less volume built (right)

At the building-costs estimate before or after public tender the ventilation is sometimes curtailed. The suddenly required extra fire compartmentalizing is a well-known phenomenon in the last phase before the building permit is granted.

Installations reviewed
Gradually we have arrived at a turning point in thinking about installations. The current installations in houses appear in practice not to be appreciated by its inhabitants.
The main reasons are noise nuisance and the easily clogged heat exchanger behind a steel hatch in the attic. It belongs to another world compared with the familiar thermostat of the central heating installation. The bigger installations are usually maintained, but take up a lot of space and render much thermal mass of buildings useless by lowered ceilings and insulation. This means less comfort, higher building costs and higher peak loads of cooling and heating. Installations have a short writing-off period and are thus relatively expensive.

Use and maintenance
When installed correctly, a long period of use and maintenance follows. According to research it appears that heat exchangers in houses with a balanced ventilation system are hardly maintained and get clogged up with dust. It also appears that two thirds of the mechanical ventilation as prescribed in the regulations is not achieved in draught-free newly built houses. The average user generally has no idea of technical installations. In large buildings, which are mechanically ventilated, the sick-building syndrome has been found; people felt locked up in non-compliant technology. This complaint is sufficiently remedied by opening windows, but the question arises: shouldn't we look for fundamentally different ventilation systems?

New highly efficient ventilation
Albert Einstein said: "We cannot solve problems with the same thinking that created them".
Let us begin again at the very beginning – the building is sustainable architecture – installations are supposed to be silent and smart. As an architect I have been hypothesing for years on the idea of constructing a Breathing Window. How this is to be achieved and what form it is going to

have is at this moment (February 2005) not yet entirely clear. Optimization of heat recovery to around 95% seems to be feasible.

As mentioned previously, the search for the best heat exchanger took many years, and to my surprise ended on a website showing a fine-wire heat exchanger designed by someone who worked only 40 kilometres away from where I live. The inventor, Noor van Andel, needed only a few months to convert the original water/air heat exchanger into an air/air heat exchanger (In 2006 Noor received an honorary doctorate from the University of Amsterdam). To test the design I chose the dimensions of a window-frame with a standard cavity wall depth.

The Breathing Window has 3 main components:
1. Balanced ventilation system with two fans
2. Smart control system
3. Fine-wire counter-current heat exchanger

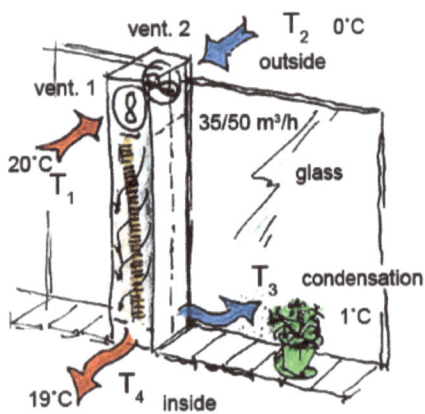
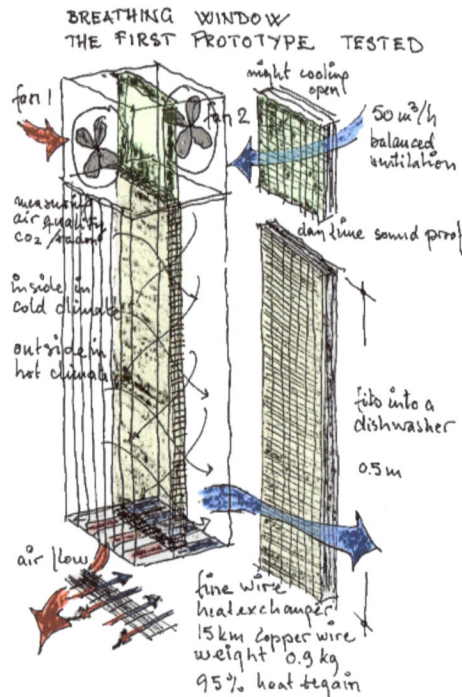

Fig. 04.32: The Breathing Window can be a jamb, mullion or built in a wall (above); the first generation prototype design (right)

The prototype has a compact semi-transparent synthetic counter-current heat exchanger consisting of 15 km (length) and 0.1 mm (diameter) copper wire weighing 1.05 kilogram. The winding of the prototype in 26 vertical layers on a washing drum takes three days to prepare. For the purpose of worldwide applications we assumed an inside air temperature of 20°C. To a heat exchanger it is indifferent whether to pre-heat cold outside air or to pre-cool hot outside air, the efficiency stays the same.

Cold climate: outside air of 0°C enters at 19°C. The Dutch building regulations state, that the height of a ventilation opening is allowed to be lower than 1.80 m, if the temperature difference between the incoming air and the inside air is less than 2K. The Breathing Window meets these regulations up to an outside temperature of -20°C, when the incoming air temperature will be 18°C. Hot climate: outside air of 40°C enters at 21°C. Fig. 6. In combination with moderately chilled surfaces, e.g. floors, walls or ceilings, the traditional air-conditioning may be reconsidered.

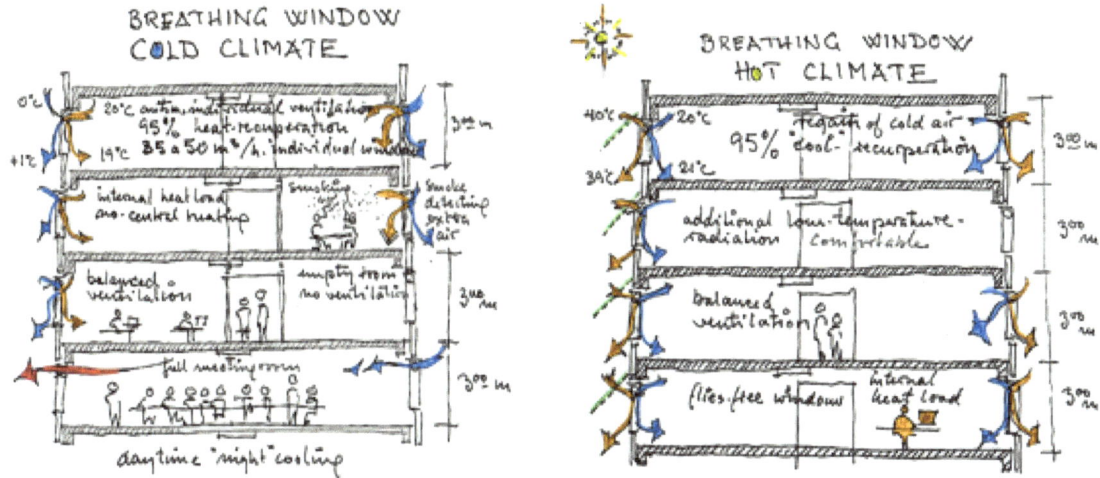

Fig. 04.33:   Schematic cross-section of a building with a the Breathing Window principle in a cold climate (left) and a warm climate (right)

Technical specifications

To make a Breathing Window prototype preliminary draft agreements must be made regarding dimensions, outward appearance and ventilation capacity. The dimensions of the first-generation prototypes are 750/200/180 mm. The fine-wire heat exchanger can be cleaned under the shower and easily fits into a standard dishwasher. The first prototypes were made with a transparent synthetic casing in order to detect pollution in the fine-wire heat exchanger. The Breathing Window functions well alongside natural ventilation, hybrid or completely mechanically balanced ventilation. The CO_2 sensor (Sense air Sweden) starts automatically at 500 ppm (parts per million) when an addition to natural ventilation is needed, but also gives a light signal at 1200 ppm (MAC value). On reaching 1700 ppm CO_2 a sound signal will be heard. This means that doors and windows have to be opened to keep a healthy indoor climate.

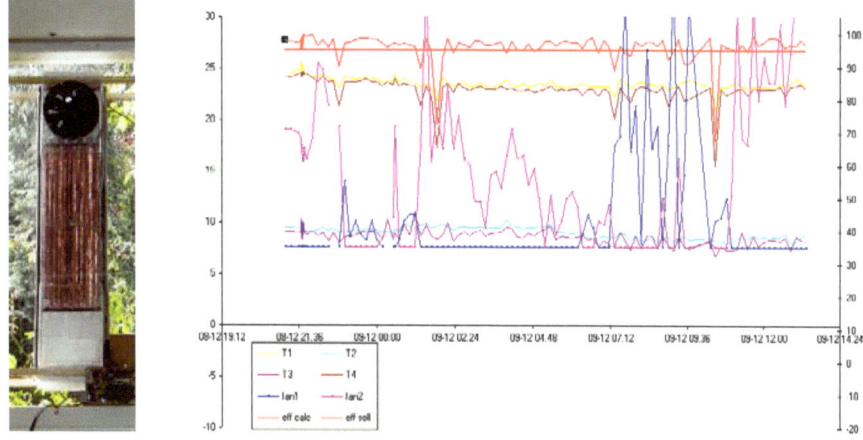

Fig. 04.34:   Test results in Iceland 2003 with reverse ventilators as the wind direction changes 180°; result is approximately 50 % less geothermal hot water needed for heating in the dwelling

What should the driving force be, what energy consumption is reasonable and which noise level belongs to a certain air velocity? Analysis indicates that the ventilators need to have a 12-Volt capacity of 2 Watts each, and the 12-Volt transformer another 2 Watts. At 50 m^3 of air per hour the noise level can stay below 30 dB. The larger the vent hole, the lower the air velocity, the noise production decreases, but the wind effects increase in high-rise buildings.

Two small reversible computer ventilators could not cope with the extreme differences in air pressure (100-150 Pascal). The ventilation systems in large tall buildings also tend to lose their balance during a storm, the manufacterers advise closing the horizontal air supply and exhaust ducts when there are heavy winds, because in these circumstances there will be enough natural ventilation anyway. According to calculations the prototype should have an average heat recovering efficiency of 95%. The prototype tested in a kitchen window on the coast of Iceland in 2003 usually had a heat-recovering efficiency of over 95% - the uppermost line. The four thermometers, which regulate the temperature of the two balanced airflows by means of the reversible ventilators, work well. One can notice the extreme rotation speed (and noise) during storm peaks, both windward and later leeward. And thus we have arrived at the realisation aspects.

Realisation

The basic idea behind the Breathing Window is a smart local ventilation system, which has almost all the qualities of large centralised ventilation systems with a minimum of disadvantages. To re-design and minimize most parts of a ventilation system is an achievable task. It is my personal opinion that minimum technology can always be realised. A second, redesigned prototype is devised from the point of view of a producer and a consumer.
The industrial-design student, Yannic Dekking, of the Delft University of Technology, received this assignment as his final project. In broad outline the dimensions of the second prototype were similar to its predecessor. Dekking succeeded in optimising the feeder channels of the fine-wire heat exchanger and fitting them into a winding machine. In the space left vacant a handle could be made to take out the heat exchanger in order to clean it. All types of ventilators were included in this research.

There are three different construction possibilities in several types of building; as part of transparent glass, as a vertical window frame, or, which seems to be the most probable solution, as part of a closed panel/wall in existing buildings. The Breathing Window functions well besides natural ventilation, hybrid or completely balanced mechanical ventilation (air-conditioning).

Fig. 04.35: Compact counter-current fine-wire heat exchanger fits into a dishwasher

Use as decentralised room ventilation
The main characteristic of every Passive House ventilation device is that it must be very well balanced because of the perfectly airtight exterior wall. The decentralized Breathing Window – one in every room – is characterized by perfectly balanced ventilation in every room with a high percentage of heat recovery. The control system measures the CO_2 concentration of the indoor air in parts per million and reacts on it immediately by adjusting its ventilation rate. The relative humidity of the indoor air in relation to the outdoor air temperature makes an optimum heat exchange possible without any condensation. Good indoor-air quality in each separate room is ensured. Low occupancy rooms are minimally ventilated. One can adjust (programme) the maximum and minimum CO_2 concentration. In the countryside the ventilation stops at 450 ppm and in urban areas at 550 ppm. When a room is not occupied or when a window is opened the Breathing Window also stops ventilating. When a room is used more often the BW will rotate faster to refresh (exchange) more air. Whereas at 50 m^3 air/hour (master bedroom) the BW is not audible (< 30 dB), the noise level in the occupied living room can reach 40 to 45 dB at a high rotating speed and 250 m^3 air/hour, however the perception of this noise level is reduced to background activities in the house or outdoor traffic.

The CO_2-controlled ventilation system is highly efficient, unoccupied rooms are not permanently ventilated. However, regular ventilation is desirable in connection with radon and paint smells. Generally decentralized ventilation as compared to central ventilation can lead to a 2/3 saving in energy with the same indoor air quality. In summer, when doors and windows are likely to be open, the BW will not rotate. The relation between humidity and the outdoor temperature ensures that the heat exchanger will never get frozen. By adjusting the rate of recirculation of the indoor air through the 'bypass' the highest possible efficiency is always reached.

Some calculations

Calculating energy saving
There are 5080 degree hours in the heating season in the Netherlands. Between October and May the outside temperature is 4.8°C, the inside temperature 20°C. The 'Breathing Window' ventilates on average (ranging from 15 to 50) 40 m^3/hour with a heat recovery efficiency (85 to 95) of 90% volume metric heating capacity, that is 1212 joules/m^3 K.
Saving, 5080 x 40 x 1212 x (20 - 4.8) x 0.9 = 3.37 gigajoules/'Breathing Window' per year.

Heating cost reduction per house
Expressed in energy equivalents: one m^3 natural gas is 32 MegaJoules in the heating efficiency of a 90% High Efficiency boiler, that is 3,370,000,000 / 32,000,000 x 0.9 = 117 m^3 natural gas/'Breathing Window' during the heating season. With 3 to 5 Breathing Windows in one house, its average multiplied by: 4 x 117 = 468 m^3 natural gas or 13.5 gigajoules. At the end of 2004 the price of natural gas was € 0.416/m^3.
Thus the calculated saving is 41.6 x 468 = € 195/year per house.

Electricity consumption
Besides the savings of the heat exchangers the primary energy consumption of the two ventilators should be deducted. At an outside temperature of 0°C and an inside temperature of 20°C and 50 m^3/hour ventilation per 'Breathing Window', the two ventilators use 8 Watts, but now with 95% heat recovery efficiency. The thermal (low-calorie) energy saving is now: 50 x 3600 x 1212 x [20-0] x 95 = 320 Watts.

The high-quality 8-Watt electricity is produced by a traditional power station (not connected to district heating), with 40% efficiency amounting to 8: 0.40 = 20 thermal Watts. The energy saving is 320 – 20 = 300 thermal Watts, therefore the net efficiency of the 'Breathing Window' is 300 / 320 x 0.95 = 89%, which is close to the 90% average efficiency assumed earlier.
The electricity consumption of the CO_2 meter and the intelligent control is negligible.

Air resistance and noise
Even when two ventilators work reversibly to control an even air current, they can be very inefficient. The heat exchanger in the 'Breathing Window' has an air-pressure resistance of 18 Pascal at 50 m^3/hour ventilation. The two ventilators produce a net energy of: 2 / 3600 x 50 x 18 = 0.5 Watt ventilation energy. Due to this modest air resistance in the heat exchanger little electricity appears necessary, but even so the indoor ventilator produces a 30-decibel noise and that is audible in the silent hours of night. We aim at 25 decibels. The simplest solution: when you halve the depth of the heat exchanger, the heat recovery will still be 85%. A sirocco type ventilator with a spiral case underneath is also an option.

Fig. 04.36:   *The test version of a double Breathing Window: two Fiwihex elements in a compact box*

Conclusion
Although the Breathing Window is still in the making (statu nascendi) it seems to be the right answer to the question of desired customized ventilation. Time will show. A coincidental, unforeseen advantage compared to the usual plate heat exchangers is that the fine-wire heat exchanger hardly freezes up. The explanation is not simple. Is it sublimation? Is the frost evaporation time so short that the forming of ice does not take place?

Applied in hospitals the fine-wire heat exchanger can easily be renewed to prevent infection. The range of applications is wide. For instance, it fits into a specific small mounting space in boats, caravans and mobile homes. The CO_2 meter is also a very accurate smoke detector, which signals fire even before any smoke develops.

After more than 10 years of product development the first Zero-series of Breathing Windows went into production in 2010. Brink Systems became the manufacturer, but to our great disappointment by early 2012 no application had been made yet, in spite of various expressions of interest from the market.

At the time of finalising this book, a slimmer, longer, more façade integrated Breathing Window is now ready for the market.

04.03.04 The Air Mover

Definition of a problem
If you have to point out the weakest link in the building trade, it is ventilation. It is often insufficient and too noisy. Too much ventilation does not exist, because the maximum ventilation level is the outside air. However, draught caused by an air velocity that is too high, can be detrimental.

If we consider the CO_2 concentration of inside air in ppm (parts per million), its most important quality standard, 500 to 600 ppm is a good air quality with 30 to 50 m³ fresh air per person per hour. The problem of draught-proof buildings is that the same quantity of air that is removed must be supplied. This balanced ventilation is common knowledge; what is new and unknown so far, is that there is a special ventilator that can produce two balanced air flows. This special ventilator, which we call air-mover, can, by itself, even replace two ventilators rotating slowly. During rotation the Air Mover ventilates six times its volume.

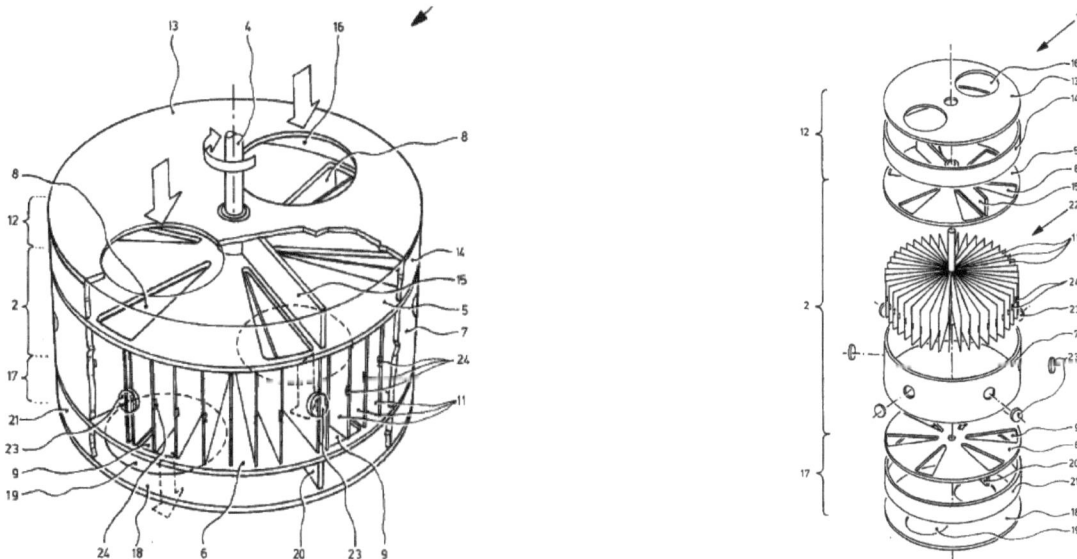

Fig. 04.37:   Drawings of the Air Mover (prototype no. 1) magnetic blades principle, from the patent application[12], 19 m³/h with 1.5 rotation per second (parallel principle)

---

[12] Image by Björn Kristinsson

The Air Mover

The air-mover can achieve not only two balanced parallel airflows, but also reach an over pressure which has not yet been measured. Therefore without air valves the air-mover is suitable for applications in high rise buildings, in ocean-going vessels or in the changeable stormy polar climate. The over pressure is produced by small magnets fixed to the cylinder wall and by small magnets fixed to the flexible ventilator blades, which slowing down a little, lag behind untill the next ventilator blade moves up and the whole procedure starts all over again. See figure 04.40 below.

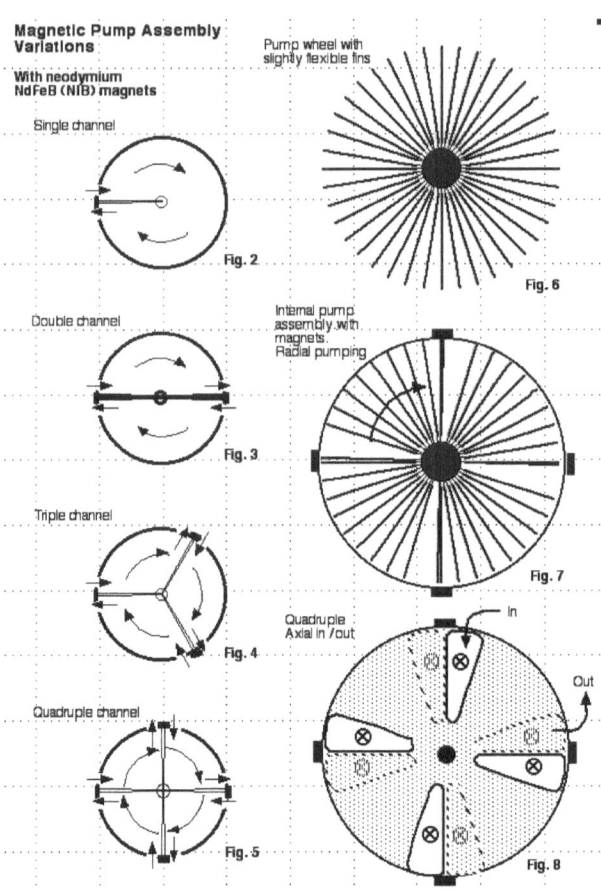

Fig. 04.38: Principle of the Air Mover [drawing by Jón and Björn Kristinsson]

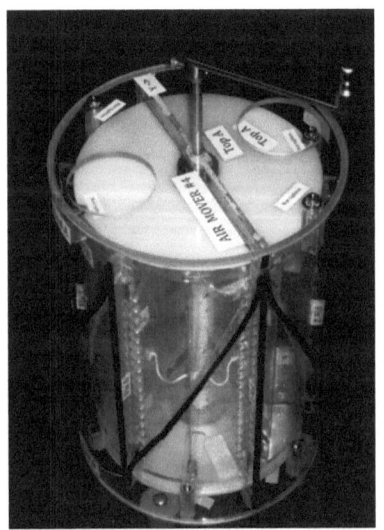

A prototype has been made and a second robust type has almost been completed. The first prototype with a diameter of ø 250 mm, an opening of 60 mm and a height of 125 mm can displace two times 2 x 20 m³ air per hour, at a rotation velocity of 1.5 per second. The rotation test at a forced higher velocity led to the damage of weak glue connections to the core of the rotor blades. A second, more successful prototype – diameter ø 200 mm, opening ø 520 mm – proved to move 2 x 15 m³ of air at a speed of 2 m/s with 1.0 rotation per second. The noise level at 3 m distance of the open installation was no more than 38 dB.

Fig. 04.39: Plexiglass model of the Air Mover (prototype no. 2)[13], double cylinder, 16 m³/h at 1 rotation per second (reverse principle)

---

[13] Photo by Björn Kristinsson

Application

The first thing that comes to mind when thinking of the application of Breathing Windows is balanced room ventilation. It stands to reason to connect a compact heat exchanger direct to this room ventilation. This small air/air heat exchanger, made of 7.5 km wound 1/10 mm copper wire, exists in the Netherlands under the name 'Fiwihex' (fine-wire heat-exchanger).

The size of this Breathing Window is not determined by the air-mover, but by the heat exchanger developed at great cost. The most favourable proportion between width and height of the 'air-mover' has not yet been investigated. The second prototype will be higher than it is wide. Due to this the magnetic ventilator blades will be a little less burdened. Thus we see that, even before the new air-mover has been put on the market, a new application field has already been found.

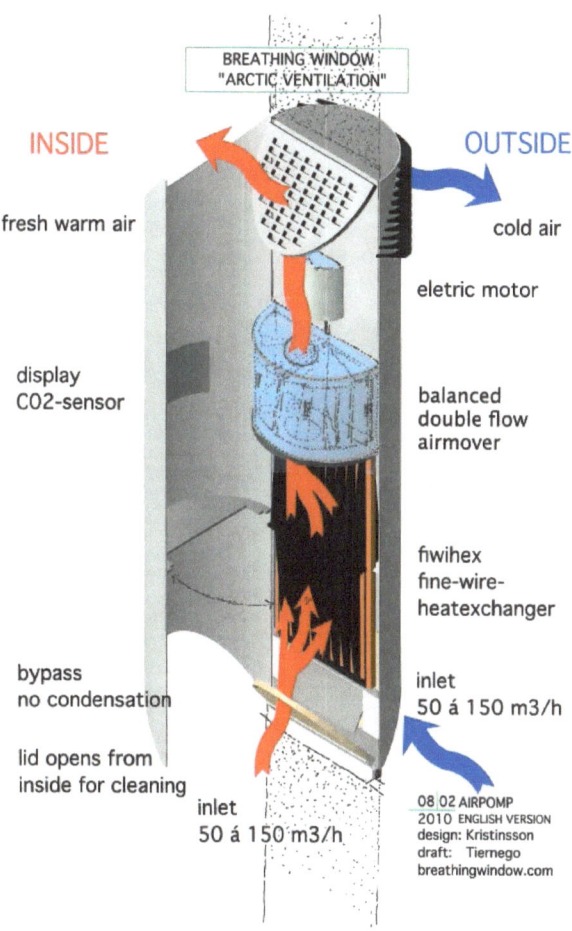

Fig. 04.40: Technical scheme for a heavy duty Breathing Window for highrises and arctic ventilation

04.04 Light

04.04.01 Daylight and roof lights

When we observe the projection of sky luminescence, we immediately see the difference between the quantities of light provided by roof windows in comparison with a window in a façade. Generally the amount of light is 5.5 times larger! Therefore a reduction of 60% on artificial light can be achieved when using this principle.

When using layered plate glass with colloidal foil (non-crystalline) in a roof, the transparent foil turns white and starts to reflect light when the temperature exceeds 30°C. It thereby prevents a surplus of irradiation and unwanted temperature increase. This automatic sunblind reduces around 50% of the solar irradiation. The incoming shortwave radiation remains quite constant, both with a clear and a cloudy sky.

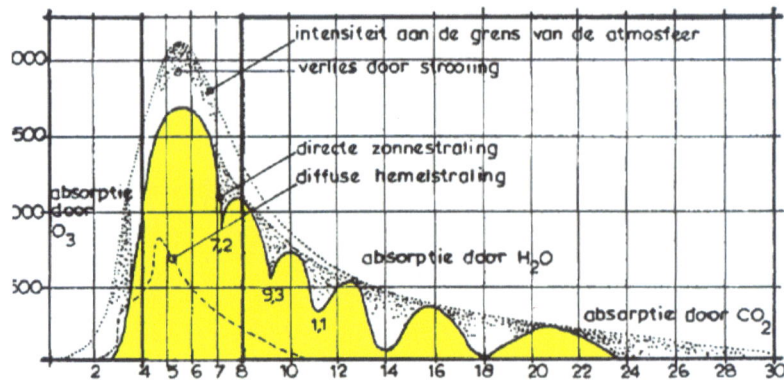

Fig. 04.44:   The spectral capacity of the solar radiation

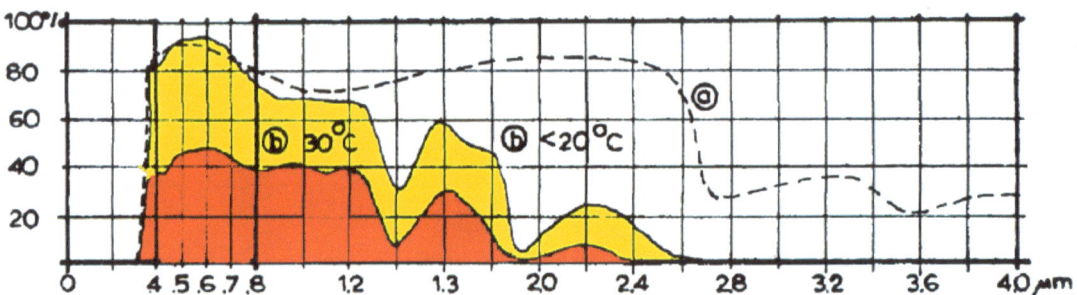

Fig. 04.41:   Spectral permeability of double pane glass with colloidal foil as automatic sun blind in the roof windows (b), compared to 6 mm of polished plate glass (a). The colloidal foil turns white in sunlight (red area: incoming solar radiation heat when the foil is white).

As well as the prevention of overheating, this light control is of a particular benefit to office workers, reducing direct daylight and glare that would ordinarily affect their tasks.

Fig. 04.42:   Image of a greenhouse with colloidal foil during cold weather (left) and warm weather (right)

04.04.02 Parabolic roof shells

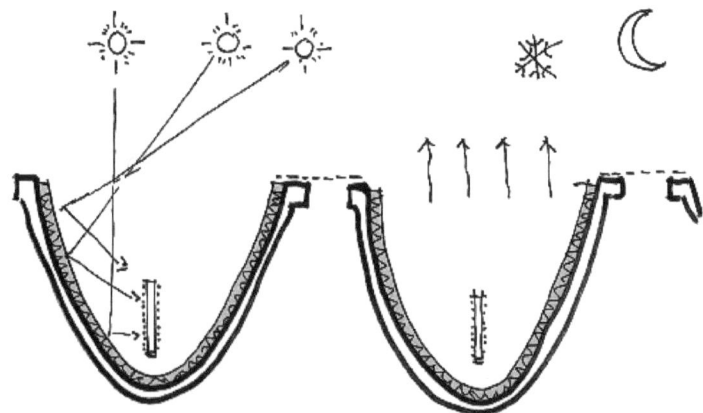

Fig. 04.43: *Functions of parabolic roof shells: collection of solar heat, PV, nocturnal cooling and water collector (from rain and condensation at night)*

Parabolic roofs can provide environmental advantages over normal roofs. When covered by stainless steel sunlight will be concentrated on focal point. This focal point could be filled with a flat plate solar collector filled with water. The warm water can be guided through tubes, possibly situated next to the rainwater discharge, to a solar boiler or to the ground for interseasonal storage.

Another solution could be PV in the heart of the parabolic shell, producing electricity, but without further measures the cells would possibly overheat, detrimentally affecting their performance and therefore gaining no advantage on typically positioned photovoltaics.

Apart from reflecting light, the parabolic shells could also have a function as a solar collector (irradiation from the sun) or cold collector (eradiation to the clear night sky) and as a collector of rainwater, to be used as water for washing, flushing and rinsing. These functions could all be integrated with a PV array in the parabolic centre.

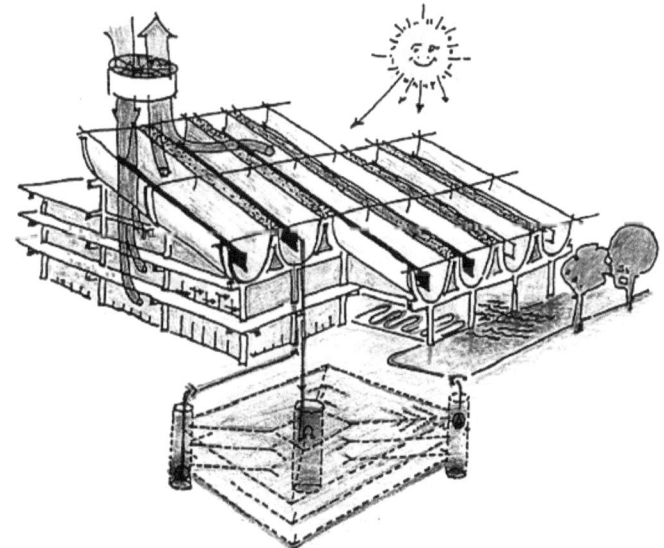

Fig. 04.44: *Parabolic roof shells as designed for the Lelystad town hall (to be discussed in chapter 09)*

Parabolic roof shells can also play an acoustic role. The reverberation time for several sound frequencies can be determined according to the Law of Sabine.

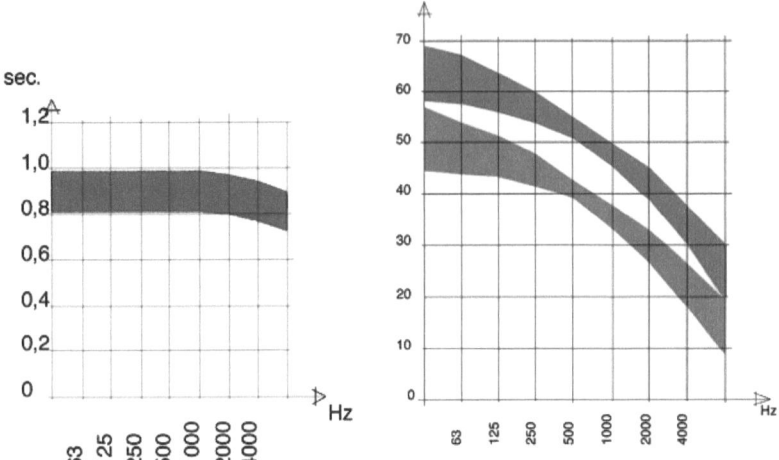

Fig. 04.45:   Resonance period in the bandwidth of 0.8 to 1 second from the lower to the higher tones of 2000 Hz (left), and the desired background noise (right) in a fully occupied office space (band above) and for the building services (band below)

Parabolic roof shells were first proposed for the 1976 Lelystad town hall. Parabolic sun boilers were recommended on the ISES (International Solar Energy Society) congress in Hamburg, 1989. It is only since 2008 that they have found a renewed purpose in Villa Flora, the greenest office in Europe.

04.04.03   Artificial lighting

Artificial lighting as addition to daylight is inevitable. In offices the artificial illumination also needs to be efficient, functional and close to the user.

Artificial lighting in offices is a large subject that could warrant a chapter of its own. The thermal colour of artificial light goes from warm (bulbs) to cool efficient fluorescent lighting, which combines well with daylight. Bulbs have a light efficiency of 5 to 95% heat. For fluorescent lighting the capacity is 20 to 25%, so 4 to 5 times higher. What is remarkable, but understandable, is that in northern countries people choose warm lights (thermal colour < 3000 Kelvin) and in the tropics for cool white light (thermal colour > 3300 Kelvin). The light spectrum of fluorescent light is not complete and therefore often extended with halogen lamps.

In Western Europe fluorescent lighting was dominant in offices. The visual perception is based on variations in luminosity. Another aspect is the relationship with user age when it comes to the desired intensity of light. With every decade of age the desired intensity of light on the desk is doubled. In the Netherlands each working space is illuminated for a person near retirement age (that is 500 lux). Even more remarkable is that according to English criteria an employee needs only half, which is 250 lux. In Finland the illumination norm for new buildings is even 200 lux.

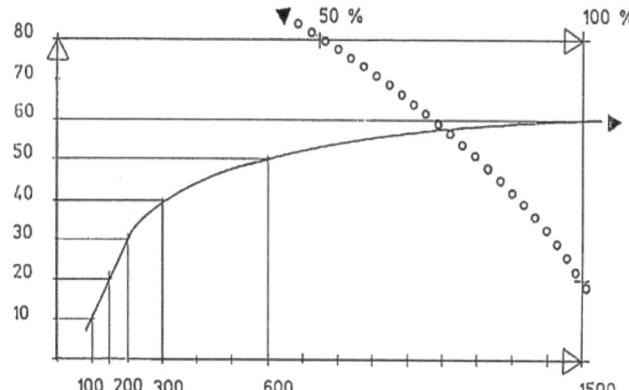

Fig. 04.46: Desired intensity of light related to ageing, in lux (lm/m^2)

Another aspect of artificial lighting is the quadratic decrease of light intensity with distance. So a seven meter tall lamppost may have an energy-saving armature, but a one meter tall lamppost principally consumes only 1:49 of the higher post with the same light intensity on ground level. Hence, from an energetic point of view it is more optimal to illuminate streets with low lampposts, instead of high ones, so that there is no illumination of an unnecessarily broad area.

04.05   Free-cooling roofs

04.05.01   The physical principle

Fig. 04.47: We all know this phenomenon: the misted up windshields of our car after a clear night. In wintertime a carport has its advantages…

When we study the spectrum of light that eventually reaches the earth's surface, we see a division in ultraviolet radiation, visible light and infra-red radiation. Free-cooling roofs consist of a spectrally selective membrane, which reflects most sunlight directly, however in a reverse way emits infrared heat radiation from the earth towards the sky. In this way an artificial night is created during the day.

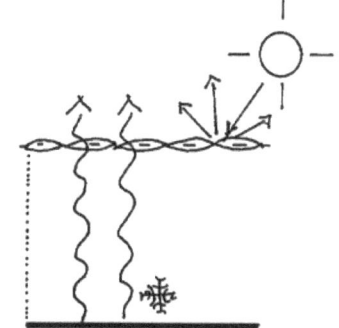

Fig. 04.48: Free-cooling roof: infrared emittance and light reflection

Jón Kristinsson — Integrated Sustainable Design

The free-cooling roof was originally an invention of TNO (report no. 86060, "Ice-rinks and Energy reduction", by Mennink et al.). We used it for the first time in 1989, as part of a holistic concept for the competition of the ice-skating rink in the sports complex 'De Scheg' in Deventer. An outdoor ice-skating rink covered by a roof with 50% free-cooling foil consumes an equal amount of energy per m² as an indoor rink, resulting in an energy reduction of 75%.[14]

Fig. 04.49: Free-cooling test roof in Haarlem[15]

The structural inflated cushions cannot be damaged by material fatigue under the influence of resonance caused by wind. There is one disadvantage however, with a relative humidity of 100% (dew-point) a water film forms under the foil roof reducing the free-cooling capacity.
A free-cooling roof in Haarlem has been tested and clearly demonstrated the influence of the roof cover: outside the ice was melting, whereas underneath the ice was still frozen.

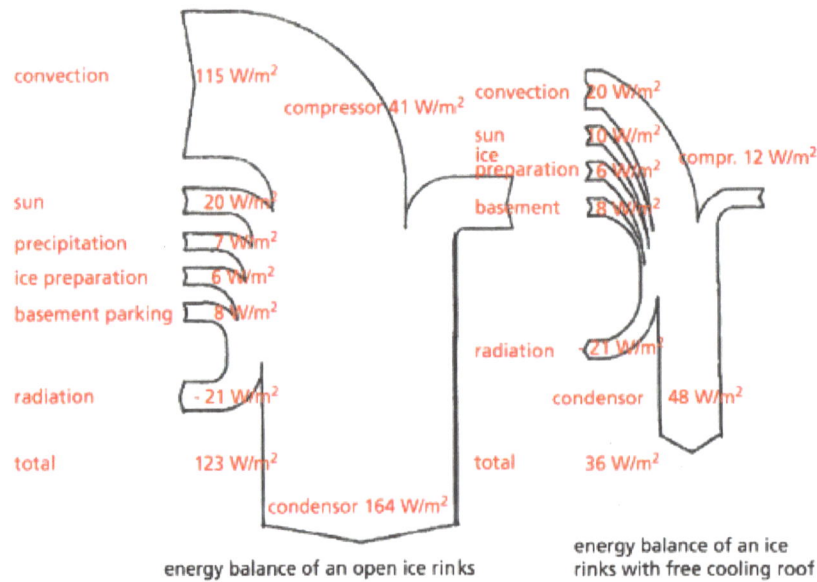

energy balance of an open ice rinks

energy balance of an ice rinks with free cooling roof

Fig. 04.50: Free-cooling test roof in Haarlem[16] (left); energy balance of an open ice-skating rink (right) and an artificial ice-skating rink covered by a free-cooling roof (utmost right) – when compared a 75% energy saving!

---

[14] Only a 50% roof covering is one asset, the free-cooling a second, and fast cooling with thin, clear, rapid ice a third option for energy conservation. Very important is swabbing the ice efficiently. In order to avoid hoarfrost on the ice a lee needs to be created with a wire mesh partition.
[15] Photo by Bertus Butter, ice-master
[16] Photo by Bertus Butter, ice-master

For clarification a division can be made between three kinds of roof: the glass roof, the traditional insulated opaque roof and the free-cooling roof:
- A glass roof always functions as a solar collector: it allows 90% of the solar heat to pass. Once inside, the wave-length of the light changes at the moment it strikes a surface, transforming into infrared heat radiation that can no longer pass back through. This leads to the greenhouse effect, is a very important principle in passive low energy design.
- A traditional insulated 'cold' roof was once ventilated with fresh air. Due to use of new insulation materials, the damp tight 'warm' roof principle is now typical with no influence from outside air.

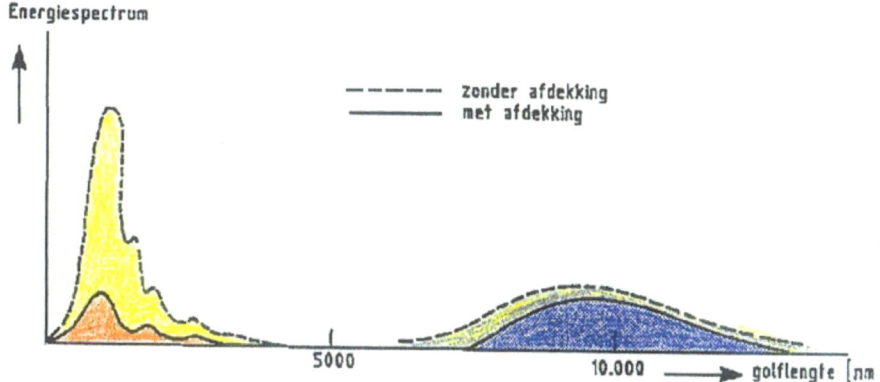

Fig. 04.51: Indication of the relationship between the short-wave irradiation of sunlight and the long-wave infra-red radiation of heat towards the sky: yellow is reflected sunlight; orange is the incoming light; blue is the radiation of heat through the roof foil; blue/green would be the radiation of heat without a free-cooling roof, i.e. in an open field.

- The free-cooling roof is made of a white membrane of polythene cushions that reflect direct sunlight. Some light enters, but with a clear sky during daytime and at night, the membrane allows infrared radiation from the earth to pass to the cold sky. This free-cooling comes down to approximately 100 W/m² which results in $-\Delta T = 3$ to $5\ °C$ of free cooling compared to the outside air temperature; a cooling performance comparable to air conditioning units. However, this principle only works under a clear and partly clouded sky, and preferably in full sunlight.

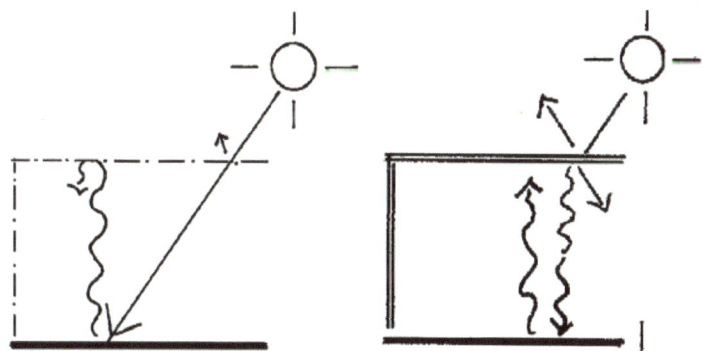

Fig. 05.52: Glass roof and a traditional insulated roof

04.05.02   Sports complex with innovative ice-skating rink, Deventer (1989)

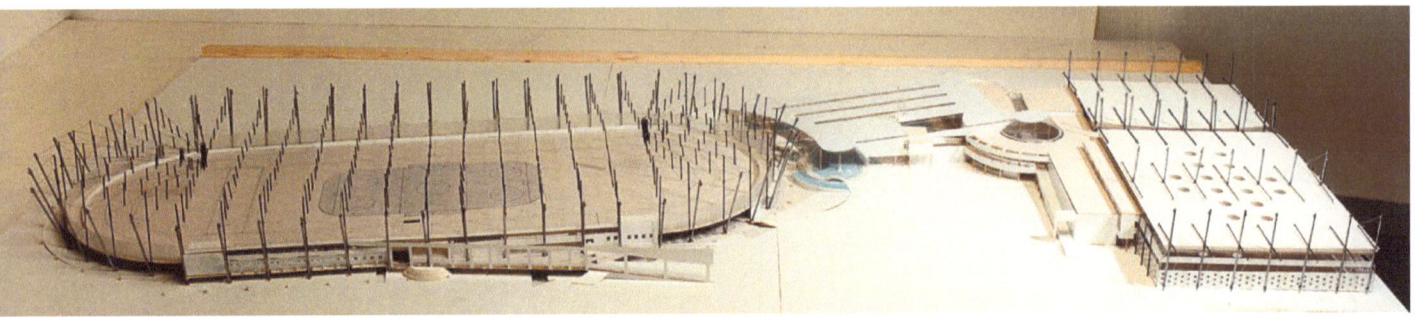

Fig. 04.53:   Photo of the 'De Scheg' sports complex scale model

Three architectural offices, including our office, were invited to submit a conceptual design for a sports centre with a partly covered ice-skating rink. The location was near the Colmschate station, Deventer East. One of the interesting and challenging criteria for us was that it would be judged by its technical innovations.

Daan Josee worked on the multifunctional sports complex and Jón Kristinsson on the innovative ice-skating rink. In the design of the sports complex the focus was aimed at the larger functions: tennis hall, sports hall and swimming pool, organised in a triangle.

At the point of intersection in that triangle the large cylindrical hall had its centre-point. From this hall all sport activities would be accessible and to some extent visible. The central hall slicing through the entire building is adapted in a route parallel to the sports hall, tennis hall and squash courts. By sloping walkways, elevators and stairs this route over two building layers connects the large square at the front (at the level of the train platforms). In the long section of this route the intensity of passengers, visitors and spectators is at its maximum. In the large and high open space of the central hall this route continues over a bridge, from which the multiple visual axes reveal something of the diverse sport activities. Therefore the restaurant is situated around this open space.

The innovation consisted of the combination of a tension cable frame construction with vertical aluminium tubes as pushrod and slanting supports with grout anchors, designed by Bartels engineering office, and the free-cooling roofs by Netherlands Organisation for Applied Scientific Research (TNO), with Bertus Butter acting as consultant on wind and fast ice.

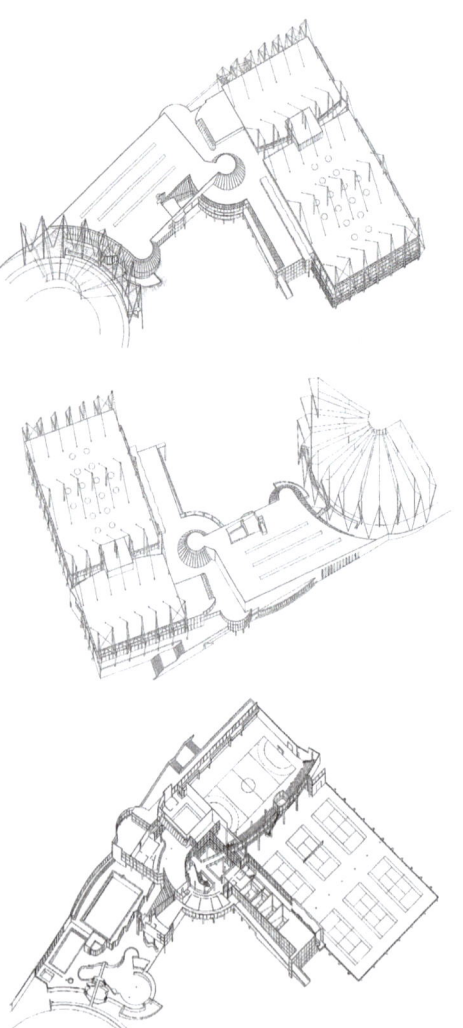

Fig. 04.54:   Closed and open axonometric views of the Kristinsson design of the Scheg sports centre

The design features of De Scheg were:

- Energy consumption was reduced by 75%, with an environmentally sound design.
- The free-bearing insulated ice-rink had super fast ice and wind lee by a semi-transparent nylon wire mesh net.
- With the aid of an automatic infra-red temperature control system the track could be frozen in one night by a small compact cooling installation.
- The roof structure had been designed with an extra-light, maintenance free, Twaron tension cable frame.
- A synthetic free-cooling roof of inflated polythene cushions, with a reversed greenhouse effect and no condensation on the underside.
- No rain delays due to a covered 400 m track.
- Visitor-friendly: feet-warming grandstand, ice-skate-friendly finishing of wood and rubber.
- The basement was partly situated in the ground and offers space for 480 cars + 480 bicycles under the ice dome.

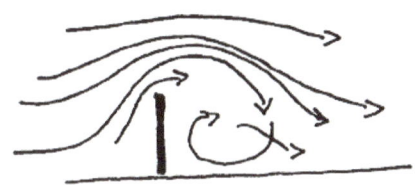

Due to far-reaching warranty requirements for new products, and a general lack of faith in the laws of nature, the free-cooling roof could not get off the ground and consequently the design was not selected.

Fig. 04.55: View of the entrance side (above) and the station-side (below)

04.05.03   Free-cooling roofs in desert areas

How it is possible to jump from optimal ice-skating rinks in the Netherlands to deserts and arid areas? It is because the laws of nature transcend national and continental borders.
The principle of passive cooling can be implemented in hot and dry, semi arid zones of the world. It can be applied, for example, in tents, shelters for cattle, market roofs, car parks, mobile homes and existing roofs. It is an important option for fossil fuel reduction and the improvement of indoor and outdoor comfort globally!

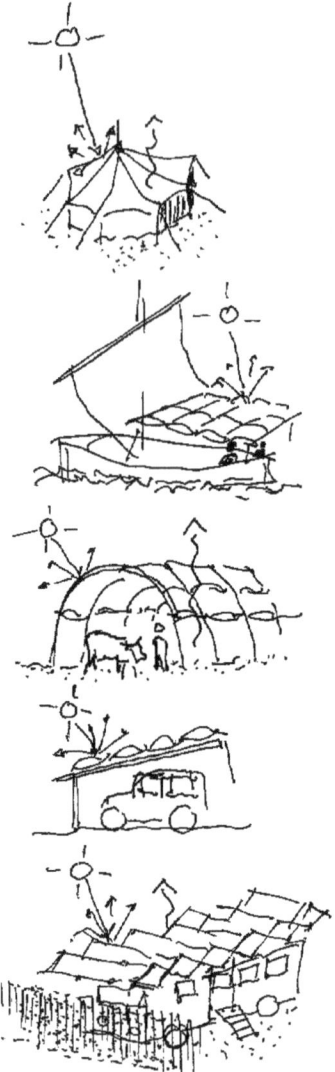

Fig. 04.56:   Applications of the free-cooling roof (top to bottom): tents, sailing ships, stables, carports, campervans

04.06   Smart Skin

04.06.01   Introduction

With regard to energy consumption, sustainable building is often directed at energy-efficient use of fossil fuels and the generation of renewable energy through technical appliances. These measures may be considered adjustments to a traditional way of building, ignoring the fact that the building itself can be innovated to an intelligent, responsive or even proactive device. As a first step to the effective use of energy, a building needs to be fine-tuned to its environs and interact intelligently with local characteristics such as climate, soil type and context [Dobbelsteen & Linden, 2007]. The building skin most logically performs this interaction: the roof (mainly for the generation of energy in whichever form), the ground floor (for the exploitation of the soil) and the façade (mainly for a response to desired or undesired climatic conditions). In changeable climates the use of building mass or the thermally constant subsoil is an effective means to smooth large temperature differences.

The Smart Skin, a translucent (light-emitting) building façade, is a sophisticated integration of three-layered glass, three registers of water pipes and underground interseasonal heat stores. The heat stored has temperatures of 8 - 25°C. The outer pane and the opaque white middle pane serve as a solar collector in sunlight. When desired, the middle pane can be transparent.

04.06.02   How to make a translucent Smart Skin

There are three qualities/aspects at issue in the design of Smart Skin; preventing sunlight transmission, gathering and storing heat and gathering and storing cold. Utilizing very-low-temperature heat > 25°C and high-temperature cold < 15°C elsewhere in the house is possible by means of new very-fine wire heat exchangers [Kristinsson et al. 2009]. The energy storage in the ground is more complicated than the smart skin itself. There are three temperatures to be stored and dynamically controlled for twenty-four hours a day, here the façade and the soil become interactive. The first prototype is based on triple-layered glass with pipes glued to each layer of glass, filled with water (Fig. 04.61).

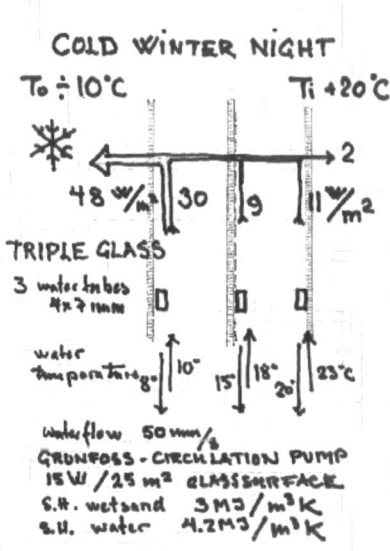 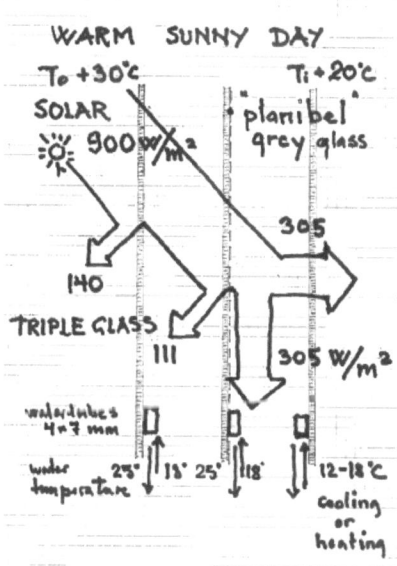

Fig. 04.57:   Smart Skin on a warm sunny day in connection with the groundwater heat and cold storage (left), and on a cold dark winter night: the inner glass plate is 21 - 22°C (right).

04.06.03 Every innovation creates a problem

The temperature of the outer layer of glass is highly dependent on the outside temperature, but in the Netherlands aquifer water of around 11°C can be used at all times, without a license, in quantities of no more than 10 m^3 per 24 hours. In this way we can always keep the outer glass pane at a temperature of 10 - 12°C, so that during freezing temperatures the heat loss is not larger than when it is +9°C. The temperature of the glass in relation to the temperature in the water pipes (mounting bars, grills) is dependent on the quality of the connection of the tube to the glass and the glasses thickness. As the glass thickness increases the water pipes can be placed further apart, for example, from 150 to 250 mm centre to centre.

Fig. 04.58: The first 'Smart Skin' prototype with clear triple-layered glass, upside down.

Cold or 'coolth' harvested in winter at the outside pane is stored underground and used for cooling in summer. Heat harvested in summer at the middle pane is stored and used for heating in winter. Cooling and heating are generated from the inside pane. When a large part of the outer wall of a house consists of Smart Skin, the lack of radiation from the cold inner glass in summer, or the back radiation of the inner pane into the interior in winter makes a large contribution to comfort. We can cool with water of 12°C, and heat with water of 18°C because of this effect. By using heat absorbing grey-tinted glass, heat harvesting at the inner pane can be increased.

The great advantage of glass is that it is translucent making any leakages in the water system immediately visible. Leakages in the connections of the 2 x 3 = 6 water pipes (per pane) may be solved in the longer term, however waterproof glass sealing with dry, kit-free glazing, and a prefabricated standard bottom rail appears to be the best solution in the short-term. In this early stage of development the bottom rail is made of sustainable wood with a large trench.

04.06.04 Heat storage in the ground

One important condition has not yet been mentioned: the temperature control system. The water in the pipes in the 'Smart Skin' is dependent on orientation, radiation and the inside and outside temperatures. The following relates to an experimental bungalow with a 0.7 m thick insulating cellular structured 'floating' foundation (Fig. 04.63).

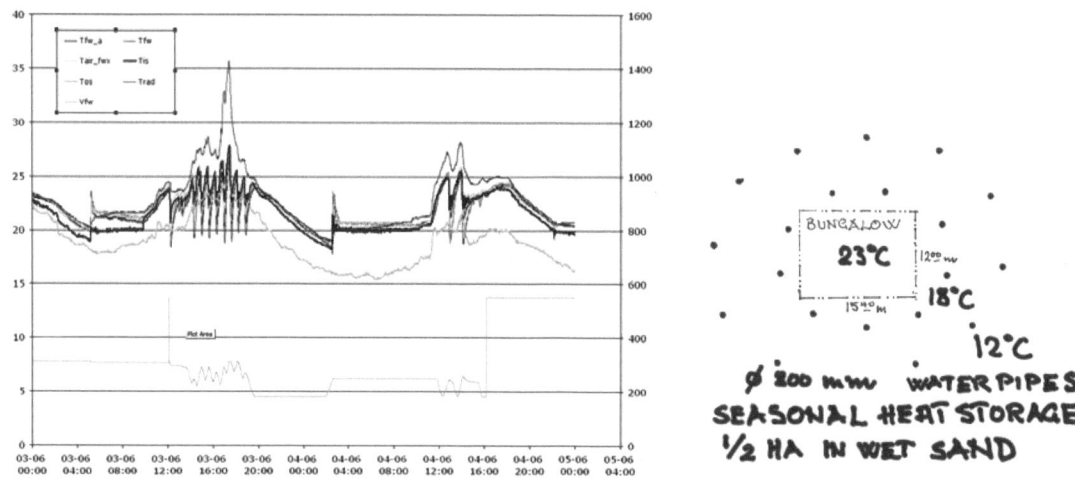

Fig. 04.59:   The temperatures within 'Smart Skin' injection during a field test in sunny weather (left), and an oval configuration of pipes under the experimental building (right)

Pipes are connected in turn to water-collecting hoses in floor ducts along the façades. Such floor ducts are not common in the building industry, but here they are necessary to connect the water-collecting hoses with short vertical heat-exchanging pipes in the ground. The connection between these heat-exchanging pipes, which are shot in the sandy soil under hydraulic pressure, is unwieldy. As the 5 to 10 m long pipes must be injected before the ground floor is poured, dimensioning inaccuracies in location and height made at the initial stages of construction, make access to them difficult. It is much simpler and cheaper to allow a dimensional tolerance of 100 mm, for example. In view of easy mounting the floor ducts are extra deep (> 200 mm) and extra wide (> 300 mm).

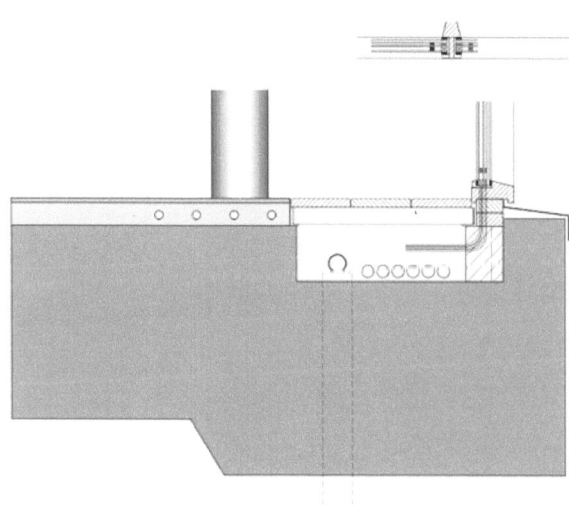

Floor ducts make construction work more complicated. The floor heating is interrupted and the removable covering can cause noise. All the water pipes in the floor ducts finally end in a pump pit inside or outside the building. In this case a prefab pump pit has been chosen. It is a concrete pit outside the building with an insulated removable cover. Not only rows of small fountain pumps are mounted on the wall of the pump pit, but also all the switches, thermo-couples and thermostats required by control engineering. The temperature regulation is computer-controlled. Heat-exchanging pipes with three consecutive temperature ranges were injected in diamond formation into the ground under and around the building.

Fig. 04.60:   Detail - Smart Skin façade connected with water pipes. The ground floor is of cellular concrete.

04.06.05 The design of an experimental Smart Skin building

The results of the first bungalow field test with a vertically mounted 'Smart Skin' (600 x 800 mm) did not match expectations. The heat output on a sunny day in May 2008 only fluctuated round 80 W/m^2, not enough for the building that requires a heat output of 200 - 300 W/m^2 (Fig. 04.65).

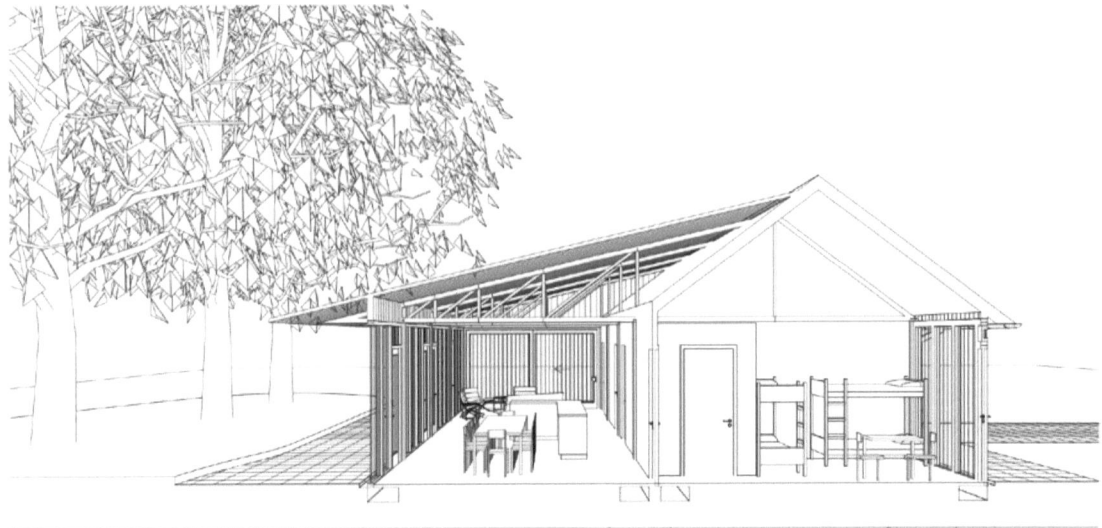

Fig. 04.61:   The experimental building will be situated in an agrarian area near Enschede, the Netherlands. The building site is a water-logged meadow surrounded by solitary trees.

The outer walls largely consist of 'Smart Skin' with large glass doors. The design is derived from the traditional country barn. The short, south-orientated saddle roof has been fitted with thin-film Helianthos PV cells, while the north-orientated roof is made of clear 6-layered polycarbonate greenhouse sheets.

Fig. 04.62:   Multi layered polycarbonate sheet applied as 'Smart Skin' roof

What is special about this roof is that it functions in a similar way to the 'Smart Skin' on the outer wall. Instead of metal pipes, black ø 6 mm synthetic tubes are pulled gradually through the polycarbonate channels. This roof also functions as a low-temperature solar collector, a heated roof and a cold collector. The technique applied to join the various diameters is often used in sprinkling devices for irrigation.

Fig. 04.63:   An impression of a 'Smart Skin' zero-energy building. Panels of thin Helianthos PV cells on the south-orientated roof

04.06.06   Conclusion and discussion

'Smart Skin' is a perfect thermal integration of a lightweight building and a water-logged building site. The future use of 'Smart Skin' will have a profound effect on the building industry, for example, in the case of energetic renovation of historical buildings. 'Smart Skin' demonstrates that it is possible to generate very-low temperature heating (18°C water) and high-temperature cooling (12°C water). A Dutch glass producer 'Betuwe Glas Groothandel' believes in 'Smart Skin' and wants to supply it. The estimated production price of 'Smart Skin' built in an aluminium frame amounts to approximately € 700/m^2 to € 1,200/m^2, exclusive of VAT. It is inevitable that the handmade installation (the first of its kind), the control system and the constructional detailing will have to contend with and overcome various 'teething troubles'.

The poor heat output performance of the first prototype can be improved by several measures, for example, the heat absorption properties of the outer-pane water pipes being enhanced by a darker back layer, or by spectral selective coatings (Polaroid principle). Another interesting application could combine the heat and cold functions with algae for water treatment. This concept was first explored by Luising [1998] and later elaborated on, and integrated into façade design by students and staff of the Manchester School of Architecture [Keeffe, 2008]. Of course these adjustments need to be tested before a working model can be presented. Needless to say that the first boilers, windmills and PV panels were not that efficient either. There is little practical experience yet, but we think that the innovative energy concept deserves every support for further development.

As a title, 'Smart Skin' does not cover the whole concept. The application of 'Smart Skin' technology in non-translucent constructions opens an entirely new outside-wall application in existing buildings and the renovation of listed buildings.

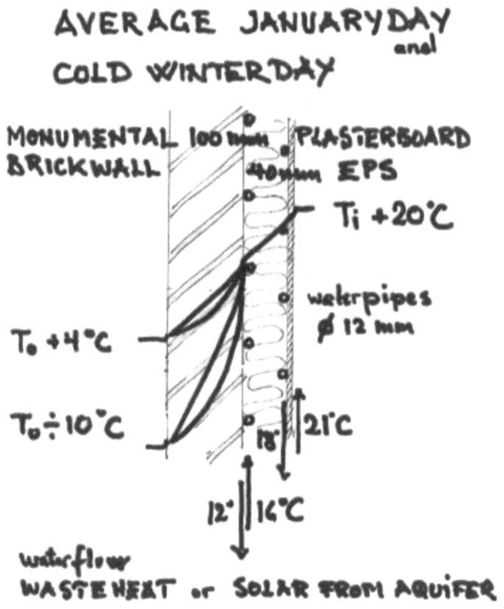

Fig. 04.64: Outline of an energetic Smart Skin renovation of 400 listed half-brick houses called 'de Hoogte' in the city of Groningen, the Netherlands.

04.06.07 Follow-up

The details for six water pipes for four orientations with accompanying pumps, management system and a seasonal storage for three temperatures, turned out to be too much technology for a small visitor building. Apart from a working prototype this translucent Smart Skin facade has not yet received a follow-up. One cannot say much about when and how these translucent facades will develop. In terms of feasibility and production, a study found that the Diamond Exchange building in Amsterdam could be heated and cooled without thermal insulation, by adopting a 'Smart Skin' concept of translucent glass facade and synthetic plated roof.

A simplified version of the aforementioned energy-producing translucent facade, has been manufactured with an opaque stone outer gable, cooled and heated by water of a very low temperature. Instead of the usual ΔT of 30°C temperature difference between indoors and outdoors pumped into a building during the heating season, the main principle is to use 10°C ground water on the inside of the outer gable, replacing thermal insulation. This energetic connection between the indoor climate of a building and the ground water temperature can be established relatively simply in renovation projects. Wall heating by water insulation is installed as floor heating with a water temperature of 18 to 22°C.

If a building is to be cooled by a 'wall heating' system, it is advisable not to go below 18°C to prevent internal condensation.

04.07 Soil energy

04.07.01 Introduction

Instead of a ventilation air inlet near the ceiling, drawing in the air through a set of synthetic tubes in the earth can reduce energy demand for air heating and cooling. This concept was demonstrated at the Poppe customs building in Oldenzaal, a project of the Dutch Government Buildings Agency.

At a certain depth the soil and ground water has a constant temperature: the local mean temperature. In the Netherlands this is 10 to 11°C. It is possible to exploit this resource in summer and winter, without damaging the deeper watertight layer of clay. In summer the soil will be a natural pre-cooler, in winter a pre-heater. Through pre-heating ventilated air in winter, the capacity of a common heating installation can be reduced by 20%. The ventilation losses of the total heating capacity are around 40%[17]. With thermal mass and optimal isolation, the living areas will keep their temperature at night. Additional traditional heating is sufficient and air-conditioning will not be necessary.

Fig. 04.65: Piping required to harness soil energy

---

[17] It must be noted however at night the outdoor temperature is at its lowest, while a lower indoor temperature can be tolerated. At this time building occupancy is typically low, and the ventilation can be switched-off.

To make this idea practical, pipes (rainwater pipes, ⌀ 220 mm, will do) can be laid under the ground floor of a building. The space between the foundation structure and the grid of air pipes is filled with 1.5 m of sand. For cleaning and discharge of condensation water the tubes need to lay to falls towards an air collection pit, from whence the air is distributed in the building.

04.07.02 Hollow heat-exchanging foundation piles

Using the soil for seasonal storage of heat has become a proven method. There are three ways to establish this system.

1. Using an underground aquifer by drilling two tubes into a sand layer between two watertight layers of clay. Water is pumped in under pressure and pumped out a bit further in a closed cycle. In this way heat (from the sun) can be stored in the sand layers. One of the disadvantages of the method is the perforation of clay layers on a depth of 50 to 150 meters.
2. To inject double 10 to 20 meter tubes with water and to connect it to a heat pump. The disadvantage of this method is the need for anti-freeze and the subsequent risk of leakage into the ground/drinking water supply.
3. A shallow horizontal network of pipes or tubes in the ground or groundwater, of the type of soil energy discussed previously.

Fig. 04.66:   Assembly of the water tubes for supply and discharge on the head of the pile[18]

Hollow piles
A new development applicable to countries like the Netherlands are hollow foundation piles. When filled with water the piles function as heat exchangers with the soil (at the first bearing sand layer), both pile and soil act as thermal mass.
With this system a low-tech, low-pressure water circulation is possible for the storage of low-caloric thermal solar energy. The system may be connected to a heat pump for domestic heating, or in reverse, for cooling of dwellings or office buildings.

---

[18] Source: IEP, Almere

In 1999 a graduation project at the Faculty of Architecture of TU Delft by Pieter Geene studied the concept of 'thermal piles'. At that time hollow pile technology did not exist, three years later they were produced by Unibeton in Zeewolde. Pieter and myself were both involved in the completion of this innovation.

Fig. 04.67:   Inventor Peter Peters and Pieter Geene in front of the storage of hollow piles

Foundation piles usually do not bear more than 10% of their loading bearing capacity. In the Netherlands 600,000 m^3 of concrete is annually processed into piles. A decrease of at least 100.000 m^3 of raw material is then possible with the hollow system. A consequent reduction in transportation removes some 2000 trailers off the roads. If we assume € 80 excluding VAT for one cubic meter of concrete, the savings are eight million euro per year.

Fig. 04.68:   Driving piles with a diesel engine[19]

---

[19] Source: Unibeton, Zeewolde

04.07.03 Deventer fire station (1990)

Fig. 04.69: South west elevation of the Deventer fire station

In 1988 we received the assignment for the design of the Deventer fire station. Two years later ground collector pipes for ventilation air were completed under the fire engine garage.

Although the predominant wind direction in the Netherlands is from the south-west, a decision was taken to allow ventilation air in at the north-eastern elevation preventing a neighbouring refuse transfer depot to the east having any adverse effects on air quality.

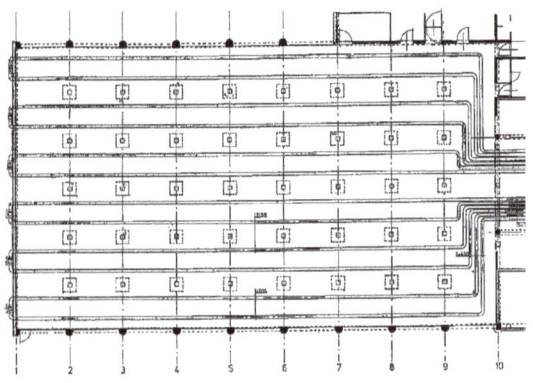

Fig. 04.70: Scheme of piping under the garage (left). The air-pipes fall 1.5 m underneath the garage floor and about 0.5 m above the highest groundwater level.

Measurements were incorporated in the National Energy Programme of the Dutch governmental energy institute 'Novem'.

Fig. 04.71: Garage (left) and north-west elevation (right). The air-pipes lay under the fire engine garage, which has a roof of steel Litzka beams. Grates for air inlet can be easily distinguished in the facade.

Summer situation
Compared to the warm air outside, the cooling of air through the soil to approximately 18°C indicates that underneath most low- and middle-rise buildings an effective environmentally sound alternative for air-conditioning is available. For large meeting rooms, which have to be extremely well air-conditioned, only additional top cooling may be necessary.

Autumn situation
This period demonstrates that there is no need for extra heating due to stored heat in the summer months.

Winter situation
In the Netherlands heating utilities are tuned to an air temperature difference ΔT = 30°C between inside and outside, assuming -10°C in winter and +20°C in summer. The lowest and highest groundwater temperatures from the period 1961 to 1990 are used in computer simulations calculating heating requirement. This temperature is still rising.

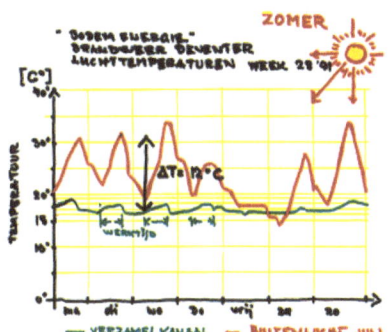
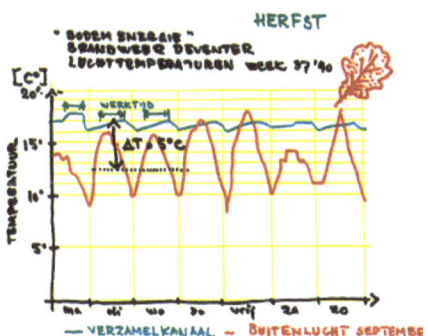
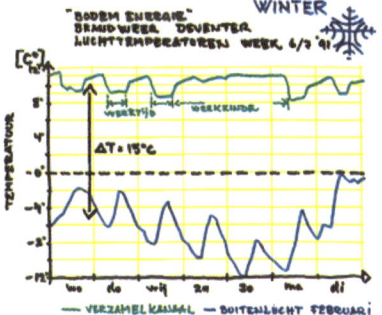

Fig. 04.72: Summer: soil energy substitutes air-conditioning, free cooling, failure free, simple, cheap.
Autumn: transition period, no heating needed.
Winter: smaller building heating service, heat exchange comparable to half the performance of a good air/air exchanger [20]

---

[20] 1990 measurements were done by EcoEnergie Engineering from Velp

Jón Kristinsson   **Integrated Sustainable Design**

The incoming air is approximately 10°C as the soil is still warm from summer. Since ventilation with soil energy is only applied during full occupancy during working hours [21], this relatively high inlet temperature is maintained for a long time. A ΔT of 15°C means that by pre-heating fresh ventilation air with soil energy, the total building heating service system can be reduced by approximately 20%. This is very important for the energy performance of a building.

To summarise, soil energy can level out temperature fluctuations in summer and winter. Soil energy has almost the same effect as air-conditioning, but in operation it costs almost nothing. Unfortunately climate consultancy companies appear to be unconvinced of the obvious benefits this approach has to offer. At present they are paid in accordance with the costs of building services applied in a building, and not by the energy reduction they achieve.

The recommendation is clear: use the thermal mass under buildings. The capacity of an air-conditioning unit becomes redundant and the building heating service for winter can be reduced significantly. Extra costs are minimal and maintenance is nil.

04.07.04 Sustainable fire station, Soest (1998)

Fig. 04.73: The Soest fire station, designed by Jón Kristinsson[22]

---

[21] The fan has a standard control with a weekly programme.
[22] Photo by Jan Derwig

Having seen the 'soil energy' Deventer scheme at the VIBA sustainable building exhibition in Hertogenbosch, the Netherlands, the municipality awarded us the contract for the fire-station in Soest. The project criteria were: use of passive solar energy, optimum daylighting and sufficient façade protection and minimal maintenance. The ground pipe concept at Deventer was repeated at the Soest fire station (figure 04.78) with the addition of a solar chimney (fire-hose tower) to induce the extraction of exhaust air.

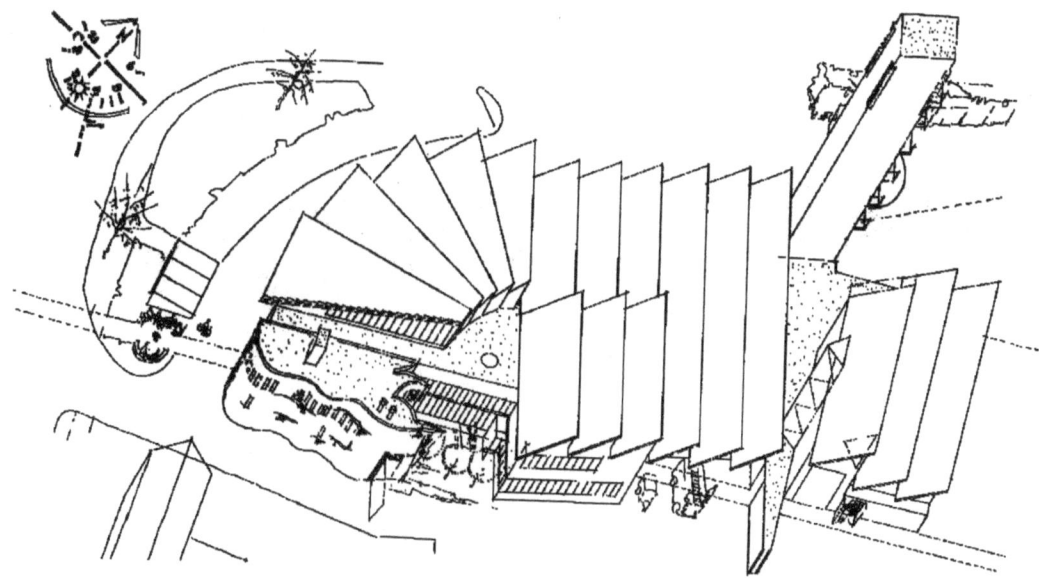

Fig. 04.74:   Bird's eye view of the fire-station, where a new fire hose tower is still drawn, which however was removed during the design process due to the substitution of the old hoses by light synthetic fire hoses that no longer had to be suspended.

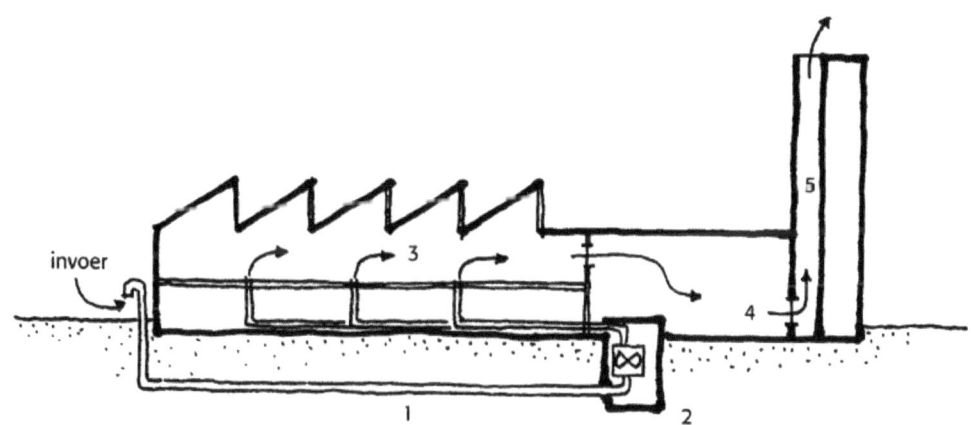

Fig. 04.75:   Soil energy principle of the Soest fire station.

Energy measures
Energy-saving and sustainable measures include:
- The garage has natural ventilation by draught through the chimney-shaft in the existing fire hose tower.
- Soil energy cools air in summer and forms an extra heating source in winter.
- Rain water is collected for fire-fighting water, washing and rinsing.
- Passive-solar energy and natural light is received from the shed roofs.
- Light regulation and energy-saving armatures have been used.
- Water-saving taps, toilets and shower heads are used.
- 40% of timber has been saved through wood with 'Lignostone' connections.

Fig. 04.76: Canteen with light from above.

Although the original fire-station was demolished, the fire hose tower was preserved. No longer in use, the tower was to be utilised in the natural ventilation strategy following the principles of the 'stack effect'. Here, natural draughts are induced by the height and the difference in atmospheric pressure between the indoor and outdoor climate.

Soil energy was applied with pipes running under the garage (see the section on the Deventer fire-brigade). These provide air-cooling in summer and auxiliary heating in winter. The offices on the ground floor have bare concrete ceilings promoting thermal mass. For the acoustics, a suspended modular ceiling was installed. General lighting was integrated into the ceiling panels, while desk lamps provided individual task lighting.

Material measures
Sustainable materials are:
- Ceramic tile cladding
- Baked tile roofing
- Inner cavity wall of sand lime brick
- Windows and frames of finger-jointed and laminated larch (durability class two), transparent varnished on base of alkali (1 and 5), as well as the balcony and stairs partition.

Fig. 04.77:   Backside of the fire-station in Soest.

The interior is also sustainable, with linoleum in the canteen and corridors, a cotton carpet in the offices and tiles in the wet spaces. The furniture is predominantly constructed of wood and steel. In the canteen a wall of glass building bricks surrounds the washroom block, allowing natural lighting to permeate during the day. In the centre of the building a large expressive timber spiral staircase forms the entrance to the canteen and the instruction area.

Awarded timber roof frame
The Soest Fire Brigade building (1998) is spanned with untreated (as placed inside the building) laminated framework beams. With a maximum length of 22 m, each beam cantilevers out to the exterior protecting the façade from adverse weather. A large canteen with balcony for the voluntary fire-brigade is located above the offices. The shed roofs catch the passive-solar energy and natural light.

Timber connections are made using the 'Lignostone' technique, originally developed in 1995, by Hylke Katsma and Ad Leijten from the Faculty of Civil Engineering at TU Delft. A galvanised thick-plated steel tube with a connective ring is pressed into the wood with tightly layered beech plywood between the joint parts. Although heavier with extra material, the frame becomes significantly stronger. Partly because the joints and tension members were made of rigid steel, the framework could be designed slimmer and lighter leading to a 40% saving in timber.

Fig. 04.78:   Tube with connective ring and tight beech plywood pressed in-between the wooden joints.

Unlike the timber beams that span from the inside to the outside, the Lignostone beach-wood connections had to be located within the building envelope due to their high sensitivity to moisture. The frames exposed on the exterior would later be covered with ventilated transparent polycarbonate plates.

Fig. 04.79:   Hammer-beam truss, covered with transparent polycarbonate plates and with the old firehose tower on the background.

In 1999 our architectural office received the European Glulam Award (for glued and laminated wood connections) thanks to this new and special construction.

Fig. 04.80:   The European Glulam Award logo

04.07.05 Greijdanus, School of Fresh Air, Meppel (2011)

Fig. 04.81:   Front of the Greijdanus School, the new build left to the original building.

Introduction
Fresh air is a major problem in schools across the world. There is strong scientific evidence that the learning performance of students significantly declines when the indoor air quality is compromised. This problem is aggravated by the limited budget of school building projects. For the Greijdanus School in Meppel we saw it as our challenge to solve this issue by integrated design, providing real-time physics lessons every year, including solar access and natural cooling. The building had to radiate its timelessness during all seasons and every hour.

Sunshading
The demand for cooling was minimised in the architectural design. Dynamics of the building were made visible from the outside by the strategic preservation and site relocation of deciduous trees. At the roof cornice a metal mesh foot-rack functions as a fixed sunshading device creating diffuse daylight. A large overhang at the north-eastern side provides a wind lee solar terrace. In addition, there is automatic external sunshading and a timber pergola.

Fig. 04.82:   Mesh foot-racks act as sunshading device at the roof cornice.

Ventilation

It is a well known that ventilation is the weakest link in school design because of overheating, limited refreshment air, excessive draughts, ventilator noise and noise leakage through air ducts. The Dutch regulation for school ventilation is 12.6 m^3/h per m^2 of floor area, a figure that is hardly ever achieved. Normally, operable windows could solve this, but the Greijdanus School location next to relatively high levels of traffic noise demanded a building design combining natural ventilation with a closed facade. Breathing Windows therefore were an appropriate solution. These provide basic ventilation and heating. Breathing Windows permanently monitor the air quality on CO_2 concentrations. The ventilators could switch off at 600 ppm and give a warning at 1200 ppm. Mechanical exhaust is used in washroom areas.

Soil ventilation

Most notably, after successful installations at Deventer and Soest fire stations, and with the help of consultant Gosse Landstra, soil ventilation was utilised for the very first time at a school. Physical investigations proved that the air quality is better than in any other schools ventilated in the traditional way.

The Greijdanus School is entirely ventilated with air drawn in through a ground-air heat exchanger consisting of a soil pipe register (30 times 30 meter, ø 200 mm) at 1.2 meter depth in the ground. This provides sufficient, naturally pre-conditioned fresh air for 200 pupils. The capacity is 8200 m^3/h, which approximately equates to 50 m^3 per hour per pupil. In winter the air is pre-heated and humidified, in summer pre-cooled and dehumidified. The air coming in is around 18°C at a 30°C outdoor temperature. When it freezes, air is heated up in the soil ducts to around 10°C. In that case a small afterburner provides the additional heating. In winter some recirculation takes place. The ducts lie at a gradient in order to enable annual cleaning by high-pressure sprayer.

Night cooling

The soil ventilation system offers simple, cheap, natural air cooling, and competes favourably in terms of efficiency against the much more expensive concrete core activation. Suspended ceilings were replaced by acoustic ceiling panels, exposing the thermal mass of the concrete floors. This helps to cool the structure on summer nights during 01:00 and 07:00. Thus, the system also provides night cooling that can be managed on each floor automatically.

In the classrooms, excess temperature hours of Ti > 28°C were reduced from 41 to 13, 40 to 10 and from 29 to 6. Despite a superior air quality and comfortable indoor temperature, the installation costs are lower than traditional climate designs for schools.

04.08   Inter-seasonal heat storage

04.08.01   Working principle

The inter-seasonal heat storage was originally designed as a horizontal one-pipe system in three layers of wet clay. In a one-pipe system, in summer the heat is transported to the ground by the same method used in winter to extract heat. The ground area equals 40 m x 40 m = 1600 m^2. The solar heat spreads horizontally from the hot core to the surrounding edges. Vertically, stratification (layered temperature increase) is made possible through three vertical water shafts (Fig. 04.86).

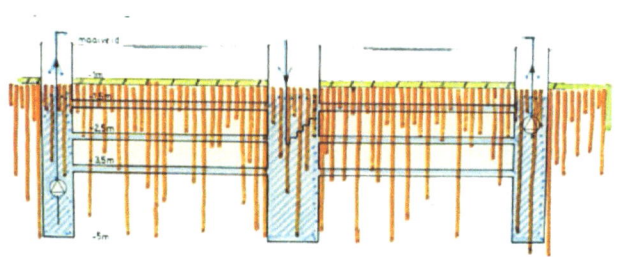

Fig. 04.83:Piping scheme of the inter-seasonal heat storage (analogue to the electrical resistance model), the charging occurs from the central shaft (above left). Section of the one-pipe system in three layers, connected to three shafts, and the temperature composition by stratification (above right).

Fig. 04.84 (right): An increasing amount of energy is stored in the 'battery'. In the second year neighbouring dwellings can also receive heat from the system.

Due to a bowl-shaped temperature profile there is no need for thermal insulation under the inter-seasonal heat storage. Following the principles developed by Prof. Van Koppen at TU Eindhoven the central shaft has a floating inlet composed of a light-weight sleeve. The inlet is filled with water of variable temperatures, this water eventually flowing to water of the same temperature and specific gravity. This principle prevents a mixture of temperatures in the shaft. The water with the highest temperature is obviously collected in the upper part. During the heating season solar heat is extracted from the inter-seasonal heat storage through the shafts on the outside. When there is a limited demand for heat the pump at the bottom of the lowest shaft is used. When the heat demand is high or when the storage is emptied, a pump at the top of the stratification extracts the heat.

Due to its 'open' character and little resistance this horizontal system with shafts enables the water to spread through the one-pipe system almost without any pumping, thanks to the different water levels or stratification in the shafts (communicating vessels). Because of the large dimensions of the horizontal water pipes that

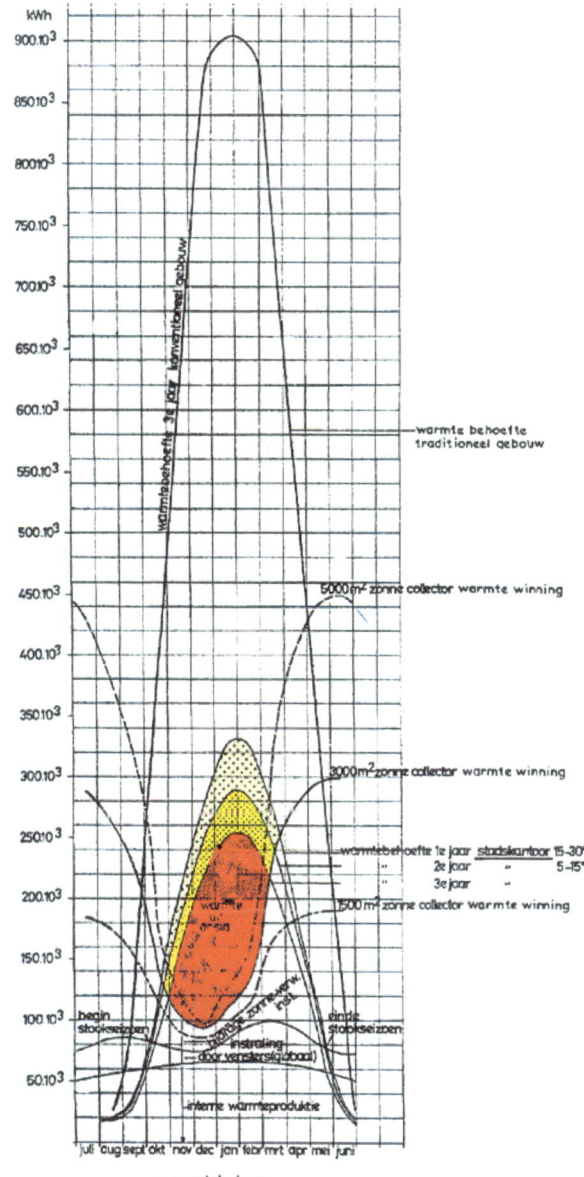

energiebalans
de eerste drie jaren van ingebruikname

heat up the clay, gravity generates the circulation of water. An additional benefit to this strategy is that an open circulation system without pressure can have simple joints and connections.

04.08.02 Beijum, Groningen (1982)

An inter-seasonal heart storage system, partly funded by the European Community, was built for the neighbourhood of Beijum, in the city of Groningen (Fig. 04.88).

Fig. 04.85: Installation of solar panels to be combined with an inter-seasonal store, extension Beijum, Groningen, 1982.

For any inter-seasonal heat storage system it is important to connect the solar panels early in the process so the heat storage can be charged one summer before the building is in use. After a few years, when the storage is completely charged, the surrounding buildings can also be connected. The estimated efficiency of 50 to 60% has since been found to be accurate.

Fig. 04.86: Dwellings with solar collectors (left) feeding the inter-seasonal heat storage (right) for 100 dwellings in Beijum.

Fig. 04.87: Early illustration of the storage strategy at Beijum, built in 1982 and still in operation.

At Beijum, a one-pipe system was used with a vertical structure, water circulation relying on pumps and not temperature stratification as described in the previous section. For peak loads in summer a tank was added to balance day and night operations. For the solar panels, highly-efficient vacuum heat tubes were preferred, similar to those installed at the residence of Professor Van Koppen the year before - a technology way ahead of its time.

Fig. 04.88: Solar panels in-situ at the Prof. Van Koppen residence (Architect: A. Hoekstra), Eindhoven, 1981 (left), with high-tech vacuum collectors and warm water storage tank of 3.7 m^3. Detail of the vacuum tube heat pipe collector (right).

05

TOWARDS ZERO-ENERGY BUILDINGS

05.01   Minimum-Energy Dwellings

05.01.01   Energy saving in social housing through limited investment

In 1980 at a symposium held in Spijkenisse, the Netherlands, there was discussion about the feasibility of utilising waste heat or geothermal energy for city scaled heating systems and, more specifically, building energy-saving dwellings at Pernis, Rotterdam (a new expansion adjacent to a Shell refinery). The investment for each housing design being no more than 10,000 Dutch guilders (now € 4,500).
Several offices were invited to propose a scheme. Our office of course presented an energy-saving concept. Although the focus was on the 120 dwellings that had to be built in Spijkenisse, the numerous solutions were also intended to bepartly applicable to other new dwellings elsewhere.

The architectural strategies and calculations applied to a new dwelling aimed to improve on the thermal insulation norms of 1978. This dwelling has a volume of 330 m^3 and consumes 74,000 MJ per year for heating (hot tap water not included); this corresponds with 2350 m^3 gas equivalent with a high-performance (90%) boiler for the central heating system.
The second proposal was closest to the specified budget of € 4,500, being € 3,900. The thermal insulation, reducing transmission losses by 42% in comparison to the index dwelling, had the highest return on investment.

A clear measure in the cost-conscious housing industry can be calculated by construction investments in euros per m^3 of natural gas saved per year. For a small consumer in 1980 we could calculate approximately € 0.14/m^3 nge/year. The smallest investment, for an isolated floor with 40 mm of insulation, is € 0.67/m^3 nge/year. When the roof insulation thickness increases from 30 mm to 150 mm, the investment amounts to € 0.95/m^3 nge/year. On top of these, other facilities became cheaper: heat recovery on the ventilated air for € 1.32/m^3 nge/year and an extra sealing of seams for € 1.70/m^3 nge/year.
The use of a 'seasonal adaptive façade' with thermally insulated shutters or shutters with external sunblinds is favourable in regards to double glazing, but when compared to three-layered glazing it is quite expensive in this stage of development: € 4.55/m^3 nge/year.

With the available money of € 3,900 (excluding VAT) a dwelling can be designed which has its energy consumption reduced to about 12,000 MJ/year (and 33.4 MJ = 1 m^3 nge). Together with a high-performance boiler using natural gas this means savings of 2350 – 410 = 1940 m^3 nge/year! In Spijkenisse, where 345*10^6 MJ of geothermal energy is available, the costs can be reduced from € 4,070 to € 1,135 per dwelling, because at the moment we start building truly energy-efficient dwellings 10,000 extra dwellings can be connected to the geothermal energy supply!

The heating demand of 12,000 MJ is almost equal to the hot tap water of 10,000 MJ per year. The building materials, the orientation, the window openings, the external sunblinds and the use of passive and active solar energy can become critical factors.

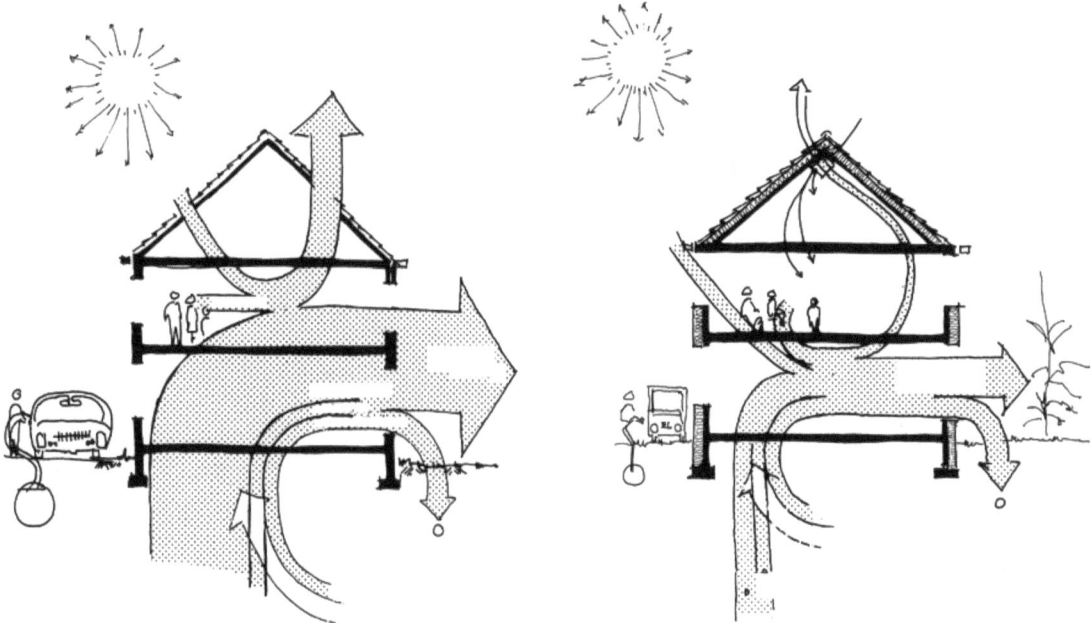

Fig. 05.01: Heat balance of a conventional house (left) and one adjusted according to the ideas proposed at the Spijkenisse symposium (right).

The conclusion of the Spijkenisse symposium was that with an extra investment of € 3,900 energy-efficient dwellings can be constructed that reduce the heating demand from 74,000 MJ to 12,000 MJ per dwelling per year. Only 410 m^3 nge/year would still be needed!
Thus, a central heating system would become unnecessary. Thirty years later, the building industry still has not shown any significant improvement in this respect: most dwellings still need central heating and still consume more than 500 m^3 of gas for heating.

05.01.02 The Dwelling without Central Heating, a giant leap forward (1981)

The Spijkenisse symposium proved that dwellings without a central heating were possible, reducing the demand for fossil fuel. Together with Peter Ghijsen as project architect, we elaborated the 'Dwelling without Central Heating' by means of external funding. Afterwards a press conference was organised in our office to make the news known to the world.

> New philosophy
> New building materials
> New building techniques
> New building services
> Passive solar energy
> Physical calculations

The design philosophy was to invest extra money in a package deal of energy-saving measures that lowered the heating demand so much so that savings could be made on the purchase of a central heating system. A part of the extra investment could be recovered, and the remaining part could be found in savings on heating expenses.

Fig. 05.02:   The team of the Dwelling without Central Heating and the Minimum-Energy Dwellings (left): Koos Slootweg, Peter Ghijsen, Willem Schuringa and Jón Kristinsson. Press conference at the Kristinsson office (right).

The overall design principles were:
- Large windows on south elevations, small windows on the north.
- Windows with thermally insulated shutters, operable from the inside.
- Zoning of living spaces on the south side, to create a heat buffer.
- Kitchen, storage and hobby spaces on the north side.
- Bathroom in the 'warm' core of the house.
- Dwellings are made extra seam sealed (no draught), by means of a closed entrance hall at the front and balanced ventilation with heat recovery.
- Extraction of air takes place in the kitchen, bathroom and toilet.
- Cheap building services that are easy to maintain.

The preferred heat source was a double-sided incinerator for wood and paper with a small combustion room, this design ensuring high incineration temperatures that transmit heat quickly. It's double-sided canal providing heat recovery from exhausted gasses.
The underlying idea was to collect papers, wooden crates and similar materials throughout the year, and to use them for extra heating when required. With this approach no central heating was necessary and therefore a major saving was possible.

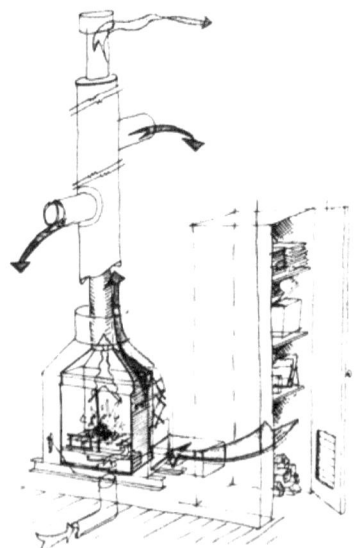

Fig. 05.03:   Double-sided incinerator for wood and paper with storage cupboard.

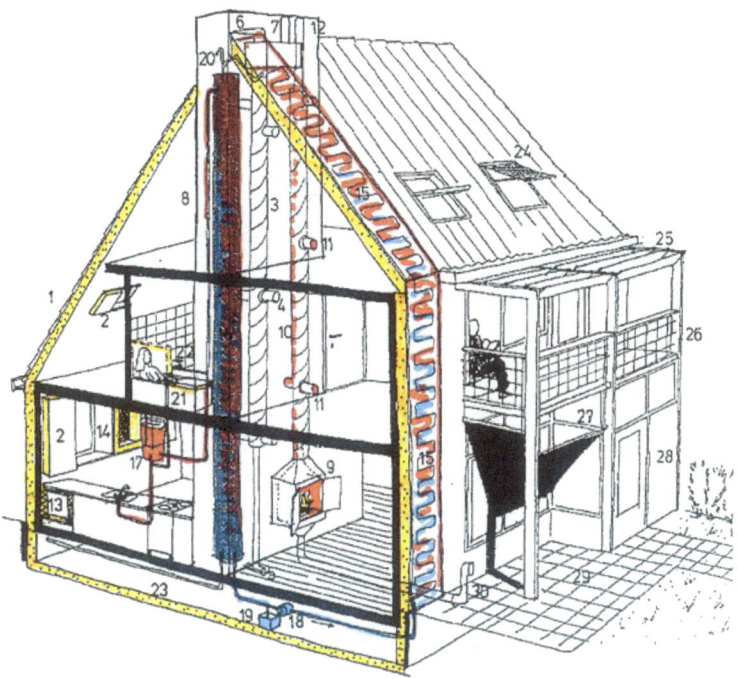

Fig. 05.04: Sketch for the 'Dwelling without Central Heating' (1981):
1. 150 mm insulation
2. Insulated shutters
3. Heat exchanger & balanced ventilation
4. Blow-in air valve
5. Extraction of air from the crawl space
6. Supply of fresh air
7. Outlet of exhaust air
8. Central pipe shaft
9. Wood/paper incinerator
10. Double-sided canal
11. Warm air valve
12. Outlet of exhaust gases
13. Insulated small fridge
14. Meat-safe
15. Solar collector
16. Hot water cask
17. Re-heater
18. Pump
19. Expansion keg
20. Overflow
21. Bath with insulation cover
22. Tap directly from the storage cask
23. Cold water supply
24. Roof window sunblinds
25. Bedroom window sunblinds
26. Balcony
27. Living room sunblinds
28. Enclosed porch
29. Terrace
30. Air supply for wood/paper incinerator

Thanks partly to TV commercials from the Ministry of Economic Affairs, on energy savings in traditional dwellings, it had widely been rightly assumed in the Netherlands that dwellings cool down at night in summer. However, a well-insulated house will not cool down at night if the windows remain shut. Through the use of balanced ventilation in combination with an inlet of fresh air, there is no need to open a window at night. Furthermore, it was possible to avoid overheating in summer by incorporating sunblinds on the outside.

A relatively simple and cheap solar collector could be made with a high storage cask using stratification (temperature gradation). Optimal efficiency of a balanced ventilation system was established through double airshafts in a vertical heat exchanger. This air was extracted from the crawl space. Extra costs of this additional installation can be paid from the savings on fuel.

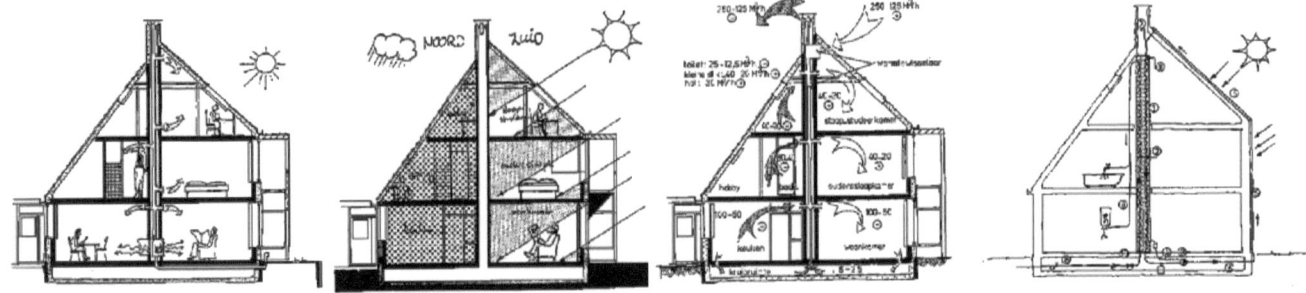

Fig. 05.05:   Principles for the dwelling without central heating: Insulation all around; retention of heat, auxiliary heating with hot air (top left). Zoning and passive solar energy: living areas on the south side (top right). For airtight dwellings balanced ventilation is a necessity (bottom left) Cheap solar boiler with temperature gradation in the tall storage cask (bottom right).

There is only a small kitchen heater for hot tap water. The large loss of energy in the cooking process is used for the dwelling heating. Usually this heat is extracted directly by the hood above the stove. All pipes and utilities are easily accessible in a specially designed shaft.

For the calculations of the heat balance we used the calculation model of Fläkt from Stockholm, because this was the most accurate programme at that moment. Incoming solar radiation, heat-accumulation in walls and floors, preferable opening of shutters (open from 7:00 till 17:00 o'clock), and separation of the internal heat gains (residents, illumination and the electrical devices) were optimised.

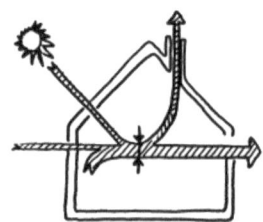

Fig. 05.06:   Heat balance of a common dwelling (above) and of the Dwelling without Central Heating, with a heat recovery of 50% on ventilated air (preliminary study, below).

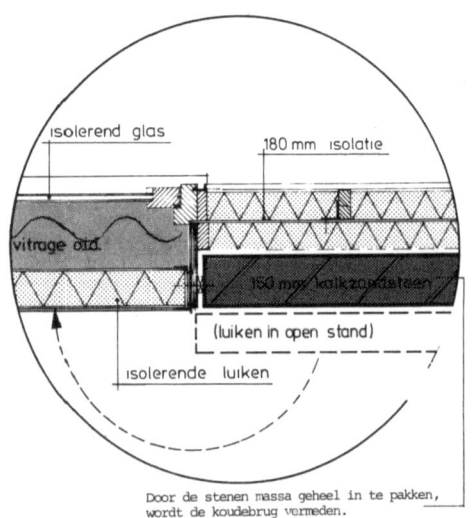

We chose to use shutters on the inside, which are easy and quick to handle, as well as low to maintain. They reduce heat-loss by transmission by around 50% in contrast to a dwelling without insulated shutters.

Fig. 05.07:   Connection detail of the insulation shutter.

Integrated Sustainable Design   Jón Kristinsson

After cooling down at night there is a peak in the heat demand in the morning of 1500 W (sunny day) respectively 2500 W (cloudy day). If the sun is shining this declines to zero at a fast rate.

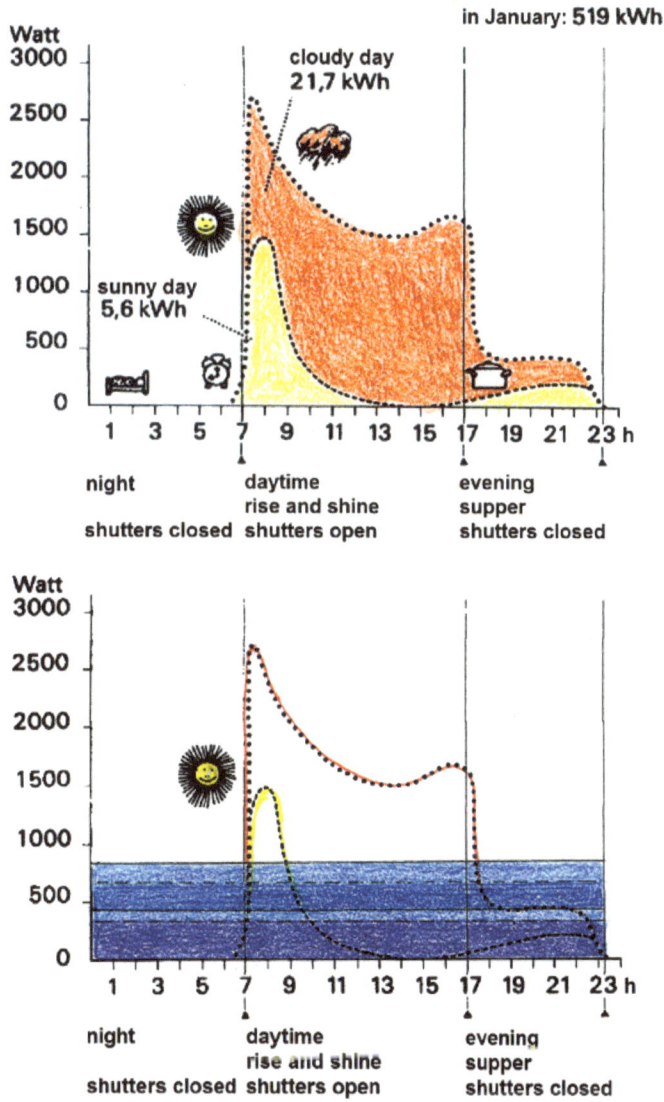

Fig. 05.08:   Heat demanded by a working family during a 24-hour sunny and a cloudy day in January per 24-hours [23]. Power x time = Energy. 1 kW (1000 Watt) x 1 h = 1 kWh (kilowatt-hour), i.e. the area in the graphs.

There is always loss of heat as a result of ventilation in the 'Dwelling without Central Heating'. Natural ventilation through seams in a common house can be equal to, or even twice the total

---

[23] Source: Adviesbureau Jongen, Vlaardingen.

volume, i.e. 250 to 400 m³/24 hours. Mechanical ventilation will operate for 24 hours a day if programmed, there will be additional ventilation of 50 m³/h (during the day) due to leakages.

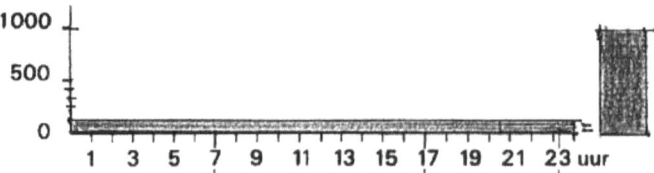

Fig. 05.09:   The metabolism of a human being: 100 Watt x 24 hours = 2,400 Wh or 2.4 kWh of heat per twenty-four hours. One person generates 2.4 kWh of heat per 24 hours (100 W x 24 h). This is complemented with 30 W of latent heat (e.g. in perspiration).

With balanced ventilation with a heat recovery of 66% to 75%, the transmission loss becomes approximately equal to the ventilation loss. We need 20 m³/h of air per person (50 m³/h for smokers). For a family, a decrease from 250 m³/h to 125 m³/h does not appear to be unhealthy.

Table 05.01: Energy savings and remaining heat demand through insulated shutters

	Energy saving by shutters		Remaining heat demand	
	MJ	kWh	MJ	kWh
January	1100	305	1900	528
February	1050	291	1200	333
March	950	266	500	139
April	750	208	200	55
October	650	180	250	69
November	850	236	1150	319
December	950	264	1800	550
TOTAL	6300	1750	7000	1943

Calculations determined that during the morning hours in winter about 2 kW of extra heat would be needed if all the shutters were open. If we assume that the desired indoor temperature is 20°C, this heat could be delivered by a small electric heater. While a common dwelling on average consumed 25,260 kWh annually (mainly natural gas), the Dwelling without Central Heating only needs 1,943 kWh, which comes down to 15 kWh/m² per annum.

Fig. 05.10:   Electrical heater with a capacity of 2 kW is sufficient to keep the Minimum-Energy House warm.

The PBE, later called Novem, then SenterNovem and currently Agency NL(an agency of the Dutch Ministry of Economic Affairs) attended the 'Dwelling without Central Heating' press conference and immediately announced their financial support for the realisation of the dwellings. It became the first pilot project of the national PREGO research programme (rational energy use in the built environment).

05.01.03 Minimum-Energy Dwellings, Schiedam (1984)

Fig. 05.11: The Woudhoek-Noord Minimum-Energy Dwellings, Schiedam.

Following the press conference on the 'Dwelling without Central Heating' (which was also broadcast on the national children news channel 'Jeugdjournaal'), Chris Zijdeveld, a Schiedam councillor and mechanical engineer, called to ask whether he could be the first to build these dwellings in his town. Zijdeveld was an advocate of solar energy applications, explaining his nickname 'the sun king'.
The opportunity to develop 76 single family dwellings and 108 apartments presented itself in the social housing sector at Woudhoek-Noord in Schiedam. All housing would follow the principle of the 'Dwelling without Central Heating'. The urban plan had a fan form, which made it possible to apply passive solar energy in repeated shifts of orientation.

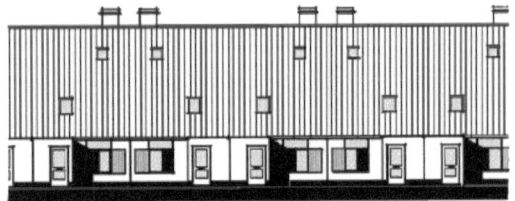 

Fig. 05.12: North elevation of the terraced houses in Schiedam (left) and south elevation of the stacked terraced-houses (right).

With an investment of € 5,000/dwelling the calculated energy consumption for space heating at Schiedam came to 160 m^3 nge/year. Although the short-term cost is an substantial one, it must be put into perspective with the long-term energy and financial demands of conventional subsidised housing. For example, in the REGO programme (1982) the energy consumption was set at 2,150 m^3 nge/year!

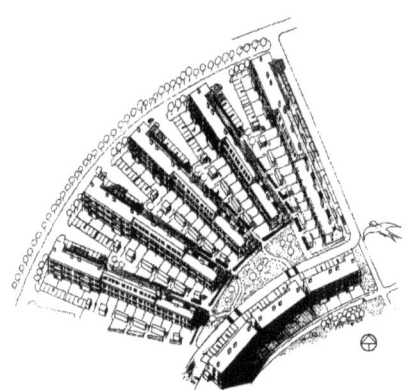 

Fig. 05.13: The Schiedam neighbourhood of Woudhoek-Noord in aerial perspective, with 184 Minimum-Energy Dwellings (left) and an impression of the plan from street view (right).

This extremely low energy consumption was achieved by implementing an extended package of energy-saving measures:
- Southerly orientated building blocks (minimal facades facing east and west).
- Optimal insulation of façade and roof (180 mm mineral wool).
- Extra insulation of the ground floor (R = 5 m^{2}K/W)
- Insulated shutters in front of windows, three-layered glazing.
- Insulated foundation piles to avoid thermal bridges.
- Avoiding thermal bridges in the construction R = 1.3 m^{2}K/W
- Insulated panel at the entrance of the crawling space.
- High quality draught sealing in the Swedish and Danish windows with architectural connections.
- Enclosed porches (at the front and back) to reduce heat loss.
- Heat storage and delay in cooling by retaining concrete mass inside the insulated building envelope.
- Benefitting from passive solar energy, large windows on the south, small windows for all other directions, living areas on the south side, compartmentalised.

- Balanced ventilation with heat recovery from ventilated air.
- Accessibility of cables and ducts in a duct shaft.
- Additional heating system that heats ventilated air with hot water from the kitchen heater.
- Electrical ignition of the geyser flame.
- Small refrigerator in combination with a meat safe (to be discussed in chapter 10).

Fig. 05.14: Window (with shutter) in the upper roof on the south provides sunlight in the northern room.

Thermal insulation is the pre-eminent energy-saving measure. It is relatively cheap and utmost effective. External insulation was chosen, which was fastened to an inner gable of stone and finished with mineral plasterwork. The insulation value of the façade was as high as possible: 180 mm of mineral wool. The advantage of the mass on the inside was that heat could be accumulated. Hereby the inside temperature will remain warmer in winter and cooler in summer. All windows are supplied with insulation glass.

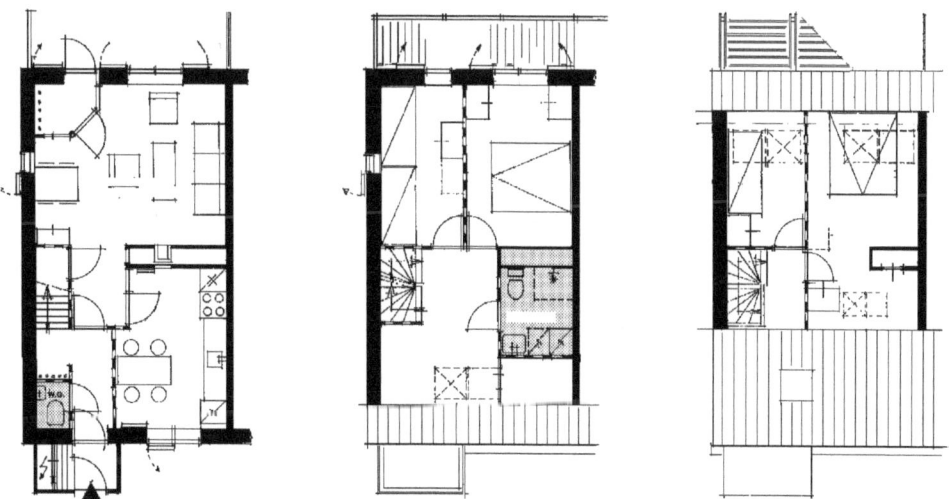

Fig. 05.15: Ground floor, 1st floor and 2nd floor of the Minimum-Energy Dwellings in Schiedam.

The heat balance indicates that, in order to guarantee a comfortable indoor climate, there has to be an equilibrium between energy loss and energy gain. Minimising the additional heating enforces avoidance of transmission losses, as well as the use of solar energy and internal heat production. This entails decreasing the ratio of surface/volume, decreasing the thermal transmission coefficient and decreasing the difference between in- and outside temperature.

Houses with a deep plan have a more favourable (outside) surface/volume ratio than shallow ones. In relation to passive solar design this measure is disadvantageous. A solution is to compartmentalise spaces and activities that have similarities in heat demand. The activities that demand a relatively high temperature should occupy minimal space and volume.

In the bathroom the heat demand is larger than in the rest of the house: approximately 22°C instead of 19 to 20°C. If the bathroom is situated in-between the bedrooms and the landing – as with low-rise dwellings – and the temperature of these spaces is around 18°C, the difference will be 4°C.

The heating demand of the bathroom is 250 W. However, if the shower is switched on there will be a surplus of heat. The water, which cools down from 45°C to 30°C, generates 500 W of heat! So, in the bathroom, before we enter the shower, there is a lack of heat, but as soon as the shower is switched on the bathroom becomes comfortable almost immediately. Conclusion: it is a waste to constantly heat a bathroom; heating by a simple lamp is sufficient.

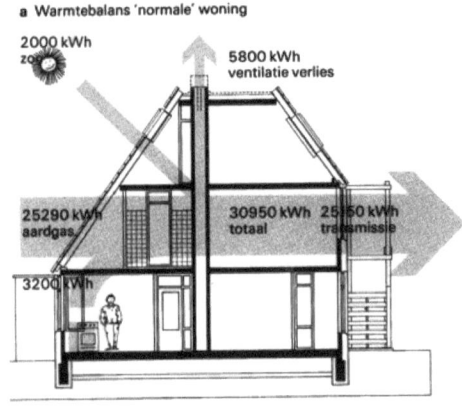

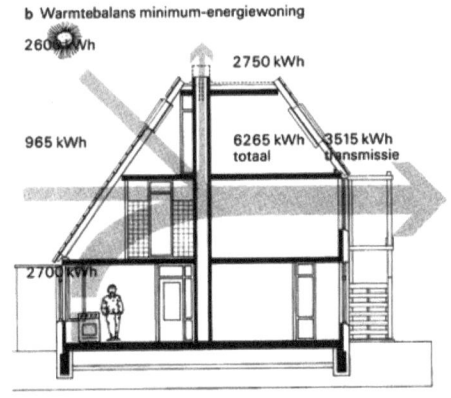

Fig. 05.16: In traditional dwellings the solar heat and internal heat are negligible, in the Minimum-Energy Dwellings these sources of free energy are used for heating.

From the calculated energy balance (Fig. 05.20) three observation can be made: (1) in the winter months there is not enough solar energy; (2) the internal heat production is equal to the amount of additional heating; (3) ventilation losses and transmission losses are similar – therefore, high efficiency in heat recovery is desirable (1 m^3 nge = 33.4 MJ).

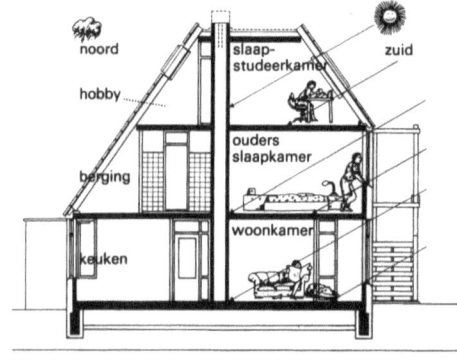

Fig. 05.17: Space zoning: the living areas requiring heat are situated on the warm south side; the (closed) kitchen, entrance, storage and hobby spaces are located on the north side.

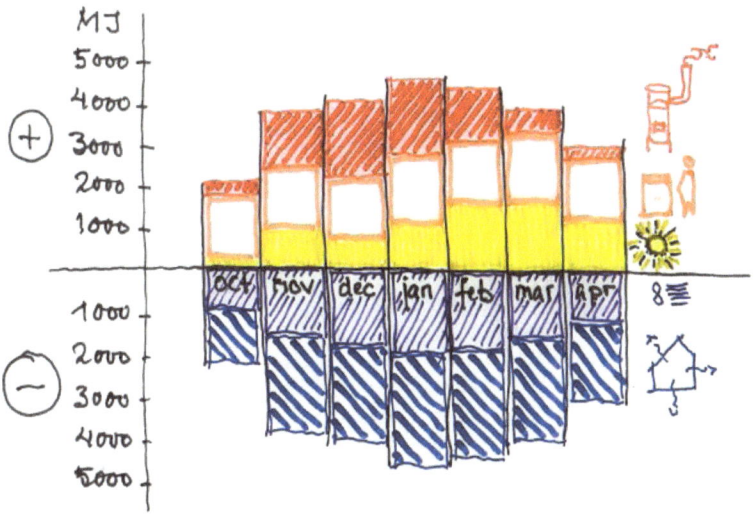

Fig. 05.18:   Calculated energy balance of a 'Dwelling without Central Heating' [source: Jongen consultancy office, Vlaardingen, with the calculation model by Flåkt in Stockholm].

The Minimum-Energy Dwelling was made air-tight by the following measures:
- Extra rabbet for windows.
- Draught-proof connection of the window-frame, wall and roof.
- Enclosed porches at the front and back side entrance.
- No ventilation or air supply grills.
- Two-points latch for windows and three for doors, against warping.

Fig. 05.19:   Insulated panel to the crawling space behind the front door.

By these measures the dwelling is almost air-tight (q < 5 Pa). The necessary ventilation was obtained by the balanced ventilation system.

A concrete inner gable was chosen for the façade. The surface of the thermal mass had to be maximized so the temperature fluxes inside would be minimal. In this experiment one house was constructed with a timber framework. Studies showed that air temperature fluctuations were hardly influenced by the concrete inner gable.

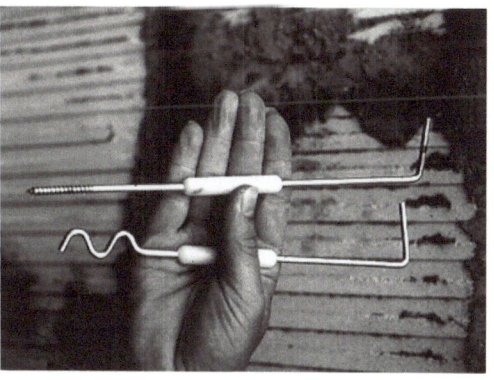

Fig. 05.20   Insulating wall-ties

In current housing developments the detailing of outer insulation is constructed in a more cost effective manner. The use of plasterboard with a vapour-proof foil is a common method together with a timber frame with insulation, vapour-permeable foil, cavity and outer gable of stone, wood or cladding.

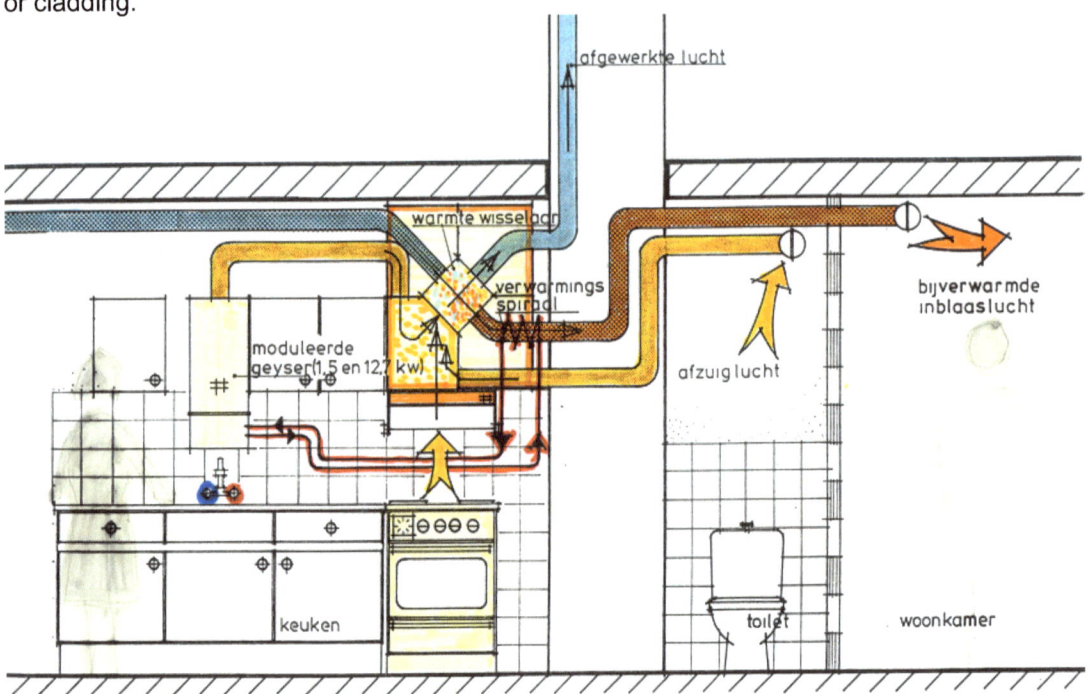

Fig. 05.21: Heating system of stacked dwellings with a horizontal supply of fresh air. The kitchen heater without pilot flame generates 12.5 kW of hot tap water and 1.5 - 5 kW of heating water. A compact air treatment device with a heat exchanger and heating spiral, integrated in the cooker hood above the stove, generates additional heating for the air supply.

The contribution of the internal heat and the use of the insulated shutters is significant. On sunny days the additional heating of about 2 kW is necessary only in the morning hours. On cloudy days this is the case from seven in the morning till five in the afternoon. More use could be made of heat stratification in the dwellings by blowing warm air from the ridge to the ground floor.

The design received a PREGO award (PREGO is a Dutch governmental organisation that tests projects of sustainable energy use).

Heating and ventilation

Only 17 dwellings were allowed to install a wood/paper incinerator due to the risk of air pollution. Therefore the design team looked for other options for air heating that met the following criteria:
- Ventilation of 150 m^3/h.
- Heating up to 4 kW.
- 100 m^3 recirculation of air

The Flåkt ventilator factory in Sweden had an air unit with too large a capacity for domestic use. After some investigation it appeared the Dutch ventilation market was not interested in developing an alternative. In response, design team member Koos Slootweg, in collaboration with geyser manufacturer 'Fasto', decided to design and build a domestically scaled prototype.

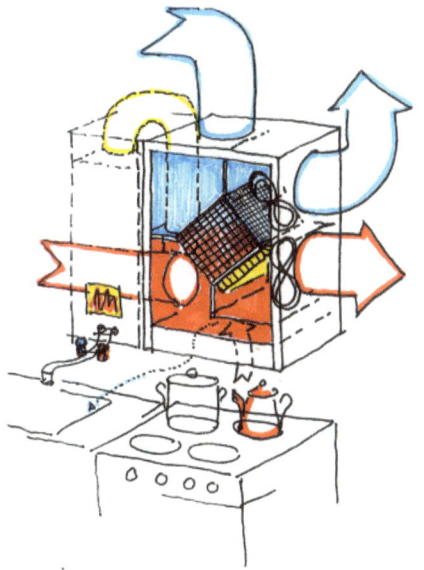

The wood/paper incinerator was to be replaced by a compact air treatment device in combination with an advanced gas geyser without pilot flame. The geyser supplied hot tap water (1.5 l/min at 60 °C and 12.5 kW) as well as heating water (1.5 to 5 kW). What was remarkable is the fact that both the kitchen heater and the compact air treatment device were integrated in the cooker hood above the kitchen stove. The solar boiler was later omitted as the system become over-complicated.

Initially the gas supply via the heat exchanger was rejected, but after the development of a special electronic control system and with results from measurements by TNO, Gastec gave its approval. This combination was used for the stacked flats. Therefore the fresh air was supplied via the façade through long insulated ducts. For the low-rise houses the municipality wanted the heat exchanger to be placed on the roof to allow easier maintenance.

Fig. 05.22:   Combined installation of the geyser with heat exchanger.

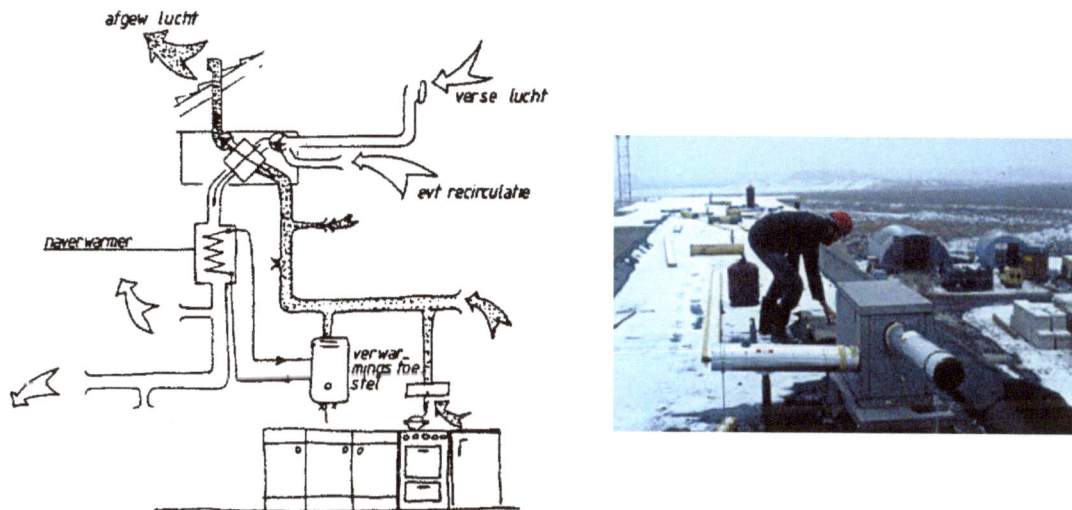

Fig. 05.23   Diagram of low-rise houses with heat exchanger on the roof (left) and roof installation of the heat exchanger, winter 1983-1984 (right) [24].

---

[24] The municipals decision to place the heat exchanger on the roof for inspection purposes was incorrect. Due to the external conditions the performance of the unit decreased by a factor of two.

With a capacity of 1.5 and 10 kW, the 'Slootweg unit' was unique at that time - an output that even modern devices would find difficult to compete. However, what was particularly fascinating about the Minimum-Energy Dwellings was that heat-losses through ventilation and through transmission were almost equal. A situation that warrants further investigation.

Fig. 05.24: Slootweg unit with Fasto geyser (left) and TNO measuring equipment in the dwelling in favour of the surface and air temperature (right)

The following products for sustainable building did not exist at the time of the 'Minimum-Energy Dwelling':
- Thermal insulation as permanent formwork for foundation beams.
- A ground floor with a heat resistance value R = 5 m²K/W.
- Impact-resistant outer insulation of mineral wool.
- Internally operated insulated shutters in front of the windows.
- Modulating kitchen geyser with electrical ignition.
- A compact air treatment device for balanced ventilation with 66% heat recovery.
- Avoidance of thermal bridges and noise insulation at the front doors.
- Air-tight dwellings with high specification draught-proofing detailing.
- Insulating wall-ties.

The average of the total measured fuel consumption was approximately 550 to 600 m³ of natural gas per year per dwelling for cooking, hot tap water and space heating. The space heating alone came down to approximately 360 m³ natural gas per year. At that time a reference dwelling demanded a total of 3000 m³ nge/year!

The 'Minimal-energy dwellings' design became a great inspiration for the energy-efficient building community in the Netherlands. A primary benefit resulting from this large experiment was that companies were now willing to develop new innovative products. Within a period of two years the Dutch market for building materials changed forever.

05.01.04 25 years ahead of the Energy Performance Code

Since December 1995, in accordance with the Energy Performance Code (EPC), any new building in the Netherlands must prove its energy credentials in order to obtain a building permit. In 1995 the Energy Performance Score (EPS) required for dwellings was 1.60; after that year it was lowered several times and currently is 0.75. For the 1981 design of the 'Dwelling without Central Heating' we were 30 years ahead of our time. In the document 'Demonstration-projects and energy-saving housing" Dr. Sacha Silvester mentioned that the energy performance requirements from 1995 had not yet reached the level of these dwellings [Silvester, 1996]. We calculated the Energy Performance Score (EPS) according to today's standards and came to 0.58-0.75, which still amply complies with the EPC regulations of 2010.

How did we achieve this?
The document 'Rules of thumb for EPC in housing' [Novem, 2002], originating from an initiative of Novem and the Dutch Architects Association, summarises EPC's main criteria:

(Urban) Architectural
- Orientation: for the EPS a north-south orientation is favourable and east-west least favourable; this is demonstrated by a difference in EPS of approximately 0.03.
- The addition of a glasshouse will only affect the EPS if the extensive calculation method is applied or if an input for the linear heat losses is quantified, in which case the EPS improves by 0.02 and 0.08 respectively.
- Ultra-high-performance glazing (U_{glass} = 1.2 W/m^{2}K) gives an improvement of EPS of 0.02 in comparison with high-performance glazing (U_{glass} = 1.6 W/m^{2}K).
- An insulated door (U_{door} = 2.0 W/m^{2}K) gives an improvement of the EPS of 0.02 in comparison to a traditional door (U_{door} = 3.4 W/m^{2}K).
- Increasing the thermal insulation of the total building envelope ($R_{c,facade/floor}$ = 4.0 m^{2}K/W, $R_{c,dak}$ = 5.0 m^{2}K/W, U_{glass} = 1.2 W/m^{2}K and U_{door} = 2.0 W/m^{2}K) improves the EPS by 0.08.
- If there are small linear heat losses it is simpler to meet the EPS requirements; in the case of high linear heat losses, as with corner houses, detached houses or houses with porches the EPC will remain the same or increase slightly.
- Submitting own values for linear heat losses (for example via reference details) the EPS will improve substantially: this can be an improvement of 0.01 to 0.06; for dwellings with a relatively high amount of linear heat loss the effect of submitting own values on the EPC is approximately 0.05.
- Applying shutters in front of the windows results in an improvement in the EPS of approximately 0.05, when only applied to the north 0.02.
- Improving the seam sealing ($q_{v;10}$) will decrease the EPS with approximately 0.02.

Building services

Ventilation
- Balanced ventilation (with 'normal' heat recovery of around 70%) instead of natural supply and mechanical discharge of air results in a lower EPS of 0.10.
- In comparison with an alternating current ventilator for mechanical discharge a direct current ventilator gives an improvement in the EPS of approximately 0.02; for balanced ventilation this improvement is approximately 0.05.

- Increasing the heat recovery efficiency from 70% (standard) to 95% (high efficiency), can reduce the EPS by approximately 0.05.
- Pre-heating the ventilated air in the glasshouse can improve the EPS by 0.01.
- The addition of demand-driven grills with mechanical ventilation gives an improvement of the EPS of 0.13.

Heating
- A low-temperature system with floor and/or wall heating gives an improvement of the EPS of approximately 0.02 in comparison with a high temperature system with radiators.
- Solar collectors (5.6 m^2) for the heating of rooms and hot tap water (solar boiler combination) will improve the EPS by approximately 0.20 compared to a high-performance combi-boiler (HR107) – a solar boiler combination is often applied with a low temperature system.
- A heat pump in combination with floor and/or wall heating results in an EPS improvement, depending on the source (soil, ground water or outside air), of approximately 0.03-0.12 in comparison with an HR 107 combi-boiler with floor and/or wall heating.
- An electrical heat pump with a ground water source is, regardless of the temperature of the water supplied, is favoured by the EPS method; with the soil or outside air as a source the EPC is about 0.02 and 0.04 higher respectively.
- Heat supply by others (STEG, industrial production process, incineration of waste, or gas engine heat pump) improves the EPS by about 0.15 compared with an HR 107 combi-boiler.
- A cogeneration plant gives, depending on its capacity, an EPS improvement of approximately 0.03-0.06 in comparison with an HR 107 combi-boiler.

Hot tap water
- The addition of solar collectors (2.8 m^2) for hot tap water (solar boiler combination), together with a high-temperature HR107 combi-boiler improves the EPS by around 0.10.
- Solar boilers and residential buildings: the application of a solar boiler, as an addition to a HR107 combi-boiler, lowers the EPS in a residential building (gallery flats) by approximately 0.03. Here the effect of a solar boiler (combination) is much smaller than in an individual house because of distribution losses.
- The application of a heat pump boiler instead of an HR107 combi-boiler results in a reduction of the EPS by 0.07; starting-point is mechanical ventilation and no balanced ventilation.
- When the piping has relatively short lengths, calculating with the actual length gives an improvement of about 0.03 on the EPS compared with the fixed lengths; therefore the location of the boiler is important.
- A lower comfort level for hot tap water improves the EPS by approximately 0.02.

PV cells
- Orientation of PV cells to the south is favourable for the EPS; enlarging the area from 7 m^2 to 10 m^2 gives an improvement of around 0.05 and from 10 m^2 to 13 m^2 an EPS improvement of 0.05.

Epilogue
Within the building industry people are questioning whether the search for a lower EPS needs to be continued. Put simply without the excessive criteria, a flexible design, offering the possibility to be built and used without construction and demolition waste, contributes greatly to the sustainable use of resources.

05.02 Solar Cavity Wall Dwellings

05.02.01 Background of the solar cavity

Solar collectors
As a response to the design for the Lelystad city hall (discussed further on in this book), our engineer Koos Slootweg proposed the installation of a solar collector system in our studio offices. In 1979, collectors were commonly filled with anti-freeze. Our experiment used an emptying principle that didn't rely on toxic additives. When the collector temperature was less than $\Delta T = 7°C$ higher than the water in the reservoir, the collector water would be drained into a small tank adjacent to the circulation pump. Draining would be repeated to prevent overheating i.e. when the water was close to boiling point. This method quickly became an obvious solution for sustainable houses.

Years later we also made two types of air collectors in our garden. The first absorbing material was a permeable black cloth. The second collector had black roof tiles as an absorber. Measurements indicated that the synthetic cloth collector reacted much faster to solar radiation, however for the total capacity the difference was negligible. The conclusion was therefore: every tiled roof can be transformed into an air collector.

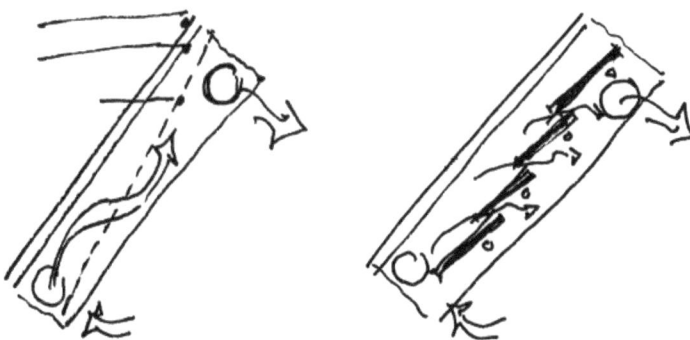

Fig. 05.25: Two principles of a solar collector with Tedlar and Teflon: above with black cloth as an absorber, below with black concrete tiles (or normal roof tiles).

Solar cavity wall dwellings with hybrid solar heating
As a result of the 'Momo' fair in the Berg church, Deventer (1979) we were asked by the Leiderdorp solar dwellings foundation to design nine terraced houses in accordance with their philosophy: "contribute to knowledge and application possibilities concerning solar energy in dwellings, with the awareness of working towards the development of a clean, safe and infinite energy source that cannot be monopolised". These became our first solar cavity wall dwellings.

The heating system by solar air collectors is based on heat storage of air in toothed cavity walls without wall-ties separating terraced houses. This principle has four advantages: saving fossil energy (no central boiler needed), harvesting solar energy, heat storage and the frost-insensitivity of air. With a difference in phasing between summer and winter, that is to say between a surplus and a lack of sun hours, each form of heat storage is appropriate for the northern hemisphere:

- Solar heat is used adequately.
- Heat is stored in the building mass.
- Phasing difference: the heat is released from the other side of the wall only after five hours.
- The temperature of the radiating surface may be low because of the large surface of the separating wall.
- There is no threat of freezing.
- The cavity wall between the dwellings is also sound-insulating.
- In southern countries the installation can be used for cooling during summer nights.
- Control of the ventilators is easily managed through a thermostat in winter and with an on-off switch in summer.
- The principle is very suited for the spring and autumn period and to a smaller extent for dark winter days.

The disadvantages are:
- In winter a secondary heating system is necessary (hence the term 'hybrid').
- Air has little thermal capacity.
- A silencer is necessary on the air supply pipe.
- In order to avoid the mixture of air between two dwellings, only one heating source can be connected per solar cavity.

05.02.02   Background of the solar garden

Our studio office resides in an old mansion originally constructed in around 1890. The building has had an interesting past. Built for Deventer's elite, damaged in the Second World War, then serving as housing for immigrant workers in 1965. Finally, with the aid of governmental subsidies this heavily neglected structure could be made suitable for living or for offices. Because of its large spaces with high ceilings no air conditioning was needed, and it was comfortably cool in summer.

Conservatories and greenhouses
In the mansion a conservatory (constructed 100 years ago without central heating) was separated from the living room by glazed sliding doors. In spring and autumn these doors could be opened to gain solar heat in the living room. In summer they were closed to keep the living room cool while the back door was opened towards the garden to enjoy summer and the garden. In winter they were closed to keep out the cold.

When we started to design conservatories and greenhouses by the end of the 1980's, difficulties arose. There are now technical ways now to direct heated air from the conservatory into the living space i.e. through ventilators, instead of opening sliding doors. This does not mean that the conservatory now should be part of the living area. It is still a separate space that generates heat in winter and is cold in summer. Unfortunately many residents expect their greenhouse to have the same temperature as the living room. They remove the sliding doors and then complain that it is too warm in summer and impossible to heat in winter.

Fig. 05.26: The high slanted roof-light in the glasshouse providing daylight to the meeting room.

Principle of the solar garden heating
This next section will discuss examples of houses we developed with a so-called solar garden: an 'outdoor' space inside a greenhouse, attached to a dwelling. This solar garden plays an important role in the heating system of the dwelling.
Operation:
In the solar garden the air is heated by the sun (in the Netherlands solar energy yield is typically 500 – 1000 W/m^2 of horizontal surface). The air is directed into the hollow space of a tie-free

cavity wall that separates two dwellings. This cavity wall forms the 'heat battery' of the house, which radiates the heat to the spaces on the other side of the wall. The bricks accumulate the heat and, after approximately four or five hours, deliver this heat as infrared radiation into the living areas (two dwellings benefitting from one system).

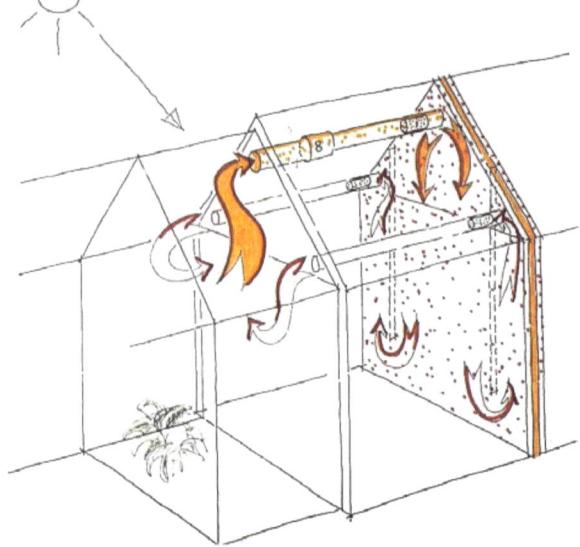

Fig. 05.27:   Airflows in the solar garden heating system

An electric thermostatically controlled ventilator is placed in the duct in the ridge of the pitched roof. The fan only runs when the air is sufficiently heated. This ventilator draws in preheated air from the ridge of the glasshouse and directs it through a spiral duct into the cavity of the separating wall. The air flows down in the middle and up again at the sides. The air returns to the solar garden through ducts in the attic floor.

Elementary components of the system are:
- Ridge of the solar garden.
- System of ducts with the ventilator in the attic.
- Cavity in the wall that separates the dwellings.

How much energy can we roughly generate by this system?
Let's assume that in the winter months (the heating season) the sun shines 10% of the time. In Western Europe the heating season measures five months, so we have 360 effective sun hours. The glass surface on the south side of the glasshouse is 5 m x 7 m = 35 m^2, and the solar intensity has a mean value of 500 W/m^2 (in winter). For a low capacity installation, for example 50%, this results in 35 m^2 x 500 W/m^2 x 0.5 = 8.75 kW.
Duration x power = energy; 360 hours x 8.75 kW = 3150 kWh.
This is comparable with a reduction of approximately 300 m^3 of natural gas per year.

The Delft University of Technology conducted research on the cavity wall, concluding that in practice, the additional heating in these privately owned dwellings is around 500 m^3 nge/year.

By 2002 the technical construction requirements of cavity walls was made more stringent: the dwelling-separating tie-free cavity with gables of 2 x 100 mm, was now increased to 2 x 150 mm. This additional mass slowing down the heating system, the effects being felt after several days, rather than within a desired twenty-four hour period.

05.02.03 1ˢᵗ generation Solar Cavity Wall Dwellings: Leiderdorp (1983)

Fig. 05.28:   The nine Solar Cavity Wall Dwellings with fixed wooden sunshading on the first floor and external sunshading on the conservatory roofs to avoid overheating.

All nine dwellings in the Leiderdorp plan had their own solar cavity wall heating. The lightweight solar air collector covered the whole southern half of the pitched roofs. A prefabricated collectors compiled from various components fitted between the roof beams with a double layer of storm-proof Tedlar foil on the outside and a heat-resistant Teflon foil on the inside sealing it off. The black glass fibre absorber (acrylic paint) was installed between two wedge-shaped spaces. From a narrow shaft above the solar collector the air was extracted into the crawling space, after which the air spread slowly through the air cavity towards the collector in the attic. The ventilator was placed in the crawling space under the ground floor.

As secondary heater, a balanced ventilation device with heat recovery, was placed in the attic. Each system was developed in such a way that it can function stand-alone. The slow supply of heated air into the living areas took place in the upper part of the inner walls and in the bedrooms above the doors. A separate solar collector for hot tap water was integrated into the solar air collector system on the roof. The cavity wall without wall-ties was made of toothed, glued limestone blocks and of aerated concrete on the neighbouring walls. As heated air was guided under the ground floor this floor was not thermally insulated.

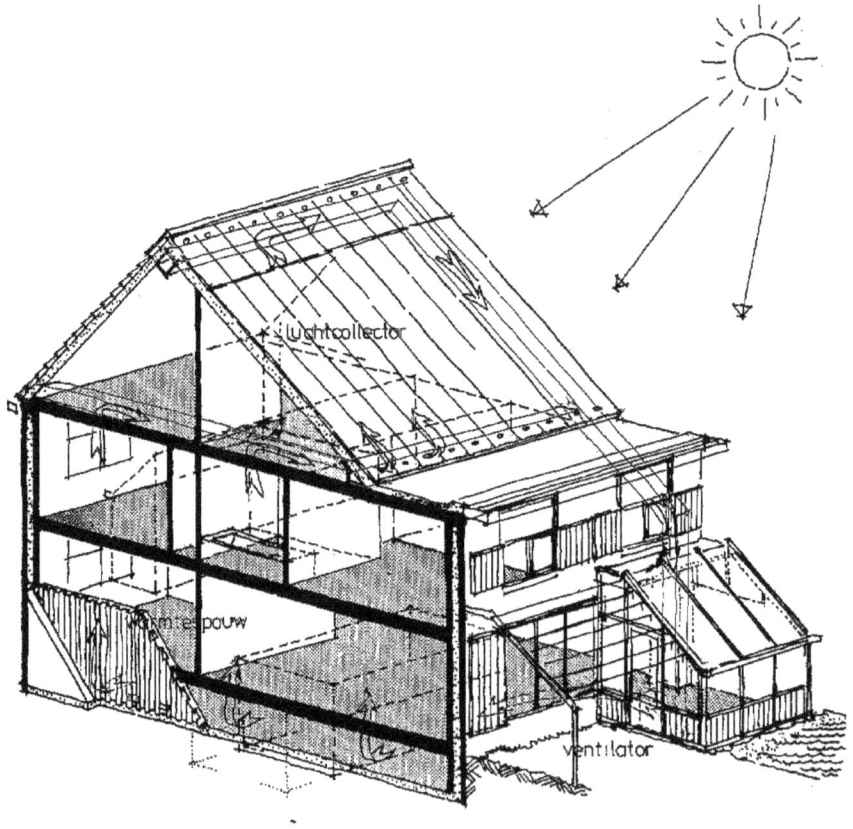

Fig. 05.29: Perspective of the Solar Cavity Wall Dwelling in Leiderdorp
01) Air duct in the ridge collects the heated air that is then led to the crawling space through a tube.
02) Air collector generates heated air.
03) Pipe in the attic transports the air from the cavity to the air collector.
04) Air duct at the bottom of the roof distributes the air over the collector.
05) Crawling space spreads air in the cavity.
06) Heated cavity toothed to increase its contact surface.
07) Ventilator in crawling space generates circulation of air.
08) Water collector for hot tap water.
09) Fixed sunshading device.
10) Conservatory constructed separately from the system, with external sun shading.
11) 'Cool' cellar.

A new technique specifically developed at Leiderdorp by Pittsburgh Corning was the floor system. Given the name 'Perinsul', the floor was completely constructed of foam glass insulation panels, this heavy load-bearing (HLB) structure was then coated with bitumen. The function of Perinsul is twofold: thermal insulation between the soil and foundation and a vapour-proof layer against the capillary rise of moisture in the brick foundation. The average pressure strength for Perinsul was 0.83 N/m^2, for which a safety coefficient of 1.8 was applied. The study of properties of this material would be partly funded by governmental energy agency PBE.

Fig. 05.30:   Placement of heavy load-bearing foam glass in the foundation.

The air-tight houses had an unheated enclosed porch on the north side, and a conservatory on the garden side. To further reduce heat losses a layer of 180 mm wall insulation was applied to the ventilated cavity wall. The lower windows had external shutters, while the upper window shutters were placed on the inside and were hinged near the ceiling. External fixed timber slats provided sunshading.

Fig. 05.31:   Insulating shutter on the inside with a telescopic operation system (left) and fixed external sunshading (right).

The Delft University of Technology investigated the dwellings by PBE commission. The conclusions were:
- The collector surface can be reduced by 50%.
- The rough (toothed) surface of the cavity wall is not necessary.
- The individual computer-controlled volume for the solar air collector can be used collectively.

These large houses had an average consumption of natural gas (1985) of approximately 230 m^3 nge/year per dwelling.

Producer Ruud van Hemert filmed the construction of the dwellings for the 'Puur natuur' (pure nature) series by the VPRO, a Dutch broadcasting company. The construction workers were particularly motivated by this media exposure, which made them aware of their involvement in a building of 'national importance'.

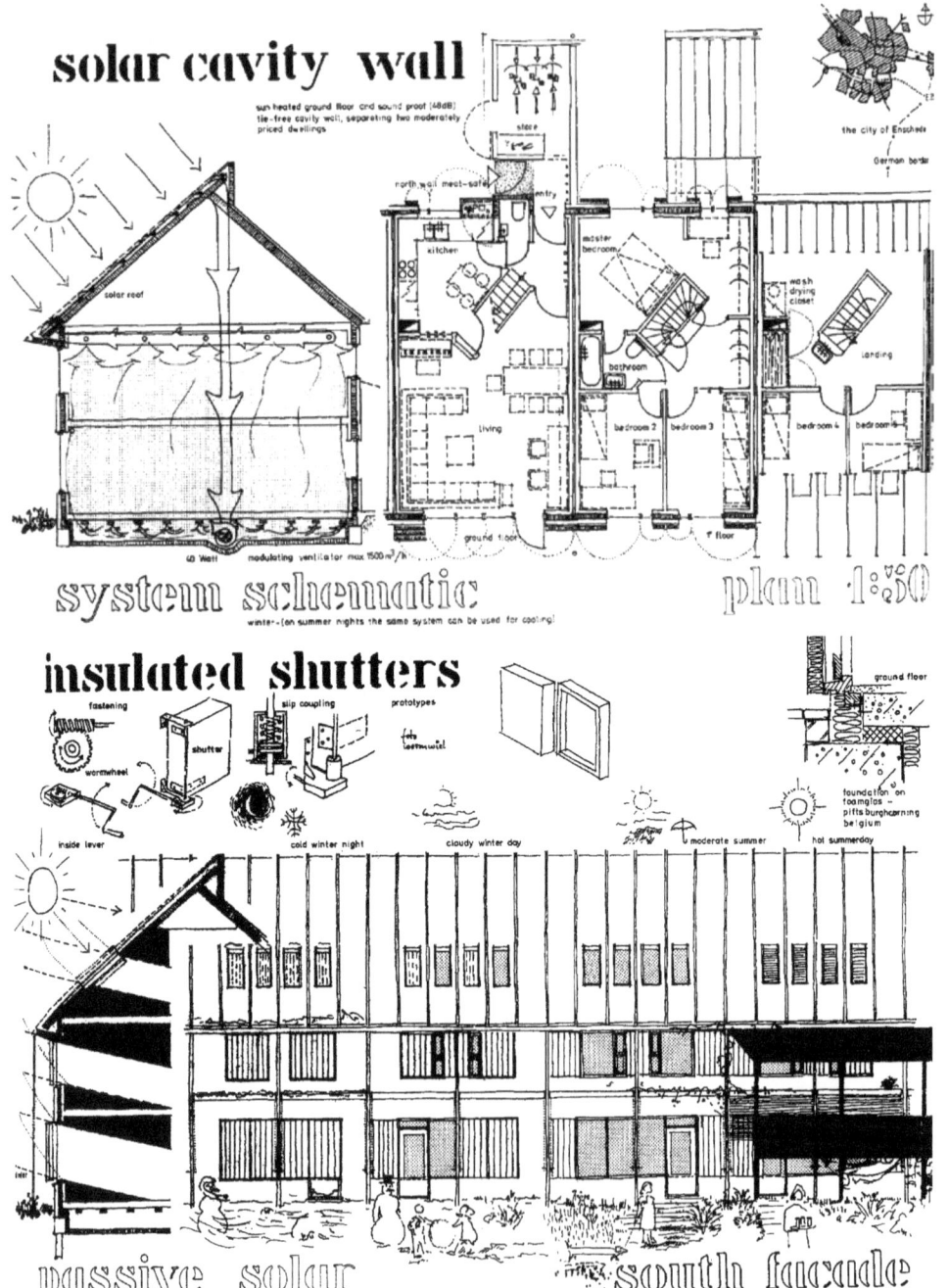

Fig. 05.32: Award winning contribution to the 2nd EEC passive solar energy competition (1982). An architecturally improved version of the Solar Cavity Wall Dwellings in Leiderdorp, with additional Slootweg type heating (Calculated heat consumption - 306 kWh per year).

In the second project design faults became apparent. The clients wanted a cool cellar in the heated crawling space, an extremely difficult design to execute. A further fault concerned the assembly of the air canals, which was confusing and the monitoring on leakages appeared not to be realisable. The programming of the temperature sensors, needed to control the ventilation of the air collectors, turned out to be too complicated. The high-tech electronic operating system was too ambitious.

This project taught us the need for simplicity and clarity in installation. After only three years following a heavy storm moisture problems occurred in the solar air collectors. Despite a life expectancy of 20 years, the collector suppliers refused to take responsibility. It was decided to cover-up the collectors and, unfortunately the experiment was terminated. The principles of the first generation Solar Cavity Wall Dwelling were however successful, and later repeated in Hoofddorp in 1984, this time with shorter air collectors that avoided excessive thermal expansion.

05.02.04 2nd generation: Drachten (1992)

Fig. 05.33: Morra Park glasshouse; roofing of the glasshouse consisting of transparent three-layered corrugated plastic sheets.

A 'creative' philosophy was adopted at solar garden dwellings at Drachten, one that provided the residents with the opportunity to develop their own environmental lifestyle. The idea being that when people have more influence on their immediate living environment, they are more likely to care for it.

Fig. 05.34: Sketch of Morra Park in Drachten. Solar gardens between the dwellings function as air collectors. Clients choose if they want a solar garden, then size, height and depth are selected within the maximum boundaries.

The solar garden can have various purposes; greenhouse, work-out space, atelier, workplace, extra living space in spring, summer and autumn, etcetera. The housing strategy was to allow each resident to decide which to use. Occupants could also choose to install a balcony /mezzanine at first floor level.

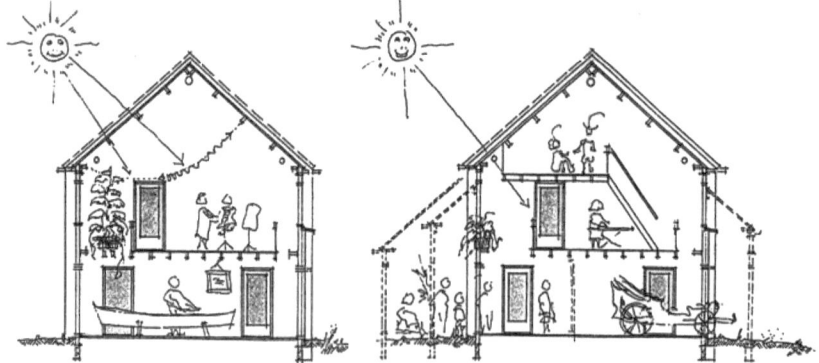

Fig. 05.35: Section of a glasshouse with a platform on the first floor (left) and extension of the solar garden on two sides (right).

The solar garden is not meant as a permanent living space, it should be regarded as covered external space or buffer zone. As with a conservatory, inappropriate usage will result in

disproportionately higher heating costs in winter. It is not practical to use the solar garden as a garage as extra facilities are needed such as fire safety and building permits.
The solar garden was delivered without an interior, with single glazing in the facades and covered with transparent corrugated plastic roofing. The northerly oriented glasshouse roof of three-layered 'Dobbelstek' slabs could in hindsight have been more effectively tiled reducing winter heat losses.

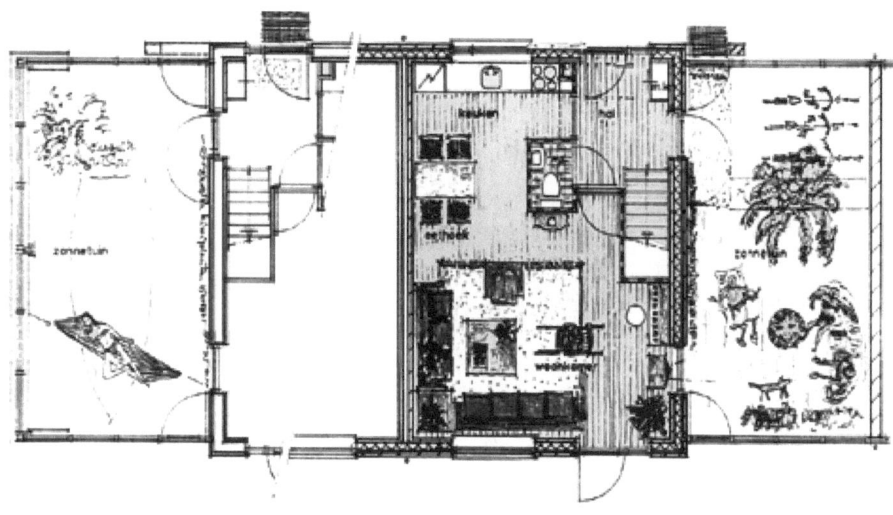

Fig. 05.36:   Ground floor with glasshouse.

The 12 dwellings have a high Rc-value (floor 3, façade 4 and roof 4.5 m²k/W) and all windows have insulation glass. Each dwelling is served by central heating with radiators and a high efficiency combi-boiler, as well as a 2.8 m² solar collector for hot tap-water. With the high efficiency boiler providing additional heating, the dwelling would be ventilated by a balanced system with heat recovery.

Five dwellings had a glasshouse constructed.
The environmental research and design office 'BOOM', in Delft, developed a method to test the environmental quality of the construction of dwellings and living environment for the municipality of Smallingerland. Observations concluded that the glasshouse radiated too much heat to the night sky; any future design developments should consider an insulated north and south roof would reduces these losses.

Fig. 05.37:   Completed glasshouse dwellings in the Morra Park along the water front.

05.02.05   3rd generation: Ede (1995)

Fig. 05.38:   South elevation of dwellings in the Rietkampen neighbourhood of Ede.

Realisation of Solar Cavity Wall Dwellings in the social housing sector was not possible without special financial measures, as we already described in the Groenekan example. The Municipality of Ede wanted to act, and the housing corporation Woonstede was willing to participate. By adding extra apartments the dwelling density was increased, extra capital generated allowing the municipality to lower the land price.

The solar collector was a bay design featuring a double façade integrated with rotating and lifting venetian blinds. A fan distributed air in the cavity wall between the dwellings. The cavity between the outer and inner façade was naturally ventilated outside of the heating season.

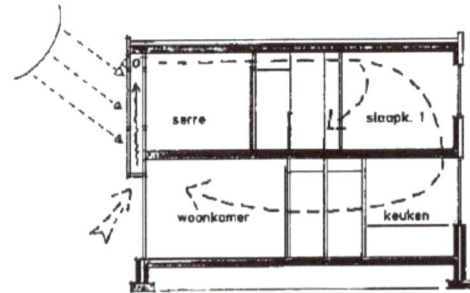

Fig. 05.39:   Principle of the solar bay with the airflow in the cavity between the dwellings.

06

INFRASTRUCTURE

06.01   Introduction

The merits and burdens of infrastructure
Because of a surplus of infrastructure people become a prisoners of themselves!

Fig. 06.01: Utrecht. Ivo Waldör, a foreign friend and architect with whom we accompanied to Utrecht, asked: "How can such a beautiful city be hidden behind so many motorways?"

The negative environmental effects of constructing in the built environment must be reduced. This does not necessarily mean that the future will only have restrictions. On the contrary, realising sustainable technology is a challenge leading to new possibilities for human society. After releasing restricting directives and legislation many cases will be reconsidered, rediscovered, recalculated and redesigned.

Knowledge about nature and environment is essential for the integrated use of space. Holistic knowledge of all primary life cycles at the building and neighbourhood scale is a requirement for optimal infrastructure under influences of change. It is a pity that the major part of infrastructure lies underground and therefore is not controllable. We only know that we are connected to an ever more extensive infrastructure that demands maintenance, that we need to pay for this and that this is registered by meters in buildings.
The supply of drinking water has another status. According to the law drinking water is a primary necessity for life, which can never be denied to a citizen even when unable to pay for it.

Fig. 06.02:   'The architect, devouring the landscape' [25].

If the environmental consequences of building have to be reduced, this should also apply to the urban infrastructure: transportation roads or residential streets, sewage, drinking water, gas, and electricity grid, phone, television and radio cabling, open and closed water flows, as well as the transportation system.

---

[25] Source: Green architecture, drawing by Malcolm Wells

Advances in the field of public health and hygiene, communication, mobility and energy, have made extensive infrastructure in our society commonplace. Within ten to fifteen years scientific and practical tests will generate new concepts such as 'dry sewage' for apartment blocks and residential streets.

Each infrastructural factor needs to be maintained, for example, to seal tunnels and pipes a powder is injected that when in contact with water forms a gel with smaller molecules than water. This gel is not environmentally harmless, and it does not deteriorate. This means that all scales are important and must be considered, from the largest oceans of the world to the smallest molecule.

Infrastructure and land planning
In 1994 the land value in a rural area in the Netherlands was € 2.27/m^2. A quarter of all land was designated for development and valued at € 10.9/m^2. However, the cost of a building site that had been prepared for building was € 163.4/m^2. This 15-fold increase of the original land price is reason enough to reconsider our planning strategies.

The initial costs for a dwelling comprise of the price of the land parcel, building costs, legal fees and extra costs. Dwellings in the free market sector partially pay for social housing and the underground infrastructure. In the costs of dwellings all external facilities are included, such as parks, sport accommodations and sewage. Unpublished research concluded that the occupant only pays a part of the actual sewage costs as sewage-fees.

Ground lease
Before the existence of Vinex-locations (a policy briefing note), the Dutch ministry of spatial planning fixed the land prices for housing construction. Later these were released with dramatic consequences for the housing market. The acquisition of construction land by investors cannot be prevented.

Because of our relatively short life spans it could be argued that private property ownership is in fact not necessary. Building on the alternative, leased land, has four advantages:
- No inheritance tax.
- Lighter, demountable and more temporal building solutions are feasible.
- The land value is relatively cheaper.
- Flexible land use is possible.

Ground lease leads to larger building lots, better build quality and the possibility of increased green spaces. This stands in contrast to the farmers who maintain the still open agricultural land, where management of the company has passed on from father to son for generations. Nevertheless, this is changing in many countries across Europe.

06.02 A different approach to infrastructure

06.02.01 Terrain analysis, soil and green

Table 06.01: Historical exploration, future thoughts

Soil & ground	
	Minimal transportation of earth, no import or export of earth.
	Maintain or improve the existing environmental conditions.
Green	
	More possibilities for the existence of flora and fauna.
	Vegetation roofs or green facades with deciduous plants as sun-shading element.
	Healthier urban micro-climate: - Balanced temperatures. - Higher humidity. - Less dust and noise.
Water	
	Well-deliberated water management.
	Retain water in the neighbourhood: buffer pools with approximately 0.20-0.30 cm of fluctuating water level.
	Slower discharge of rainwater.
	Circuit of surface water.
	Self-purifying helophyte fields.
	Use rainwater for washing, watering the garden, toilet flushing.
	Reduce consumption of drinking water in and around the house, use B-quality water.
Transport	
	Division of the street in functional zones: - Pedestrians, cyclists, smooth pavement for buggy's - Roads with brick pavements. - Parking: grass cobblestones/slate pavement.
	Shorten streets, limitation of pavement.
	Divert car routes, concentration of main roads.
	Good walkways and bicycle paths.
	Car parking at the end of a street, edge of the neighbourhood.
	Choice: either parking near house costing extra (because of extra pavement) or a central parking free of charge.

Fig. 06.03: Japanese water-closet where the washstand is usually integrated with the flushing cistern (and mini-landscape).

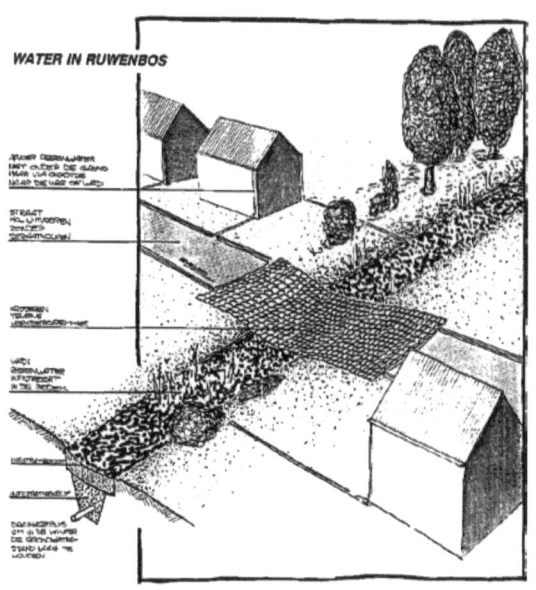 

Fig. 06.04:   *'Wadi', underground water buffer, in the Ruwenbos neighbourhood of Enschede (left) and dwellings in Ruwenbos with a 'wadi' in-between.*

06.02.02 'De Kersentuin', Leidsche Rijn district, Utrecht (2003)

We were commissioned by the society 'De Kersentuin' (the cherry garden) to design an ecological neighbourhood of 67 houses and 28 rentable social dwellings, including a project house in Leidsche Rijn in Utrecht, the assistant designer was Edo Keijzer.
When, as the architect, you have 68 clients, it is essential to have a flexible mind-set and organisation. It turned out well and after three years of meetings and sessions we started building in 2002.

The genesis
Important links in this fantastic building process were BIEB (building in own management) from Eindhoven who managed the development valiantly, and Portaal Ontwikkeling, a passionate individual who represented the social dwellings. The project was a risk financially but we all persevered. Sometimes we could not see the wood for the trees. Idealism everywhere, men and women who sorted out every detail from building process to funding. The organising of the floor plan, demanded by the association beforehand, caused a tremendous delay. A consequence was that many nice, interesting and enthusiastic participants had to drop out in the middle because they couldn't wait any longer for their house.

Once in a lifetime, as an architect, you have to join a group of people who wish to make a better world, where the mind exceeds the money by far!
1   In what kind of surrounding do I wish to live?
2   Which environment and neighbours do I choose?
3   Environmental awareness is the key behind every decision.
4   Freedom of choice brings happiness.

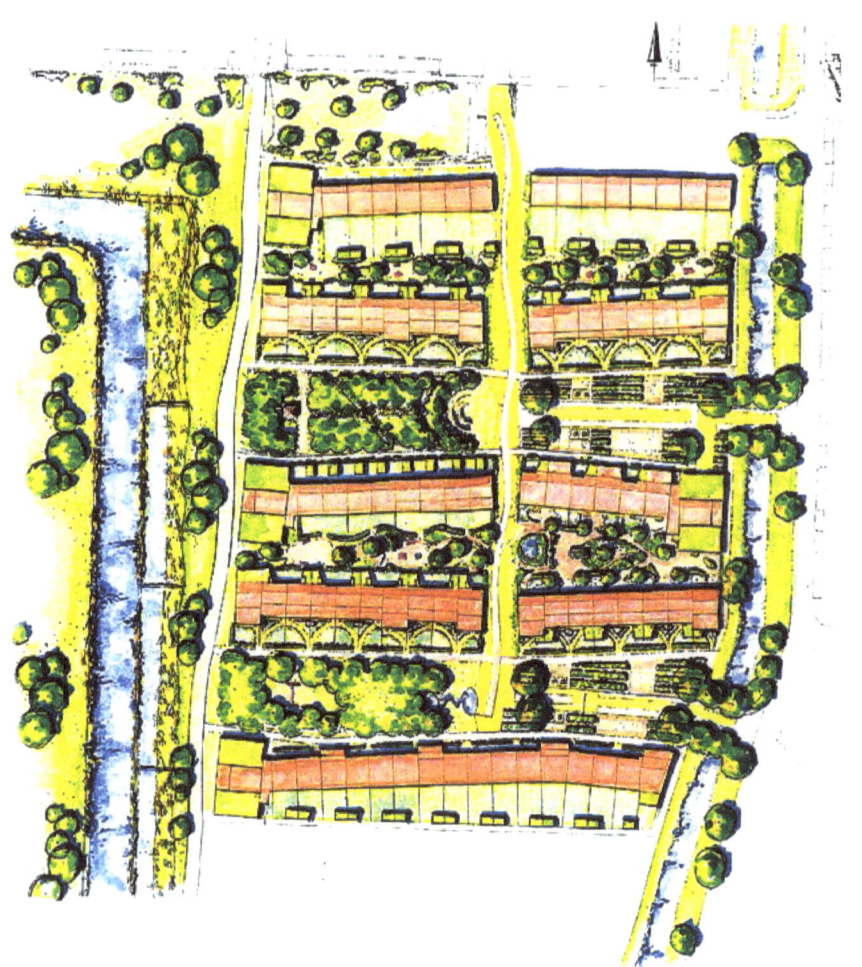

Fig. 06.05: Garden design in collaboration with Hyco Verhaagen of Copijn garden and landscape architects (above) and living space above and adjacent to parking and the project house (right)

The list of requirements was extensive; the following is a brief summary of the main topics:
- Construction in private ownership.
- Initiative development.
- Sustainability, flexibility and participation as keywords.
- Technical sustainability and social sustainability are equal.
- Lifecycle proof and adjustable to new phases in life or circumstances.
- Flexible cabling.
- Prefabricated PV grow-roof elements.
- A revolutionary small-scale water purification system.
- Large diversity in dwellings for sale and rent.
- Ecologically responsible natural (living) environment.
- Residents participation in maintenance and use of (semi-)public space and facilities.
- Car-free infrastructure.
- Combined car ownership with an aim of 0.5 a car per household.
- Underground parking garages beneath two building blocks and a roof garden.
- Project house at the head of garage parking.
- StIR-subsidy (stimulation of intensive use of space).
- IFD-subsidy (industrial flexible dismountable).

Fig. 06.06:   Three basic floor plans for low-rise dwellings; these were necessary for the building permit and an indication of the building costs.

One exceptional aspect within this housing project was that people wanted a car free street environment. After receiving a StIR subsidy the planned underground parking garage and water purification system for drinking water became realisable. The water piping company Hydron organised an accessible technical installation under the project house. As the people of 'De Kersentuin' owned the land no extra costs had to be paid to a developer. The front facades, adjacent to the public area, are permanent and have been constructed with bricks, whereas the rear facade is a timber framework that is demountable and extendable.

Fig. 06.07: Street view of the Kersentuin dwellings.

Public, semi-public and private spaces normally have a financially motivated hierarchy in housing projects. Here, private gardens were given up in favour of the semi-public space, an experimental and harmonious move that has potential. Our aim is that children that grow up here will treasure the best memories from this place.

06.03 Water

06.03.01 Water at all scale levels

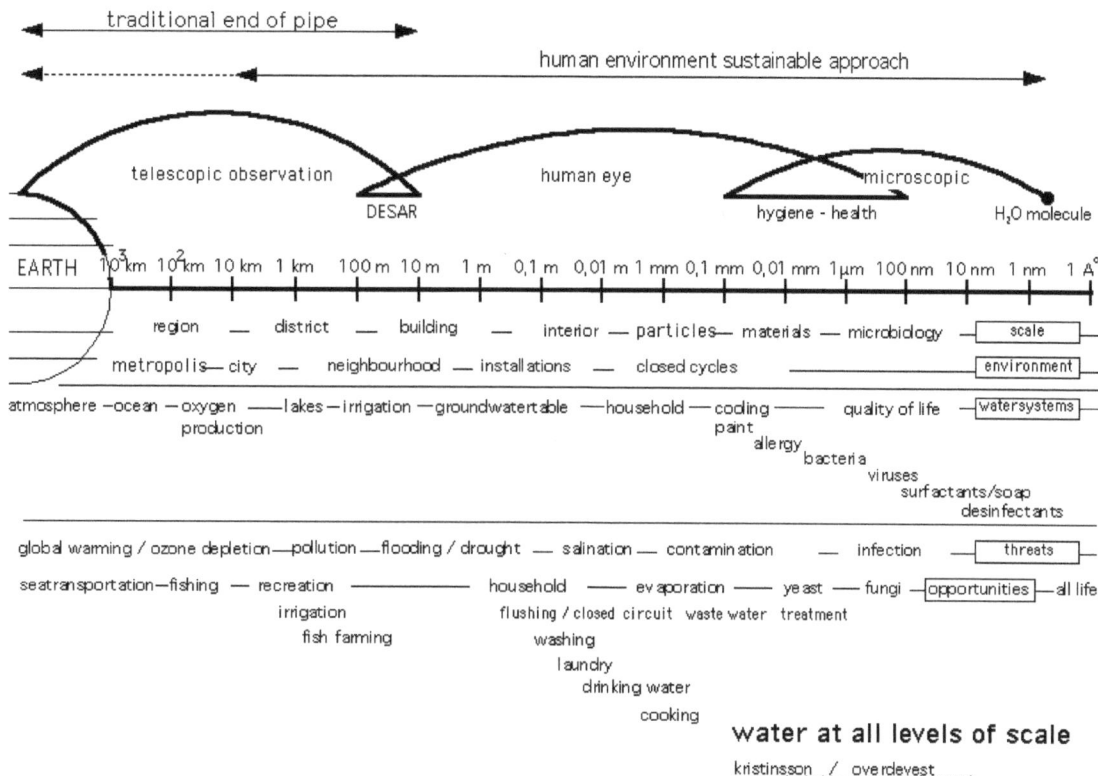

Fig. 06.08:   Water at all levels of scale

Oceans
The world's oceans cover 72% of the earth surface. They contain 97.5% of all the water on this planet and are our largest oxygen generators.
The sea level rise is mainly caused by the increase in volume of the oceans water due to 'global warming'. At 4°C water reaches its maximum density; above this temperature water expands.

Fresh water
The following table depicts how fresh water supplies are distributed.

Table 06.02: Distribution of fresh water supplies.

	Total water supply	Fresh water supply
ice caps	2.05%	68.70%
lakes	0.01%	0.16%
rivers	0.0001%	0.01%
groundwater	0.68%	30.15%
atmosphere	0.001%	0.04%

From the table it is clear that the share of water supply from ice and groundwater are significant contributor. Not mentioned here is the pollution of large parts of fresh water in rivers, brackish water (water that has more salinity than fresh water, but not as much as seawater) from the oceans and estuaries.

Perception of rain
Sun worshippers have the opinion that it is always raining in the Netherlands. Even though it differs by a factor two per region, we can say that the average precipitation amounts to 800 mm per year. Most wet periods coincide with the cold season, however, on average precipitation is equally divided throughout the year. Heavier showers in summer balance long winter drizzles.

Rivers
In delta areas such as the Netherlands, much more water comes from the mountainous hinterland by means of large rivers. This polluted water is treated for drinking and consumption in large cities in the western part of the country. Water from the Rhine, with its origin in Chur in Switzerland, has travelled 1340 km before it runs into the North Sea. As a consequence of altered water supplies, canalised shipping routes, meltwater and precipitation, the water reaches our delta area three times faster than 50 years previously. River banks have a height of 18 m above sea level. The water level at Lobith, where the Rhine leaves Germany and enters the Netherlands, is usually 6 m above sea level, with a water flow of 6,000 m^3/s.

Fig. 06.09:   Flood of the IJssel river near the ferry in Deventer, the Netherlands, December 1993 and early 2011.

In contradiction to all statistics, a high water level was reached twice within a short period. In 1995 the water level rose to 16 m above sea level, with a water flow of 18,000 m^3/s.
The incoming water filled the rivers passing the summer dikes, causing a serious threat of collapse and flooding, leading to the evacuation of those in imminent danger.
We should remember the captain of an inland vessel that manoeuvred his ship along a collapsed dike at Capelle aan de IJssel preventing Rotterdam and Delft from flooding!

Water
The names of development areas as *Hooiland* and *Rietkampen* remind us of the flood areas. These new expansion areas in the river basin of the Maas disappeared after the rain period of 1995. These exceptional situations are unfortunately defining spatial planning. The Netherlands

needs to keep the water as a friend. In order to retain water in the broad river landscape, regions demand for a completely different building method.

From an ecological perspective all aspects of water should be considered equally. From a global approach to the atmosphere around the earth to a water molecule of 3 Ångströms (a unit of length equal to one ten billionth of a meter) can be made quite comprehensible on a logarithmic scale.

We chose three parallel approaches:
1. The built environment down to microscopic dimensions.
2. Water systems as a condition of life.
3. Threats within the water systems.

Due to limitations, which will later turn out to be inevitable, the attention is mainly focused on closed water cycles, infrastructure and hygiene.

06.03.02   Integrated water management

Precipitation

There is an ecological, economic or administrative battle for every drop of water, from all kinds of participants:
- Plants
- Animals
- Individuals
- Municipalities
- Farmers/gardeners
- Water boards
- Government river department
- Polder boards
- Mobility societies, water sports
- Drainage sluices
- National department of waterways.
- Ministry of transport and public works
- Rhine treaty
- Maas treaty

The government takes responsibility for water, while the individual water drinker becomes more and more ignorant.

Drinking water

Clear water has a pH value of 7. The surface water around Loenen on the Veluwe is basic water, with a pH > 7, i.e. more alkaline. The numerous laundries in these regions only need 30 to 40% of the soap in comparison to areas with acidic water. Periodically we have contended with acid rain (pH < 7) caused by the emission of acids from industrial processes. As a result, the lifeblood of trees fails to reach its maximum and the trunk begins to grow leaves instead of the upper branches. When there is no longer a transportation of lifeblood, the tree dies [26]. Once it reaches Lobith at the Dutch border, the water has been used many times, making the inlet inappropriate for the water supply of agricultural land in summer.

---

[26] Rome gradually killed itself when extra drinking water was needed and transported from new sources by aqueducts. This new water was slightly more acidic, causing the lead pipes in the ancient city to oxidise, slowly poisoning the entire populace of Rome.

The Japanese scholar Masaru Emoto has made several studies of water crystals at varying phase changes. Each drop of water crystallises differently, some appear to erode more than others indicating quality. It is a surreal experience to see these differences, beautiful angular ice crystals characterising good quality drinking water. According to Emoto this has to do with the energy of life. In Tokyo chloride is added to the tap water and it hardly crystallises.

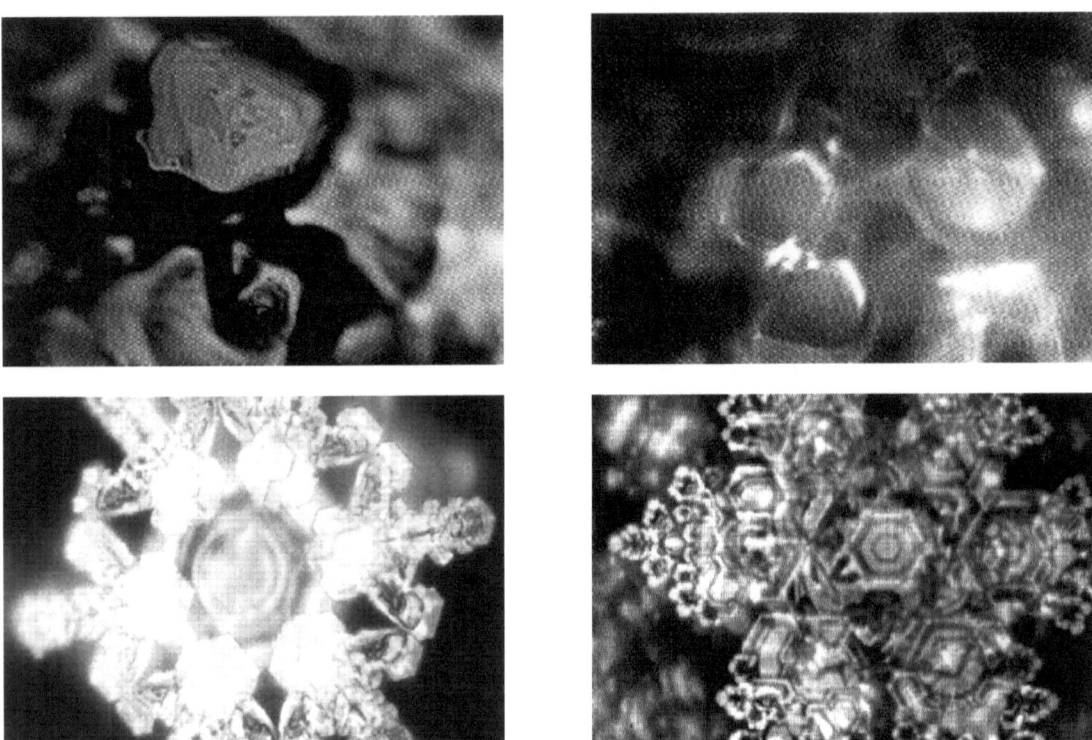

Fig. 06.10: Water crystals studies by Masaru Emoto [27]. Clockwise from top left: 1. Tokyo tap water; 2. Paris tap water; 3. Eater from the Sabu-ichide Yusui source, Japan; 4. Antarctic ice: 370,000 years old.

Chloride is added to drinking water as a disinfectant against micro-organisms. Considering that we have a larger body than micro-organisms, and cannot be killed so easily, are these additives really necessary? Our body consists of 60 to 70% water therefore it has a stark influence on our health.

Due to the low cost of drinking water in the Netherlands, the Dutch people do not limit their consumption of it, or realise its origin. The ground water table is lowered drastically in many countries in the world. In western countries this is mainly due to the irrational use of high quality water for flushing toilets and washing clothes. We need to understand that by doing this we are going beyond our limits: we are limiting the use of clean, fresh water by our children and grandchildren and opposing the principles of sustainable development.

---

[27] Source: Fertile Earth no. 4 / 2001.

B-quality drinking water that is safe, but has a less taste, should be cheaper than our valuable drinking water. There have been projects that incorporated B-quality water, one being the extension area of Leidsche Rijn, near the city of Utrecht, the Netherlands. However, poor installation and grey water connection led to problems and put B-quality household water in a bad light.

Water consumption

In only a 50 year period water consumption has multiplied by 5. Water represents wealth, its consumption is expressed by thousands of m^3 that a person can use on average. Strange as it may sound, 'water-deficient' countries such as the Netherlands and Bangladesh have 1000 m^3 of available water per person, whereas 'watery' countries have more than 5000 m^3. The Netherlands disposes over 860 m^3 of water per person per year [28]. Citizens personally consume 53 m^3 of water per year, yet need only 3.5 m^3 of real drinking water, the remainder is used for flushing, rinsing and washing.

In 1995 5% of the world's population had insufficient water, by 2020 this figure will increase to 25% of humanity, a situation compounded by the fact that the worlds population will probably increase from 5.7 billion in 1995 to a predicted 8 billion by 2020.

For every 145 litres of consumed in the Netherlands, 127 litre ends up in the sewage system. It is evident from these statistics that rainwater should be retained as long as possible and the water management in urban and rural environments should have a more dynamic character. Collected rainwater should be utilised for toilet flushing, car-washing, watering of gardens and even for the common washing of clothes and dishes.

Waste water treatment

Envisage a scenario with better recycling and a slower discharge of water. We would use surface water and rainwater, and reduce to a third the amount that is currently used in kitchens and washbasins. Precipitation water would be disconnected from the sewage system and drained to open surface water, as was the case in the past. The substituted sewage would only carry 'black' wastewater, now reduced to a tenth of the capacity. The black wastewater (generally organic waste) could be purified through anaerobic fermentation or processing by green algae. By 2045 the amount of drinking water can be cut back to 11 litres per day per person, or have turned completely into bottled water, as is common in many countries.
The amount of surface water and rainwater (as B-quality water for flushing, rinsing and washing) has significantly decreased. The dish-washer and washing machine that binds soap and dirt, while purifying the water at the same time, is yet to be invented. Once it is, connection to the sewage system will be unnecessary and the water can be re-used.

60 years ago Russian astronauts consumed their own faeces that had been transformed into proteins by green algae. A version of this odourless closed cycle process will by 2045 be commonplace in the building sector when applied to flushing toilets. The yield of algae is then used as fish nourishment and fertiliser. An aerobic decentralised water treatment plant together with a septic tank and a tank for the algae yield with a robust 'black' wastewater pump will be a normal feature in buildings of the future.

---

[28] Source: Prof. H.L.F. Saeijs.

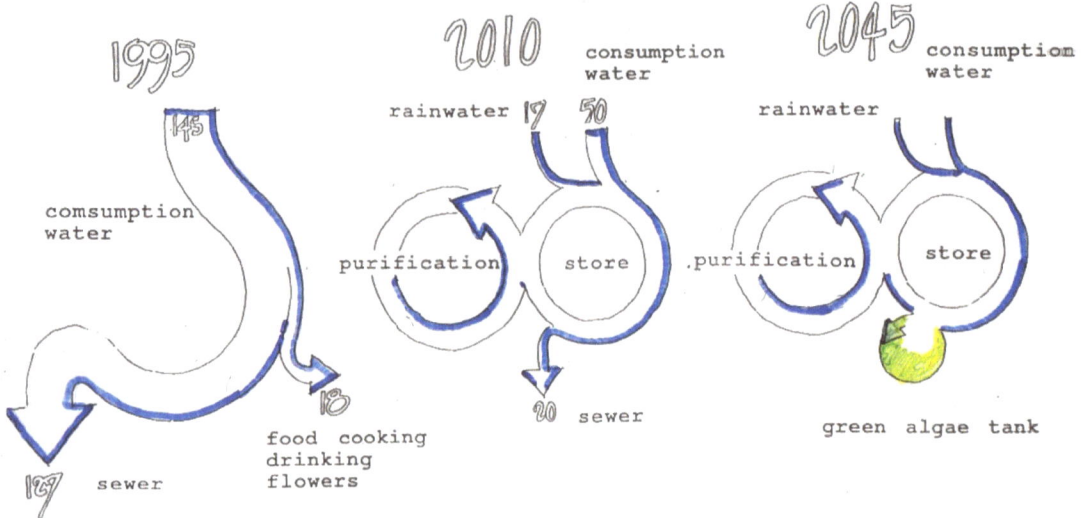

Fig. 06.11:   Water cycle in 1995 and future proposals for 2010 and 2045.

The completely sealed aerobic process of purification and composting by algae could eventually lead to the complete removal of the sewage system. Only then can we speak of sustainable water management.

The domains of architecture and urbanism tend not to concern themselves with water. From their perspective as soon as precipitation has reached the rainwater drain, the technical job is done! By pumping out water from the building pit during the construction stage, and draining water during the operation period, we're able to control the water level. Trees, even some distance away die as a result. The closed cycle of water on the construction site and the built surroundings require a totally different approach.

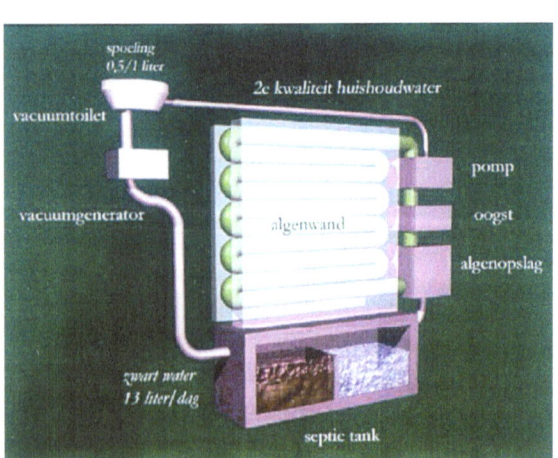 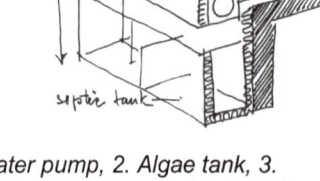

Fig. 06.12:   Algae façade element (designed by Alexia Luising [29]): 1. Water pump, 2. Algae tank, 3. Translucent isolation on vertical pond cultivation, 4. Sewage water siphon, 5. Septic tank.

---

[29] Source: Cobouw 08-10-2002.

The introduction of the sewage system solved many problems relating to comfort and public health. Nevertheless, a sewage system connected to water purification plants raises ecological questions concerning all known environmental themes:
- Squandering of materials.
- Threat of over-nutrification.
- Acidification caused by materials from calamities and emergency deposits.
- Removal of waste by purification sludge.
- Disturbance of existing ground ecosystems.
- Desiccation through direct discharge of rainwater to the sewer.
- More desiccation caused by extra drainage, because of leaking sewers.
- Extensive and expensive construction with a limited lifespan.

Holistic water system at different levels
An integrated water system can be established at the city, block and building scale. At the urban level we return to ancient times when water was the most significant structural bearer:
- Water is made visible.
- Canals are reintroduced and interconnected again.
- The ground water level is almost released uncontrolled.
- Rainwater is slowly discharged.

At the level of an apartment block:
- A grey water circuit (closed process) through all gardens and office buildings.
- Black water purification (closed process) by means of green algae under new offices.

At the building level:
- Rainwater filtering to drinking water standards.

Plants love people:
- Roof garden with hardwood as open-air meeting spaces.
- Rhythmic pumping of rainwater in flow forms [30].
- Linear plants: reed, rush, iris, horsetail for water purification.

Conservatory with subtropical plants:
- Mimosa di bata climber.
- Olea europeia.
- Magnolia grandiflora.
- Passiflora.

Bougainvillea eduls

06.03.03   Waste water treatment

DESAR (DEcentralised Sanitation And Reuse)
DESAR, a multidisciplinary research project, attempted to purify 'black' wastewater from faeces at the domestic scale using similar processes to those tested by early Russian space technology (mentioned previously). If successful, underground sewage systems in our living environment would become redundant.

---

[30] Advice by tree consultant Jörn Copijn.

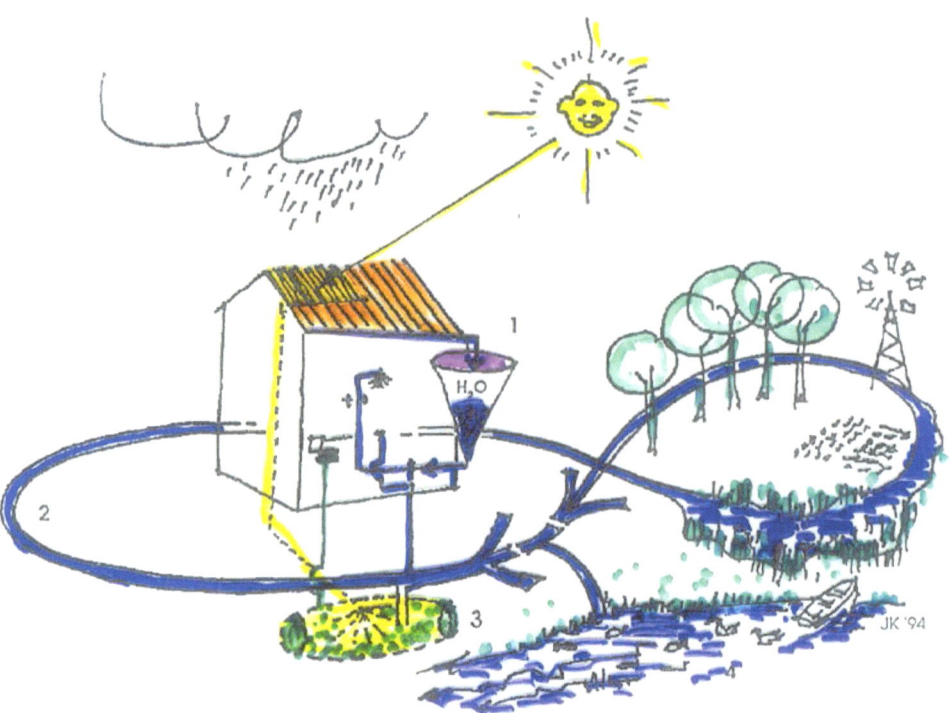

Fig. 06.13:   *Schematic of a conceivable new balance: "closed process of water in the built environment":*
- *rainwater – sand filter – drinkable water*
- *- 'grey' wastewater track, runs slowly through a neighbourhood, purification by sunlight and reed and rush banks, windmill with small pumping station*
- *- 'black' wastewater track: small, warm green algae tank illuminated with glass fibre cables fed by Fresnel lenses on the roof, transformation of faeces into pure proteins that serve as fish or cattle feed*
- *- open water as emergency drainage; no further purification required.*

A few examples are ready for implementation; others are 'in statu nascendi'. One of these solutions is a 'green algae purification plant', a research project that was started by the Wageningen University and Vrije Universiteit of Amsterdam, both from the Netherlands. This contributed to raising awareness that sewage systems form a large economical and ecological problem. One should understand however that a public opinion poll highlighted that water closet was the most appreciated invention ever!

The UN summit in Johannesburg 2002 agreed on reducing the number of people living without water and sanitation by 50% by 2015!

06.03.04   Morra Park, Drachten (1990)

Nijhuis Construction Company in Rijssen asked our office to participate in the development of environmentally sound dwellings in Morra Park in Drachten, the Netherlands. It had been accepted for elaboration into a demonstration plan for the Dutch Fourth Note on Spatial

Planning, with the theme 'dealing carefully with resources and waste'. The municipality lowered the land-price by € 4,60/m^2 and the municipal energy company gave discount on the solar boilers.

Through a holistic design process a large multidisciplinary team set about resolving the blatant over-dimensioning of development infrastructure. The urban designer preserved the Frisian coulisse landscape in the new neighbourhood, including the old alder canals and existing ditches. The hydrologist designed a water system that purifies itself with a varying rush waterside. The Koningsdiep water board did not demand the usually pre-described five meters width of space on both sides of the waterways for slush machines.

Fig. 06.14: Morra Park. The calculated costs for the sewage system, water management, site preparation and planting vegetation turned out to be slightly cheaper than usual. The green and water applications were more expensive, but the savings on pavement and sewage infrastructure compensated.

Rainwater from roads was drained into oil collection pits near the parking spaces at the start of construction. This was disconnected from the sewage system, allowing for a smaller pipe diameter. The implementation of a second B-water system from waste and/or rainwater for toilet for applications that do not demand drinking water i.e. toilet flushing, was based on ideas referred to previously and by purification via plant roots. The water circulation was partly driven by wind energy.

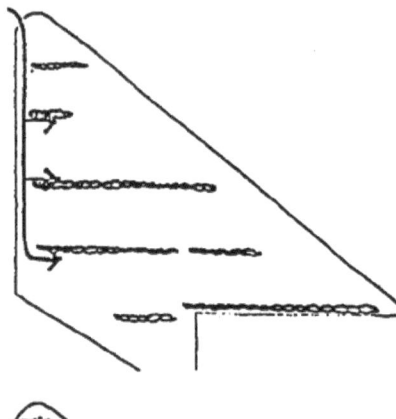

The quality of surface water is determined by means of typical ion indicators, which are chloride, nitrate and phosphate. Already in 1993 Morra Park turned out to be the only location in Frisia that met all requirements for these indicators. The very low concentrations of nitrate are a result of the current maintenance strategy.

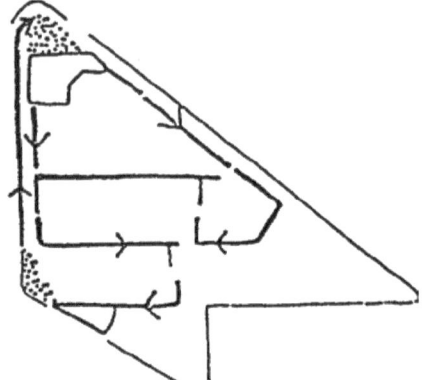

Fig. 06.15: The existing coulisse landscape of ditches and trees as a basis for the urban design. Banks with reed and rush for water purification, retention ponds and pumping station. The water system is closed; water is pumping around by a windmill (right).

06.04 Building in nuisance zones

Considerable area in the Netherlands is unbuilt or contains only low-value functions, especially zones along transport lines in cities which form large areas of potential development. As part of the doctoral research by Evert de Ruiter, these zones were considered for the development of high-value buildings, specifically housing. However, along such highways substantial noise reduction is essential.

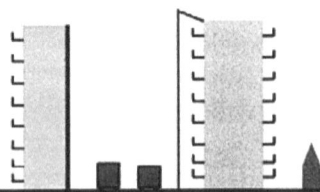

For now this entails long and high shielding objects. When these are screens, well designed or not, their application will receive much public resistance, due to their length and height. However, when buildings function as noise barriers, heights of 10 to 30 meters are easy to fit in, especially when they comprise of interesting architecture.

Fig. 06.16: Two types of sound barriers on tall buildings adjacent to an urban canyon [31].

---

[31] Image by Evert de Ruiter.

But the starting-point is that in these 'front-line buildings' a comfortable living environment should be achieved; other functions – offices, retail – can then be applied effortlessly.

06.04.01   Manifesto 50/50, Midden-IJsselmonde, Rotterdam (1995)

Smitshoek, in the municipality of Barendrecht. Our input, in contrast to the architecture office MVRDV, was sustainable development of city and infrastructure.
The transformation from a consumption 'hire purchase' led society to a global sustainable society is imperative. A direct problem for technological development is that the lack of time and the analytical way of thinking taught to us since childhood makes us too slow in delivering innovations. If we, as a society, do not want to be submersed by scarcity, wars and chaos, nomadically looking for water and food, then it is time for a fundamentally new approach.

By replacing analytical thinking with lateral thinking, creative solutions are possible that are leaps ahead. We will also seriously look at the effects of climate change.

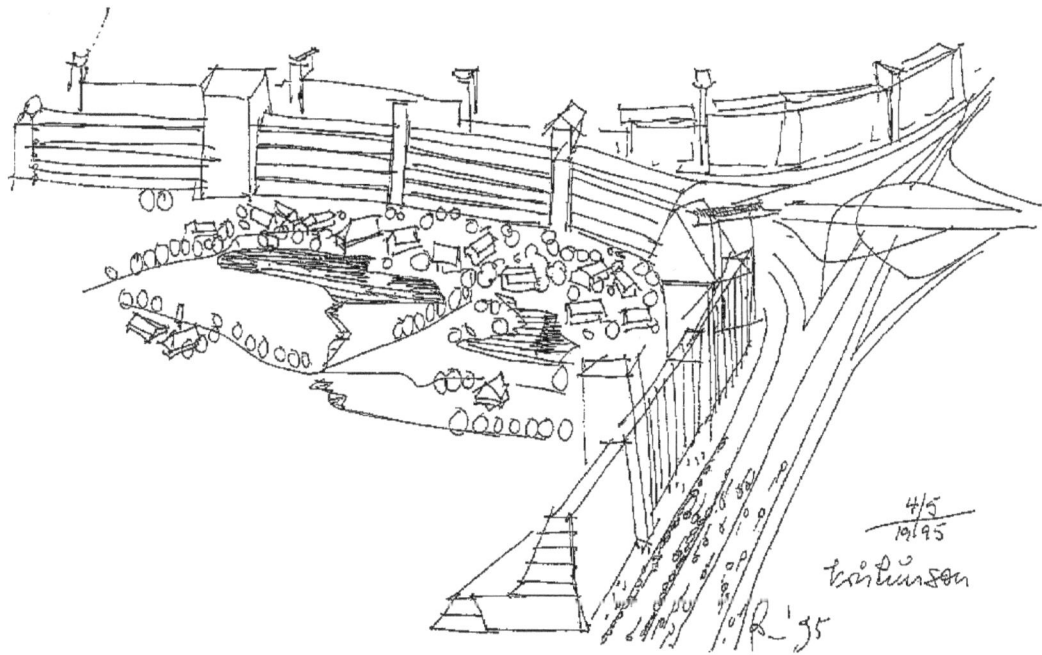

Fig. 06.17:   Concentrated high-rises in the nuisance zones along the A15 and A29 motorways at Smitshoek. 'Llight' urban design, for the expansion of Barendrecht, in the noise protected hinterland.

When we limit ourselves to the sustainable development of the slowed-down cultural city, it will only be achievable if look at the city holistically. Sustainable housing has to be flexible, reuse of building materials and building elements will have to be developed as demountable technology.

Fig. 06.18: Mainport of IJsselmonde.

The issues that need immediate action are accelerating and increasing, while the short-term solutions of politicians fall short. People have to choose from scenarios that can be adjusted. A slowly manoeuvrable filled oil tanker that can alter its direction only after a few miles could be an empty oil tanker in fifty years, but even when its course is on autopilot and supported by satellite navigation, a route still needs to be determined.

Table 06.03: Contrasting propositions for a sustainable IJsselmonde (1995).

	Scenario II: Slowed-down city	**Scenario I: Mainport Rotterdam**
Experience value	water as structural element Living Landscape park Biotic Nature Small-scale Familiar Known Ancient concept Soil – soft Temporise Existing landscape Farming industry	Road as structural element Transport Technology in nuisance zone Conceptual technological Culture International 24-hours industry Variation New building concepts Concrete – hard Modernise New road concept Transportation
Physical aspects	Silence Peace Slow Clean Trees	Noise Dynamics Fast Polluted, becomes cleaner Lampposts
Social aspects	Health Privatise Ecological economy Full employment Voluntary support Equal payment level Closed cycle We = you and me Dwelling, services, education Municipal policy Invulnerable Stable Singing birds – ducks Own vegetable garden Self-governance Social control Integration of immigrants Schools – knowledge Variety Sustainable, timeless	Wealth Collective Market economy Automation Labour market Different payment levels Defined environmental impact They Port, industry Multinationals, Rijnmond Vulnerable Unstable Sea-gulls – pigeons International fruit Governable Order police Indigenous Trade Flexibility Economical conjunction

06.04.02 Sustainable playgroups in a noise barrier, Amersfoort (1996)

Design by Daan Josee (Kristinsson Architects & Engineers)

Fig. 06.19:   The south side of the children's playgroup rooms next to the ring-road.

The architect Daan Josee executed this project that the municipality of Amersfoort assigned to us. The two playgroups at the northern ring-road of the district of Nieuwland are situated in a noise barrier, in a location that is visible from both sides of the wall. The children experience two worlds, one of peace and quietness at the end of the neighbourhood against the noise barrier, and one of fast traffic on the other side.

Fig. 06.20:   North side facing the Nieuwland district (left) and the interior (right).

The initial 'noise buffer' glasshouse design integrated with a solar heating of the cavity air, was later dropped for financial reasons. Extra thick glass on the outside, the concrete reversing wall and placement of the building in the body of the dike ensured an acceptable indoor climate. The toilets for common use were placed in the centre of the north side of the building leaving more space for playgroup room. At the south side rooms are divided by a glass wall so that children can see each other play.

Because of the buildings round form a strip foundation would have been labour-intensive. The inventive solution was a well-insulated floor of 40 cm aerated concrete with a floor on top reinforced with steel-fibre (R ≥ 4.0 km^2/W). Aerated concrete is easy to apply. It was built up in two layers. The first layer was poured in a foundation excavated pit, until the top of the raft foundation was 69 cm high. The second layer was applied a week later against the foundation of the sand-lime bricks, which rests on the first layer. Where extra reinforcement of the steel-fibre floor was needed, the aerated concrete could easily be removed, for example around the columns and walls. The steel-fibre floor of 12 cm thick had the advantage that the reinforcement did not have to be applied in a circle. There was no risk of frost damage, because the aerated concrete has a closed cell structure.

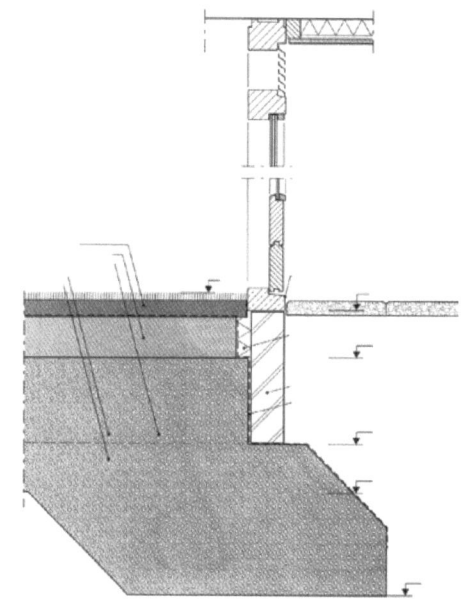

Fig. 06.21:   Detail of the aerated concrete ground floor connection to the façade.

The roof was loaded heavier than usual as it was incorporated in the walking path over the noise barrier.

Fig. 06.22:   Walkway over the noise barrier and the round space on the roof of the playgroups, which can function as an open-air theatre.

06.04.03 Study of noise barrier dwellings, Ede (1998)

As part of a feasibility study for Bouwfonds housing development we were asked to design dwellings along the A30 motorway and the Laan van Kernhem in Ede, a noise nuisance area. The most important weapon in urbanism is a pair of dividers, a method that ignores the problem instead of looking at it as a challenge that can be solved by architecture. Fortunately the way of thinking has changed and some alterations in the rules can be noticed. Solving a problem creates a tension that will only benefit the design.

Fig. 06.23:   Housing containing offices along the Laan van Kernhem, large dwellings with high rooms and broad parcels, diversity in housing typologies, such as ground level or first level dwellings, basement dwellings in which you live above street level, half-span roof to benefit from the sun, and quiet zones to the rear.

What is positive about a location with noise nuisance?
Until the 1950's a person was regarded as having a high-class position if they lived along an important road or street. When the importance of the road increased, the buildings would become more prominent. In the many buildings along canals and lanes a conversion took place in their use: law offices and other high-value office functions began to dominate, and the housing function decreased.

The causes of this change are:
- Market pressure: Large/grand buildings became too expensive to live in.
- Good accessibility, prominent location and the visibility made them desirable for companies to establish themselves.
- Less attractive for families: noise nuisance, bad odours and infrastructures for children.

In Kernhem front-line dwellings along noisy roads are part of an extraordinary neighbourhood expansion. If we succeed in ensuring a quiet and car-free area, the location will become attractive to families, the housing row operates as a separating element for these two functions. Bad odours and noise nuisance will be solved by good zoning and detailing.

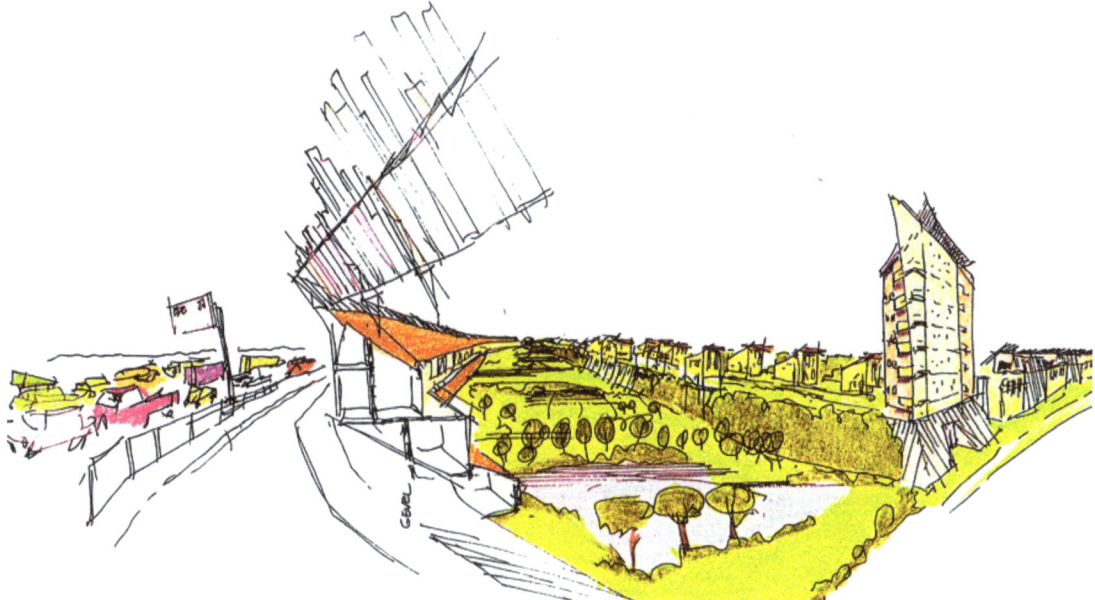

Fig. 06.24: Buildings along the A30 motorway with 'quiet' areas, the Broekbos is behind them.

Noise nuisance is easily dealt with in technical terms, juristically the problem is tougher. For the government location of a building façade is important. For the designer the start of the dwelling is important i.e. what part is the barrier, glasshouse, office function or storage area? The noise barrier has to be created by adding a second cavity wall and a second air-filled screen at the outside. In terms of finance and space this has potential.

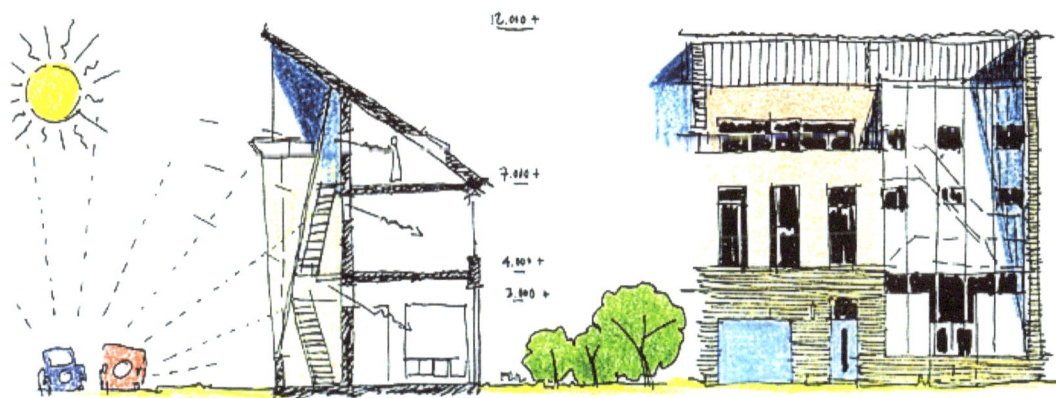

Fig. 06.25: Cross-section and elevation of dwellings for living and working along the Laan van Kernhem.

Inventions such as earth hills placed against a building are especially effective in filtering high tones. These hills need space and, as we see it, do not form an architectural addition. The lower tones have larger wavelengths that pass over.
We received the material for the noise barrier as a 'present' from additional excavations on the A30 motorway, at the point where you can find the current slope.

Along the A30 it is possible to realise beautiful sound barrier-dwellings, dike house typologies being appropriate for this location. At the foot of the slope we think of houses on poles. The orientation of the quiet space is to the east, with a view to the Broekbos. At the foot of the slope are the bedrooms. Accessibility by road is from above, at the existing slope, here the living or office areas would be situated.

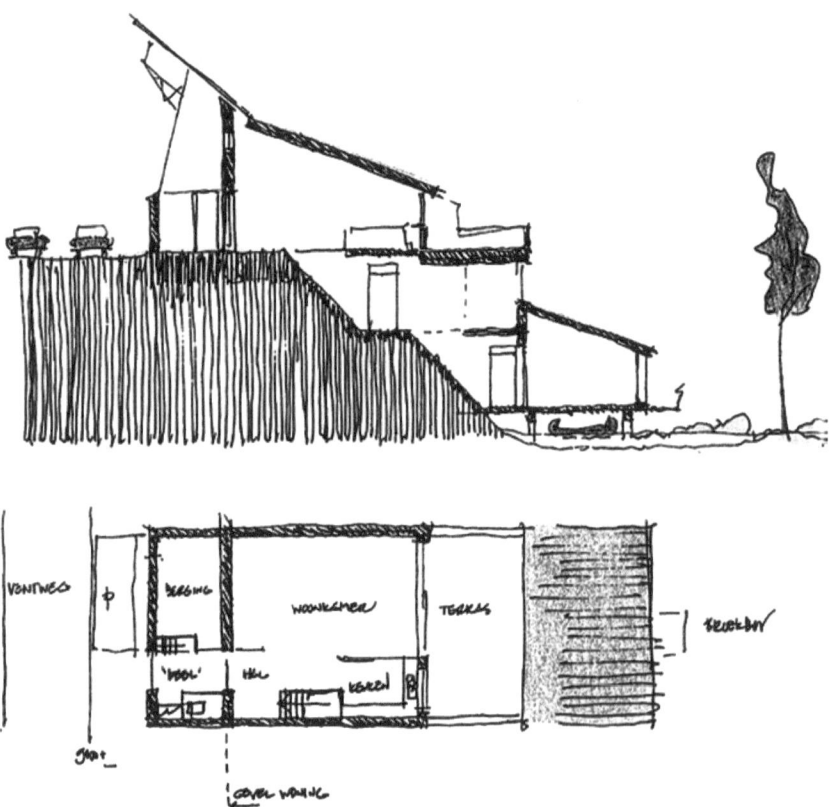

Fig. 06.26:   Ede Sound barrier dwellings – section and floor plan.

In the valley, in-between the slopes, a wet environment can establish and flourish. Living quality improves if we lift the parallel road one meter above the motorway. Another option is to avoid dwelling functions on the top layer, the ambiance along the motorway not being the same as that along the Laan van Kernhem. Ventilating air from the noisy polluted side can also lead to obvious problems. In Drachten, we proposed to incorporate greenhouses into the ventilation system. By means of the chimney effect it is also possible to supply clean and 'silent' air from the hinterland.

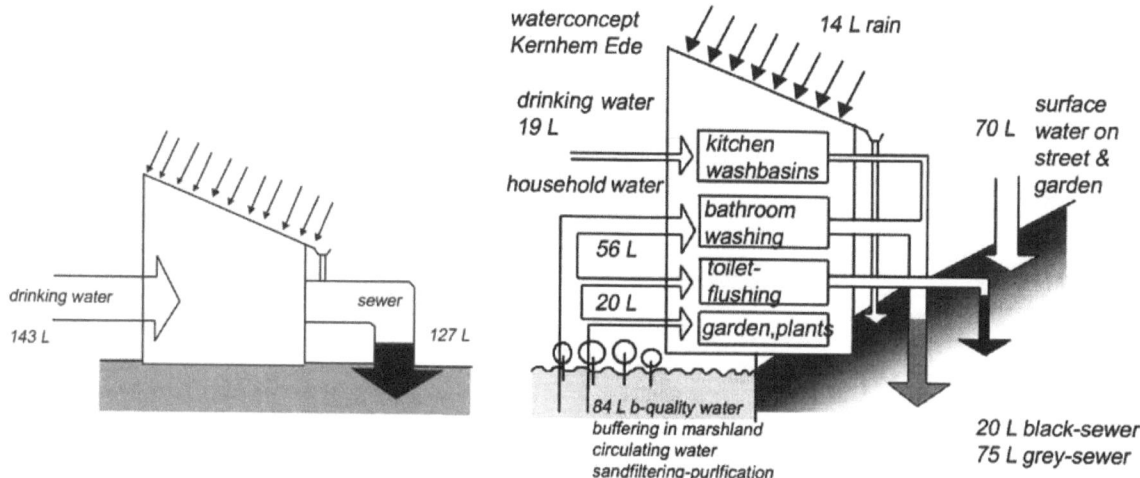

Fig. 06.27: *Average water consumption per person per day in the Netherlands, 1997 (left) and the water concept of Broekbos, Ede (right).*

Water story of Broekbos
The surface water of Kernhem flows downhill towards the western Broekbos. The sewage was omitted and the road structure was adjusted. The Broekbos is filled with many plant roots, reed and rush, that can purify the surface water. Once filtered through sand, water is finally pumped back to the neighbourhood where it is used as B-quality water. From the 143 litres of water we use on average per person per day in the Netherlands, one-sixth is used for washing and flushing. Water used in the kitchen, and the 'cold water' for brushing teeth, amounts to 11 to 19 litres per person per day. This water can be salvaged from the neighbourhood, without supplements, using a closed cycle system integrated into the built environment.

06.04.04 Railtrack-view dwellings, Elst (1998-2002)

Building developers Gerritsen asked us to design 52 sound-proof dwellings along the railway near the station of Westeraam in Elst. By adopting an half-span roof and cantilever design it was possible to reach the maximum of 60 dB through the construction of a 7 meter high façade. The roof material needed to have stone-like properties, foundations were 'springy' and therefore vibration-free, which is not necessarily required by law. All operable windows are oriented on the garden side, the railway-side windows are sound-proof. As the dwellings were, in effect, made 'deaf' by an acoustic cavity wall, the view on the railway could be enhanced by large windows.

The dwellings contain an inner courtyard and a bedroom at ground level, and two bedrooms on the second floor. The garage adjacent to the inner courtyard can also function as a home office. The bilateral connection of the blocks is formed by a glass noise barrier screen so that the entire row of dwellings function as a noise partition for the neighbourhood of Westeraam located behind them.

Fig. 06.28: Dwellings along the railway in Westeraam in Elst.

Fig. 06.29: Street side railway dwellings with inner courtyard.

Unfortunately the amount of dwellings was reduced drastically because of new insights in spatial planning. This made a traditional noise barrier imperative. Only eight dwellings were built in 2002 when the new railway tunnel was constructed. It could have been the first Dutch example of new housing that also functions as noise buffer.

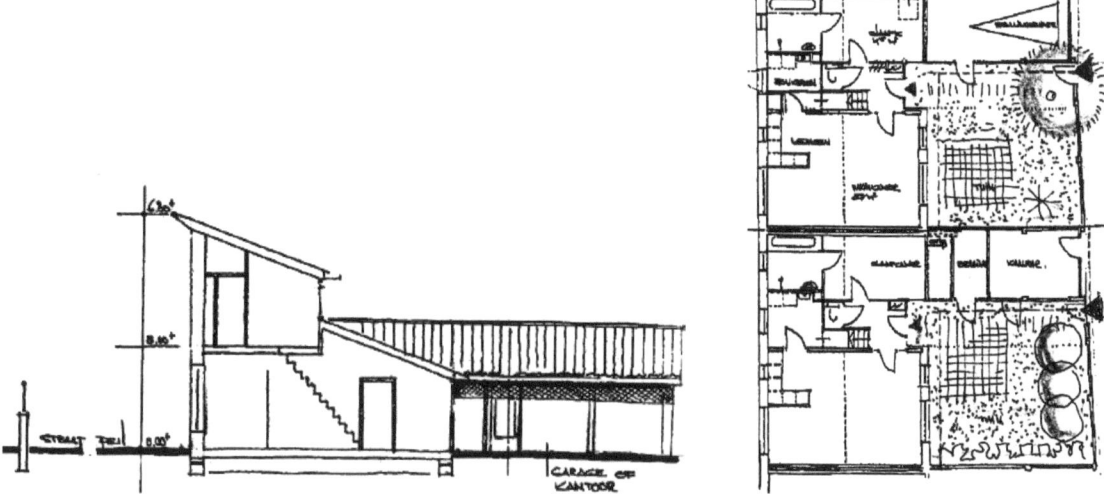

Fig. 06.30: Ground floor plan and cross-section of the Elst dwellings.

06.05 Transportation

06.05.01 The necessity of a sustainable collective transport mode

A preliminary study concerning multifunctional transport at two Dutch universities (TU Delft and Erasmus University Rotterdam, 1994) resulted in an unconventional approach that fits the current western lifestyle, meets the Kyoto targets of CO_2 reduction, and is universally applicable. Although this study named 'Icarus' was set up in a very broad way – in terms of transport means, logistics, storage, customer demands, finance and telematics – implementation in the short-term was set as a prerequisite.

> *Instead of heading for Las Palmas when the weather is bad, improvement of living conditions could be a justified alternative. Each kilometre by plane or car costs around 0.1 m^3 of natural gas equivalent (nge), so on an energetic basis, per person, a return trip from the UK to Spain is equal to the annual heating of an energy-efficient dwelling.*
>
> *In other words, assuming a large car that consumes 1 litre of gasoline per 10 kilometres, the owner of a Minimum-Energy Dwelling (using less than 500 m^3 nge/year) who annually commutes a common 20.000 km, uses the energetic equivalent of four dwellings for his travelling.*
>
> *The moral of this story is that commuting has a larger energetic impact than an environmentally benign dwelling. We need to make holistic designs: the distance to work is an important aspect to ecological building.*

Traffic and transport are traditionally an artery of a growing economy and wealth. On the other hand wealth is only maintainable when ecological balance forms the foundation of economic expansion. Long-term growth eventually leads to a trend-break. This will also happen in the transportation sector, where ecology suffers from the strong growth of auto-mobility.
The individual car has exceeded all its reasonable boundaries for growth due to its enormous success. Roads and cities are filled with cars, both driving and standing. Perhaps we can draw a parallel to wine yeast, which eliminates itself at an alcohol percentage level of 12%. Small public transport is often deserted, reduced and subsidised.

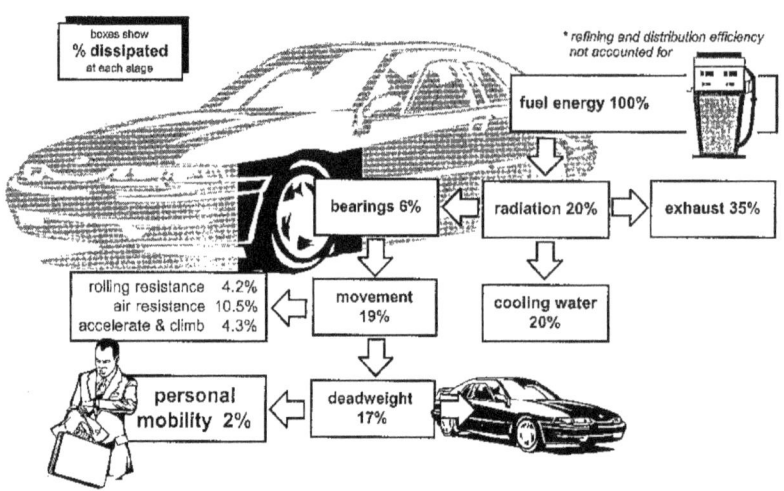

Fig. 06.31:   Car efficiency calculation by Claude Fussler, an authority on energy efficiency.

The several studies that need to support a holistic transport system regard adjustments to the existing system and possible trend-breaks:
- An acceptable substitution for the car in commuting.
- An addition to public transport during weekends and at night.
- The elderly and people who do not own a car are able to travel cheaply and safely.
- Rural areas, villages and cities will be accessible for people and goods.
- Evenly distributed occupation of main roads, 365 times twenty-four hours per year.
- The periphery of the city relieves the city centre.
- Warehouses form a noise barrier along motorways.
- Decentralisation of stations for storage and transition.
- Decentralisation and decrease in the scale of goods transport.
- Transportation of small goods without packaging.
- New personal approach to collaboration.
- Optimal public/private partnership.

Not least: minimising the environmental load to 1/12 or 1/20 becomes achievable.

The new twenty-four hour 'light-weight transportation' of people and goods would provide a totally different view on the system of transport and use existing roads more efficiently. The new multifunctional transport vehicle is similar in appearance to a biplane-carrier. Transportation of people is primary during rush hours, but at low-traffic hours and at night there would be mainly transportation of goods. Transition stations for goods and people on a nodes on the outer city rings are on the one hand unmanned high-tech warehouses and on the other hand welcoming shelter for travellers.

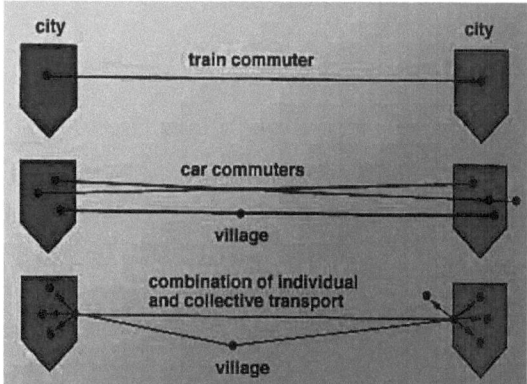

Fig. 06.32: Difference between a traditional collective traveller using public transport, a traditional individual traveller using a car, and the Icarus system with travellers using collective transport over long distances but individual cars for the first and final short stretches.

The Icarus system makes a connection between the individual transportation of car-loving people and the collective public transportation of people who are more economically and/or environmentally conscious. Implementation is expected to happen because of the double use decreasing operational costs, hence promoting growth. Sparsely populated regions of Norway already have combined buses for the transportation of goods and people. Companies that only deal with personal travel can start transporting goods outside rush hours and manufacturing companies can transport their own employees together with their products in the same Icarus system. It goes without saying that in some countries the law will have to be adjusted. The international standardisation of infrastructure, properties of carriers, secondary vehicles and transit stations will soon become urgent.

The traveller

The traveller, of any kind, is welcomed in a warm space facilitated with information, a call system, a phone and telematics. Each traveller is a registered member of Icarus. Payment and transport orders, with departure and arrival times, are organised in advance, making it possible to anticipate the individual need of mobility. Pedestrians, cyclists and disabled people, also with their mini-car, are welcome. People can leave their personal transport means safely behind at the stations where goods from elsewhere are also stored, supervised and distributed.

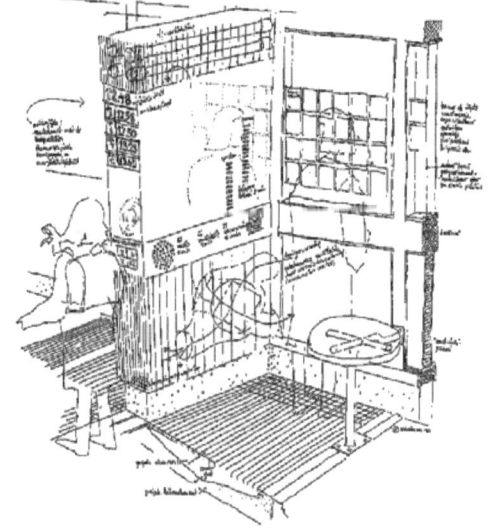

Fig. 06.33: Communication pillar for bus stops and waiting rooms – competition idea, Reykjavik 1980, set aside as 'fantasy' [32].

---

[32] Design by Björn and Jón Kristinsson.

06.05.02 Future commuter traffic – individual/collective

A joint project by the Delft faculties of Architecture (DOSIS research) and Industrial Design Engineering (Design for Sustainability), involving interdisciplinary graduation projects by Niels Peters and Peter Welleman.

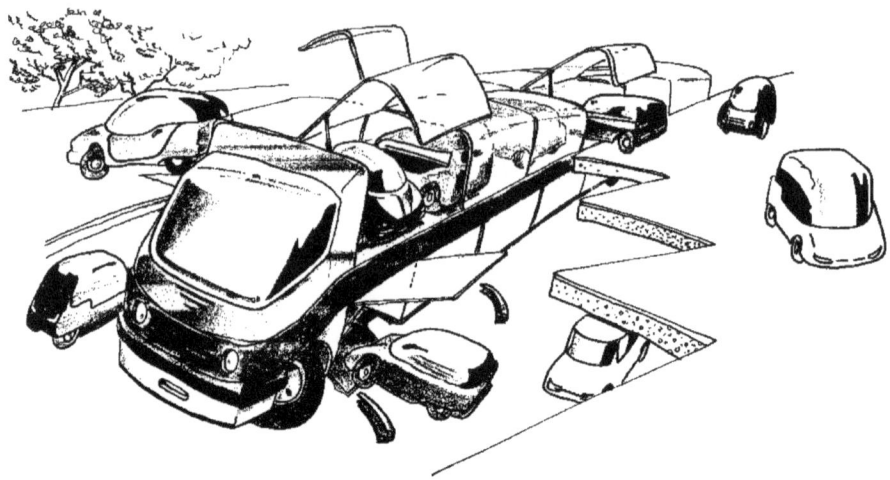

Fig. 06.34:   The C(ollective)-carrier with I(ndividual)-cars at a STIC (Station for Transfer between Individual and Collective).

Icarus
The Icarus idea resulted from shipping and road transport with flexible working hours and self-organising ability. Icarus is a multiple transportation system, privately and centrally commanded, which can function as a small means of transport under development as well as a large international system connected to rail and air traffic. The Icarus system functions optimally through high-tech telematics.

I-car – C-carrier – STIC
With an addition of the current rail and road infrastructure, all commuter traffic can undergo an incremental capacity enlargement. Through better accessibility and usage of highways, new functions are attributed to city border railway stations, which become STICs (Stations for Transfer between Individual and Collective)[33].

The C-carrier
The C-carrier of the Icarus system resembles a Swiss post-delivery bus, a truck holding a carrier trailer, is technically feasible in its most simplified form. The C-carriers can have various dimensions. On long distances these are thought to be biplane vehicles with a trailer wagon. The C-carriers will not only be appropriate for transportation at short distances in densely populated industrial countries, but also on long distances in sparsely populated areas with extreme weather conditions. The reliability of collective fast transportation should also attract lightweight individual transport.

---

[33] Or GOOS (Getting On and Off Stations)

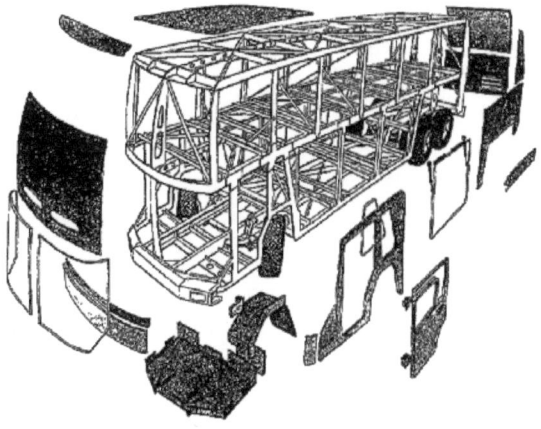

The STIC (Station for Transfer between Individual and Collective)

The infrastructure for loading and unloading of C-carriers needs to be standardised e.g. the dimension of doors, for a fast interchange of the pneumatically driven storage pallets. The STIC, change-over station for goods and people, is the 'transfer machine' between fast traffic and diverse slow traffic. Despite standardisation, the form and capacity of STICs may be different. They unite architecture, storage technology and chip culture. The expected growth of rental and lease cars, just as the electric car, will stimulate charging and parking facilities at the STICs.

Fig. 06.35: Exploded view of the C-carrier.

In addition to pedestrians and cyclists, I-cars (individual cars) will be introduced on the road. These are advanced lightweight, non-crashing two-seater vehicles. As a result of implementation of flexible C-carriers (collective carriers) for commuting traffic – and the transportation of goods in low-traffic hours – parking spaces along the motorway become equivalent to train stations. In the mean time, rail tracks that are not used by I-cars can be used as a secondary rail network.

06.05.03 Sustainable individual/collective transport, Zwolle (2000)

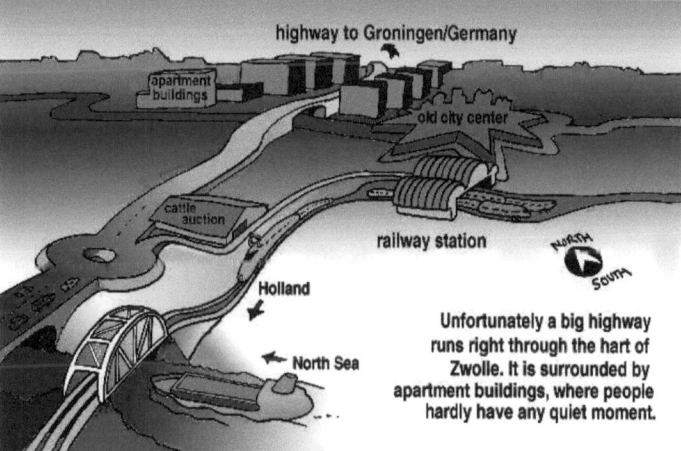

Fig. 06.36: The transport situation of Zwolle.

With reference to sustainable transport studies, the municipality of Zwolle asked us to collaborate on a website for the generation of ideas about the problems relating to the A28 motorway that cuts through Zwolle. The motorway would become the economical artery, as is illustrated in a sketch by Peter Welleman. The first step towards a solution lies in the creation of a sound barrier next to the motorway, formed by buildings parallel to it (Fig. 06.37).

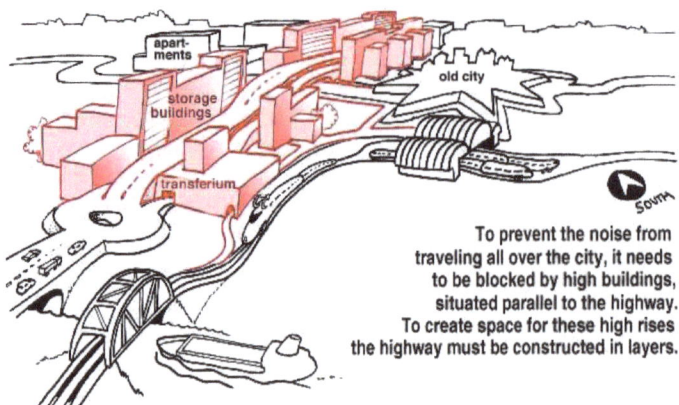

Fig. 06.37: Noise blocking by buildings parallel to the motorway, Zwolle.

These buildings could also function as STICs, discussed in the previous sub-section.

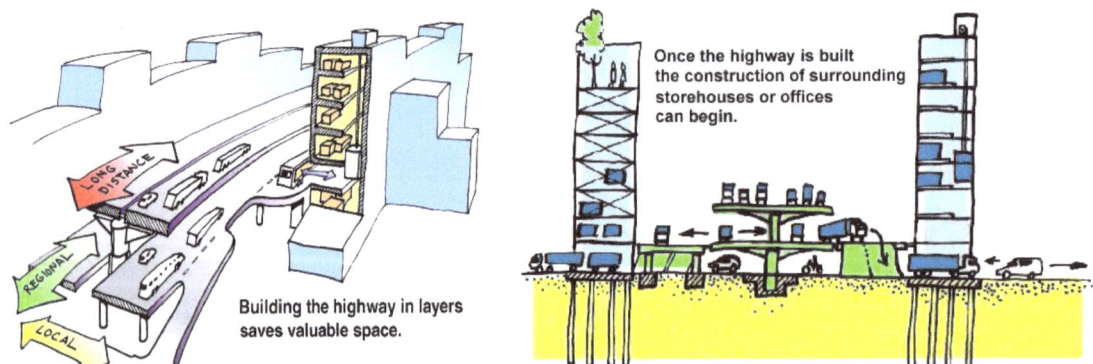

Fig. 06.38: The Zwolle plan: buildings along the motorway function as a sound barrier and Stations for Transfer between Individual and Collective transport.

The new tangent-connection between the main road and the city has not been tested before but can be favourably compared to the system applied in Curitiba, Brazil.

07

NEW SUSTAINABLE URBANISM

07.01 Introduction

> *"Panta rhei"* – all things flow and pass, and all things constantly change.
>
> *Philosophical principle of Heraclitus*

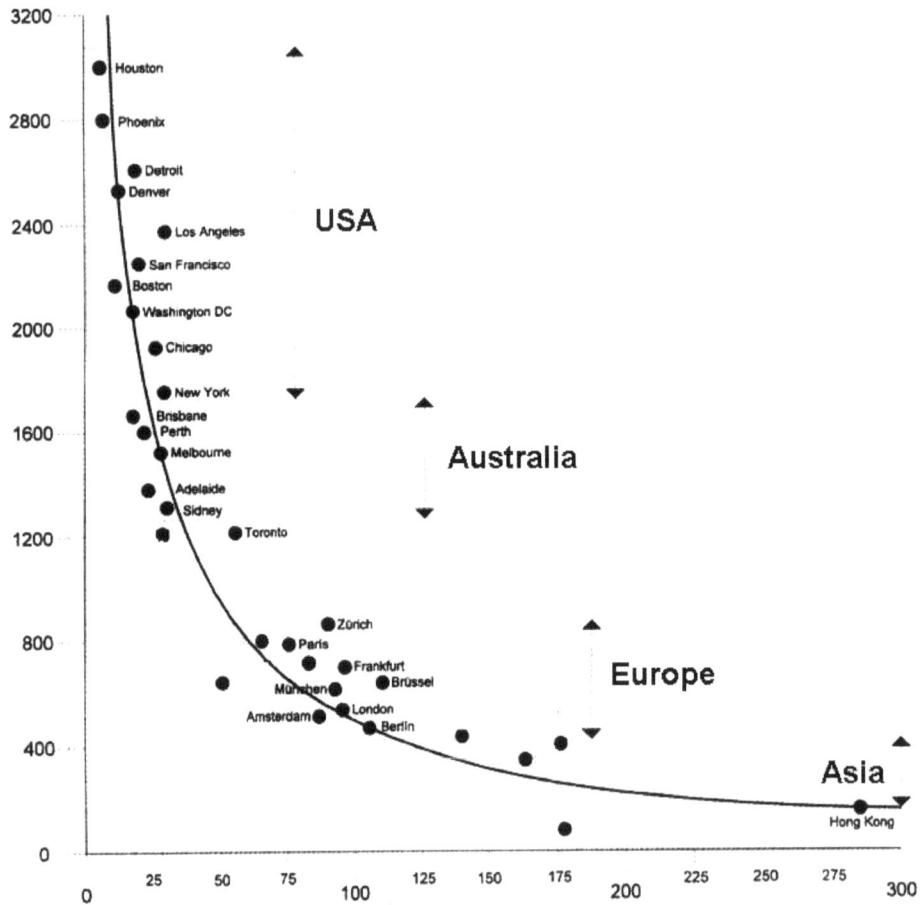

Fig. 07.01: Influence of urban densities (horizontal, inhabitants per ha) on the energy consumption for mobility (vertical, MJ per capita) in 32 cities [Newman & Kenworthy, 1989; 2001]. The graph indicates that the energy consumption for travel increases with low-density housing. Moreover, this leads to excessive commuting times and extra costs per family.
The world knows many housing cultures and models. Each continent appears to have a recognisable pattern in regards to fossil fuel and the commuter traffic. Energy reduction in commuter traffic demands five measures: 1. densifying the built environment, 2. prioritising cyclists and pedestrians, 3. reducing the maximum speed for cars, 4. making the city centres compact, 5. improving the capacity and quality of public transport.

The 1987 Brundtland rapport, "Our common Future", had worldwide influence. Gro Harlem Brundtland's definition of sustainable development states: **a development that meets the needs of the present without compromising the ability of future generations to meet their own needs.**
As a result from the environmental convention in Rio de Janeiro in 1992 several sustainable developments were continued by a group of supporters and spread fast, such as the 1997 Kyoto protocol, which focussed on the reduction of greenhouse gasses. Unfortunately the 2002 UN convention in Johannesburg, with the theme of 'environment and combating poverty', did not lead to major breakthroughs. The result was smaller than hoped for, yet more than expected.

Sustainable urbanism consists of the integration of our environmental system in new urban development concepts. The design of human settlements can be achieved in several ways. One person pays more attention to aspects of the landscape, another on the biological aspects and a third on the financial feasibility or political support. An extensive holistic approach however will be most sustainable. In practice some priorities appear to be just short-term politics. New developments will be discussed later, here, we will examine sustainability and the occupied space per individual.

Table 07.01: Uncontrolled growth – Past, present and predicted population figures (in millions) in the world's largest cities, listed in ranking order [United Nations, 2007].

City	Country	1950	1980	2010	2025
Tokyo	Japan	11.2	28.5	**36.1**	36.4
Mumbai (Bombay)	India	2.9	8.7	**20.1**	26.4
São Paulo	Brazil	2.3	12.1	**19.6**	21.4
Mexico City	Mexico	2.9	13.0	**19.5**	21.0
New York City	USA	12.3	15.6	**19.4**	20.6
Delhi	India	1.4	5.6	**17.0**	22.5
Shanghai	China	6.1	7.6	**15.8**	19.4
Kolkata (Calcutta)	India	4.5	9.0	**15.6**	20.6
Dhaka	Bangladesh	0.3	3.3	**14.8**	22.0
Buenos Aires	Argentina	5.1	9.4	**13.1**	13.8
Karachi	Pakistan	1.1	5.0	**13.1**	19.1
Los Angeles	USA	4.0	9.5	**12.8**	13.7
Cairo	Egypt	2.5	7.3	**12.5**	15.6
Rio de Janeiro	Brazil	3.0	8.6	**12.2**	13.4
Beijing	China	4.3	6.4	**11.7**	14.5
Manila	Philippines	1.5	6.0	**11.7**	14.8
Osaka-Kobe	Japan	4.1	10.0	**11.3**	11.4
Lagos	Nigeria	0.3	2.6	**10.6**	15.8
Istanbul	Turkey	1.0	4.4	**10.5**	12.1
Paris	France	6.5	8.7	**10.0**	10.0
Seoul	South Korea	1.0	8.3	**9.8**	9.7
Jakarta	Indonesia	1.5	6.0	**9.7**	12.4
Guangzhou	China	1.5	3.0	**9.4**	11.8
London	UK	8.4	7.7	**8.6**	8.6

We are conditioned to think that development equals growth. But growth does not automatically mean improvement: it can also mean a change for the worse. How can we prepare ourselves

for stagnation or even negative growth? Very little is done about this issue because it does not match our analytical thinking that tends to extrapolate.
The search for solutions must be broadened, where new forms of organisation and technologies must be found. The strategies may be different, for example from centralised to decentralised small-scale facilities. The level of self-sufficiency becomes important.

07.02   History

07.02.01   Early civilisation

The foundation of our western civilisation consists of the rational thinking of the Greek, the organisation of the Romans and the combating faith of Israel [Prof. Bismo Suwondo Sutedjo]. Hence the apostle Paulus, founder of the church of Rome, whose father was a Roman citizen, who studied in Israel and was frequently seen in Greece, became the first western man in new style.

- The first cities arose 8000 years ago in the Asia Minor: Cathal, Huyuk and Jericho.
- The city is the hart of civilisation.
- Art and culture develop with city wealth.
- The organisation of a city is stable, otherwise the city would have never exist.
- Cities arise, grow and will eventually shrink.
- In 1994 the largest mega-cities with the most inhabitants were Tokyo, Sao Paulo, Mexico City and New York.

Fig. 07.02:   Urban grid of the heart of Rome (left) and arial photograph of the ruins of the grid built Roman city of Timgad in Algiers [34] (right).

---

[34] Source: Winkler Prins encyclopaedia

Around 100 BC Rome was the largest city of the world, with almost one million inhabitants. After having been seized by the Goths from the East and with the rise of the Byzantine Empire (555 AD), Rome shrank substantially to 30,000 inhabitants. In the Renaissance (1536 AD) its numbers climbed again to 55,000. Which tourist can imagine today that in the year 1800 the Forum Romanum, centre of the once powerful Roman Empire, would used for grazing by cows? Only after Rome became the capital of Italy in 1871 did the city start to grow again.

In the historical Hanseatic city of Deventer on the IJssel river, our home town, the theologist Geert Grote (the enlightened predecessor of Luther) died in 1384 of a plague epidemic, due to terrible hygienic conditions.

Fig. 07.03:   Map of Deventer around the year 1650, by Joan Blaeu, with earthen walls as defensive system.

Table 07.02: Number of Deventer inhabitants through the ages.

14th and 15th century	5 to 10,000
1570	10,000
1600	4,500
1650	7,000
1800	8,000
1900	16,000
1921	32,000
2002 (incl. Dieperveen)	85,000
2015	100,000

Fig. 07.04:   De Waag (weighing house) of Deventer.

The number of inhabitants in Deventer has followed an unstable course partly due to several migrations (Table 07.02)[35]:

1950: Maluku people
1958: Indonesian people
1960: Foreign labourers from Italy, Spain, Greece, Portugal and Turkey (currently 6.6% of the citizens is from Turkish origin)
1975: Surinamese and Antilleans
2000: Iraqi, ex-Yugoslavians, Somali, Ethiopians and Afghans and 'chain' migrants by marriage

By the year 2002, in the four big cities in the Netherlands 50% of the children until the age of 4 did not have a Dutch origin.

---

[35] Data source until 1975: Municipality of Deventer, P. Holthuis, 1993; data source after 1975: NRC Handelsblad, 30 July 2002

Were our cities sustainable in the past?
Regarding their existence in that time, they were, but very bad to disastrous for their natural surroundings. Urbanisation led to deforestation, as one effect among many others. Every human being aggravates the environment. In the mediaeval cities in Europe people lived, dwelled and suffered differently than they do today. Inside the city walls the land was completely built, even the backyard. There was no space for trees. Streets were filthy, dusty and muddy. Waste accumulated. Church bells announced the times for the evening prayers or mass. People feared imminent death and sin.

07.02.02   Cities and energy

The city had the tendency to 'eat' her own children because the net fertility was low due to the bad living conditions and hygiene. Wars, epidemics, fire, silting up of ports and salinisation of the hinterland due to irrigation were re-occurring interruptions. The medieval city also had a natural limit to its growth and this was mainly related to the capacity in the fuel supply.

Historically Amsterdam has proved to be sustainable. The buildings along the canals, from the sixteenth and seventeenth century, still stand upright and are used and maintained. The key to this sustainability is beauty, building materials that can be easily maintained and the flexibility in use thanks to over-dimensioning, which made it possible to transform the warehouses into dwellings or offices.

How could Amsterdam have had more inhabitants than London in that time?

Fig. 07.05:   *Map of the historic centre of Amsterdam and an Image of a typical canal with merchant's houses.*

The secret lies in the accessibility by boat, fuelled by peat from the 'high-altitude' areas (everyone knows that in the Netherlands, high altitudes are very relative...). Already in the 13th century peat was cut in the province of Drenthe, near Zuidlaren along the Hunze.

Peat as fuel for small-scale industries and the heating of dwellings in Amsterdam had large consequences for the landscape in the provinces of Drenthe and Groningen. In the 'Peat Colonies' peat was extracted at a fast pace in order to supply Dutch cities. The Delft street named 'Brabantse turfmarkt' indicates that also in the province of Brabant peat was cut. The Delft Schie canal had already been dug by the Romans partly for its acquisition.

Fig. 07.06:   Peat cutting in the late 1800's.

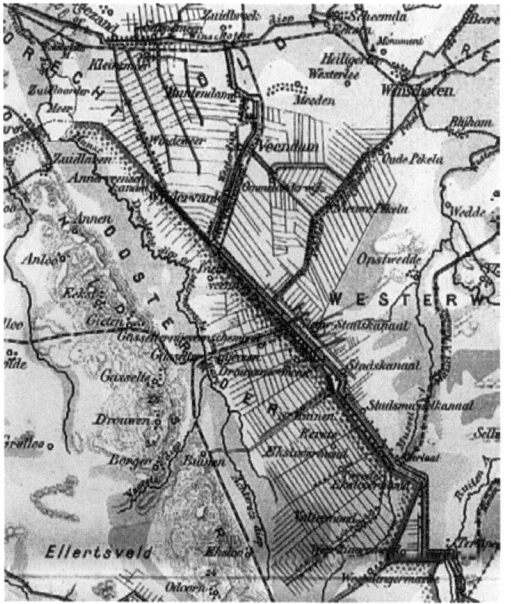

Peat as fuel supply is not sustainable, since it is a fossil fuel just like natural gas that is now extracted from rock formations under the northern provinces and the North Sea. However, wooden ships with peat were controllable and visible to the consumer. Natural gas is supplied through invisible underground tubes and automatically paid for through your bank account. With the arrival of highly efficient fossil energy, coal, gas and oil, cities can easily expand to mega-cities. The Dutch city of today does not know scarcity, but a surplus and over-dimensioning of infrastructure. Pavements are kept free of vegetation by the use of herbicides.

Fig. 07.07:   Map of the peat areas in Drenthe and Groningen, from the 'Bos Schoolatlas' of 1912.

07.02.03   Cities and water

A second important aspect in the development of a city is drinking water. A city was usually supplied with fresh water from a river. Amsterdam was dependent on its surrounding lakes from which boats supplied drinking water. The Roman aqueducts are monuments of civilisation, we you observe the water cisterns next to the Aya Sofia in Istanbul, you realise how valuable the collection and underground storage of drinking water was to its inhabitants.

Fig. 07.08:   Aqueduct of Segovia, Spain (left) and Byzanthean water cistern in Istanbul, Turkey (right).

In lowland cities water flows slowly, up to this century the hygienic circumstances were poor as a result with the toilet discharge ended up in the canals. Drinking water was collected from polluted water sources in inner courtyards and from open water in the countryside. Reliable drinking water was beer and therefore the beer brewers were important for public health.
In Nijmegen, university city and once the Dutch seat to Charlemagne (742-814), pure groundwater was pumped up at great depth in 742 to use it even for toilet flushing! In a wealthy and democratic country, with a well-educated population, this plunder on the drinking water supply has to be stopped for the sake of the next generation. The recovery of the groundwater level will take centuries rather than a few decades to rectify. The ecological alarm bell should have tolled a long time ago.
In modern large Dutch cities people choose a remarkable direction of filtering and purifying polluted water from the Rhine and Mass rivers, draining the pure rainwater that falls between the rivers within a 36 hour period, then discharging it to sea. A situation that needs to change. Upstream more retention basins for rainwater should be created. These have to avoid the inlet of polluted water from the river in dry periods to supply agricultural land.

07.02.04   Monofunctionality of industrial and commercial districts

During the twentieth century cities underwent industrialisation and two world wars. The city of horses and bikes became one of cars. The expansion of monofunctional office districts and industrial sites will strongly diminish. As a result of the low net occupation rate of offices new concepts evolved, such as flexible workspaces and business centres. These do not offer personal rooms, but personal trolleys that can be taken to empty workstations. A good example of this is the office of the Dutch Governmental Buildings Agency in Haarlem. Production processes become ever more compact and products smaller and lighter. The present-day, half-empty industrial sites called commercial districts are swallowed by stores, transhipment, transportation and logistics. These areas should be reallocated for new companies and for the 24-hour living and working of young entrepreneurs. The automation industrialisation has already announced itself and will have a great influence on transportation.
Producing without any reserves is asking for production stagnation. Motorways have become driving warehouses, and due to delivery 'just in time' strategies an over-loading of the road network. Distribution centres in favour of chain stores have nocturnal logistics as an effect.

07.03   The sustainable city

07.03.01   The sustainable city, backcasted from 2048

This was a project by the TU Delft, Faculty of Architecture, Building Technology Department, Chair of Environmental Design: Jón Kristinsson, Arjan van Timmeren and Andy van den Dobbelsteen. Discussions on sustainable directions provided innovative insights into the future of urbanism.

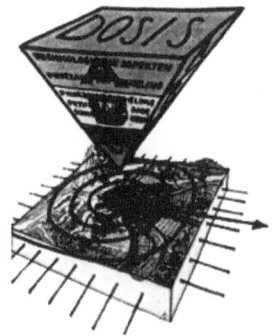

Between 1992 and 2002 DOSIS (Dutch abbreviation of sustainable development of city and infrastructure) there was a broad and comprehensive educational and research programme, which has its predecessor in the Green Building Innovation programme. The positive attitude of DOSIS was a holistic approach to the most probable future scenario: a drastic decrease in the environmental metabolism within the coming half-century. Through 'backcasting' new concepts were developed in many areas and on various scales. We aimed for a reduction of consumption in materials and energy of least one twentieth the current figure.

DOSIS research
All DOSIS studies were based on the idea that within sustainable technological development great progress will only be made when we collaborate interdisciplinarily, interdepartmentally and (inter)nationally with a lateral way of thinking. What do our grandchildren wish for us to decide today?

For the built environment reconsideration and completely new concepts were needed, some of which have been developed since:
- Closed cycles: tackling waste at all scale levels.
- Individual/collective transport for commuter travel.
- Integrated water management with green algae technology.
- Self-sufficient housing: zero-energy dwellings.
- Building concepts for hindrance zones (no expansion in natural areas).
- Convenient living areas for the unemployed.
- Reduction of infrastructure with clear, self-regulating land prices.

07.03.02   The two urban structures: water and roads

The two most important structures in urbanism are water and roads. What is missing in our way of thinking is the question: what are closed-cycle processes or, put differently, are we able to restore ecological cycles?

Water, as the carrier of life, has a vital role in life cycles. Therefore water should be given priority as a primary structure in the urban environment. Roads form the economical structure in urbanism. The consequence is that roads will have to become secondary to waterways.

However, this does not mean we have to completely desert our current systems. The redesigning, reconstruction and execution will take at least 50 years.

For a sustainable society, which functions with an environmental metabolism, a completely different water strategy is needed. Holistic design demands a zero from the outset. For water this means that we try to make a completely closed cycle; only in this way can we achieve the necessary reduction of (technical) infrastructure. Highly necessary, because the costs keep increasing year after year, while the price of a sewage pipe is already between € 200 to € 600 per meter! The money literally lies on the street. We simply just don't see it.

Sometimes 'wishful thinking' becomes reality. In October 2002 Cobouw published "Pavement with characteristics of sewage". This pavement system, developed by Prof. C.J. Pratt from the University of Coventry, has a water storage capacity depth of 40 mm and utilises biological purification. A capacity depth of 20 to 28 mm storage will suffice for the Netherlands.

Sometimes the Netherlands looks like a big sandpit, in which all civil and other brother and sister engineers are playing, including 'Betuwelijn', a commercial rail track project from the Rotterdam harbours to Germany. This big business could also become 'smart business'. To continue this 'playing in the sandpit' we not only need extensive regulation, but also a sustainable philosophy:
- What is not needed should not be constructed.
- What can be visible should not be hidden and made uncontrollable.
- How do we get to a balanced spatial planning where cohesion and logic prevail.

07.03.03   Light Urbanism

Light Urbanism is the intelligent, sustainable and human settlement of the 21st century. Light Urbanism comes and goes and, as a good traveller is supposed to, does not leave a trace. The infrastructural designers develop new integrated technological breakthroughs through backcasting from the year 2050.

- Light Urbanism originates and responds to highly dense, compactly built nuisance zones surrounded by infrastructure. This well-designed, multifunctional fringe development forming the sound barrier between heavy and light urbanism.
- Light Urbanism is resistant against expensive and unnecessary infrastructure. People can utilise the increasing facilities for buildings, mainly because of the upcoming technical and ecological developments. In the design concept for buildings and the city it is possible to have a strong influence on the consumption of water and energy, and therefore also on the necessity of a sewage system and gas or electricity infrastructure.
  The meter box behind closed doors is disputed. Openness and responsibility for the community should be natural.
- The introduction of new individual and collective transport concepts, as well as transforming social structures, has direct and diverse, derivative effects on the built environment.
- Light Urbanism starts with image building, but in spite of the ecological and economical advantages, current building laws and tradition are incapable of making great leaps in development.

Fig. 07.09: Avant-garde imagination of Light Urbanism (1995): living in caravans, tents, train units or houseboats, in the sound lee behind an occupied high sound barrier wall in Barendrecht, in the background the Euromast of Rotterdam.

- Light Urbanism mainly follows the housing demands from survey reports [36].
- Light Urbanism, in principle, is low-rise. We know that people with a low income are less likely to prosper in high-rises. Unemployed people benefit from organised social activity and allotment gardening. The grey economy around recycling needs more structure for environmental reasons.
- Light Urbanism has to be resistant to unfavourable influences of negative economic growth.
- Light Urbanism can grow from an 'inframedion'. This is a village square with central facilities. But also a farmhouse can function as catalyser for a slow growth of a settlement. A new neighbourhood should develop toward a village at a slow rate with closed cycles in its infrastructure.
- Light Urbanism has light-weight buildings, which are possible when we use the soil as thermal mass, hereby creating a balanced, comfortable indoor climate. All thermal isolation materials are light-weight. As natural building materials we can think of wood, natural fibres, cork, flax, hemp, loam, etcetera. 'Drily' connected demountable materials can be based on wood, metal and glass. Sand-lime bricks, clay bricks and concrete are heavy and with the current knowledge hard to dismantle. Pre-stressed bricks and dry mounting of concrete elements for facades are possible.

---

[36] 71% of the Dutch population wish to live in rural environments and 24% in a highly urbanised environment. This comes to approximately 10 dwellings/ha, respectively more than 100 dwellings/ha, in contrast to the 30 to 35 dwellings/ha (the 'Vinex' ratio), which has been used extensively for a long period by the Dutch government.

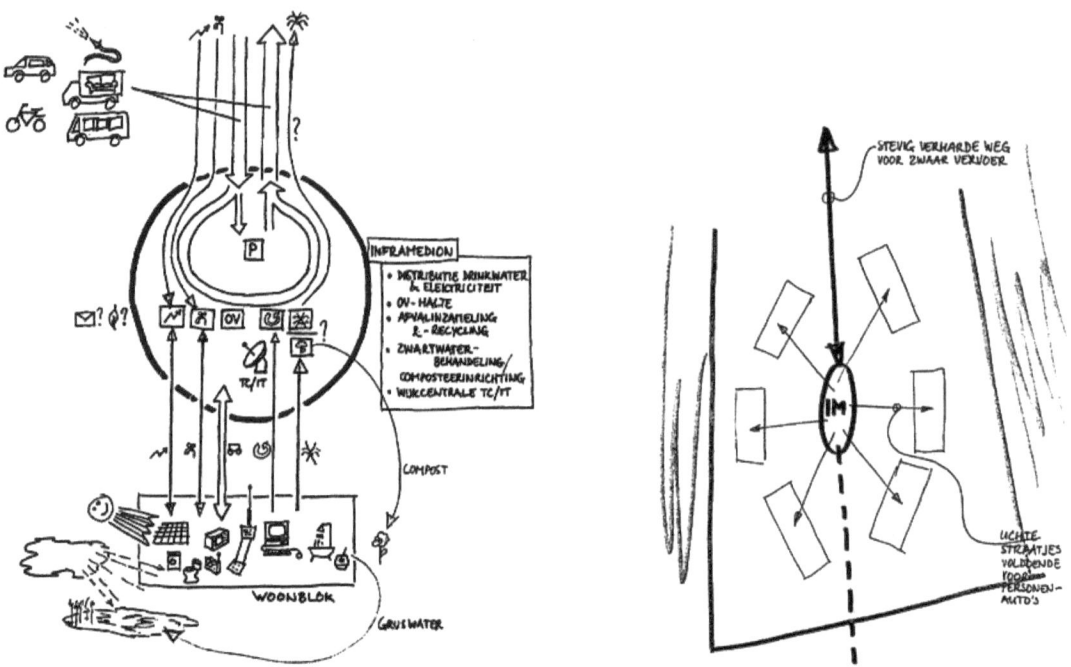

Fig. 07.10: Principle of the Inframedion and all functions involved (left) and location of the Inframedion in an urban extension neighbourhood (right).

Holistic design based on building physics is, for now, the most probable direction for sustainable architecture within Light Urbanism.

Fig. 07.11: Humorous impression of extreme light urbanism.

07.03.04 Drachten urban border vision, expansion avoidance (1994)

This concerns a research assignment from the Municipality of Smallingerland (awarded as a consequence of our well received ecological contribution to Morra Park). The brief was to develop a proposal for the expansion of Drachten. In collaboration with IBN (institute for forest and nature research) and Kuiper Compagnons urban planners the outcome was a remarkable vision on the city borders, in the rural area to the west of Drachten. Our aim was not to expand in Boornbergum, but instead to 'inpand' i.e. find expansion inside the urban boundaries, close to the town centre.

Fig. 07.12:   Drachten circa 1925 (left) and 1990 (right).

Drachten was formally a Frisian village whose appearance has changed drastically through its transformation into a town:
- The open water of the canal had been filled up.
- The blonde clinker pavement had made way to grey concrete tiles and black asphalt that stretches to the front of the town hall.
- Bridges, image-defining elements, had been replaced by traffic lights and road signs.
- The urban border is a frayed silhouette of solemn high-rises, crowned with installations and lift towers.

The characteristics that should have been preserved in the historical centre had not been developed in a sustainable way due to an excess of money and determination. Each individual has the right to grow old and decay, but a city has the right to grow old and to rejuvenate itself. Expansion occurs or can happen by growth circles around the city. However this was not the case for Drachten. Expensive infrastructure for industry, waste, roads and sewage 'metropolitanly' closed off the village, between nuisance zones and motorways. It became a car-town, closed off from the marina and the surrounding beautiful landscape with Frisian lakes. Why do growth circles often result in ugly tumours that cling to the edge of a city while the city core turns rotten?

New image: the image of a 'liveable city' should be a timeless human settlement that can expand and incline by ecological rules. The name of this timeless human settlement, a slowed down society, has to be replaced by a new magical word for sustainability yet to be conceived. It comprises housing, working and recreation and offers a holistic balance. It includes village, city, suburb, rural area, ribbon development and agricultural area.

An area where:
- One dreams and thinks.
- Many and diverse activities are allowed.
- Freedom is the norm.
- People enjoy staying.
- Demand and supply are balanced.

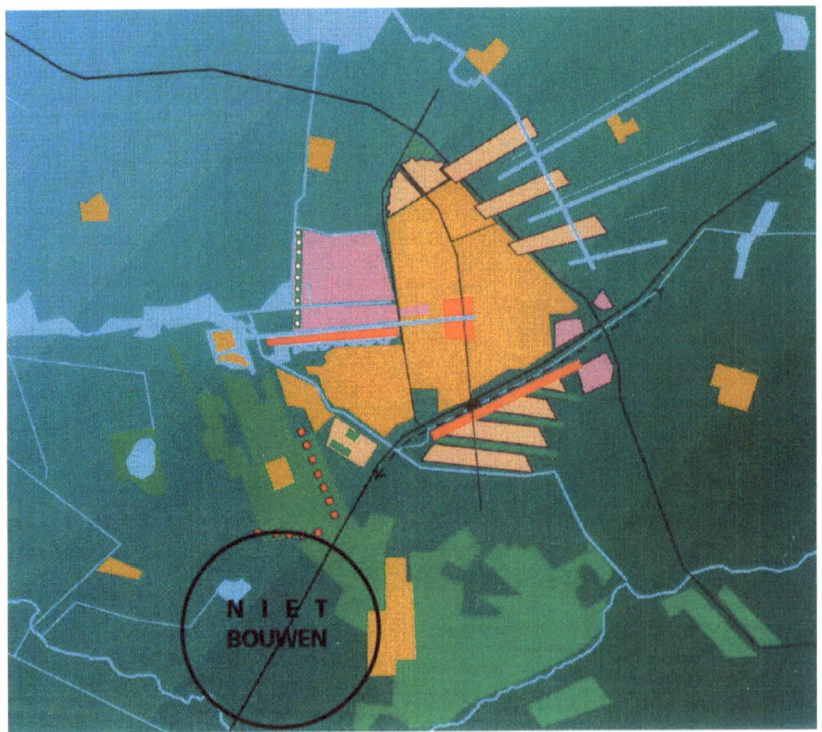

Fig. 07.13: Proposed extension plan for Drachten, as proposed in the urban border vision of 1994. 'NIET BOUWEN' indicates the rural landscape to be left undeveloped.

If we move to a liveable city model, then we return to the basic principles of timeless self-sufficiency. How does the liveable city differ from the current expansive city? The scale of size and density per hectare, the richness in differentiation and choice define human happiness. Beauty is the first criterion for sustainability, because people inherit something beautiful.
The following keywords help define aims and objectives that ordinarily are omitted in comprehensive brief descriptions:
- Village: intimate, secure, personal, small-scale, timeless, appropriate for children, safe, kitchen gardens, cycling.
- City: lively, cosy, cultural, good ambiance, schools, safe, committed neighbourhood, freedom, industrial activities, buildings determine the overall image, gardens, tourists, small cars.
- Suburb: flats, separate villas, no human scale, impersonal, distance, unsafe, good dwellings, parking spaces, bus stop, parks, subways.
- Rural area: luxurious lifestyle, rural living, freedom, tree lane, not accessible, villas with added buildings, "the happy few", boats, vacation, jeeps/SUVs.

- Agricultural area: open, seasonal changes, farms, cattle, odour of manure, farmland, ecological processes, tractors and horses.
- Marina: guests in high season, wooden landing stages, no social structure, heterogenic income, sterile polluted sea bottom, antifouling.
- Camping site: low threshold, oasis of first names, shorts, noisy and united, self-imposed discipline, no democracy, dictatorship of the owner, avoiding building permits.

The sustainable city should be capable of self-renewal, be compact, inter-connected and in-tune with former and future generations. The image of the city border can be built and completed, the carrier of infrastructure is usually new and unknown and has to be developed without harming other developments. The liveable city needs to be checked on other ecological requirements than those of the current urban design plans. At a very low level of abstraction, understandable for everyone, the design, the construction, the funding, the maintenance, the growth, the replacement of the timeless contact with neighbours and social and cultural life, should be determined in logical rules until the end of times. Within our democratic society only 1.5% of population actually determine what happens.

Technological forecasts are complex and difficult. If time, politics and technological developments were linked to democratic decisions of free citizens, nothing would change.

Fig. 07.14: Wrapping the industrial area, and buildings along the Drachtstervaart.

In 1995 the Faculty of Architecture, Department of Building technology, Chair of Environmental Design received the assignment from the Rijksplanologische Dienst (governmental spatial planning agency) to elaborate on some aspects of the Drachten urban border vision. opMAAT, office for architectural and environmental research and design in Delft, was asked to collaborate on the water issues. The outcomes were published in the report 'Van blokkades naar potenties' (from blockades to potentials).

The results from the study are summarised here:
- The juridical sound barrier zones are contested physically.
- The water is revaluated at all scale levels.
- The Drachtstervaart canal will transform into a semi-dynamic waterway.
- Sailing ships can reach the centre for food.
- New locks make it possible to purify the landfill site.
- The concrete industry encloses itself.
- A building strip of 1.5 km arises.
- A new free automatic public transport system is introduced.
- Buildings along the highway function as a sound barrier.
- The 'Inframedion' is applied as utility and facility core of the new urban expansion.

1. Drachtstervaart
- Stretched to the city centre as it was before.
- Transition from industrial to housing area.
- Using the barrier zones, juridical issue.
- Verifying the potentials for a good living environment.
- New slow transport means.
- Restoring the relation of Drachten with the Frisian lakes and marina.

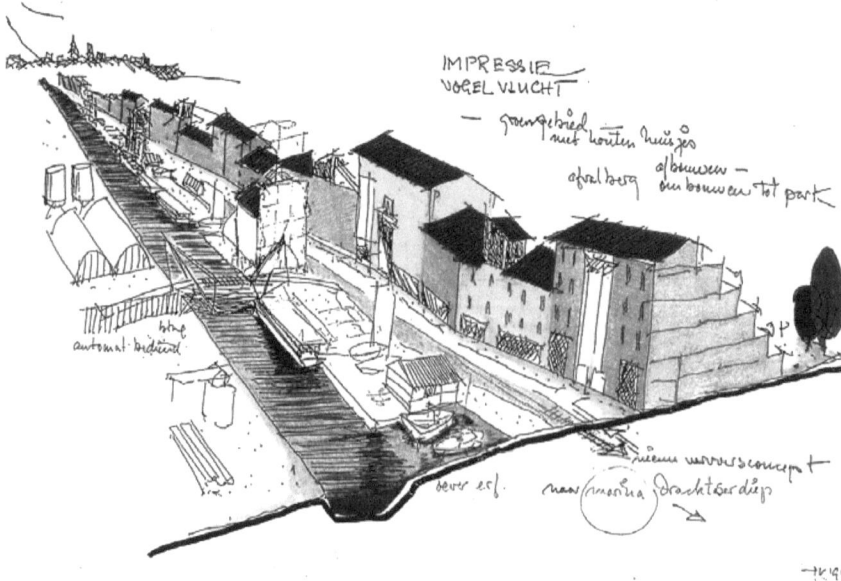

Fig. 07.15: The Drachtstervaart canal stretched all the way to the town centre, living in a 'sound barrier'.

2. Industrial area De Haven
- Start with the organisation of maintaining the environment.
- Cleaning the landfill site.
- Wrapping the industrial area.
- Elaboration of water maintenance, transitional industry landscape and industrial living.

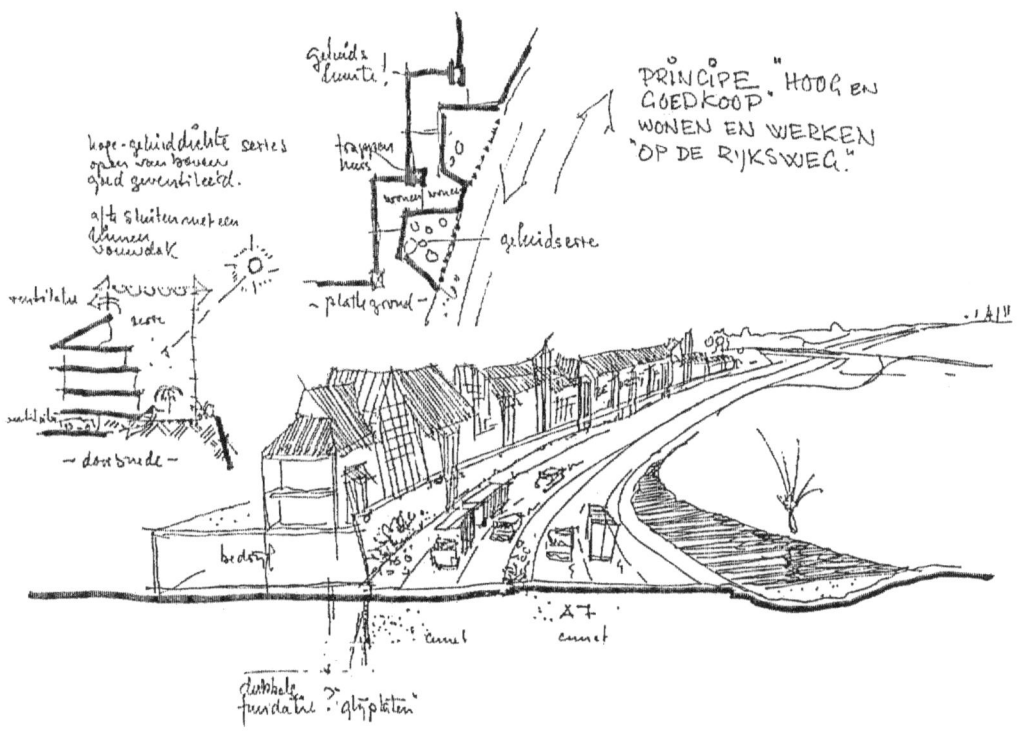

Fig. 07.16: The functional urban border development needs to be situated very close to the road in order to form an efficient sound barrier. In this way the necessary building height can be limited to 15 to 25 meters. Through the use of closed verandas along the highway as a sound buffer the dwellings receive preheated air that is generally 6°C warmer than the external air. When the chimney effect is applied fresh air from the neighbourhood can be induced from the rear. Behind a noise-reduced façade one can live healthily along the highway!

3. Possible developments to the south and east of Drachten
- Building in the nuisance zone along the motorway.
- Tackle problems at source.
- Roads and water as carriers of urban and landscape developments.

An interesting field of tension develops between spatial planning, juridical aspects and environmental management:
- Industrial noise and housing developments.
- Nuisance zones along busy roads.
- Nuisance zones on the border of dwelling and agriculture.
- Infiltration and retention of rainwater on industrial sites.

The 'Aanzet stadsrand Drachten' and 'Van blokkades naar potenties' reports think and act in accordance with the Rio conference 'Our Common Future'.

> Environmental metabolism is one of the few known distant future factors.
> No wealthy country will escape the changes in quantity of consumption.
> It sounds as a paradox, but taking into account the known an unknown future will give great stability to urban developments. People understand why a certain autarky and consideration in scale levels is unavoidable to maintain our living environment.

07.04   Zonneterp, the Greenhouse Village

07.04.01   The Energy-Producing Greenhouse

With Noor van Andel and Gatze Lettinga

Dutch glasshouse horticulture as a source of energy (without high consumption of natural gas) is becoming a reality. The Energy-Producing Greenhouse concept is attributable to high-quality and innovative Dutch glasshouse horticulture in the moderate West European climate and thick sand/clay-layers in the Rhine delta as a substrate for seasonal heat storage. In March 2006 four municipalities and their local market gardeners' organisations planned to collaborate and realise the Energy-Producing Greenhouse.

The trick of the trade is a fine-wire heat exchanger that can heat and cool air efficiently. Technical innovation has led to a fundamentally new heat exchanger, much better climate control and a better use of low temperatures. The basic idea and French patent dates from 1927. The concept had never been used however. Even laboratory experiments by Akzo Nobel in Arnhem failed to find an application for this fine-meshed-wire heat exchanger (proved to be approximately 22 times more effective than plate heat exchangers). When this renowned laboratory was dissolved, the unused patent passed into the hands of Dr. Noor van Andel (former corporate research director), who in 2001 received an honorary doctorate from the University of Amsterdam for his subsequent efforts.

For many years nobody had been interested in the device or its application. In their workshop, father and son team, Eur van Andel continued to develop low-temperature air-heating by means of this technology. Finally, The Innovation Network of the Ministry of Agriculture and Environment discovered the existence of this innovation and the realisation of the energy-producing greenhouse was accelerated.

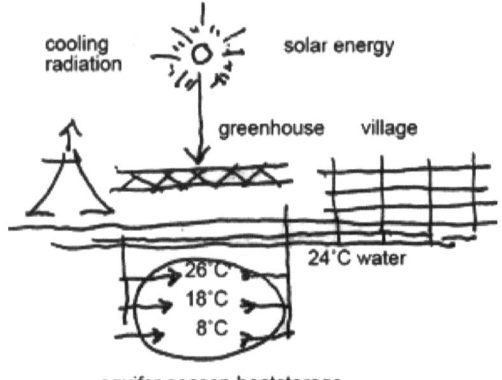

Fig. 07.17:   The Energy-Producing Greenhouse plan as a concept for climate control and annual heat balance.

In 2002 three ministers decided to make the experimental phase financially possible. The largest cost items were the new fine-wire heat exchangers. After serious delays (due to professional deliberation on the payment of development money) new weaving techniques and looms were developed and are presently fully-operational. It has been calculated that the energy-producing greenhouse has a heat excess of 24°C, a very low temperature. This temperature is too low to be able to heat adjacent greenhouses with traditional heating installations.

Newly built blocks of minimum energy houses would be more suitable to use a heat surplus. In this stage, Jón Kristinsson was approached to help think about a concept for minimum energy houses in a Greenhouse Village. The energy department of Rabo Vastgoed rural bank became involved in the project due to their interest in the redevelopment of glasshouse horticulture areas and also in the financing of house development. As luck would have it Professor Dr. Gatze Lettinga of the University of Wageningen and his staff members, among whom Adriaan Mels (Lettinga Associates Foundation: LeAF) were involved in the Energy-Producing Greenhouses. As a result the project acquired a new ambitious dimension by producing all materials by means of closed cycles beside raising the possibilities of heating control. The standard of attainment was raised and the Energy-Producing Greenhouse project (Fig. 07.18) changed its name to the Greenhouse Village ('Zonneterp' in Dutch).

07.04.02 Closed cycles

The symbiotic existence of greenhouses and village houses
The former symbiosis between the town and the surrounding countryside can be partly regained, although it is no longer the greengrocer who, with a horse-drawn cart, delivers the seasonal vegetables, and the waste-food collector who collects kitchen waste for his pigs. There is a balance between the sunlight radiation towards the earth during the day and the permanent radiation from the earth towards a clear sky. When the greenhouse is double-glazed the radiation from the sun is 7 times the radiation emitted from the earth.

The greenhouse must release excess heat. The surrounding houses need to be heated. The aquifer under the greenhouse has minimum dimensions, otherwise the marginal loss will be too great. There is a reasonable energy balance between 2 ha greenhouse (150 x 150 m) and 7 to 8 ha residential area with 200 houses. This appears a simple and complete story. Nevertheless, ask any heating installer to heat your house with water of 24°C and he will seriously scratch his head.

Home radiators are typically set at 90° and 70°C discharge temperature. Heating houses with water of 23 to 24°C is therefore a new challenge. First of all there are the possible material cycles, which form the most important symbiosis. It is wishful thinking to expect that soon all metropolitan citizens will start thinking in cycles, but one day it will be inevitable that they do.

If we do not achieve a sustainable society humanity will be disappear in a hundred years' time. The basic type of heating and cooling from this aquifer in the Minimum Energy Houses is radiation heating supplemented with fine-wire air heating. The challenge of supplying the required ventilation in super-insulated draught-proof houses is solved by using "Breathing Windows", a product that is also based on fine-wire heat exchange technology.

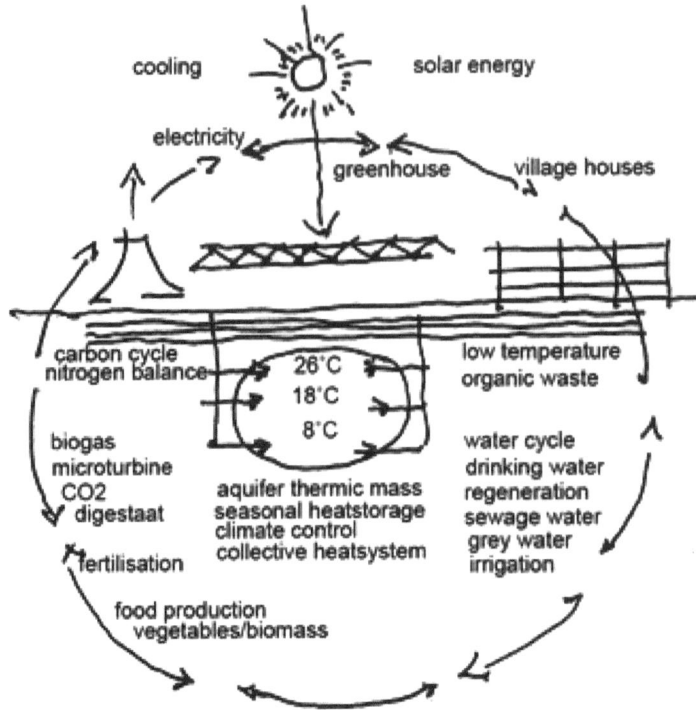

Fig. 07.18: Concept of a sustainable greenhouse and dwellings with their closed cycles and CO_2 balance, based on the Dutch 'Zonneterp' Greenhouse Village.

The Greenhouse Village
The realisation of the Greenhouse village, an ecological residential area as a further development of the Energy-producing greenhouse, is a new demonstration project for closed material cycles (Fig. 17.19). Beside the climate controlled heating and cooling such as the energy-producing greenhouse, the Greenhouse village concept has four more closed material cycles: Food production, drinking water purification, irrigation water regeneration and organic waste management for biogas production.

Climate control
The energy exchange between the sun and the earth and between the planet earth and the universe, finds a balance in our climate via the diurnal cycle and the seasons. To determine the order of magnitude of this energy balance we assume that the solar radiation during daytime and the radiation from the earth during 24 hours are almost the same. If not we will have a problem of very fast global warming.

The heating of the greenhouse is not our problem. The design works with a double polycarbonate (zig-zag) glazing developed by General Electric Bergen op Zoom, with a heat transfer of 3.5 W/m^2K. When we want to heat the greenhouse in winter to 19°C, and it is freezing -11°C outside, we have a temperature difference of 30°C, and should heat with 30 x 3.5 = 105 W/m^2. For cooling purposes, we should cool away 600 W/m^2 however when the sun shines maximally in June and it is hot outside. Therefore we install minimally 55 W/m^2K heat exchangers to cool this heat away with ground water from 10 rising to 26°C. When heating with 105 W/m², we need water of 105 / 55 = 2 degrees higher in temperature than the 19°C we want to reach in heating: 21°C. But we produce water of 26°C when cooling, store it under-ground, and expect a half year later still a temperature of 23°C. It really comes down to a few degrees, but we are sure that it will work. The aquifer takes 2 years however to reach this performance, so in the first year we have to use a supplement of natural gas for heating. (In existing non-airtight greenhouses a heat-pump is a good solution).

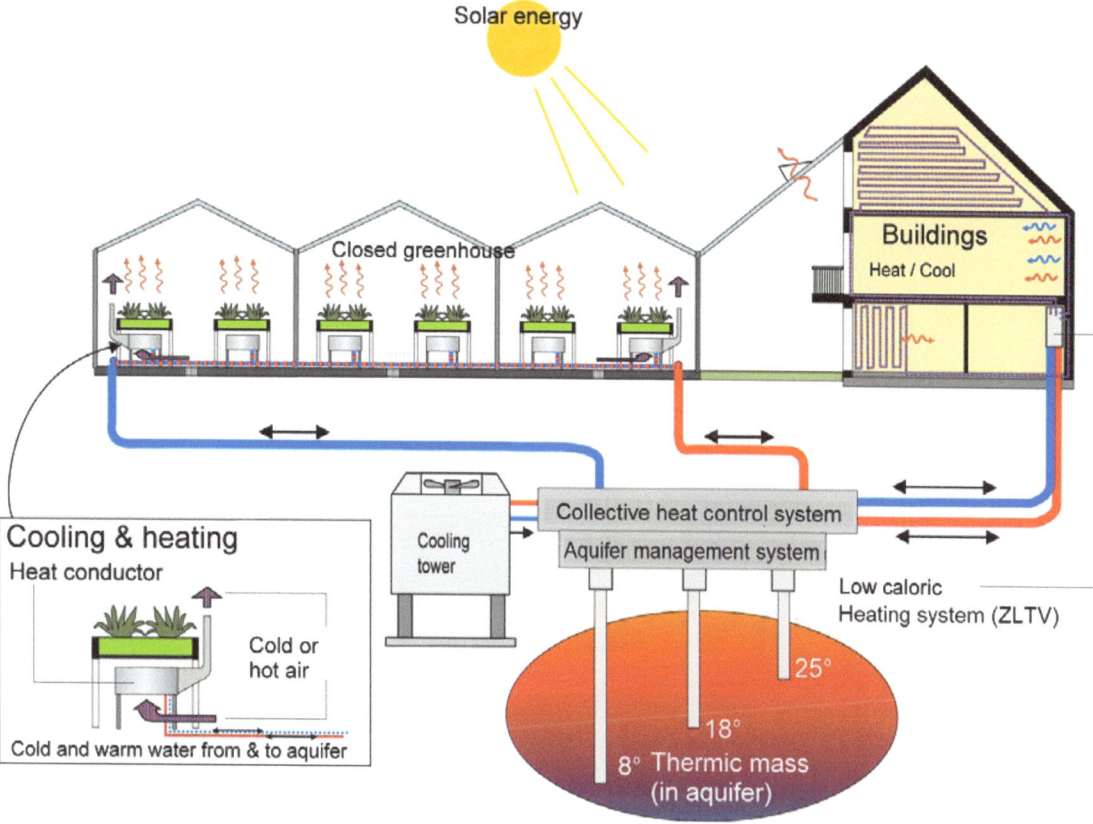

Fig. 07.19:   Heating system, CO_2-neutral living.

At a peak load of 1500 W/m² on a summer day and clear sky radiation cooling of 300 W/m2 during a winter night, the thermal mass of the seasonal storage has to solve the problem of the difference between the maximum greenhouse temperature of 28°C and the minimum one of 15°C. Wind and precipitation we leave aside. However, if the short-waved sunlight falls through a greenhouse roof and touches a plant or the floor, the wavelength changes into the IR-radiation which will be radiated again in some measure via the glass. Throughout the year 7 times more solar heat will enter the greenhouse than the greenhouse with double-glazing will give off as transmission loss.

The essential difference between present greenhouses and the energy-producing greenhouse is that the latter is closed, will not be cooled by opening roof windows and furthermore it can be built low-rise compared to modern glasshouses. The excess heat at 25°C is absorbed by 50

W/m²K fine-wire heat exchangers on the greenhouse floor and carried off to a heat and cold aquifer storage at 30 m depth. These 2 m long heat exchangers, which have the structure of an open car battery, have tangential blowers for the forced air circulation. In anticipation of the description of the houses in the Greenhouse Village we can already reveal that there are two types of fine-wire heat exchangers: a. the woven water/air heat exchanger and b. the winding air/air heat exchanger. The cooling of the greenhouse from the bottom of the aquifer is equal to its solar heating. The cold 'battery' in the ground of approximately 8°C is charged in wintertime. There is also a cooling tower on at night. The first generation of the greenhouse as a source of energy, such as in Huissen in the Netherlands, satisfies these conditions. The glasshouse horticulture can become CO_2 neutral. Whereas the Energy-Producing Greenhouse can function independently by means of a thermostatically controlled annual programme, the Greenhouse Village is interactive through the participation of the occupants, who also benefit economically (Fig. 07.20).

Organic waste
Technically and socially the organic cycle near to home is hard to imagine. We were born and bred in a society with water closets and GFT containers which are collected and emptied. Vacuum toilets, crushed kitchen garbage, separated urine and vegetable waste processing in a biogas fermenter is an inevitable ecological process. By processing in a central fermenter all the organic waste matter from the greenhouses and the private houses, including grey and black waste water (faeces + urine), biogas can be gained, which can operate a diesel engine for the production of electricity for the private houses.

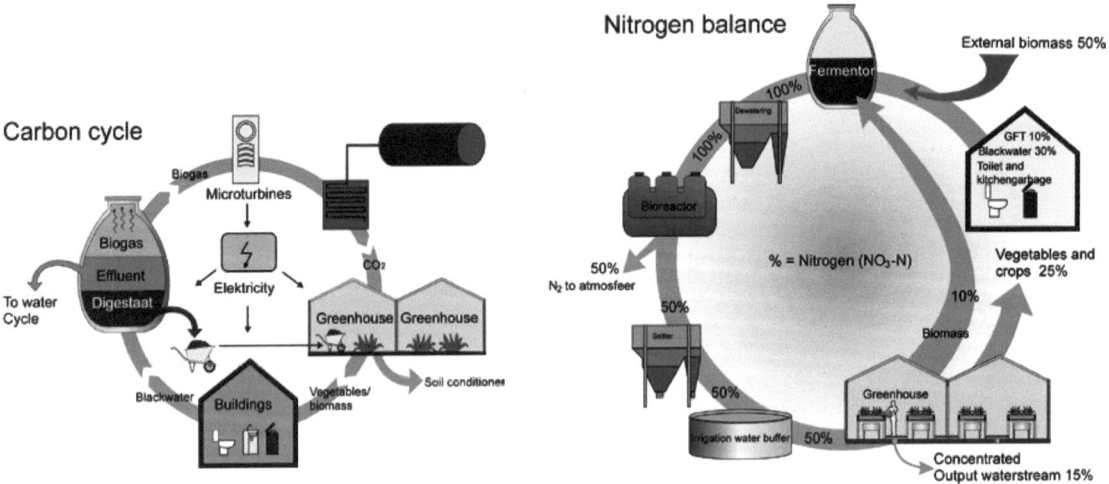

Fig. 07.20:   The carbon cycle (left) and nitrogen balance (right).

The waste matter is manure that, among other things, can be used as a substrate in the greenhouses as well as the CO_2 that the plants need in daytime in a concentration of 1000 ppm (Fig. 07.21). Raising CO_2 from 500 to 1000 ppm yields roughly a 20% larger crop. Due to the fact that the greenhouse is closed there are fewer troublesome insects and the fact that 85% relative humidity is maintained.

Biogas exists of approximately 2/3 methane (CH_4), 1/3 CO_2, some H_2 and inert N_2 and, the weak link, a little sulphurated hydrogen H_2S. The village of 200 households is too small, 50% more biomass is required. Garbage from a hotel kitchen would be very welcome.

Three water systems
Inside the closed greenhouse, which has also to be cooled to keep the temperature below 28°C, a special inside climate arises, even apart from the CO_2 content and the condensation produced by drinking water. This condensed water lacks the flavour of minerals and is not permitted in the Netherlands as drinking water (fig. 07.22).

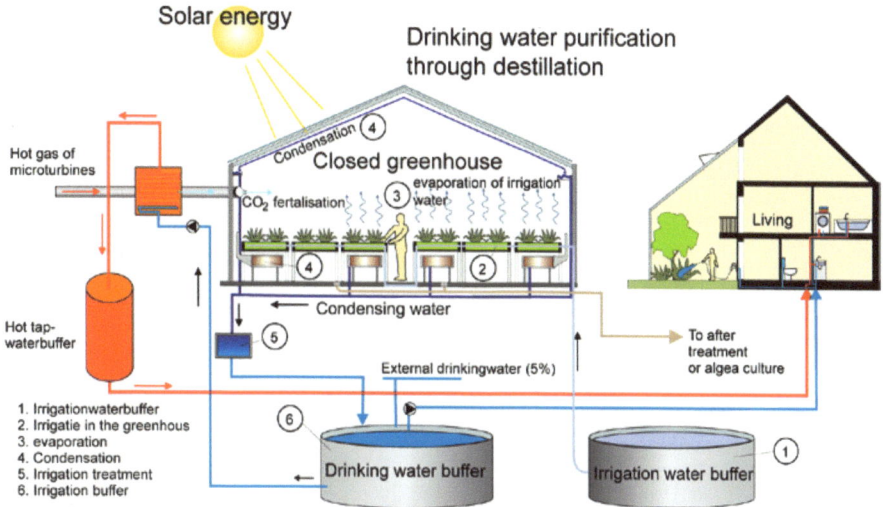

Fig. 07.21: Three water systems: condensed (drinking) water, grey waste water and rainwater used for irrigation.

Irrigation
If the grey waste water from the private houses can be kept apart, irrigation water can be gained from it. Very little irrigation water is needed in a closed greenhouse that is not ventilated. Closed ecosystems within the built environment are professional installations. They are entirely dependent on the willingness of the occupants and their guests not to disturb the short closed cycles.

Food production
The Greenhouse is commercially productive. Who should be the owner has not yet been settled. Also unclear is the relationship between work and joint use by the occupants of the area around the greenhouse. Areas which could be used for facilities such as a school, local coffee house and pub or swimming-pool. The greenhouse itself must be able to create an added value for the participating occupants, as a supplier of food, employment, income guarantee and low recurring household expenses. The greenhouse can also have an educational value showing how the bio-industry can be sustainable. The technical installation space needed for a greenhouse of 2 ha is about 10% - (15 x 15 m) of the greenhouse surface. The cooling tower is a new visible element that gives some shade. The cooling tower forms the skyline profile of a greenhouse village.

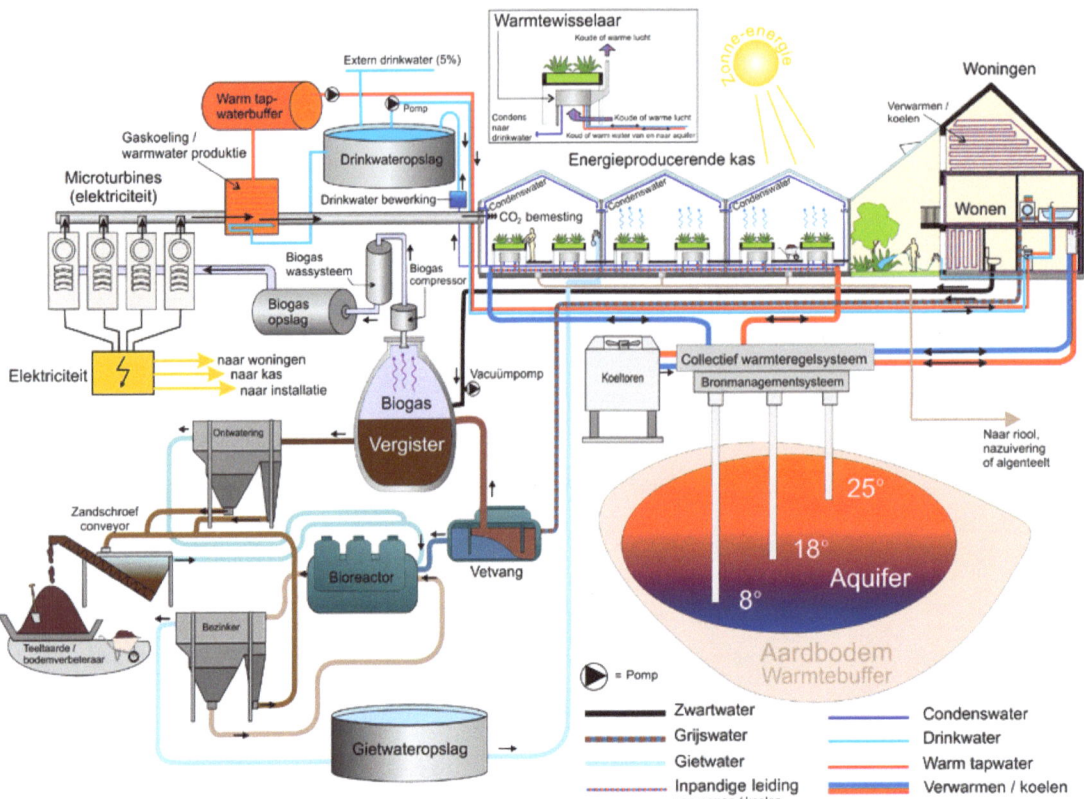

Fig. 07.22:   Complete greenhouse installation (terms in Dutch)

The village houses

The very-low-temperature energy houses are by far the most expensive parts of the Greenhouse Village. The investment for 200 houses is almost 10 times the cost of the greenhouses with their fine-wire heat control and the seasonal aquifer storage. The list of requirements for the new village contains regulations for various measurements and building costs of cheap houses for young couples, one-family houses, houses for senior citizens and eventually houses suitable for every age.

Division of land charges from hereditary tenure to property offers many possibilities. The very low water temperature from the aquifer is a challenge. Some technical innovations are needed in these minimum energy houses. This extremely low temperature heating is floor/wall radiation heating of 20 to 22°C, which may be too low for bathrooms as well as elderly occupants. As there is little experience with regard to very low temperature heating, air heating of 23 to 24°C is locally added. Therefore, each house needs 3 to 6 Breathing Windows, depending on the number of rooms.

07.04.03 The Solar Village

Based on the principles described above, the Solar Village is a Greenhouse Village located in the horticulture area of Westland in the Netherlands.

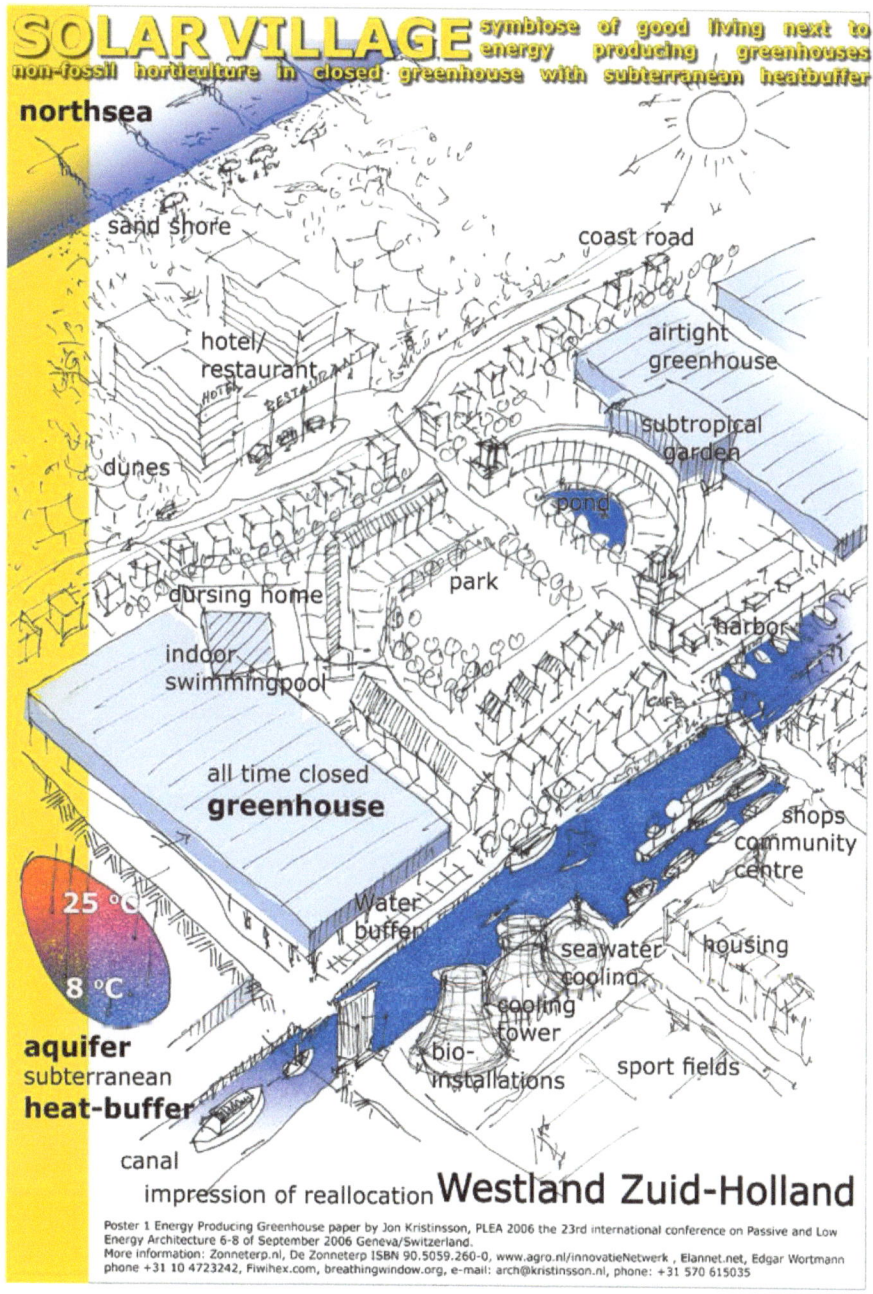

Fig. 07.23:   An impression of the Solar Village reallocation in the Dutch Westland.

The only disadvantage to living in a Greenhouse Village is that it is unknown as a new way of living (Fig. 07.24). The advantages are evident: No dormitory towns as a living environment, no commuter traffic, mainly biological food and small-scale living around village greens. The recent know-how to gain low-temperature solar heat and store it as seasonal heat has never before been possible on a large scale. Solidarity is certainly required, but without joint responsibility for a sustainable living environment within an urban area, our western culture will crumble away very soon.

Fig. 08.24:   Senior greenhouse apartments at Hengelo, the Netherlands (Kristinsson Architectural Engineers).

The fine-wire heat exchangers may be small, but can have great world-wide energy-saving consequences, both for heating/cooling and for ventilation devices in all types of buildings. At the time of writing this book the Shenzhen botanic gardens, China, are seriously interested in the Energy-Producing Greenhouse.

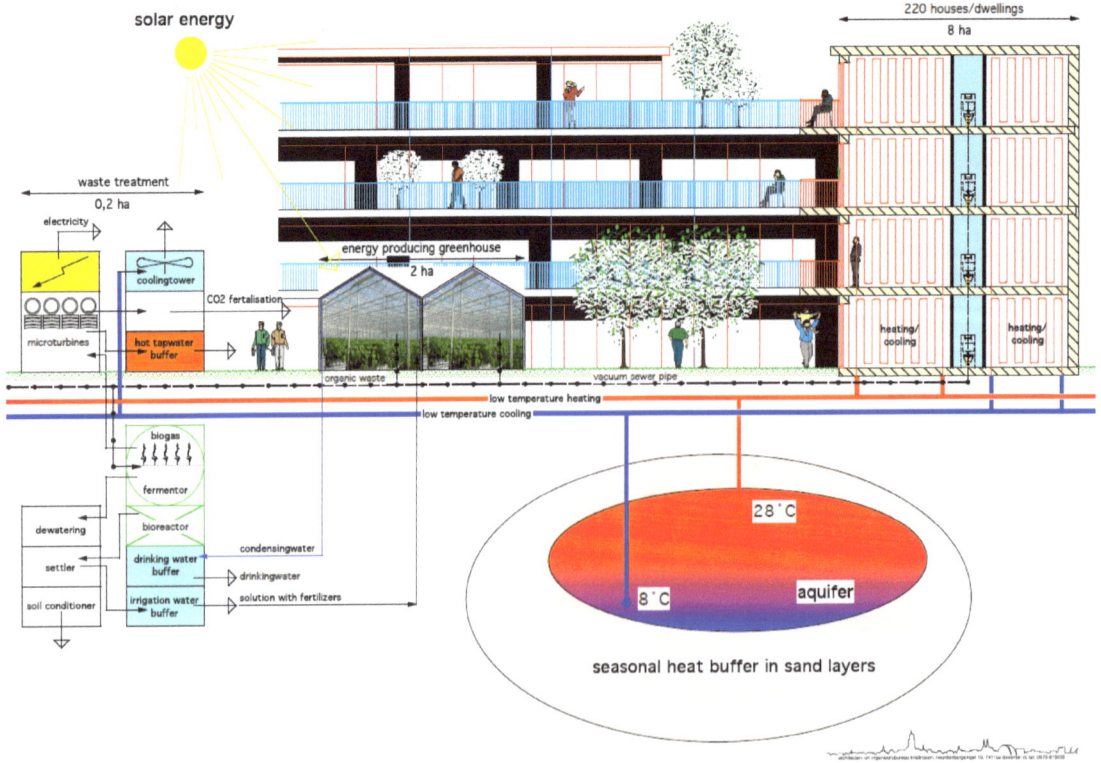

Fig. 07.25:   Technical scheme of a medium-sized Greenhouse Village.

08
HOLISTIC ARCHITECTURE

08.01 Autarchic town hall, Lelystad (1976)

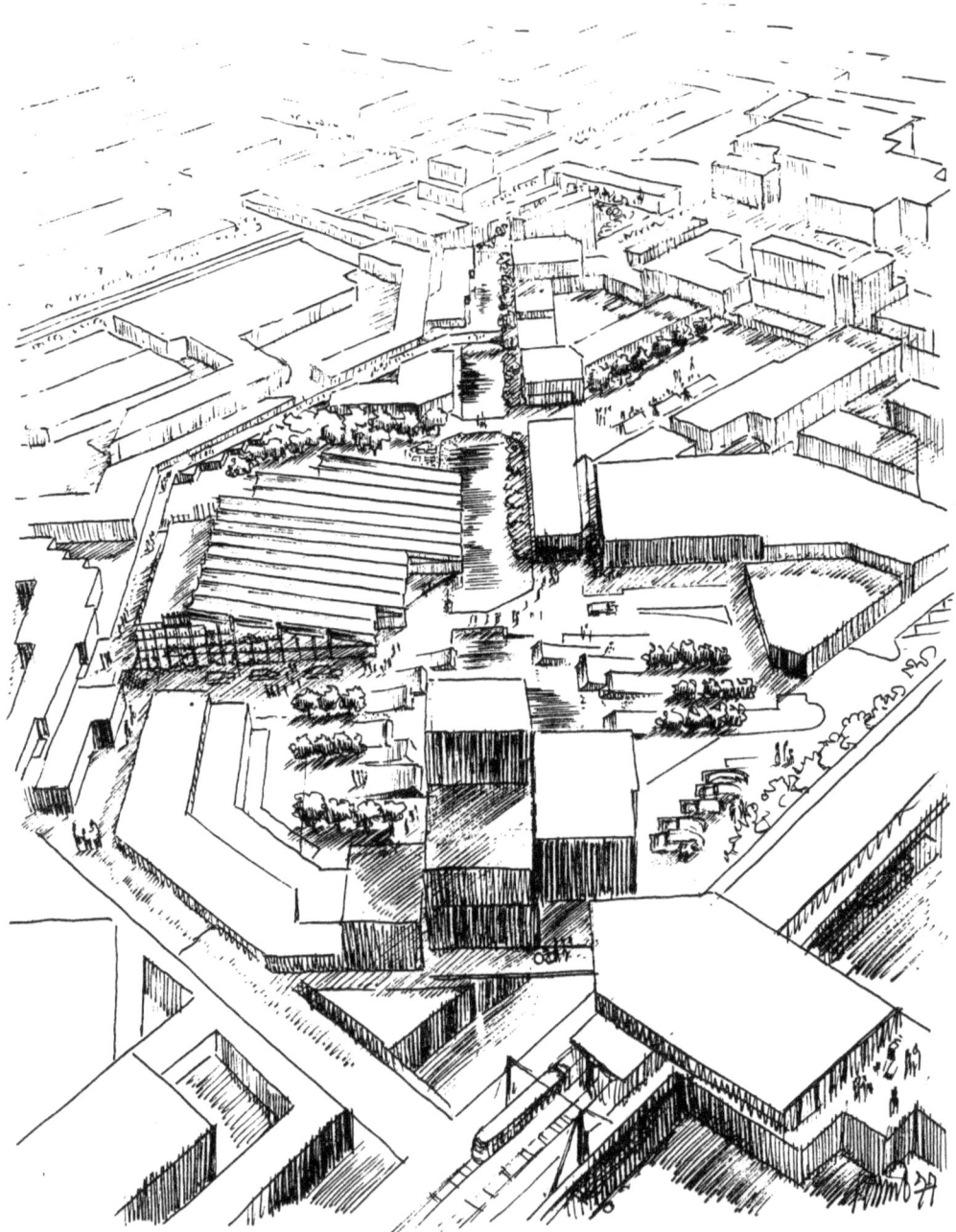

Fig. 08.01: Ariel view of the Lelystad town hall.

The first example of an integrated design consists of a design competition for the town hall of Lelystad. Our office were invited to design a multifunctional office space of 82,000 m^3. Here we tried to find a new synthesis between urbanism, architecture and human-oriented techniques by analysing and summarising the environment, building physics, business organisation and economics. This integrally designed town hall, which has not been built, would have been the first building in the Netherlands that could function completely on solar energy, in summer and winter, without additional heating.

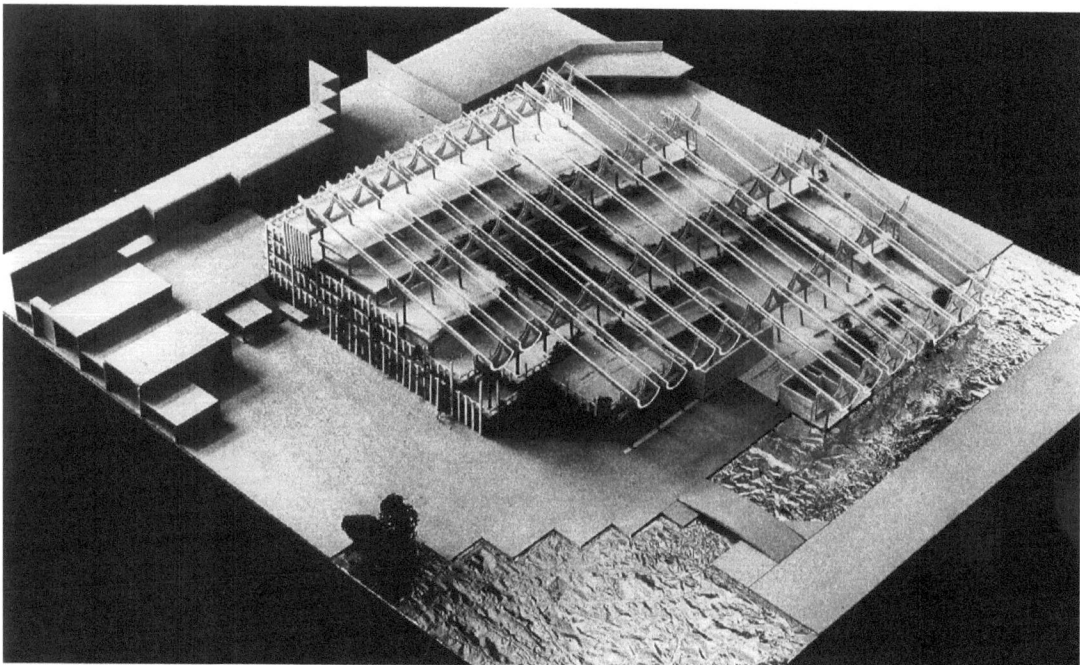

Fig. 08.02:   Sketch model of the first autarchic building in the Netherlands.

Starting-points were:
- The integration of form and function can lead to a very high level of self-sufficiency.
- A good indoor climate with few installations and a minimal consumption of fossil fuel can be achieved with the knowledge of building physics.
- A plain construction enables adjustments by the user and flexible organisation.

08.01.01 Background philosophy

Openness in politics supports a healthy democracy (without extremes) and stimulates the re-evaluation of political activities through more involvement and insight by the common civilian. Points of attention were:
1   The possibility to participate in politics for everyone.
2   The possibility to exchange and discuss ideas in a relaxing atmosphere with the mayor, aldermen, councillors and other politicians.
3   The possibility to have a chat and a coffee or drink with other civilians, governors and directors.

This was achieved within the design by:
a   Making the city hall accessible to the public in evenings, while allowing the departments to remain closed after working hours (by way of sliding doors).
b   Aligning the pavement outside with inside (no doorsteps) and automatically opening doors
c   Leaving the restaurant/bar open (also in the evening), guaranteeing supervision of the building.
d   Creating a good ambiance: a pool with many plants and footbridges with seats (terrace islands) in the water, reflecting lights as an extension of the restaurant instead of a council cellar.
e   Locating the faction chambers adjacent to the restaurant.
f   Illuminating the citizen hall and its surroundings - a festive sight due to its location along the canal and the reflection in the water.
g   Keeping the functional walking lines short and clear.

Fig. 08.03:   External perspective of the pool with the bar/restaurant

Fig. 08.04:   North-West elevation of the Lelystad town hall design.

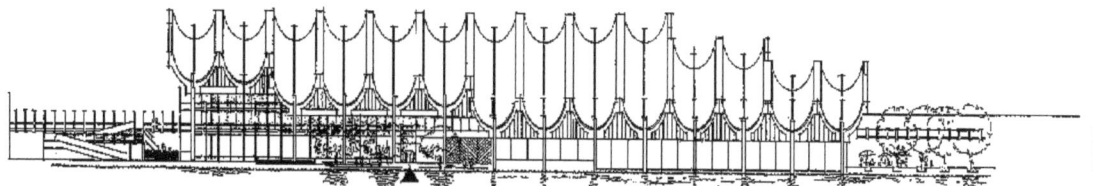

Fig. 08.05:   South-West elevation.

Environmentally sound

The environmentally sound credentials of the Lelystad town hall design were:
- Strips of daylight between the roof shells decreased the use of artificial light (the terraced building form reduced the use of artificial light by 60%).
- Benefitted from active and passive solar energy.
- Stainless steel mirrors were placed in the parabolic concrete roof shells; in the focal line of these parabolic shells were traditional plain solar water collectors.
- Solar-heated water was inter-seasonally stored in the clay soil under the building.
- The building contained balanced mechanical ventilation with recovery of heat and moisture.
- Four forms of sun shading were applied:
    - Vegetation growing on the wooden posts of the balcony (seasonally variable façade).
    - Balconies.
    - Hinging louvres.
    - Roof lights between the concrete shells.
- Pool with vegetation, fountain and planters with flowers along the up-going office-gardens evaporated naturally, moisturising the air during dry freezing weather.
- The balcony consoles contained round holes for small birds such as tits (insect eater).
- The citizen hall could be used as concert hall due to applying sound-absorbing material on the roof shells.
- The plan was based on a Dutch average of 1820 hours of sunshine a year, of which only 8% occur during the heating season. Thanks to the inter-seasonal storage all solar hours are utilised.

What was unique about the design process that successfully led to an autarchic, ecological and functional building derived by solar and wind energy was that none of these innovations were a prerequisite of the design brief.

Fig. 08.06: Example of a green façade that varies by the seasons (left), and an office room with a balcony, resembling a living room that can be changed into a residential building in the future; this was applied earlier in Kristinsson's design for the Twijnstra Gudde office building in Deventer (1979).

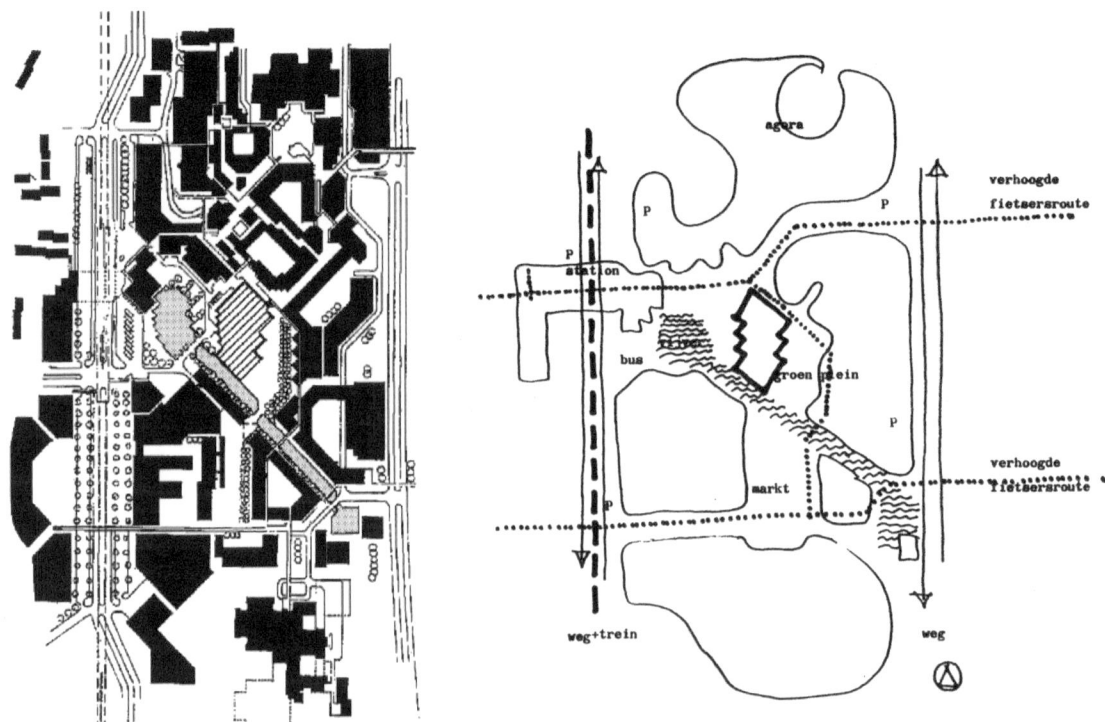

Fig. 08.07: New plan for Lelystad, with the diagonal urban canal (left) and sketch of connecting lines on site (right). The orthogonal structure of Lelystad becomes more spatial through the implementation of a diagonal.

Urban measures

The existing bicycle and walking routes were redirected along the eastside of the centre.

- The design brief required only one entrance, two at the most.
- If an entrance is not desired at a height there is no sense in directing the route along the building (during the day this will distract, in the evening and at night it is unsafe).
- Because of another experience value (in contrast to the northern centre) slow traffic was kept at street level:
    - Natural vegetation (trees, grass, shrubs, flowers).
    - Water.
    - Less wind.

Water was introduced in the plan:
- A monumental city pond as landmark of the centre of Lelystad;
- A diagonal canal to break the stringent orthogonal structure of the urban plan.
- Bridges and residential buildings along the water with arcades, as a contra-form to the roof shells of the city hall.
- Canal ending in a natural pond with reed and water plants at the north-east corner.

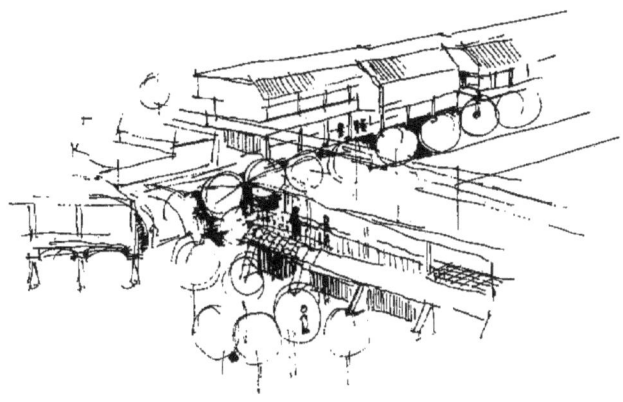

The square at the east could be seen as a green court surrounded by dwellings. The southern square was a marketplace surrounded with 'merchant' activities. The rail track was elevated and combined with a car route underneath, allowing an efficient use of space and reducing the impact/emphasis of high-speed traffic. The bus station with taxi stands was situated on the opposite side.

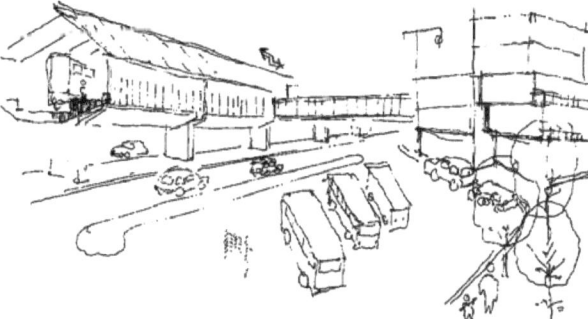

Fig. 08.08: Top to bottom: 1. canal houses opposite the city hall; 2. monumental pond opposite the station, and the diagonal city canal; 3. elevated train station, with the bus station at ground level in front .

08.01.02 Functional description of the building

The departments had internal connections through stairs in the office gardens. The office gardens were placed at the end of the floor slabs (under daylight strips in the roof). The office cells were situated on the outer side, north of the elevators and stairs. The organisation of the floor plan has been made as flexible as possible: rooms could be added or removed (open or closed). The planted area in the architecture department was situated in such a way that it provided the possibility to control the conditions of the vegetation.

08.01.03 The parabolic roof shells

The roof shells of the Lelystad town hall were not oriented in an optimum north-south direction as urban geometries of diagonals prevailed in this case, however the chosen south-west direction was sufficient as the generation of heat only differed slightly due to the roof inclination. The collectors were standard and cheap, had a high efficiency and were not sensitive to hail.

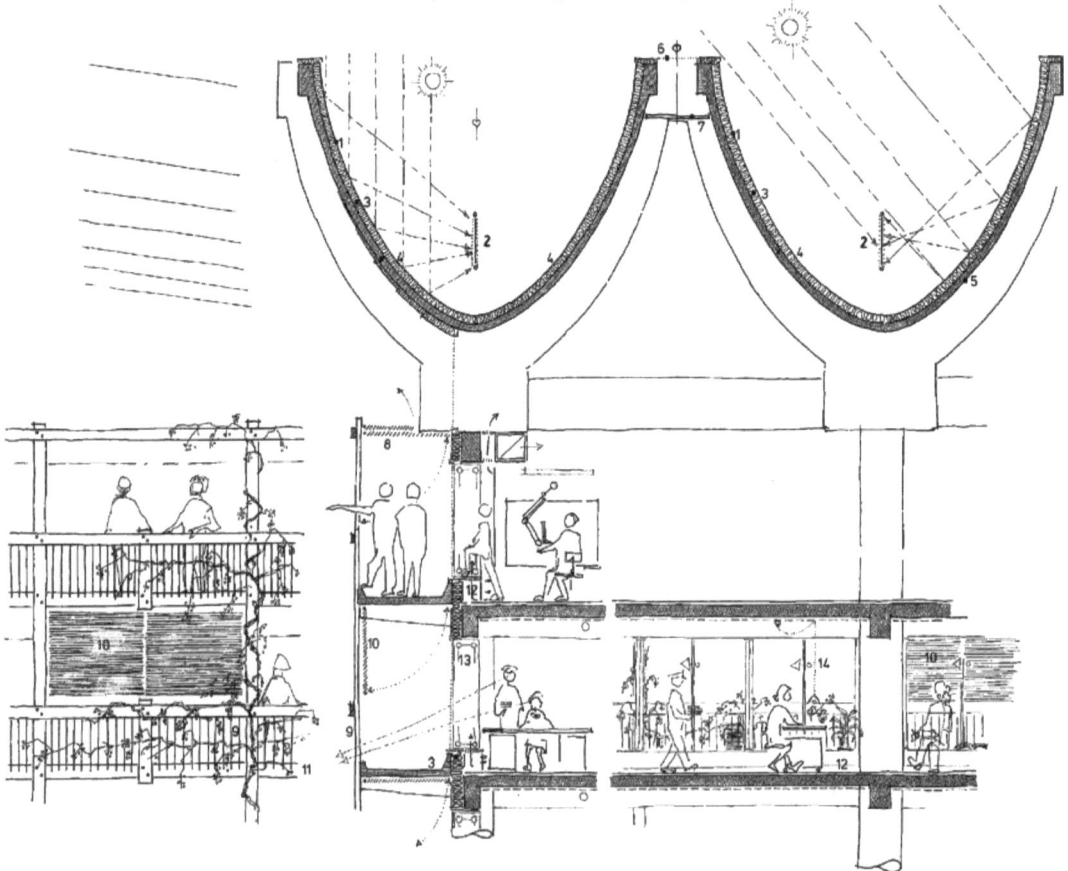

Fig. 08.09:   Front elevation and section of the Lelystad town hall.

The exterior form of the roof was made of kinked parabolic roof shells, with a width of 6 m and span length of 21 m. The facades at the south-western and north-eastern elevations revealed the size of the building by the idea of pitched roofs (with the scale and repetition akin to Amsterdam's 17th century canals houses). The roof shells were coated with stainless steel on the outside. The solar radiation would be reflected towards a plate-collector filled with water. The heated water was directed through pipes next to the drainage system towards the soil where it would circulate in plastic tubes, heating up the clay. In winter, pumps would extract this heat from the clay. This served the floor heating and the additional heating by convectors beneath the windows.

Through acoustic plaster on the inside of the roof shells it was possible to use the citizen hall in a multifunctional way such as a music auditorium for example. Other sound-absorbing materials were: wood against the flat parts of the ceiling and walls with in-between sound-absorbing material, front side of the balconies with plant troughs padded with sound-absorbing material, as well as fixed soft flooring and plants in the office gardens. In the daytime, noise level and the ability to have uninterrupted conversation were the most important aspects for the office landscape. Roof lights were located in-between the roof shells, the properties of which allowed them to change state in direct sunlight, preventing sunspots being cast on desks and drawing boards (this was still before the computer era).

The spaces between the façade columns (repetition of 7.20 m) are divided in six parts, onto which partition walls can be attached. In this area, 2 x 2 sliding doors and 2 x fixed glazing could be installed. These were combined with six insulated shutters on the outside, which had to be closed after working hours to keep the warmth inside. The sliding doors with double glazing all provided access to the balconies along the east, north and west side. A wooden grill covering the convectors under the sliding doors could function as a step to the balcony, a seat and partially as extra desk space. All desks were placed perpendicular to the facade to catch maximum daylight, and they were all supplied with an individual lamp that is not automatically switched on in the mornings.

08.01.04 Interseasonal heat storage

Every situation is unique. As part of the great Zuiderzee 'southern sea' plan of hydraulic engineer Cornelis Lely, the town of Lelystad was founded in the dry-milled Flevo polders on a thick layer of clay from the bottom of the former sea. The horizontal groundwater flow is less than 2 m/year. This offers the possibility to realise long-term (interseasonal) storage of heat.

For the Lelystad town hall the interseasonal heat storage was designed as a horizontal one-pipe system in three layers in the wet clay. In a one-pipe system, in summer the heat is injected into the ground by the same system used in winter to extract the heat again. The ground area equals 40 m x 40 m = 1600 m^2.

In the West of the Netherlands, along the North Sea coast, the soil retains salt water on various depths. Under Lelystad salt water seepage is at a depth of 22 meters. To avoid the leakage of this water to the seasonal heat storage, a large margin was maintained: 13.5 km of piping of ø 75 mm was 'pushed' into the ground by bulldozers to a depth of -1.5, -2.5 and -3.5 meters under the surface. Because of the heat stratification discussed above only the top and the sides of the heat storage needed thermal insulation. The heat demanded annually from the storage was approximately 760,000 kWh. This was established by a storage efficiency of around 50 to 60%. Passive solar radiation through windows and roof lights (calculated during the heating season) was around 450,000 kWh/year. Heat transmission of the building came down to 1400 kW.

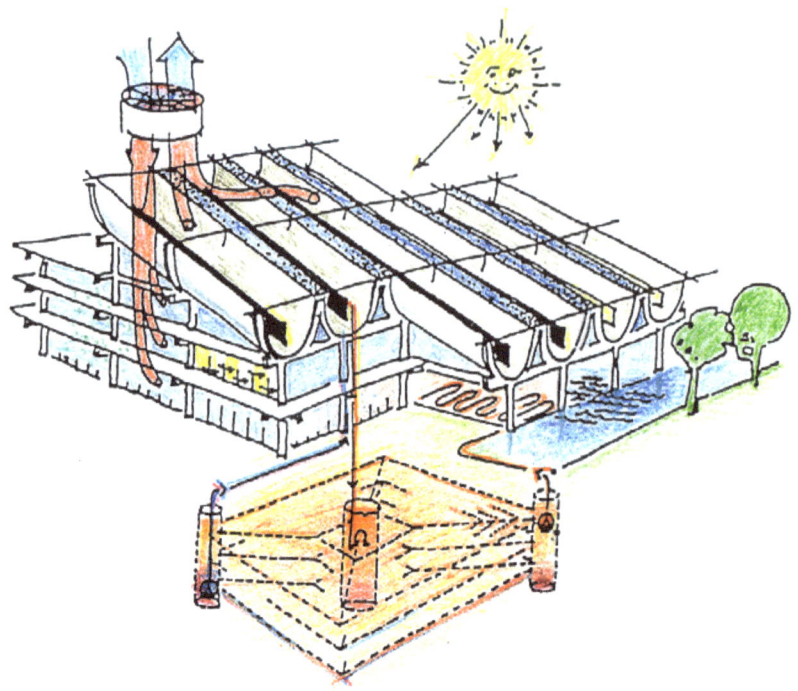

Fig. 08.10: The interseasonal heat storage of the Lelystad town hall, isometric indicating principles of integral design. Total primary energy saving and heat recovery is more than 85%. The system chosen was based on selection in stratification of the water and soil temperature with isolation only at the upper part.

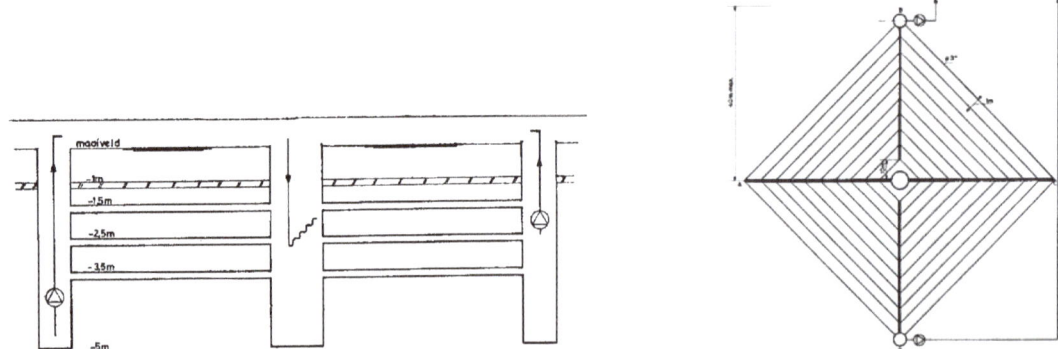

Fig. 08.11: Piping scheme of the inter-seasonal heat storage (left, analogue to the electrical resistance model), charging occurs from the central shaft – and section of the one-pipe system in three layers (right), connected to three shafts, and the temperature composition by stratification.

At the time of the proposal the design for the town hall appeared to be an 'eye-opener' for specialists in the installation field, due to:
- The amount of energy saved.
- The share of the seasonal heat storage within the overall heat balance.
- The clear dimensions of the seasonal storage in the ground.
- The accuracy in the required quantity of m^2 of solar collectors.
- Novel possibilities in the application in the greenhouse agriculture.

For interseasonal heat storage it was important to connect the solar panels early in the process so the heat storage could be charged one summer before the building is in use. After a few years, when the storage would be completely charged, the surrounding buildings could also be connected.

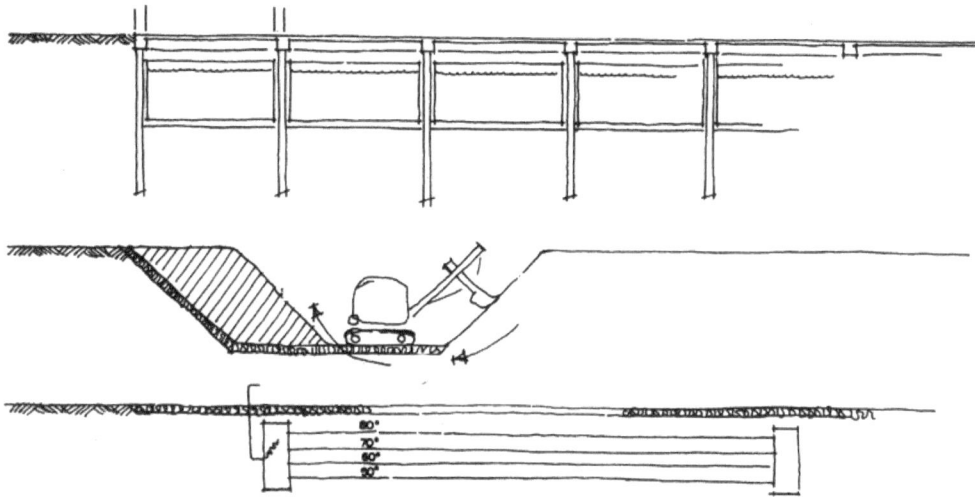

Fig. 08.12: Construction process of the interseasonal storage system: working with water cellars (above) and establishing an insulated ground layer on top (below).

The estimated efficiency of 50 to 60% turned out to be correct when, later, the neighbourhood of Beijum, in the city of Groningen, was built with this system, partly funded by the European Community. Here also a one-pipe system was used, yet with a vertical structure (a simpler technique in which water is pumped around and therefore doesn't rely or gain from stratification). For peak loads in summer a tank was added for a levelling of day and night. The solar collectors used are highly-efficient vacuum heat tubes.

08.01.05 Daylight, roof lights, sunshading and insulating shutters

Over the full length of the parabolic roof of the Lelystad town hall design, glass strips were placed between the roof shells. The high daylight that enters the building with terraced office storeys provided a high light output.

The glass between the roof shells had special characteristics and components. It was layered tempered glass with colloidal foil (non-crystalline) in-between. When the temperature of these glass strips rises above 30°C, the transparent foil turns milky white and starts reflecting light, thereby reducing a surplus of radiation and corresponding heat entering the building. This way of automatic filtering of sunlight diminishes the incoming sunlight by approximately 50%. The shortwave radiation remains quite constant for both a sunny and a cloudy sky.

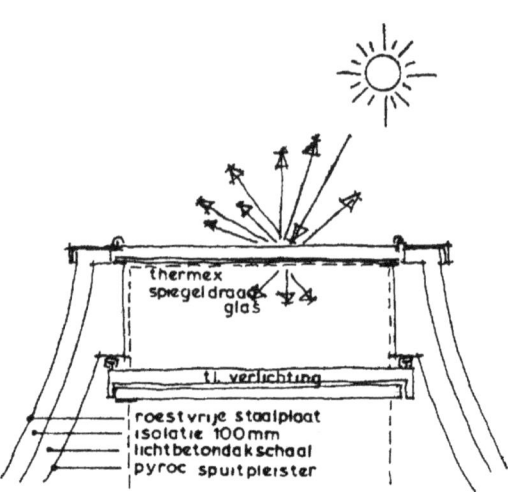

Under the balconies (eaves) sunscreens were integrated and attached with hinges on the outside, so when the sunscreens were pulled down the view was preserved. When the screens were in a folded state against the bottom of the balconies they absorbed sound. In this way the traffic noise was reduced even when the sliding doors were open.
All windows in the facade had insulated shutters, which improved the limited heat resistance of the windows after working hours, so the heat loss was kept to a minimum in this period. During the heating season this comes down to 164 hours – 60 hours = 104 hours a week, so we could say we achieved triple heat insulation two-thirds of the time.

Fig. 08.13:   The roof lights with 'Thermex' double-glazing with a colloidal foil in-between, which turns white in direct sunlight, making the light diffuse.

08.01.06 Artificial illumination

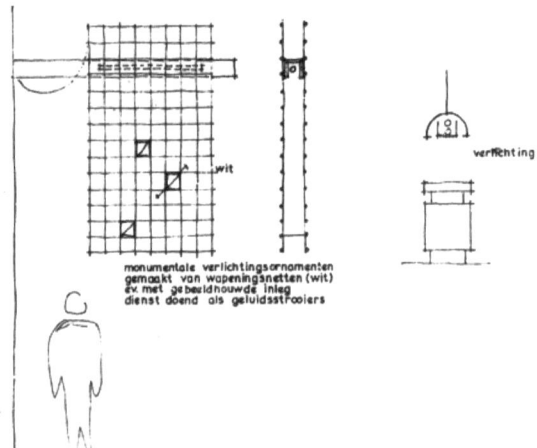

For the citizen hall little choice of monumental fluorescent lighting was available. A sketch of a self-designed armature shows a fluorescent tube that is screened by strips of milk white glass between two white metal grills. For decoration some glass crystals and gemstones were integrated in the grills. These lamps could be either hung from the wall or a lamppost. For desk lighting fluorescent lamps were chosen, these were hung in an open suspended acoustic ceiling. In this ceiling additional equipment was installed, such as telephone, intercom and additional sockets, so lights can be removed or added individually.

Fig. 08.14:   Monumental fluorescent lighting for the reception room of Lelystad.

08.01.07 Balanced ventilation with heat recovery

The Lelystad design used balanced ventilation with a thermal recovery wheel. The chosen amount of ventilated air was n = 0.6 at 50,000 m³/h. This way of heat recovery drastically reduces the tremendous energy loss through ventilation. Outside the heating season natural ventilation is possible, for all workplaces have a sliding door to the balcony.

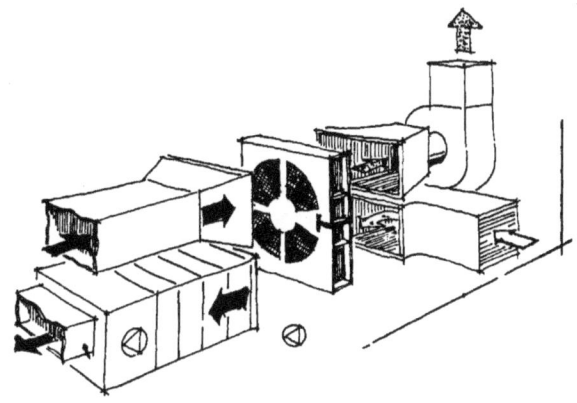

Fig. 08.15: Image of the balanced ventilation system with heat recovery by thermal wheel.

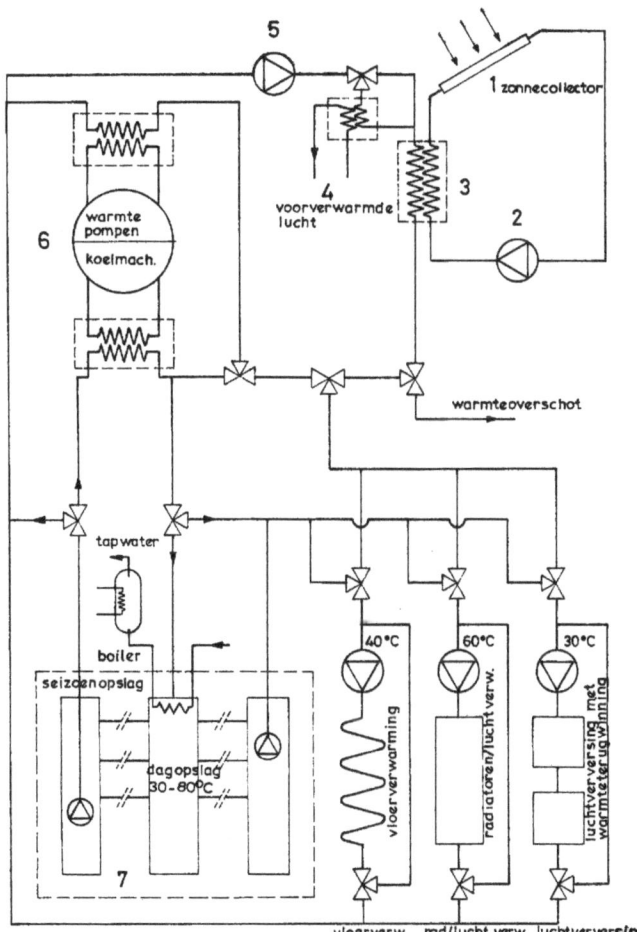

Instead of the conventional additional humidification of ventilated air in winter, we used natural evaporation of 350 m² of (low-tech) plant troughs on the railings of the (open) offices that ascend in terraced steps. The mist from small inner fountains provided sufficient humidity during winter periods.

Fig. 08.16: The installation scheme is simple to explain in its main aspects. Under 1, 2 and 3 are the solar collectors, water pumps and heat exchanger. Under 3, 5, 6 and 7, the interseasonal heat storage. Under 8 three different heating systems are indicated.

There were two types of users: people who work in the building and visitors. Politicians and administrators who have contact with both the local officials and visitors usually do not have a permanent place. Building a traditional bar in the basement of the town hall was technically difficult and financially unfeasible, and further excavation and draining led to unnecessary risks regarding the seepage of salt in the seasonal heat storage. Instead, the canal that according to the urban plan partly ran through the building at the entrance hall, was used for the council bar. It was situated on the water but upon floating pontoons.

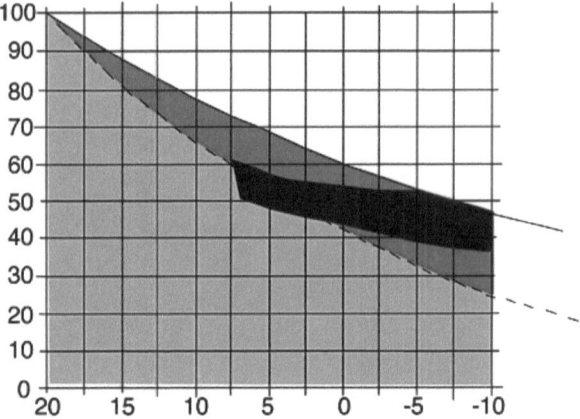

Fig. 08.17: Comfort lies between 40 and 70% relative humidity.

The water in the pond acted as an easily accessible thermal mass with a nearly constant temperature, preventing large fluctuations in temperature. Sunlight striking the south-west façade was filtered by deciduous trees.

08.01.08 Wind energy

As a grand statement it was suggested to mount turbines on top of the parabolic roof shells in order to generate electricity. The plan was eventually not incorporated in the design due to:
- The fact that fast rotating blades were not desirable in the inner-city for fear of incident.
- Noise nuisance both inside and outside the building.
- The fixed attachment of the rotors would decrease the effect at differing wind directions.

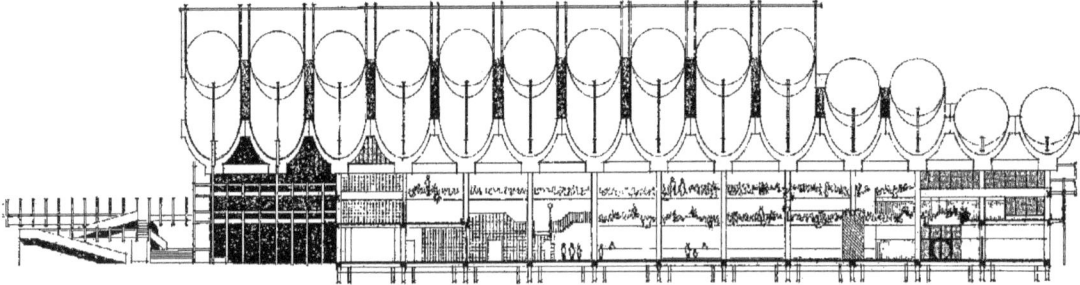

Fig. 08.18: Rear side view with 'fixed' wind turbines.

Due to ascending floor planes and an inclined roof, the gain from solar energy was more than sufficient, reducing the need for wind turbines and their associated limitations in an urban context.

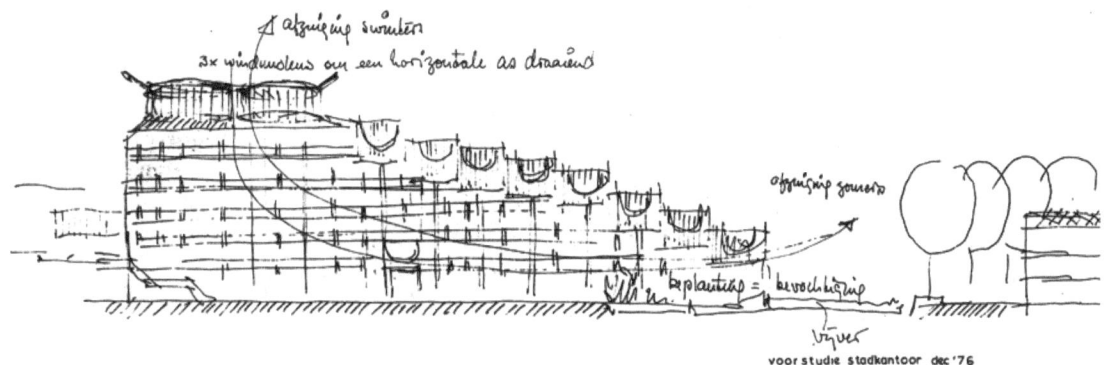

Fig. 08.19: Preliminary study of the city office Lelystad, December (1976). A building form more suitable for wind energy than the final design, which focussed on the production and storage of solar energy.

08.01.09 Conclusion

It is extremely sad that the Lelystad town management, in spite of much support from town council factions, did not have the resolve to support Kristinsson's integrated design over another competitor. In retrospect this seemingly futile decision held back drastic developments in sustainable building for many years. The Lelystad autarchic town hall would have been a valuable learning project, potentially feeding other large-scale sustainable projects then, now and in the future.

Fig. 08.20: Impression of the building skeleton during construction. Alas, this was never seen in practice[37].

It is testament to its 'sustainable' credentials and indeed 'longevity' that the Lelystad town hall design can now still be built, and be regarded as an innovative concept 34 years after its conception.

---

[37] Drawing by Jo Pessink

08.02 Intermediate projects 1976-2006

08.02.01 Salland Water Board office, Raalte (1980)

Fig. 08.21: South side of the Salland Water Board office (1998). The pond in front of the large meeting room does not freeze because of a permanent supply of seepage water. Vegetation separates the building from the public road.

We obtained the contract for a new office building for the Salland Water Board over numerous architects, because of our design for the town hall in Lelystad.

The building is located in the green belt on the western side of Raalte, along the Burgemeester Kerssemakersstraat, a major access road. It is accessible via a road to Drostenenk, where you mostly find small-scale buildings. The area at the front side, the south, has a park-like character. The building responds to this by shrub vegetation on the side of the access road. At the rear the building connects with small-scale buildings of the Drostenkamp by a pent roof on the main entrance and a bicycle shed next to the service entrance.

Fig. 08.22: Entrance to the Salland Water Board office.

The building is recognisable as a water board office because of the following features:
- The use of wood on the exterior.
- A smooth talus clinker brick for masonry.
- The protruding conference room of the general board with a roof that resembles a sluice-gate.
- The slanting masonry foundation of the conference room, partly standing in a natural pond in which it reflects, strengthening the effect of water.
- A jack-screw at the entrance.

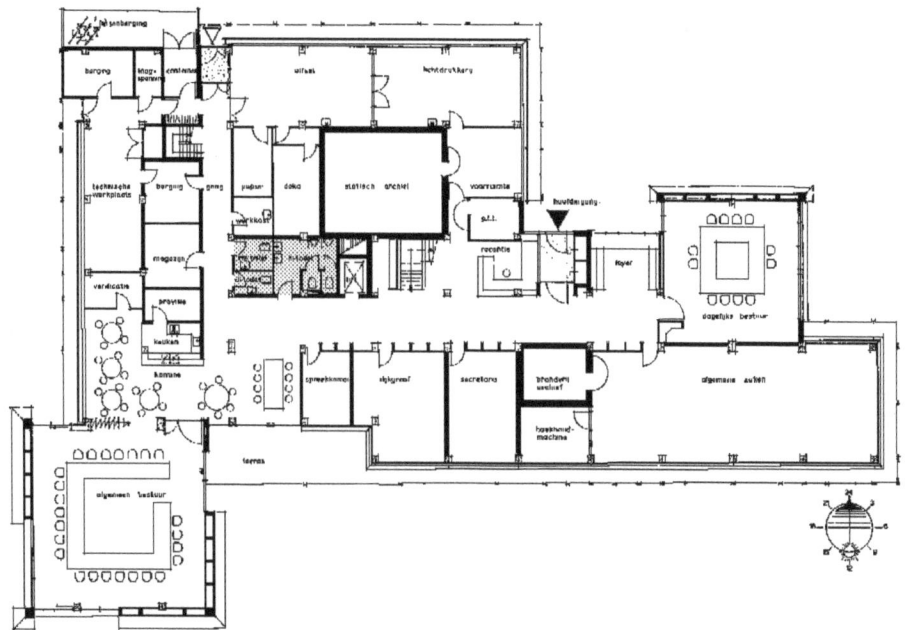

Fig. 08.23:   Ground floor plan with general board on the south side.

The facades were similar to those designed for Lelystad, although without insulating shutters (which turned out too expensive). The design also incorporated:
- Precast concrete balconies around the office wing.
- Seasonally variable façade by vegetation on the wooden balusters of the balconies and the wooden blinds.
- Convectors along the wall covered with wooden grills as extra desk space.
- Standard aluminium sliding doors (double-glazed), placed between the convector grill and the concrete beam at the ceiling.
- Desks placed perpendicular to the wall (again, this was before the computer era).
- Individual fluorescent lights (with on-off switches) at the desks.
- Acoustic panels attached to the ceiling covered with wooden strips.
- Glass strips above the door, providing general lighting to the offices through fluorescent lights in the corridor.
- Floor heating connected to the 'TOTEM' plant (to be discussed later).

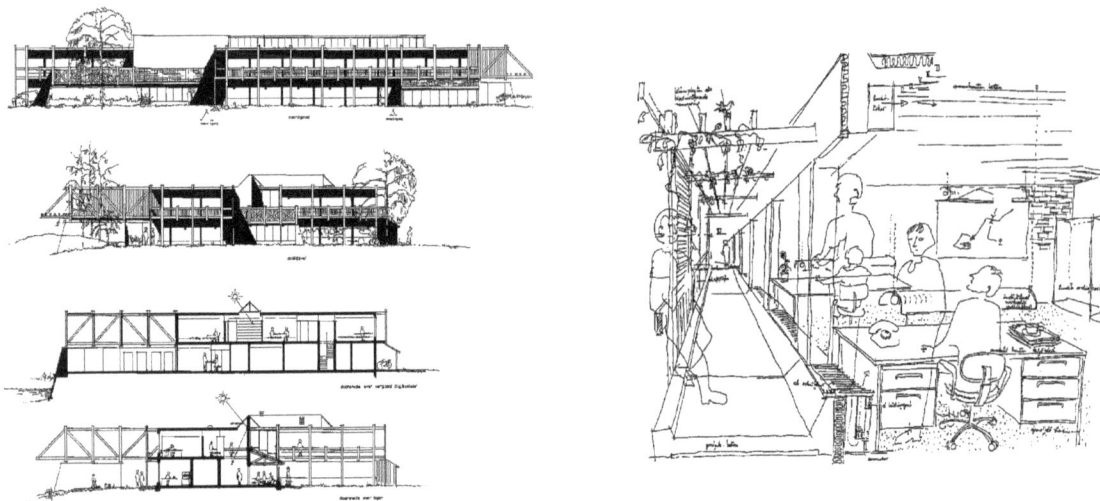

Fig. 08.24:   *Facades of the Salland Water Board office and open section including the balcony, façade and office.*

The interior is environmentally sound:
- Interior walls made of porous stone that has an acoustic damping effect.
- Tiles in the hallways and the cafeteria on the ground floor.
- Cotton carpet in the offices and the two meeting rooms.
- Cotton curtains.
- Timeless furniture, mostly oak.
- The furniture in the two conference rooms consisted of oak tables and leather chairs retrieved from the refurbishment of the provincial government hall.
- Wooden cabinets and shelves.

Fig. 08.25:   *The corridor, cafeteria and view into the large meeting room (left): sound-absorbing porous wall stones where only natural materials were applied; Indoor library connected to the office with high skylights (right).*

By placing the desks along the facade, the individual lights at the desk are mostly switched off during the day. The completion of a new office during an energy crisis motivated employees to use the building in an energy-efficient manner. The skylights on the first floor provide daylight and clarity to the corridors and the entrance. The meeting room of the general board is only heated with hot air when occupied (approximately 12 times per year). The acoustics of the large meeting room is controlled by noise reflectors made of glass, which hang above the tables and wherein the fluorescent lighting are integrated. In this way there is no need for amplified microphones.

Due to favourable calculations it was possible to add floor heating (low-caloric heating to a maximum of 55°C). By connecting it to a 'TOTEM' gas engine powered by a small cogeneration plant (a demonstration project by Novem that draws heat from the surface water of the seepage pond) the building can be heated almost whole year-round. Only during extremely cold days is convector heating, connected to the central gas boiler, switched on.

Fig. 08.26:   Plant room with TOTEM system

The average gas consumption is 4.3 m^3 gas/m^3 of building volume, compared to the normal 6 m^3 gas/m^3 (mean value for offices of the Dutch Government Buildings Agency, 1980). The average electricity consumption is 4.3 kWh/m^3, compared to mean value of 10 kWh/m^3, even though the ventilation required for the archives is extremely high.

In 1997 many water boards merged, including our client the Salland Water Board. Its office was then sold to Beafar, a pharmaceutical company. They have essentially left the building as it was. The building remains looking new.

Fig. 08.27:   Meeting room of the general board. Glass above the table serves as a transparent noise reflector. The room can be enlarged by opening the door to the cafeteria and corridor.

08.02.02 Economical office, The Hague (1994)

Fig. 08.28: Perspective of new design with 'water terrace', view from the Schouwburgstraat, on the corner of Casauriestraat.

Along with three other architects we were invited to participate in a workshop with an imagined/aspirational assignment to accommodate 'the office of the future' for the year 2044 in an existing building. Our input included thoughts on the city, the urban planning and architectural concept, the heating and ventilation, and an integrated water system.

The city
Living as well as working in the city is strongly encouraged. Segregation of functions is reduced. If we actually want children to live in the city the small-scaliness should be restored. Intelligent human-friendly vehicles in commuter traffic allow narrow roads and prevent pedestrians from being hit. There will be plenty of open water and greenery in the city; permeable brick pavement replacing asphalt.

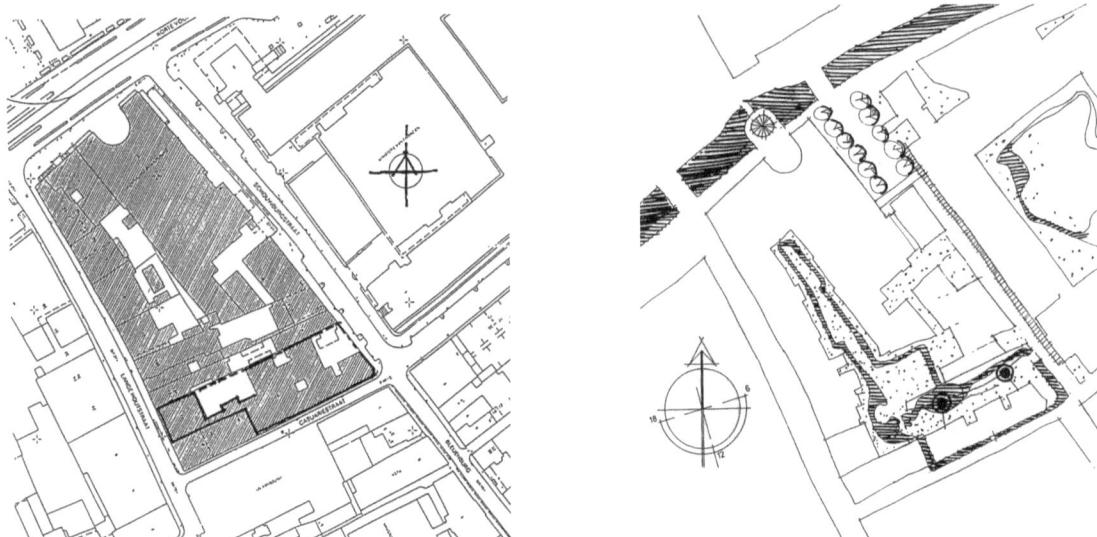

Fig. 08.29: Casuariestraat as existing (left) and new design with water circulation (right).

Urban Concept

Lange Houtstraat is the main access for visitors. All buildings on the former garden of the Lange Houtstraat 11 are demolished on site and reused elsewhere. The Casuariestraat alters in profile because of the vegetated pond along the south side. The water flows nearly at the height of the seats and is enclosed by a wide 50 cm high wall. Two greenhouses indicate that this building incorporates new features.

On the corner of the Casuariestraat and the Schouwburgstraat-Bleijenburg the pond broadens and through a cascade and turns into a 'floating' terrace in the closed circuit of grey water/reed purification. Most radical is the further reduction of the profile of the Schouwburgstraat with low rise, a high meeting-tower and a bridge connecting the theatre with the Ministry of Finance.

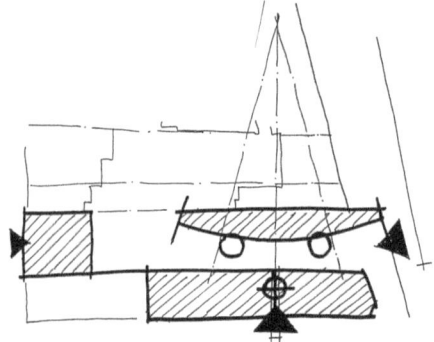

Fig. 08.30: We respected the former context by building on the existing building footprint. The main staircase was centrally located in the old building. This delivered an axis that structured the new building.

Architectural concept

The city is changing too fast. Selective demolition is a cultural and moral assignment. We chose to preserve the building in the Casuariestraat. In this building wing optimal light penetration and air is available. The roof shape of the new building is determined by the orientation of the sun and the desire to allow neighbouring buildings minimal solar obstruction. The greenhouses on the south side are a contemporary and thermally insulating addition, which preserves the value of the 19th century facade.

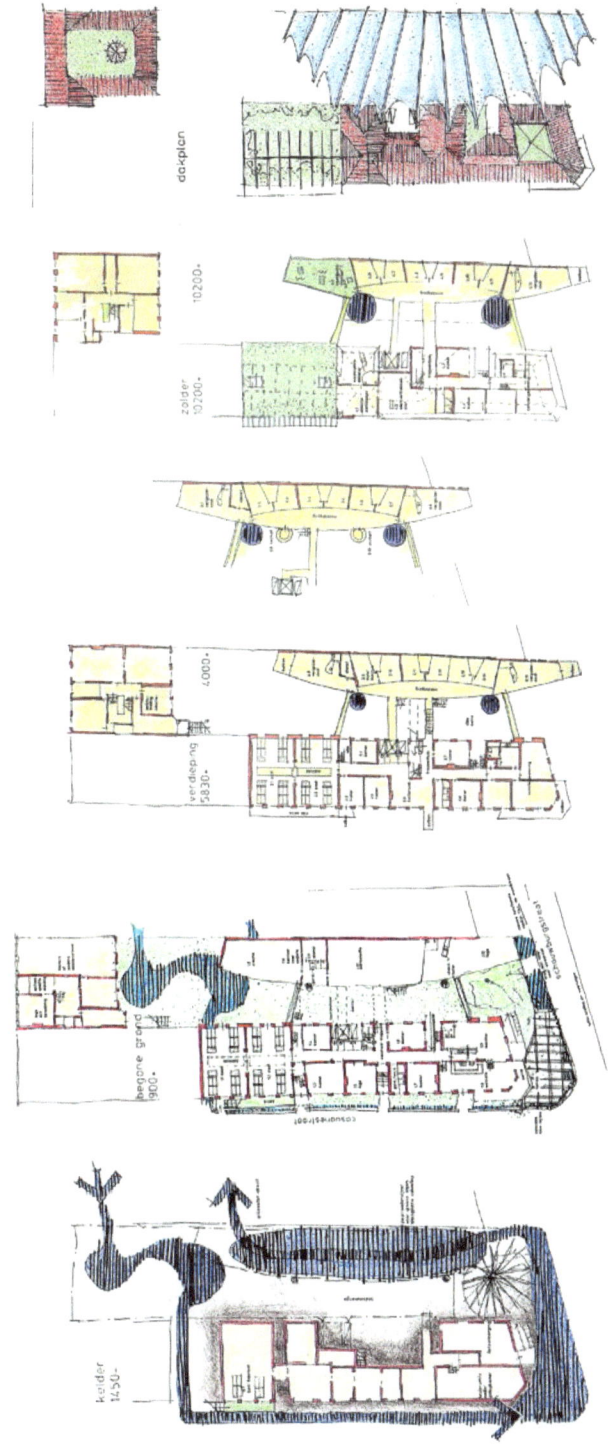

Fig. 08.31: From top to bottom: Roof, attic, mezzanine, first floor, ground floor and basement.

Heating and ventilation

Heating and ventilating in winter is provided as follows:
- Free solar heat from the ridge of a glasshouse can be directly used yet also stored in the ground.
- Internal waste heat can be stored.
- Waste heat from the other nearby urban functions can be delivered to the ground storage and used by others. This example uses waste heat from shows in the Royal Theatre.

The ventilated air ($\Delta T = 15°C$) can be pre-heated in winter.

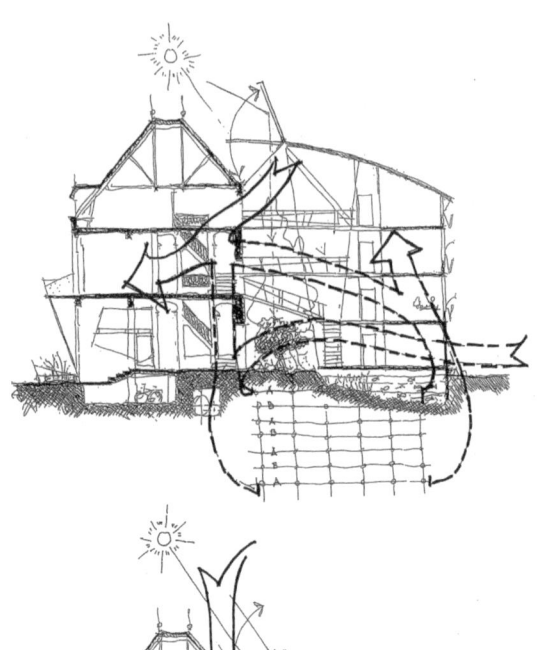

Fig. 08.32:   Sunny day in winter.

Cooling and ventilating in summer is provided as follows:
- Drawn in fresh air and if necessary blown in through the storage in the ground ($\Delta T = 12°C$ is attainable).
- Ventilated air of approximately 18°C can be sent to other functions for cooling, in this example the Royal Theatre.

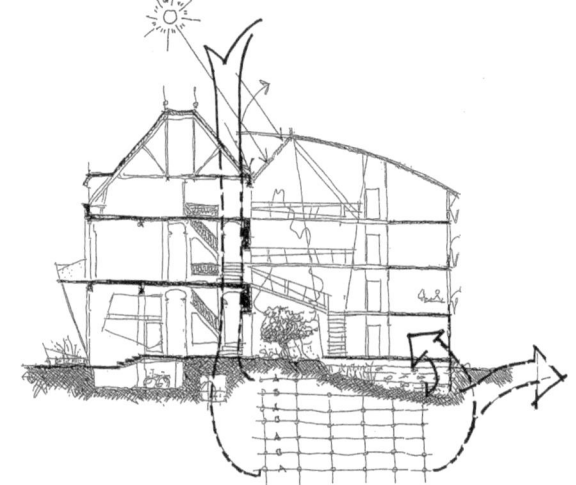

Fig. 08.33:   Hot day in summer.

Additional heating during cold weather and a cloudy sky is also provided by:
- Old buildings having local heat-radiating walls.
- New buildings heat ventilated fresh air.

Transmission losses are reduced by:
- Closed insulation shutters on the roof.
- Radiation curtains in front of windows and façades.
- Lowering the air temperature in the old building and glasshouse.

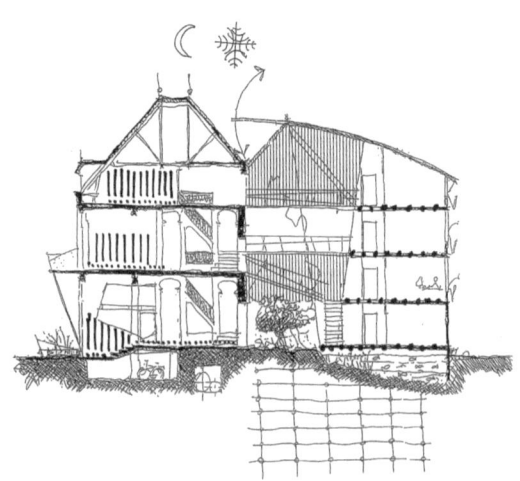

Fig. 08.34:   Cold night in autumn.

Integrated water system
The water system works at the city, block and building level.
At the city level, we go back to ancient precedent when water was the primary structural support:
- Make water visible.
- Re-introduce canals.
- Connect the Hofvijver with Koninginnegracht.
- Re-open the Hague brook.
- Release groundwater level control (almost completely).
- Drain rainwater slowly.

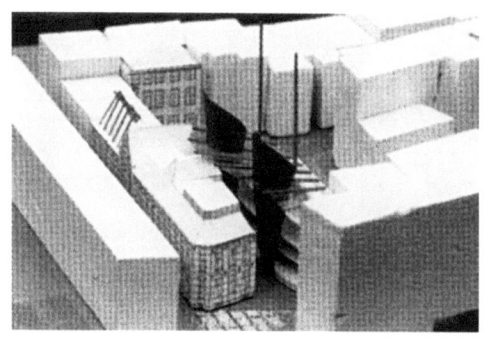

Fig. 08.35:   Model of the The Hague office.

At block level a closed grey-water circuit flows through all gardens and around the entire office building. Black water is treated in a closed process using green algae under the new office. At the building level rainwater is purified and refined to drinking water quality.

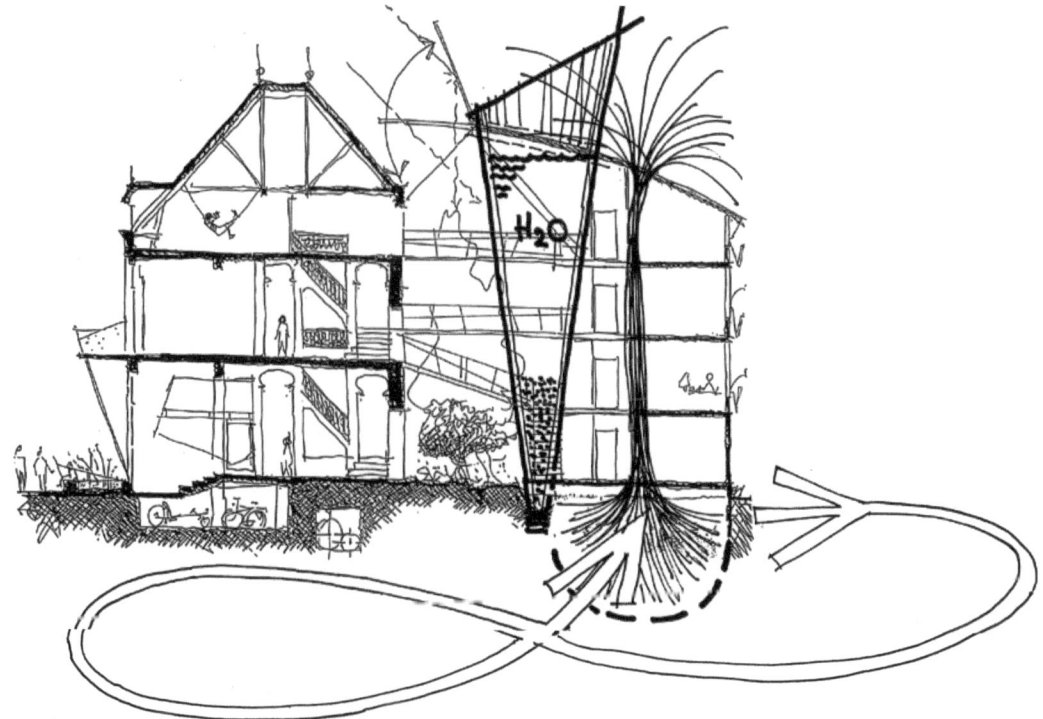

Fig. 08.36:   Integrated water system of the The Hague office.

A green algae tank situated underneath the ground floor operates all year-round and is heated by 'soil energy' as a closed treatment process for black wastewater. In addition, tilapia fish (a useful protein) can live in another warm pond basin and feed on the algae.

Jón Kristinsson   **Integrated Sustainable Design**

Autarkic drinking water facility
- Rainwater is collected in two tanks on ground level.
- Rainwater is pumped through the roof garden with helophyte filters.
- Inside the tanks the water is kept in movement.
- The final filter stage before consumption takes place inside a funnel filled with sand.

Closed treatment process
Grey wastewater:
- Grey, slightly polluted, water is filtered per building block in a closed water cycle through the gardens.
- The last stage is made visible on street level.
- Extra discharge occurs in the gardens as a supplement for larger trees.

Black wastewater:
- Black wastewater from toilets is purified in large green algae tanks through photosynthesis.

Plants love people and vice versa. Therefore the conservatory contained tropical plants including Mimosa di Bata climber, Olea Europaea, Magnolia Grandiflora, Passiflora Edulis and Bougainvillea. Linear plants as reed, rush, isseuse and horsetail are used for the purification of drinking water. Rainwater is rhythmically pumped around in flow forms, as recommended by Jörn Copijn. A roof garden with tabernacle was designed as an outdoor meeting space.

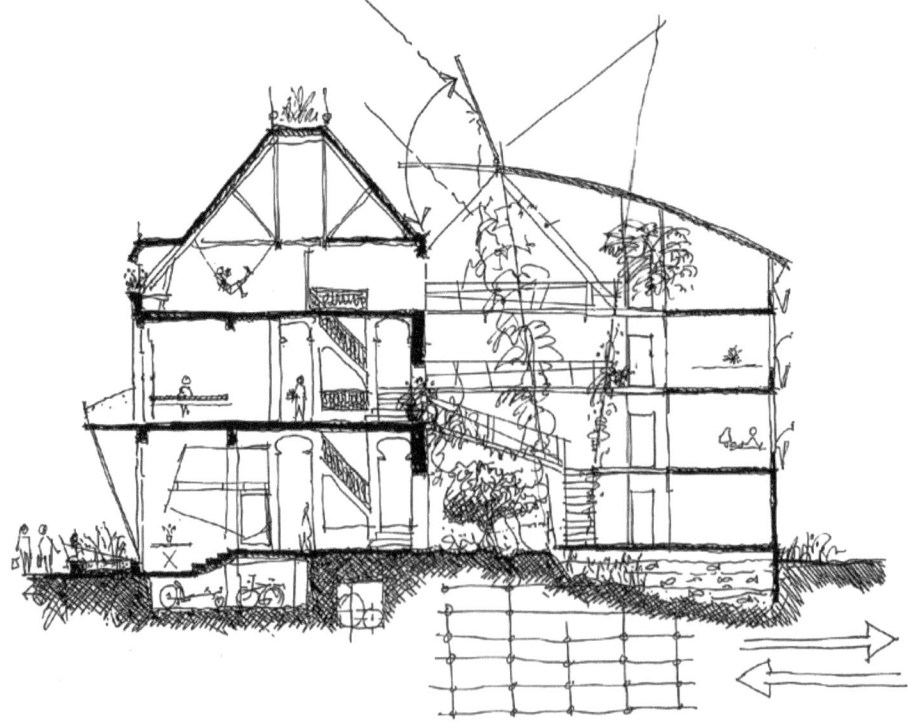

Fig. 08.37:   The green office.

Fig. 08.38:   Market hall (left) and styling room (right).

Fig. 08.39:   Open air office (left) and 'workaholic cockpit' office with 24-hour occupation (right).

Fig. 08.40:   Bar with habitués table (left) and the hotel office (right).

Working concepts
Not least important to the DTO proposal was the basis of new working concepts, which could take on humorous forms.

> **The working man**
> - We assume full employment and meaningful time-spending for everyone.
> - Social and cultural information distribution should be a stabilising factor in a multiracial society.
> - Plenty of staff, therefore no lack of maintenance on buildings and no coffee machines with plastic cups.

Fig. 08.41:   Home to the new civil office worker.
- *In the attic, on the left hand side a mosquito from the press is seeking news.*
- *Underneath, an official studies an old file of Asterix & Obelix.*
- *Right of him, beadle no. 13 moves down the stairs.*
- *Underneath, a meeting lasts long because of afraid men.*
- *On the ground floor, a review takes place in the bar.*
- *Outside, technical weather specialists work hard.*
- *In the basement, a rummager does his best.*
- *In the atrium, a smoker oversees the whole problem.*
- *Next to him, a last wave meeting is held.*
  - *Beneath, the civil servants make themselves comfortable in the hotel office*
- *Above the fish pond, it's the habitat of the department of openness of government and lobbyists.*

Environmental performance
The aim for 2040, a factor of 20 environmental improvement, was accomplished through this the use of this sustainable energy design. A GreenCalc index of 2400, or environmental improvement factor of 24, was scored.

08.02.03   Apartments for the elderly, Hengelo (1994-2001)

In 1994, for their 75th anniversary, the St. Joseph / Onze Woning housing association organised three parallel competitions, including a sustainable and environmentally sound building for seniors, called 't Vendel', which was assigned to our office. The location along the Mussenstraat and the Hengelo-Oldenzaal railroad was a challenge. Our design won overwhelmingly partly due to its feasibility, and although a simplified version without a solar cavity was constructed in 2001, it was an interesting case study and warranted its inclusion here as it epitomizes the principles of integrated design.

The project architect was Marnix de Man. The plan consisted of 26 dwellings, including 8 dwellings at ground level and 18 stacked flats. A differentiation was made between one- and two-person households.

Adaptable senior housing
- A colour that is also clear to the visually impaired.
- Fully accessible to wheelchairs: a sink without cupboard underneath, balcony doors and bathroom floors without thresholds.
- Separate kitchen.
- Closed, secure building ensemble, no basement boxes.
- Greenhouse on the south side, 6°C warmer in winter than outside.
- Use of the chimney effect for induced ventilation of the high greenhouse on hot days.
- Balcony or garden on the sunny side as well on the cool north side.

Fig. 08.42:   North elevation of Apartments for elderly, Hengelo.

Fig. 08.43:   Building oriented to the south along the Hengelo-Oldenzaal railway line.

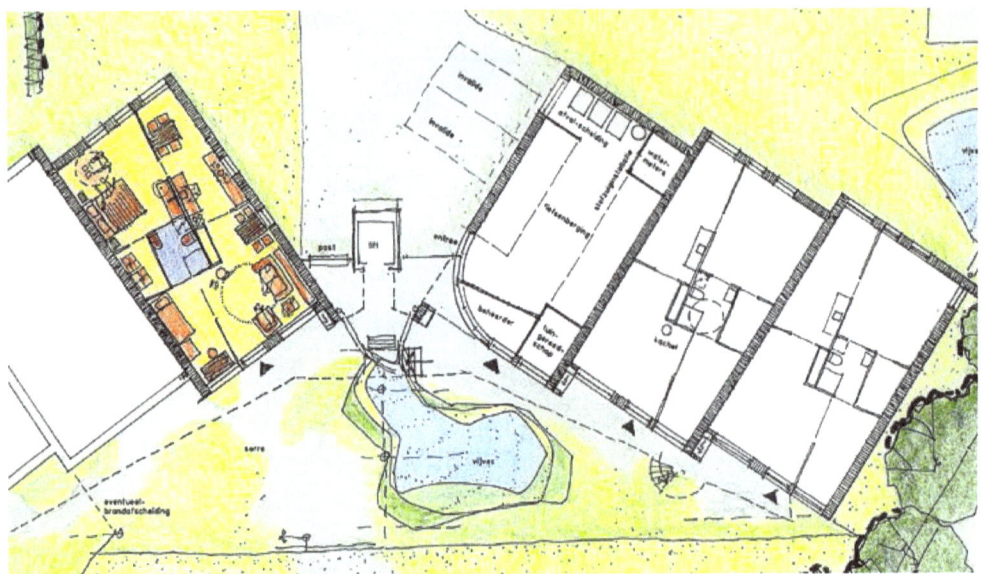

Fig. 08.44: Floor plan with staggered balconies on the side of the greenhouse/winter garden and proposed solar cavities for heat radiation.

Lifestyle
- Though small living areas, prevention of traffic occupation facilitated spacious homes.
- Large areas without a clear function: living, sleeping and hobbies can be tailored to individual needs.
- Seating in the bend of the gallery enables more informal contact with fellow residents.
- The separate upper and lower part of the front door make it easier to make contact without fully opening the door.
- Storeroom was indoors, hence easier to access, including the safe-keeping of valuables.
- Greenhouse is suitable for group activities.

Healthy building
- Avoidance of materials with toxic emitting fibres.
- No mineral wool in the cavity, but a cavity filled with air and thermally insulating blocks.
- Avoidance of allergy-inducing materials and materials with background radiation.
- Replacing regular formwork oil with a natural substitute.
- Avoiding evaporating materials.
- No use of chipboard.
- Using materials with low emissions, including natural water-based paint and, considering maintenance, exterior windows at the north facade with 'high solid' alkyd paint.
- No synthetic foam in the roof or under the ground floor.
- Building vapour-open constructions: avoiding all types of synthetic foils.
- Avoid the combustion of dust and circulation of air by using wall heating with a solar cavity and stoves instead of a central heating system.
- Bicycles within easy reach of the entrance, car parking slightly further away.
- Central vacuum cleaning system; with a regular vacuum cleaner the finest particles would be blown back into the environment.

Protected housing
- Dwellers have two front doors.
- The complex is completely closed-off, an intercom system is in operation.

Fig. 08.45:   Entrance to the 19 apartments for the elderly, Hengelo.

Noise
- A greenhouse as a screen in front of the houses, to reduce the train noise.
- Sound insulation by using tie-free cavity walls between dwellings, applying sound-proof building materials and zoning in the dwellings (whereby the storage and bathroom between the various living areas act as a buffer).
- Avoidance of noise sources such as mechanical ventilation units.
- Roof elements filled with cellulose insulation, which absorbs environmental noise more efficiently than lower density foam elements.

Fig. 08.46:   The front door is accessible by a gallery with a high glasshouse opposite.

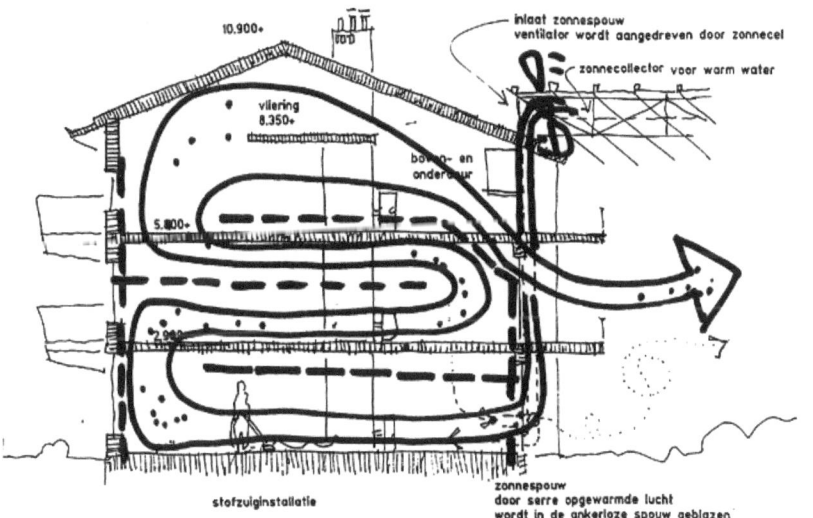

Fig. 08.47:   Ventilation strategy.

Jón Kristinsson   Integrated Sustainable Design

Energy intensification
- Maximum use of free-flowing energy.
- Greenhouse/winter garden.
- Favourable solar orientation.
- Solar cavity heating - heat storage in the cavity between the dwellings.
- Solar boilers for hot tap-water.
- Slow elevator alongside a generous passable stairway.
- 2x sound-insulating block walls with cavity, calculated R value of 3.
- Improved R value by building without crawl space.
- High-performance glass, possibly with secondary glazing on the north side.
- Local additional heating by a heater with a high proportion of radiant heat.
- The pond in the greenhouse reflecting winter sun, humidifying the air and lowering temperature peaks.

Fig. 08.48: Circulation of air in the solar cavity and greenhouse/winter garden during winter day, summer day and night.

Greenhouse/winter garden
- Micro-climate improvement by variations in height and a pond.
- Natural humidification.
- Selection of plants based on their ability to filter air pollutants such as formaldehyde and dust.
- Thermostatic control of opening ventilation windows.

Clean water
- Using water-saving taps and showerheads.
- Solar boilers.
- Water-saving toilets.

Rainwater
- For toilet flushing, car washing, cleaning common areas, etc.
- To avoid contamination by metals, water is collected and used as a decorating element in the form of ponds or drains across the site.

Waste water
- Considered: drainage from showers, sinks and washing machines on a reed field.
- Resident discipline/awareness needed with the choice of soap and washing powder.
- On-site car wash with hot untreated wash water.

Fig. 08.49:   The greenhouse.

Choice of building materials
- Recycled concrete.
- Pinewood for window-frames and recycled demolition wood for the galleries.
- Lime/sandstone inner walls.
- 'Wood-concrete' block facades for the greenhouse.
- A layer of expanded clay beads and anhydrite finish for the ground floor.
- Ceramic roof tiles.
- Polypropylene instead of PVC sewers.
- Polyethylene instead of PVC gutters.
- EPDM instead of zinc gutters.

Integral chain management
- Recycling/reuse of demolition construction materials for the parking space pavements, terraces and paths.
- Applying recycled concrete and demolition wood.

Maintenance
- Tiled roof, maintenance free.
- Maintenance platform/balcony to greenhouse roof for cleaning.
- Extended eaves providing façade protection against weathering.

Waste
- Waste separation.
- Organic waste processed on site in compost bins – resident discipline required.
- Shared compost used in the common garden areas.

Transport
- Bench for waiting taxi-passengers placed at the entrance.
- 0.7 parking space per dwelling, rather than required 1.0 per dwelling.
- Two parking spaces for disabled close to the entrance.

Residential area and urban aspects
- Special buildings such as this complex have a recognisable character.
- The building volumes should be related to the human-scale and well-integrated into the urban environment.
- The roof shapes are consistent with the surrounding context.
- The building engages with surrounding neighbourhood with an entrance and façade orientated to the street.
- The building frontage is clear; this aids security and increases visibility.
- The entrance area is collectively controlled/monitored by overlooking dwellings.

08.02.04 Exergy Dwelling competition and realisation (1996-1997)

In 1997 we won the Exergy Dwelling competition, a Dutch national competition for the best, low-exergetic dwelling design. Our plan offered optimal living benefits in a dwelling that can grow, with evolutionary equipment over a long life span. Exergy in regards to housing means the use of low-temperature heating and waste energy. The design decreased the domestic heating demand from 52 GJ/year to 5 GJ/year and for hot tap-water, 14 GJ/year to 5 GJ/year. The energy performance score was between 0.84 and 0.58, in a time when the legal obligation was still 1.60.

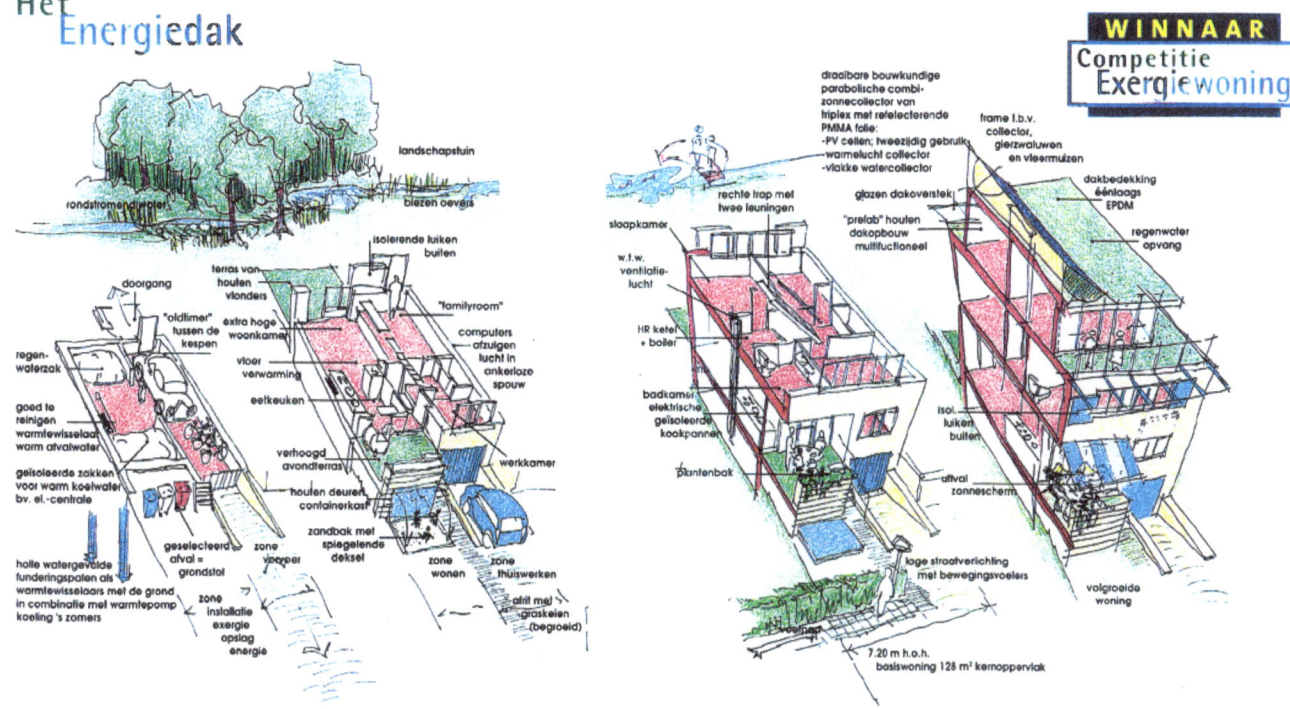

Fig. 08.50:   The exergy dwelling.

Innovation
- Water storage in the crawl space.
- Heat pump connected to hollow piles filled with water.
- 15% more building volume.
- Seasonally variable facades.
- Lightweight parabolic combined solar collectors that turn towards the sun.

Fig. 08.51:   Floor plan for terraced houses based on the exergy competition design, in the Nieuwland neighbourhood of Amersfoort (1996).

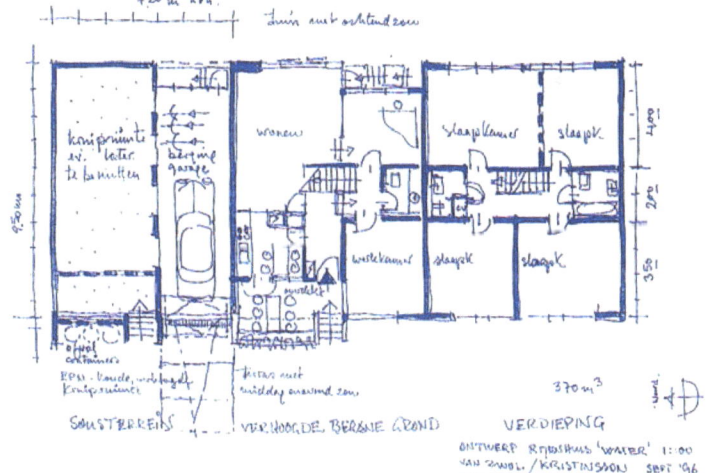

Better use of space
- Enlarged crawl space for car parking, storeroom and water storage.
- Wide house, small heated core.
- Variable future roof expansion.

Albeit in a slightly modified form our winning proposal was realised in Amersfoort. This assignment was commissioned by the project group Exergy Dwelling, involving the EnergieNed (energy trade organisation), GGR/GAS (gas provider), Novem, NUON (energy company) and the SEP (collaborating energy-producing companies).

Fig. 08.52: In 2000 the project was built in Amersfoort, the Netherlands.

08.02.05 Sustainable highrise, Dordrecht (2000)

Fig. 08.53:   The Dordrecht living tower, next to the railway station of Dordrecht

The first high-rise building of Kristinsson Architects & Engineers was built in 2000. Jón Kristinsson had observed that housing towers often had a clear distinction of quality between flats, especially outdoor quality, which varied strongly with orientation. In response he designed a floor plan in which each flat had a balcony that could receive southern sun at least two hours per day, the whole year round.

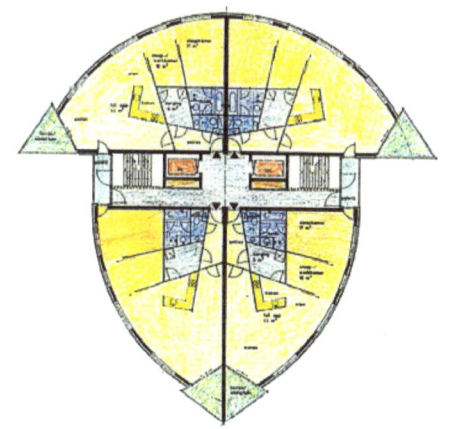

Fig. 08.54:   Floor plan, demonstrating that each of the four flats had a balcony that could benefit from the south sun.

Jón Kristinsson — **Integrated Sustainable Design**

08.02.06 Housing for life, De Marsse, Nunspeet (2002)

Fig. 08.55: Housing for life, De Marsse. Each dwelling was 350 m^3, including a storeroom.

We designed 38 sustainable rental 'Housing for life' dwellings for the ProDiA housing corporation. Like many of our clients ProDiA had ambition, reflecting the principal aim of the project which that was to gain experience in sustainability in preparation for the future.

Fig. 08.56: Site plan, Marrse-West in Nunspeet.

Social aspects

The future tenants were asked in advance for their desired floor plan. Various options were offered enabling the renter to play an active role in the design process. The design also allowed the renter to choose from three energy concepts. These were predetermined per apartment and therefore less easy to change, for example, the all-electric home had no connection to the gas grid. Nevertheless within the home and the energy concepts many user options could be attained in a simple, direct or subsequent manner.

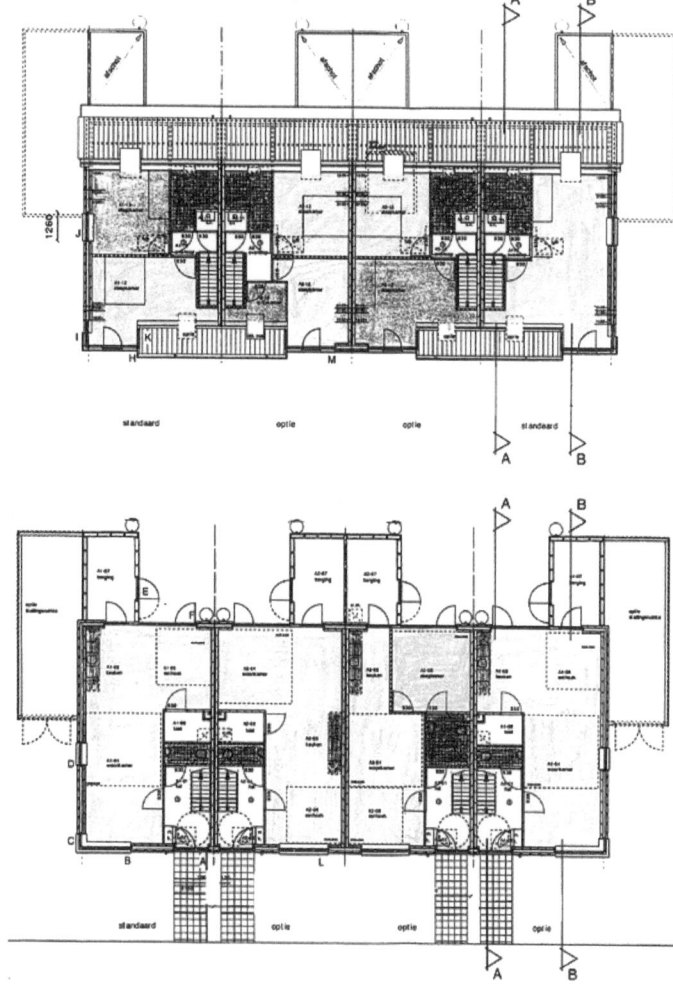

Fig. 08.57: First floor and ground floor of the houses for life in Nunspeet.

The possibilities and options:
- Living oriented to street or garden side.
- Accessibility to wheelchairs.
- Sleeping on the ground floor.
- Bathroom on the first and/or ground floor.
- Kitchen setting at front, centre or back, with flexible connections
- Demountable, movable interior walls.
- Interchangeable equipment for future developments.
- Innovative use of a gas heat pump and 'Vento' system.
- Straight stairway, allowing the installation of a stair-lift.
- Higher ceiling of 2.80 m (standard height 2.40 m) for the ground floor, 2.50 m in the utility/storage block.
- Possible layouts: dining room in shed, expansion of the living in garage, etc.
- Dormer at the garden side already prepared in roof construction.
- Timber frame structure for the utility/storage block.
- Rainwater collected in rainwater butts behind the house.

The dwelling dimensions complied with the requirements for Dutch certificates as Aanpasbaar Bouwen ('adaptable building'), Seniorenlabel ('senior label') en Toegankelijkheid ('accessibility').

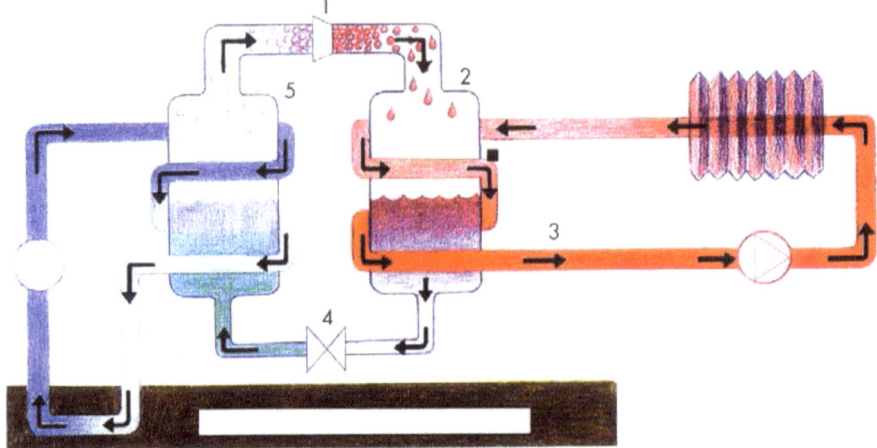

Fig. 08.58: The heat pump system [source: Statens energimyndigheten ET 2001/10000]
1. Compressor.
2. Condenser (approx. 55°C).
3. House heating system.
4. Expansion valve (approx. + 8°C).
5. Evaporator.
6. Soil heat exchanger.

Energy concepts

Considerable attention was paid to the heating and ventilation of the houses. The calculated EPS was 0.64 to 0.92. We decided to apply low-temperature concepts, as this offers the greatest potential for the future. In the brainstorming stage six concepts were discussed, of which three were selected: Concept 1: Combi unit, 22 dwellings; Concept 2: 'All electric' (no gas connection), 12 dwellings; Concept 3: Gas heat pump, 4 dwellings.

  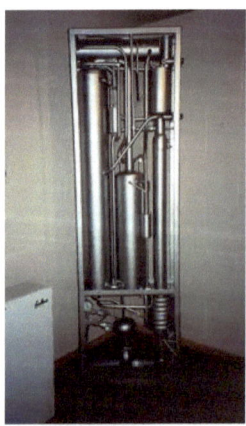

Fig. 08.59: Concept 1: Central heating tubes in the floor (left), Concept 1 and 3: Balanced ventilation with heat recovery, double ducts (middle) and Concept 3: Gas-fired Nefit stainless steel heat pump (right).

Fig. 08.60: The building site surrounded with prefabricated elements – the building process finally became a mounting system.

Thermographic analysis

In 2003, Nieman, engineering consultants for building physics and quality control, monitored the energy performance of the De Marsse dwellings after delivery. The thermographic images demonstrated that the overall insulation was sufficient, but that many seams were present in the junctions between roof, façade or ventilation duct.

Nieman's study identified a worse than anticipated energy performance at De Marsse. If this dedicated sustainable design has issues with heat loss, imagine the many cases where energy consumption has no significance in the building design – an alarming prospect.

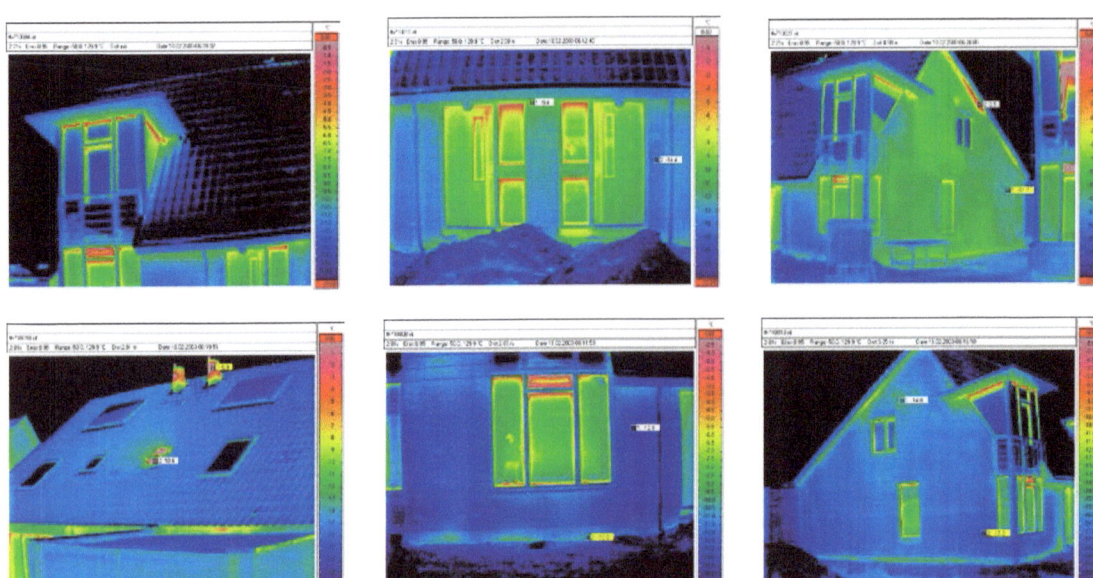

Fig. 08.61: Thermographic images of the exterior of De Marsse; the more the colour tends to red, the greater the heat loss. Window frames and seams stand out. Note the different head walls on the right: one apparently is better insulated than the other, or there is cleft leakage.

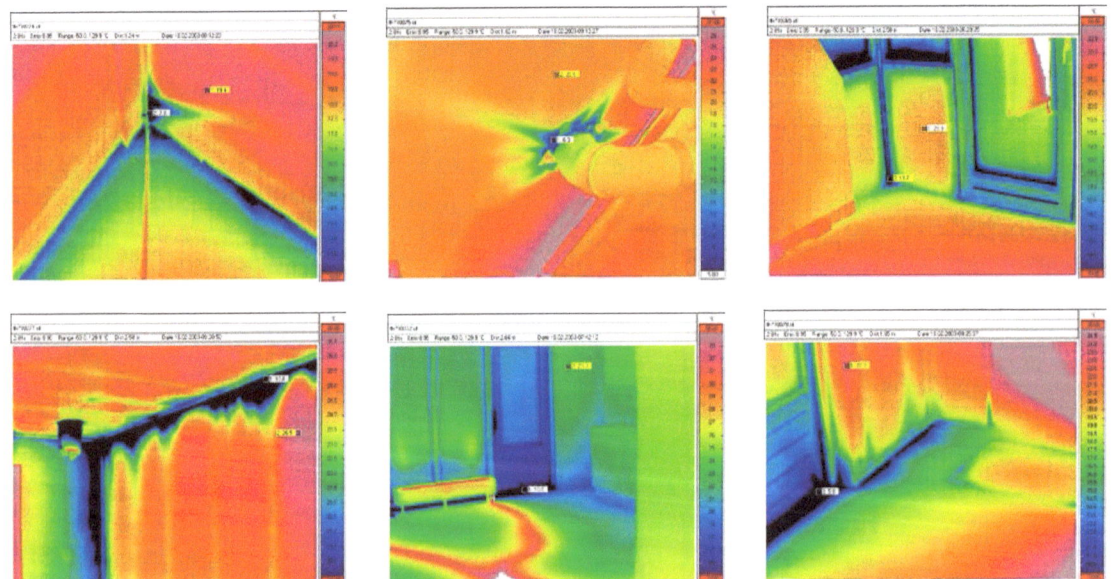

Fig. 08.62: Thermographic images of the exterior of De Marsse; this time the more the colour tends to black, the greater the heat loss (other parts stay warm indoors). Seams are more clearly visible than from outside. Visible below left: poorly connecting insulation panels; below centre: heating pipes running to a radiator. These images clarify the importance of thermal connections between different building elements.

08.03 World Sustainability Campus, Afsluitdijk (2009-)

Joint project in association with Witteveen+Bos and West8

Fig. 08.63:   Artist impression of the World Sustainability Campus

The Afsluitdijk is an impressive landmark as well as a representation of innovative and historical engineering. This victory for mankind has also meant changes for nature; instead of a natural estuary with herring and mussels, the IJsselmeer lake became an isolated fresh water basin. In the current situation the monumental value, however, remains undiscovered by many people and the natural system is left unbalanced.

08.03.01 The World Sustainability Campus

Concept

Based upon an existing integral plan a comprehensive concept is presented. In this vision a long island is created which encloses a water basin with brackish water to restore the natural gradient of the IJssel Delta from fresh to salt water. The new island forms the location for a world sustainability campus. A campus which consists of small scale, mobile laboratories, hotel boats, lodges, two harbours, a wetland wild park and the impressive World Sustainability Centre (WSC), shaped as a Lapwing's Egg (Kievitsei), referring to an old Frisian tradition.

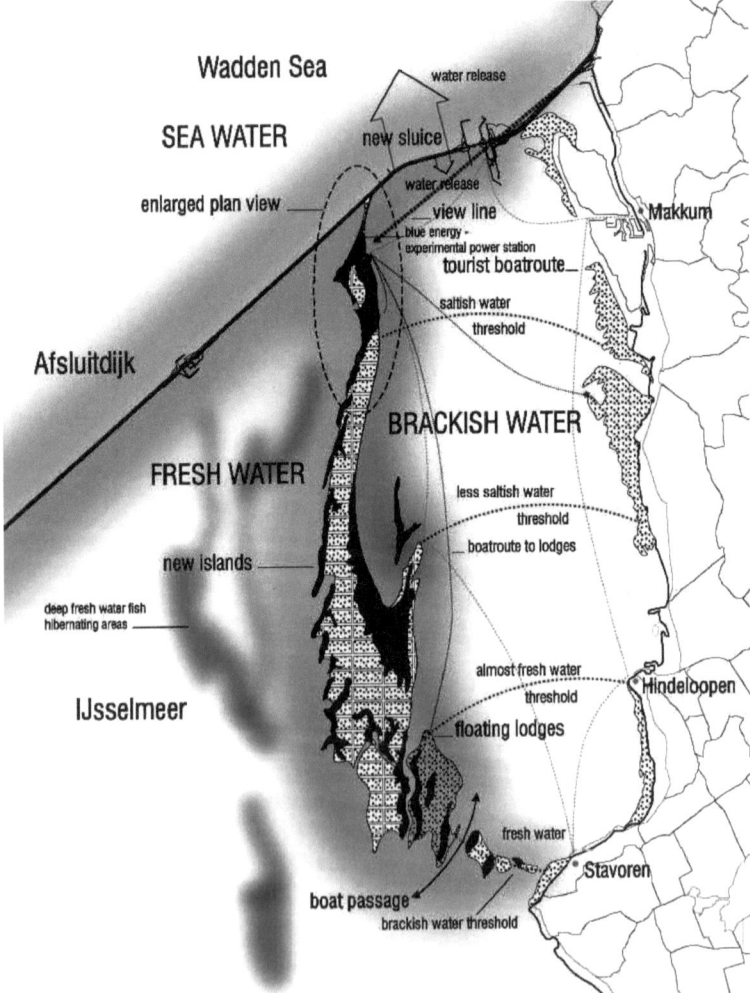
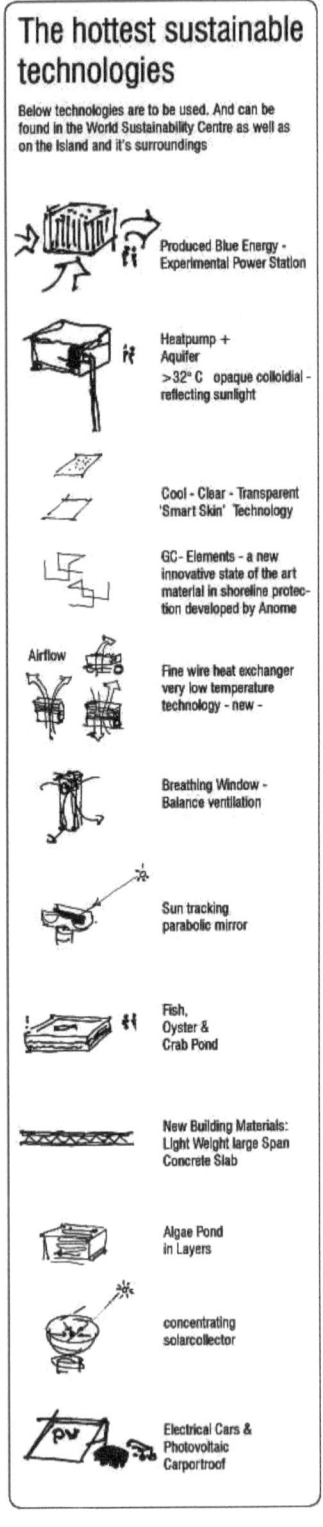

Fig. 08.64: Master plan for the Afsluitdijk and Lapwing's Egg (left); A showcase for novel sustainable technology (right).

The World Sustainability Campus will be a hub of scientific development in the Frisian area with a global importance in the field of sustainability. It is intended that if constructed leading research platforms like Wetsus, Energy Valley, universities and other educational institutes, can use the WSC as a cradle for innovative research and development. Focal points may be found in the areas of sustainable energy, ecology, hydrology and water sciences. WCS will act as a gateway of knowledge transfer from scientists to scientists, from scientists to politicians and to the general public with a worldwide impact. The campus concept offers flexibility in scale, capacity and according to the programme of requirements, the possibility to change the look and feel of the campus every 500 days.

Technologies
The internal and external spaces of the WSC will be a showcase for companies to publically present and test their 'hottest' sustainable technologies. These demonstration vehicles will be renewed on a regular basis to reflect the latest developments. The optimal location of the experimental Blue Energy Power Station also offers scientists a perfect opportunity to gain knowledge about the process of producing electricity by reversed osmosis.

08.03.02   The Lapwing's Egg

Symbolism
From a historical point of view an egg always has been a symbol of new findings. Columbus' egg for example is used to indicate creativity and new insights. An egg is also a symbol of self-sustainability and evolution. A Lapwing's egg combines all these features with a shape that fits in its natural landscape, it also refers to the Friesian tradition of the search for the first Lapwing's egg each spring. It will be a true landmark that in its appearance, setting and function, will attract scientists and researchers, as well as students and tourists from around the globe.

Energy
The Lapwing's Egg contains a double shell, the first layer consisting of a new type of flexible high efficiency photovoltaic panel. The second layer is made from a smart colloidal foil that changes from transparent to opaque white at higher temperatures, thus providing effective sunshading when necessary. Auxiliary heating and cooling are supported by fine wire heat exchangers (as described previously in this book) a revolutionary Dutch technology that can extract energy from the environment even at temperature differences of just five degrees centigrade. This new very low temperature technology will be of major importance in future energy saving in buildings. Besides the use of the IJsselmeer water for free cooling or heating, seasonal heat and cold storage is accomplished by means of an aquifer in sand layers 30 to 80 meters deep below the centre of the Lapwing's Egg.

The nest
To protect the Lapwing's Egg from the beating waves it is situated in a nest of Ground Consolidators (GC). GC's are a state of the art material used in shoreline protection. The wire elements are shaped to hook up and form a cohesive armoured layer. Behind these elements a protected environment is created. The elements are made of re-usable biocomposites. Also acting as a niche for breeding fish and birds, the GC could also be used to protect other parts of the island.

Fig. 08.64:   WSC interior with restaurant (left) and ground floor with view on the Cornelis Lely Hall (right).

The egg yolk
The heart of the egg building is the yolk. It is in the egg yolk itself where knowledge is transferred and new ideas form. These goals are reached by giving the space flexibility with interchangeable flooring allowing the possibility to turn the yolk into a conference centre or IMAX theatre. The IMAX theatre would create an experience respondent to the human senses with 3D images showing visitors real life views of theme related film on sustainability.

The conference centre would draw ideas from scientists around the globe. As a tribute, as well as reference to the Afsluitdijk, the conference centre would be named after its founder Dr Cornelis Lely.

The restaurant
A restaurant is situated at the rim of the egg yolk where guests can have a taste of science in "status nascendi" while enjoying a fantastic view of the surroundings, a large LED-screen separating the exposition space from the café restaurant. No need to say that a wealth of local biologically produced delicacies will be on the menu.

Exposition Space
The WSC would offer full day visitor programmes, the infrastructure of the Lapwing's Egg creating flexibility, in keeping with inspiring and appealing expositions that can change periodically. The small 'showcase' mobile laboratories will attract innovations from other countries to the WSC. The guests and researchers would stay overnight in a comfortable boat hotel or lodges on the island. These lodges forming low-rise housing, flexible in time and space.

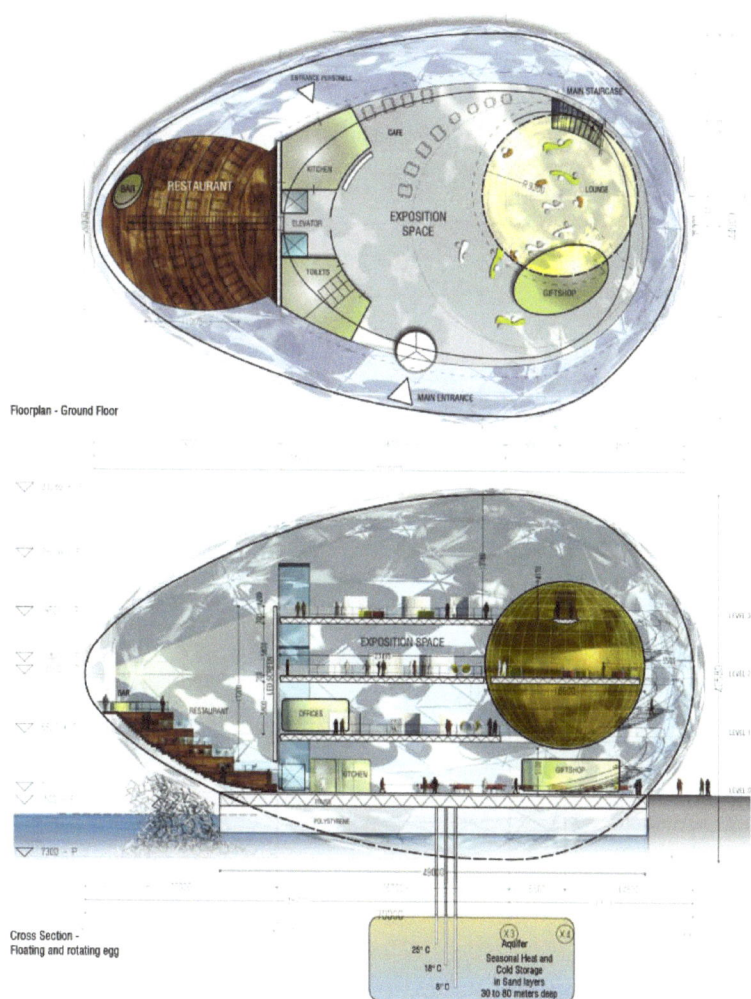

Fig. 08.65: Exhibition floor plan and cross-section of the Lapwing's Egg.

08.03.03 The Island

Natural estuary

The creation of the new long island makes it possible to solve one of the largest existing ecological problems of the Afsluitdijk: the loss of fresh water fish. Through discharge sluices huge amounts of freshwater fish migrate into the salt water of the Wadden Sea resulting in high rates of fish mortality. Re-establishing brackish transition zones east of the Island will restore the natural character of the estuary. In a natural situation the fish turns around when the water changes gradually from fresh into salt water. These brackish water zones are created by letting in an amount of seawater of approximately one sixth of the discharge volume. At the west side of the island, new 20 m deep gullies would be excavated in the Ijsselmeer (currently 5 m deep) providing an environment suitable for fish to hibernate in fresh water. The sand from these gullies being used to form the long island.

Energy production
The new island would offer great opportunities for renewable energy production e.g. blue energy. N.B. In the end energy saving is always more effective and cheaper then any energy production, as mentioned before.

Recreation
Guest harbours on both the east and the west side of the island would accommodate water based recreation and attract both private sailing boats and the historical "Bruine Vloot" to the WSC. Zuiderzee harbour towns like Makkum and Hindelopen being part of the summer boat network. The Island offers the possibility for education and recreation beyond the WSC. Activities such as mudflat walking, searching soap glands, shells and enjoying the sheer environment of the location. Visitors of the Campus' lodges would experience this first hand.

Fig. 08.66:   The WSC Egg at night. The 'Cornelis Lely' conference centre emanating light and disseminating knowledge.

Summarising
In the world of tomorrow sustainability will form the only answer to the global challenges in the field of energy, food and water. The world sustainable campus would form an international breeding ground that contributes valuable knowledge to these issues in a unique location where history, ecology and technology are one.

08.04 'Boskantoor', forest office of Staatsbosbeheer, Ugchelen (2010-2011)

08.04.01 Modest, small, yet beautiful

Fig. 08.67: The Forest Office, beautifully situated amidst the trees.

For her new office for 24 employees, Staatsbosbeheer ('state forest management') had the ambition to design an integrated sustainable building that could serve as a showcase. A design competition was initiated with six architects' offices. Our office was selected and awarded the assignment.

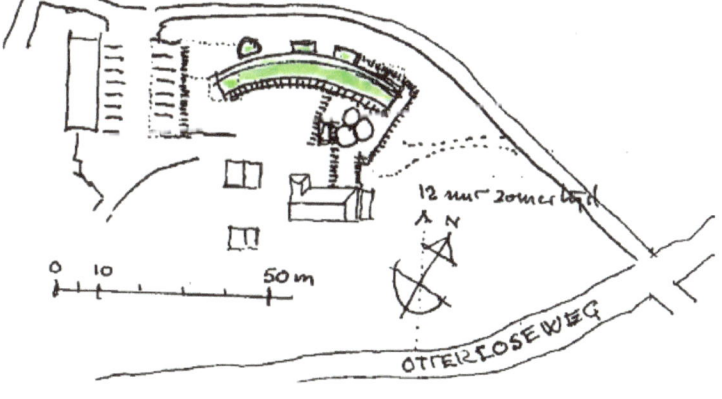

Fig. 08.68: Site plan sketch of the Boskantoor.

The site contained old black timber warehouses, in line with the integrated theory we wanted to reuse them, in practice however the buildings could not be demounted, the stone floors were not insulated and it was not permitted to reuse material in a new building.

Fig. 08.69: On the left hand side, the newly constructed office, on the right hand side the old hunting mansion, where the heat pump system was installed.

The on-site hunting mansion – listed as an 'image-defining' building – had a third life as Staatsbosbeheer headquarters with canteen and meeting facilities. The renovation was executed with small glass surfaces, exclusive radiant heating and three Breathing Window units for meeting room ventilation. The new forest office only contains air heating via Fiwihex fine-wire heat exchangers, insolation and natural ventilation.

08.04.02 Timber structure

The new forest office, which sits to the north of the hunting mansion, is slightly concave in plan, 1-story high and largely transparent due to its of glass and timber construction. The timber was sourced from Staatsbosbeheer's own forests. Wood detailing ensures that daylight is admitted without direct sunlight entering during the summer months. This level of building transparency is uncommon for such an energy-efficient building. The structure is completely demountable. The large roof overhangs and timber external solar shading protect and reduce maintenance to the facades. All rainwater is collected and utilised.

Fig. 08.70: Quality and environmentally responsive timber detailing of the Forest Office.

Part of the Integrated Sustainable Design principle is expressed by the possibilities for future reuse of the building elements. Apart from the foundation the entire building is demountable. Moreover, the timber originating from the client's own forests is FSC certified.

08.04.03 The energy system

Heat storage
Traditional inter-seasonal heat storage in the ground could not be realised in the relatively high sandy area of the Dutch Veluwe nature reserve as the ground water table lies at a depth of 50 m. In order to increase the efficiency of the soil heat exchangers at a shallower depth, excessive toilet flushing water from the rainwater storage bags from the crawl space discharges onto the heat exchanger pipes. Thus a better conduction of heat is established.

Fine-wire convectors
Heating and cooling comes from free-standing, tailor-made Fiwihex convector boxes (Hydro Systems Holland) in front of the glass facades. The heat source is the same heat pump with the vertical heat exchangers as in the main building, and also here the coefficient of performance is triple that of a traditional heating system: the COP = 10. This low-temperature heating is being made at 900 W supply at 30°C and 600 m^3/h of air through-put. The electrical contact for the 24 Volt ventilators enables the easy inclusion of vertical wiring ducts for electricity and ICT connections inside the convector. Thus a virtue can be made of a necessity.

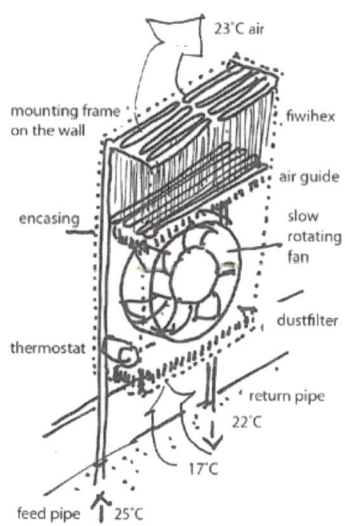

Fig. 08.71: Fiwihex heat exchangers next to the facades of the Forest Office.

Fig. 08.72: The Fiwihex convector, separate (left) and integrated into a convector box (right) that also serves as power socket.

The forest office has natural cross ventilation, so no heat recovery. In the adjacent forest there is no background noise, so every ventilator requires an extensive calculation of the heat capacity of the Fiwihex convectors.

Other energy measures

In the old hunting mansion the heating during winter is provided by a highly efficient electrical heat pump with a COP of 3 to 4.

The southerly-oriented roof was to be coated by thin-foil Helianthos PV cells, however, the budget did not permit for this – even with an innovative project as the Forest Office, additional costs could not be factored in.

Fig. 08.73: The old hunting mansion has Breathing Windows attached to the outer wall

Fig. 08.74: Interior of the Forest Office.

08.04.04 The Bird Hotel

Another striking feature of the forest office is the so-called Bird Hotel, which drew a lot of attention from local media. We attached different birdhouses to the sanitary block of the new office building. In combination with a rustic masonry brick wall, this northern part of the building has become a lovely contribution to the local ecology.

Fig. 08.75:   The 'bird hotel' on the outer facade of the bathroom block of the Forest Office.

Fig. 08.76:   Detail of the 'bird hotel' guest rooms.

09

MAGNUM OPUS: VILLA FLORA (2007-2012)

09.01   Villa Flora, Venlo

Villa Flora is Jón Kristinsson's magnum opus, a design that to incorporates all aspects of integrated sustainable design, and in many ways heir to his design of the Lelystad town hall, 35 years earlier. Finally, one could state, the master of sustainable architecture got the opportunity to demonstrate his ideas and construct a building with a comprehensive programme that completely closes the cycles of energy, water and materials and provides a comfortable indoor climate.

As is often the case with building projects subject to tight financial margins, not everything aspect from the original concept was realised, but the icon stands and presents a precedent for building designs for years to come.

Fig. 09.01:   *CAD rendering of Villa Flora – The forest is reflected in the glass of the inclined north facade, which camouflages the height of the building, rooftop parabolic solar collectors undulating across the skyline.*

09.01.01   Background

The Floriade
Every decade the Dutch horticulturalists host a great world exposition event, the 'Floriade'. For the Floriade 2012 the sector wanted to spectacularly announce itself. 2-3 million visitors are expected (with 35,000 per day at peak times) and these need to be thrown into elation by the vision, fragrance, sense and taste of flowers, vegetables and other plants from the exotic flora of Dutch and international agriculture and horticulture. Visitors also get the opportunity to see and understand the accompanying sustainable technical toolkit.
In 2007 Kristinsson Architectural Engineers received from InnovatieNetwerk/Agro and SIGN (Dutch foundation for innovation in horticulture) a study assignment to develop a large

sustainable landscape office 'with green and glass' at the Floriade complex. Innovation and novel technology was encouraged to go beyond the current 'state of the art'.

Jón Kristinsson approached this task with his appropriate knowledge the will to seek advanced experimental techniques and applications.

Architectural concept of Villa Flora

Villa Flora is one of the two iconic buildings of the Floriade 2012, built in the 'Green Engine' theme field. The building came out of a study assignment, for which the initiators demanded high ambition. The ground-floor exposition space for horticulture had to comprise 10,000 m^2; the energy-producing greenhouse formed the main theme for a sustainable building.

Villa Flora is a greenhouse building characterised by ergonomic office workplaces in green surroundings. Offices are located within the greenhouse under differing climates and vegetation. The building has a clear wedge shape with a lower south side and a five storey high north side. The sloped roof begins as an optimal closed glass roof, which gradually decreases in glass percentage. In the northern office block indirect light replaces direct light from the greenhouse. In this manner external sunshading is avoided. In addition, the northern elevation is slightly tilted, serving as a mirror for the surrounding forest.

Fig. 09.02: Jón Kristinsson explains his plans to amongst others Jo Coenen, one of his supporters and designer of the Innovatower, the other iconic building at the Floriade 2012.

Summary of technical features

This literally and environmentally greenest office is also the greenest building in the Netherlands, lacking public utilities, except ICT. The floor area of the building is 42,500 m^2. A low glasshouse roof on the south side climbs up till six floors of office on the north side. Large parabolic solar collectors dominate the silhouette of the building (Fig 09.01). Seasonal surplus of heat and cold from the solar power system is stored in the aquifer approximately 50 m beneath the building. The building is equipped with a heating system based on very low temperatures (24-25°C), enabled by Fiwihex fine-wire heat exchangers. The cooling of the indoor climate in summer is based mainly on the reverse operation of the same system.

The vacuum sewer system and organic waste collection are aspects of ecological innovation. By means of an anaerobic bioreactor and a micro-turbine, electricity can be produced on location with the addition of organic waste. Filtered exhaust gases are used as nutrients up till 1,000 ppm, in order to achieve a CO_2 balance. Pure water can be retained within this process, which takes two or three days. An important aspect of the greenhouse landscape office is the healthy work environment. It appears from research that domestic plants have a surprisingly wholesome effect. We know the process of purifying air from CO_2 and producing O_2, but reducing stress, skin irritations and headache are the little known contributions of plants to the improvement of the living/working environment.

The parabolic solar collector roof construction is the most striking architectural innovation and aesthetic. A mirrored coating enables parabolics to harvest boiling water and PV electricity on a sunny day, and cold and condensation water on a clear night sky.

09.01.02   The complex indoor climate

Energetic innovation
The export of Dutch greenhouse horticulture products amounts to 7 billion euros a year. In the Netherlands greenhouse cultivation largely depends on natural gas: greenhouses account for almost 10% of the national natural gas consumption. A greenhouse annually uses 50 m^3 of gas/m^2. With increasing environmental awareness and rising fuel prices new innovative methods had to be found. Villa Flora encompasses the results of this innovation in horticulture, translated into the integral design of a multipurpose greenhouse office building. It is anticipated that the office islands in the different climatic zones will produce evidence that working under glass and amongst vegetation is healthy and relaxing.

Fig. 09.03:   Interior view of south facing glasshouse of Villa Flora.

Different climates
The first thing visitors experience is the division of the horticulture exhibition into different climatic zones, each with specific humidity, temperature and planting. The specific climates are, the Netherlands (temperate maritime climate), the Mediteranean, the hot arid Middle East, the warm humid Amazon area and the cold climate of the polar circle. The high temperature and low or high humidity levels present no technical problems. Offices in the Middle East and the

Amazonian climate will have 'stand alone' climate working places. Also in the Netherlands the maintenance of the polar climate will be possible with a sustainable strategy.

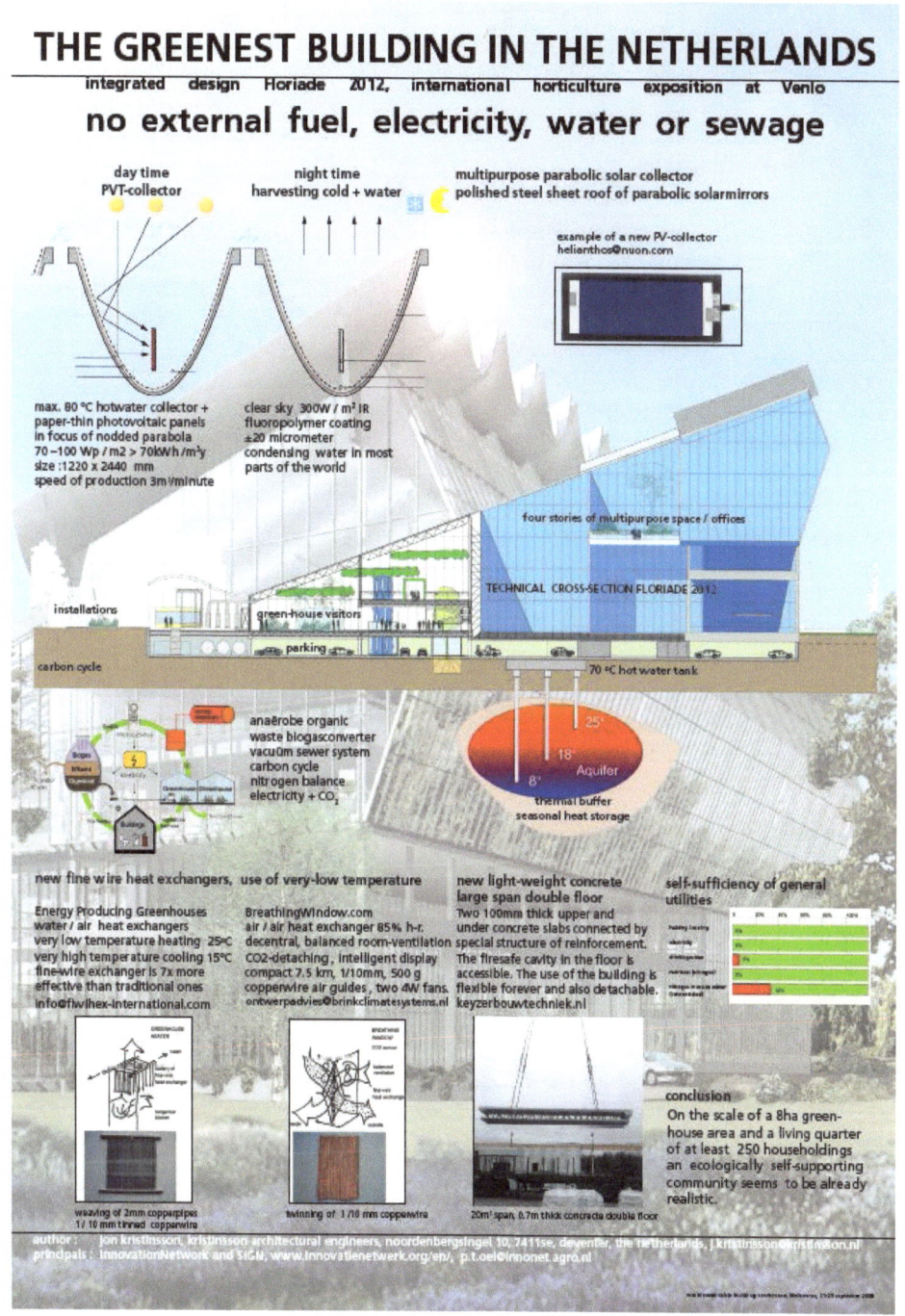

Fig. 09.04:   Early poster of Villa Flora, presented at the World Sustainable Building Conference 2008.

Metabolism challenge
A possible weak point of the greenhouse landscape office is the difference between the metabolism of the sedentary human being and that of a plant. The working climate is usually conditioned by radiant and air temperature together with a localised fan for cooling at the workplace. It has to be a good, healthy workplace, wherever on earth. So to make pleasant green workplaces in various climates was a very special challenge at Villa Flora.

09.01.03 Requirements

The client's ambition is the most important design factor for every building. Two clients initiated a spear point project to surprise the international Floriade 2012 visitor. A special point of the programme was the greenhouse office – healthy work places in green spaces as part of the 10,000 m^2 greenhouse exhibition space on the ground floor. The originality of the recently developed 'Zonneterp' Greenhouse Village (see chapter 07) was to serve as a precedent – the beginning of the Edible City.
Villa Flora embodied Integrated Sustainable Design. This is the weaving of all building functions into a sustainably holistic entity that is greater than the sum of its parts.

09.02 Integrated Sustainable Design

09.02.01 Location

The location of Floriade 2012 is a natural setting close to the city of Venlo, at a junction of two motorways towards Germany and Belgium. The invisible locational properties of sand layers and groundwater were critical for the installation of an inter-seasonal heat storage with aquifer temperatures of 8° to 28°C.

Fig. 09.05:   Floor plan of the original design – ground floor of 15,500 m^2 with four indoor climates.

09.02.02 Parabolic solar collectors

Multifunctional parabolic solar collectors have a vertical solar collector for hot water (70 to 80°C) located in the trough of each parabola. On this solar collector black thin 'Helianthos' PV cells are pasted on both sides (1.20 m wide). The solar collector also cools down the PV cells (max. 80°C) providing more electricity and promoting a longer life span. By applying spectral selective coatings on the mirrors, more IR (infrared) radiation can be achieved on clear nights. This yields more cold for the aquifer, but also condensation and glazed frost, which can be collected and used for drinking and irrigation water in dry climates. A closed greenhouse requires little irrigation water.

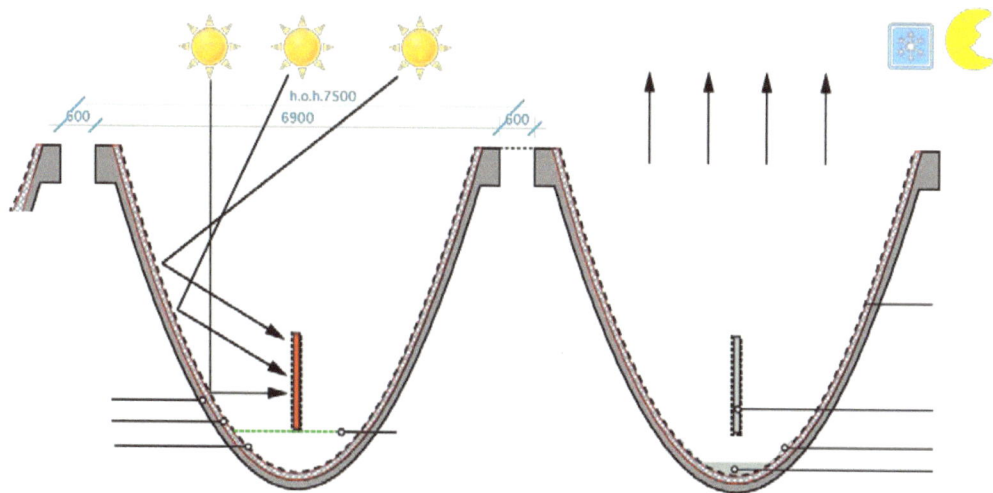

Fig. 09.06: *Principle of the parabolic roof shell during the day (left) and at night or in winter (right). PV coating on solar collectors in the parabola trough produces electricity and heat, optimised by the reflecting shell. With a clear night or winter sky the solar collector can passively cool water, while condensation water is collected in the parabolic shell.*

Fig. 09.07: *Steel frame of the parabolic roof shell.*

09.02.03 Heat and cold storage

Excessive heat is stored underground in an inter-seasonal heat storage in an aquifer, a sand layer between watertight layers of clay. Cold from nightly radiance to the sky is also stored in this system. The stack effect occurs in an aquifer, so warmer water will rise. Originally, the heat and cold storage was meant to have fixed locations for the warm and cold well, but strong groundwater currents along the river Meuse made this impossible. This however was considered as a challenge.

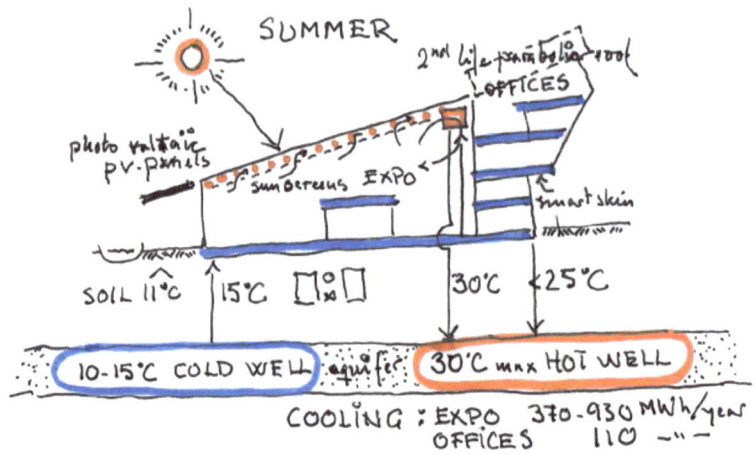

Fig. 09.08: Principle of the heat and cold storage in summertime: heat is extracted from the greenhouse and injected in the upper aquifer, while cold water from a deeper aquifer is extracted at a point where the cold water has arrived after 6 months of underground current.

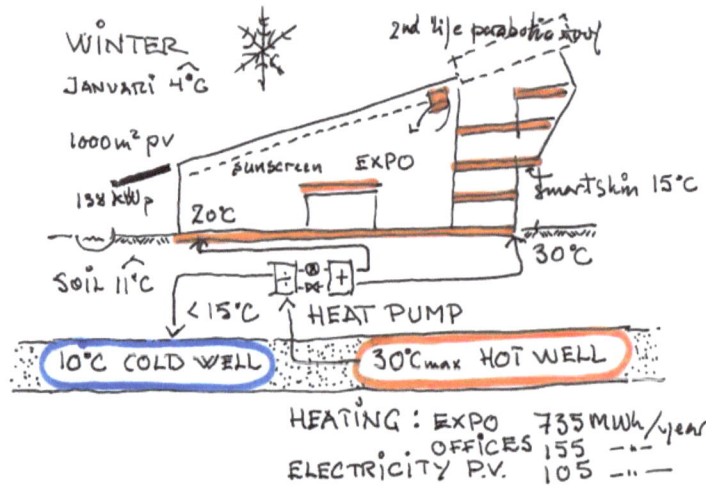

Fig. 09.09: Principle in wintertime: warm water is extracted from upper aquifer, at the point where the injected water in summer has arrived with the underground current. A heat pump brings it to the desired level of 30°C. Simultaneously, cold water from this heat pump and from colder external sources is injected into the deeper aquifer, for use in summer.

At Villa Flora, warm water (in summer) has to be pumped into one well and extracted from another. This extraction takes place at a meticulously calculated location where the heat stored in summer (or cold stored in winter) will have flowed to in 6 months time, by a speed of 50-75 m/year. Likewise, the cold storage is injected into a second, deeper aquifer layer and extracted at a point further down the groundwater stream.

09.02.04 Fine-wire heat exchangers

As you, the reader, will understand well, the sun is the primary source of heat. Night radiation towards the clear sky forms the primary cold source. The characteristic properties of sustainable utilities are that they are based on the physics of the open field more than on mechanical engineering. New fine-wire heat exchangers enable very low temperature heating and cooling within the closed greenhouse. This principle of the closed greenhouse forms a contrast with the traditional greenhouse, which is open, meaning that through the skin fresh air is admitted and warm air exhausted without heat recovery. By the time of Villa Flora's design, Fiwihex had developed two fine-wire heat exchangers: water-to-air and air-to-air. The Fiwihex heat exchanger based on ø 0.1 mm copper wire is around 8 times as efficient as a plate heat exchanger. A greenhouse receives around 7 times more solar heat than the thermal loss at night and in winter. Each greenhouse therefore functions as a hothouse, and the closed greenhouse certainly functions as a solar collector, which needs to be cooled down by means of the cold well of the aquifer.

09.02.05 Organic waste

As discussed with the Energy-Producing Greenhouse and Solar Village (chapter 07), vacuum sewerage (for faeces and urine) and a complete collection and disposal of organic waste is a condition for closed carbon-nitrogen cycles. By means of anaerobic fermentation, methane gas is made to power a micro-turbine during a period of 2.5 days in a bioreactor that supplies itself with electricity. The filtered exhaust fumes are used as fertiliser for the greenhouse plants. With a CO_2 concentration of 1,000 ppm within the closed greenhouse plant growth increases by 20% and the building can become totally CO_2 neutral. Apart from cooling, which can be limited by adjustable outside awnings, a closed greenhouse has two advantages: the relative humidity can be kept high and constant without considerable water from outside, and there is significantly less nuisance from insects. The end-product being compost that can be used as mould for gardening.

The Edible City
As discussed earlier in this book, in the Netherlands 2 ha of closed greenhouse with aquifer energy storage is adequate to heat an equivalent 8 ha of a 200 dwelling neighbourhood. A greenhouse of 8 ha produces sufficient organic waste to also provide the same number of houses with electricity. The so-called 'Edible City' requires new town planning.

09.03 Indoor climate

09.03.01 Air heating

The desired indoor climate – the temperature, humidity and ventilation – with four different continental climates is achieved by a design completely without air conditioning. The basic heating and cooling is provided by slow radiation heating, supplemented with fast-reacting air heating and cooling as used in the 'Zonneterp' Greenhouse Village. However, a transition is needed from the effective utilitarian fine-wire heat exchanger in the closed greenhouses to silent heating and cooling in office work places with a noise level of < 25 dB in the cell offices.

Fig. 09.10: Wall of the office block of Villa Flora, in the top corner Fiwihex boxes hanging from the greenhouse roof.

09.03.02 Ventilation

The greenhouse has four artificial indoor climates, subtropical, Middle Eastern, Amazon, and the polar circle area. Research has proven that plants have a beneficial effect on patients. The plants produce carbon dioxide but the offices have Breathing Window (BW) ventilation which monitors CO_2 levels. As discussed in chapter 05, the BW is an intelligent, balanced way of ventilation, which measures the indoor climate and ventilates according to one's needs.

Adjustable, but at a CO_2 level of 600 ppm the ventilation stops automatically. The fine-wire-heat exchanger in BW's consists of 15 km ø 1/10 mm copper wire and weighs 500 gr. The dimensions of the heat exchanger are 100/200/450 mm, so that it can be easily cleaned.

09.03.03 Radiant heating

Temperature control for radiant heating or air heating takes place from the seasonal heat storage in the ground. The constant indoor temperature benefits from the thermal mass of concrete. In Villa Flora, thermal concrete core activation is relatively fast and effective thanks to the structural design of 'Holcon floors' (to be discussed further on).

The concrete core is thermally activated by oxygen-tight heating pipes in the floors and ceilings. As described, auxiliary quick heating and cooling is arranged by means of air.

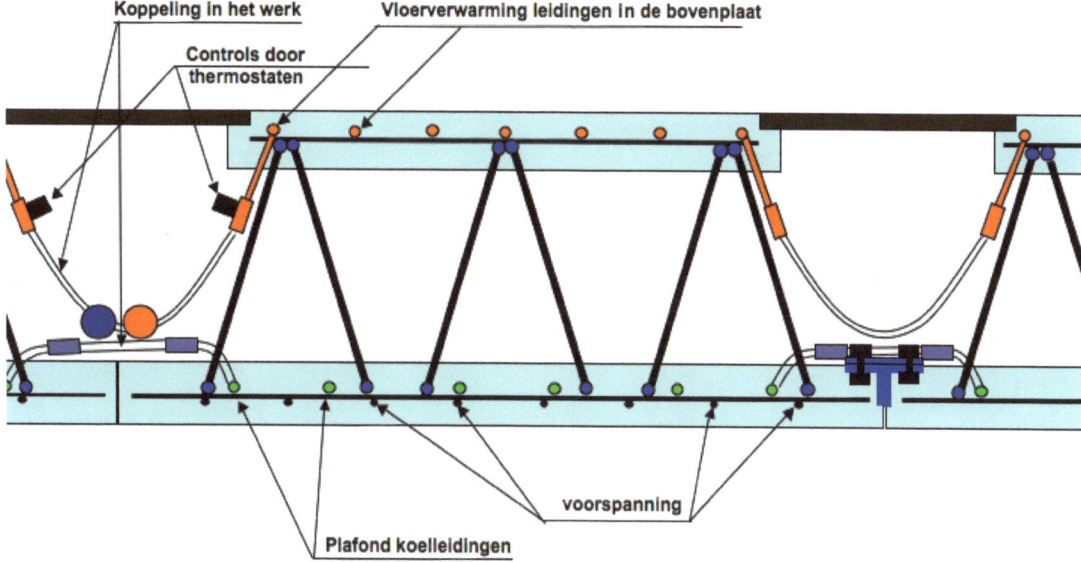

Fig. 09.11: Floor heating (red) and ceiling cooling (blue/green) system in the demountable Holcon floor system.

09.04 The Holcon floor

Architectural visitors will notice that the primary structure is also the finishing structure. A concrete skeleton with the novel, very stiff, double-layered 'Holcon' floor with diagonal steel reinforcement is applied throughout in the building.

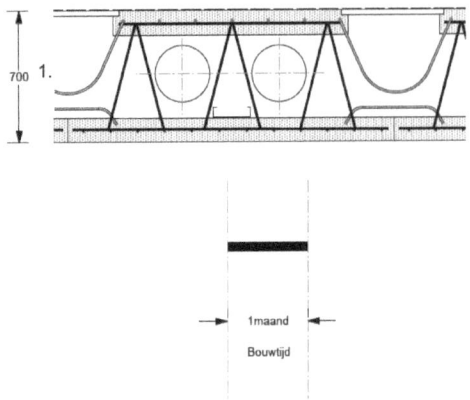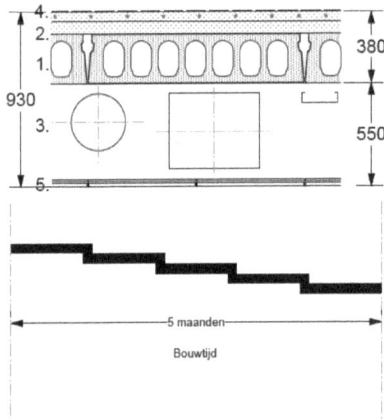

Fig. 09.12: Comparison of the Holcon floor with a traditional floor structure, both in technology, height and construction time.

The 0.7 meter hollow floor was developed by structural engineer Chiel Bartels and manufacturer Holterman from Markelo. The system can span 18 m, the distance required for the garage basement. This 18 m dimension, which allowed a large degree of layout flexibility, formed the basis of a structural grid pattern that was used throughout the plan. Even with a full loading at a span of 18 m, the floor structure hardly deflects.

Fig. 09.13: The Holcon floor, load tested at a maximum span of 18 m.

Fig. 09.14: Holcon floors mounted in the Villa Flora office block (left), leaving slots for the replacement of piping and wiring; the void between the upper and lower concrete layer, the non-bearing infrastructural space (right).

09.05 The process to delivery

09.05.01 From design to construction

Eventually the City of Venlo became the commissioner for Villa Flora, together with the regional municipalities. When public private partnership did not materialise, these municipalities took it upon themselves to build a large exposition greenhouse for the Floriade. This persistence can be applauded.

Volantis technical consultants participated enthusiastically from the first presentation of the plan. Collaboration in the translation of different innovations into construction drawings, budget and specifications was exemplary. Volantis also became the first firm to rent offices in the 'attic space' of Villa Flora. It was of great importance to have a creative local partner during the long period of realisation and political decision making.

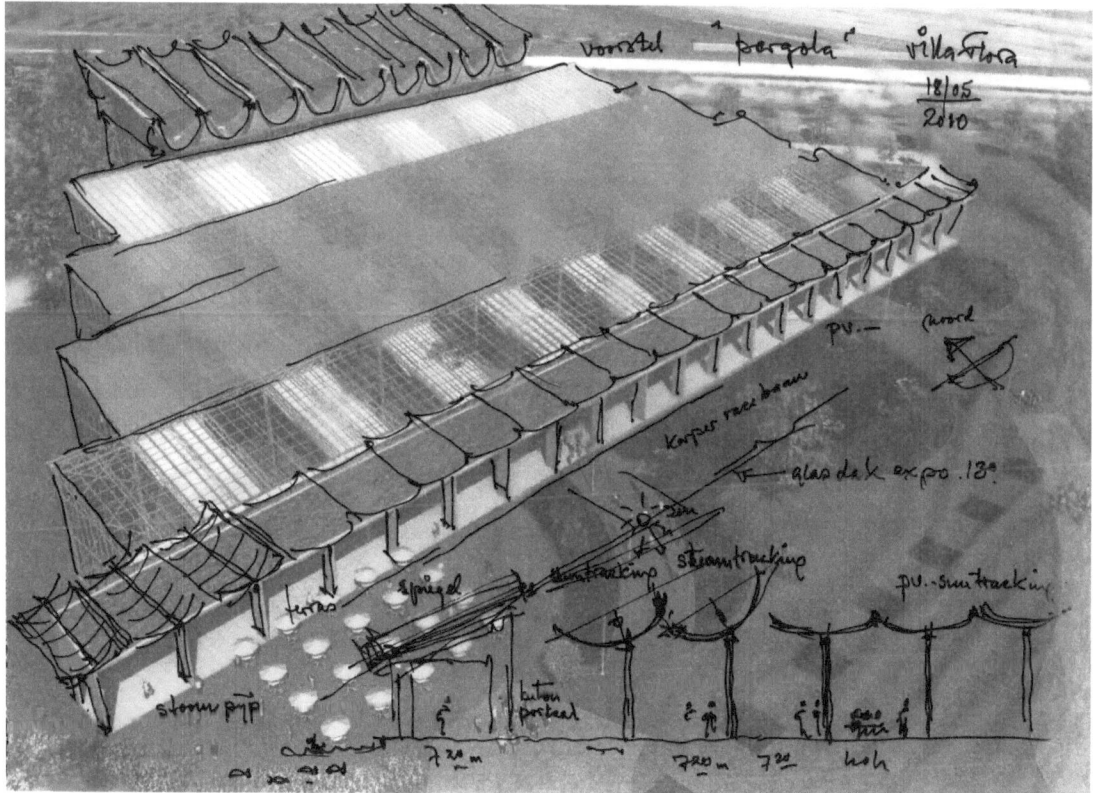

Fig. 09.15: Sketch by Jón Kristinsson for sun-tracking solar pergolas in front of Villa Flora, an alternative to the originally proposed electricity production by bio-fermentation.

The ambitious plan to provide Villa Flora with electricity only from biogas from the anaerobic fermentation of all organic waste from the Floriade and the adjacent flower auction, was eventually only realised on a small scale. Villa Flora's energetic self-sufficiency has now been established through PV panels. Similarly removed from the programme was the method to yield extra coolth and produce condensation water for drinking purposes (to be applied in arid areas of the world).

09.05.02   Encountering Murphy's Law

The prefabricated concrete structure with double Holcon floor elements was produced in Frankfurt am Main, Germany. The reinforcement steel was welded by Holterman in Markelo, the Netherlands.

Fig. 09.16:   Blocked by the 2011 Lorelei ship accident, prefab concrete portals and Holcon floors are trans-shipped to a quay in Germany[38]

The floors were transported from Frankfurt am Main by ship, over the river Rhine, in winter 2010-2011. Then an interesting sequence of events occurred. First the river Meuse flooded. Subsequently there was an early, long-lasting frost. Mid January 2011 a ship containing sulphuric acid sank in the famous Loreley bend of the river and obstructed all other ships for six weeks. Our ship was also halted and had to trans-ship the prefab concrete elements to a quay nearby. Here a second disaster struck when the Rhine swelled and flooded its banks, including the quay with our concrete floors.

---

[38] Photography courtesy of Sjaak Peters

The end of this story was that eventually all elements had to be transported to Venlo by truck after all. So in spite of our good intentions to use the most ecological transport possible, anthropogenic and natural calamities changed the storyline.

Fig. 09.17:   A river flood occurs after the trans-shipment of the concrete elements of Villa Flora [39] (left); the beautiful plan of sustainable transportation encountered Murphy's Law twice and eventually had to be solved by traditional road trucks, 16 in total

In spite all of this, ten weeks were won again by 7-days working weeks and easy assembly of the Holcon floors.

09.05.03   Delivery and further use

1st of October 2010 Twan Beurskens, alderman of the City of Venlo, performed the first official act submerging a capsule containing information about the events in Venlo into a concrete block. Pellikaan Construction Company (Tilburg) and Terberg building services (IJsselstein) delivered the building. Arcadis designed and constructed the garden.

Construction costs amounted to € 12.4 million or € 1,050/m² excl. VAT, including innovative building services.

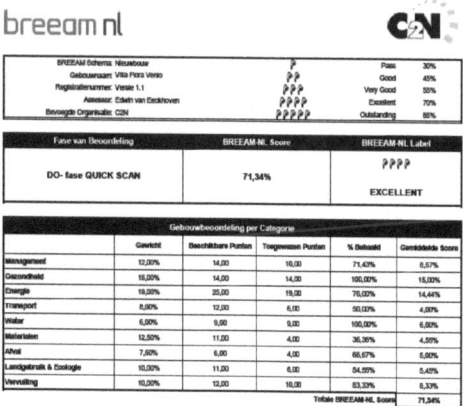
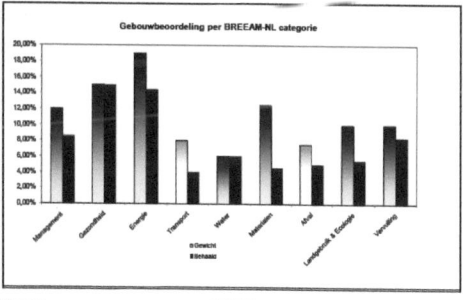

Fig. 09.18:   Scorecard of BREEAM-NL's assessment of Villa Flora.

---

[39] Photograph courtesy of Sjaak Peters

Interestingly, Villa Flora closes every cycle of energy, water and materials, but when tested on these aspects by BREEAM-NL, the building only received an 'excellent' rather than 'outstanding' accreditation. This confirms that innovative designs should not to be assessed by tools built on traditional technology alone.

The second life of Villa Flora, starting in early 2013, was known even before the official opening of the Floriade by Queen Beatrix of the Netherlands. The offices will remain rented, but the greenhouse, with catering and theatre facilities, will get a surprisingly new function as the 'Kids university of cooking'. Thus a visit to Villa Flora remains possible for the foreseeable future!

Fig. 09.19: View of Villa Flora from the Floriade cable car.

08.06 Conclusion

The Province of Limburg (where Venlo resides) strongly supports the Cradle to Cradle principle. The Holcon floor structure of Villa Flora perhaps is the only global concrete structure that can be completely dismounted. It can be installed rapidly, is relatively light-weight, fire-safe and provides great function flexibility in the building. A revolution.

Villa Flora is energetically self-sufficient, proof that for heating in buildings, low-temperature solar energy, even without a heat pump, can be a reasonably simple and cheap replacement for depleting fossil energy sources. The integration of horticulture in the built environment is a new option. Furthermore, seasonal storage of solar energy in aquifers, abundantly present in the Rhine delta, offers countries as the Netherlands a solution to be proven in Venlo.

Fig. 09.20:   Villa Flora[40].

Finally, what will be experienced as the uppermost environmental profit resulting from Villa Flora - the very low temperature heating and high temperature cooling by means of the Dutch Fiwihex fine-wire heat exchangers. These are the evidence that it is possible in horticulture, by just one step, to go from 50 m^3 of natural gas per m^2 to 0 (zero) m^3. The demonstration of this novel technique alone justifies the construction of Villa Flora.

---

[40] Photo by Marco Vellinga

10

ADDITIONAL IDEAS AND INVENTIONS

10.01 The bookshelf ceiling (1966)

Fig. 10.01: Fish-eye photograph of the Kristinssons' first home taken from the basement of the house (above), the bookshelf ceiling can be seen top left, and the article in the local newspaper discussing the remarkable intervention: 'Architectural couple uses basement as living space', upper heading: 'Room walls of six meter high' (below).

As in many other cases of smart ideas, the solution of ceiling bookshelves originated from lack of space. After their studies in Delft, the newly wed couple, Jón and Riet Kristinsson, purchased the basement and ground floor of a house in Deventer, in the eastern part of the Netherlands. As is expected from architects, they completely renovated the place, providing more space and light for living by opening the ground floor. It drew the attention of the local newspaper.

Fig. 10.02: Application of ceiling bookshelves in the basement(left) and round waste wood table (right) of the second and present home of the Kristinssons, at the Noordenbergsingel in Deventer.

Having to live within a confined space where every square meter of wall is precious and ceiling beams limit the height, why not give these beams an extra function? By nailing or screwing shelves to the beams, which often are significantly over-dimensioned, meters of library space can be created under the ceiling. This is what Jón and Riet Kristinsson did in their first basement home, and later copied in their second home and the Schildkamp-Peterse house.

Fig. 10.03: The first application of ceiling bookshelves in the first home of the Kristinssons (left) and a reprise of the idea in the refurbishment of the home of Mr. and Mrs. Schildkamp-Peterse

10.02 Energy-saving cooking (1991)

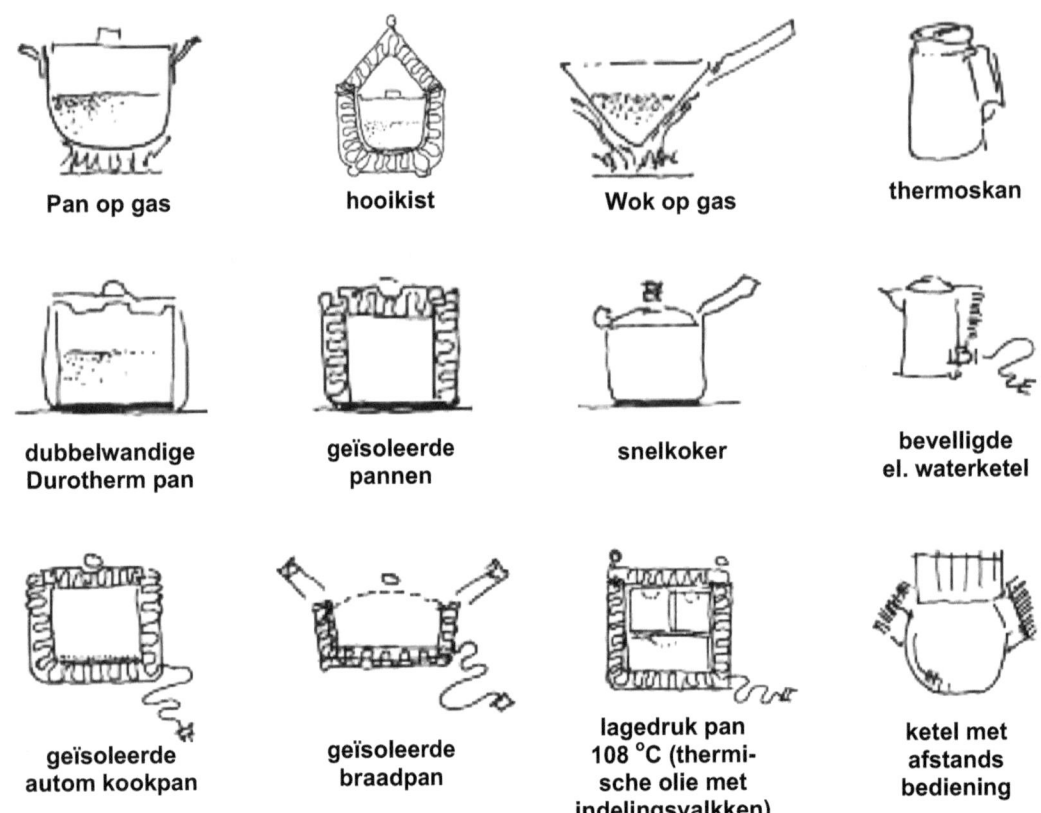

Fig. 10.04:   A full set of smart cooking devices.

'Normal' cooking by natural gas, as happens mostly in households across Europe, is dubious because of the production of water vapour and carbon dioxide. The energetic efficiency of the traditional saucepan on the gas stove is 4 to 6%. An eastern 'wok' frying pan achieves a top performance of 12-15%.

Good, intelligent and especially efficient cooking equipment is a necessity. It is recommended that novel thermally insulated cooking saucepans (with insulated lids) are developed, which serve as an old-fashioned hay chest, keeping food at temperature whilst using no energy, after food has been brought to boiling temperatures. Cooking on a gas stove will not last long much, not least due to the depletion of natural gas. In the previous decades electric cooking (including induction cooking) has evolved, but energy-saving solutions for saucepans are still absent.

10.03 Meat safe of the cool façade (1984)

Fig. 10.05: Sketch of the façade-integrated meat safe.

Present-day kitchens are a torture to the mind of an energy-conscious designer. Energy-sipping equipment can be installed wherever the customer wants, to whichever orientation, and fridges and freezers are collegially placed adjacent to heat-emitting appliances, drastically decreasing the energy performance found in the catalogue statistics of the manufacturer. The living environment is the best proof of an energy price still too low to start thinking smart.

Probably the most energy-consuming equipment of a kitchen, year-through, is the fridge and/or freezer. The technology of these cooling devices is based on the heat pump principle, a cycle of fluid being expanded, evaporated, compressed and condensated, providing cooling on the one side and heating on the other. A fridge's heater is the grill at the back, and for an optimal cooling performance this radiator needs to rid its heat easily, which becomes complicated when combined with another heat emitting device, such as an stove, oven, microwave or dishwasher.

A large proportion of energy could be saved if the fridge and freezer were situated to the northern façade (northern hemisphere) of a building, keeping the content cooler next to a (poorly insulated) façade that hardly receives solar heat. This would make the removal of heat from the fridge itself easier, enhancing the cooling process.

Not all food needs to be refrigerated down to 7°C or lower, but can be stored, just as in the old days, in a cool, dry place. In that respect, in most countries away from the equator a hole in the ground is not a bad idea, as the soil airducts described in chapter 05 demonstrated. Likewise, using the north façade as a passive fridge or 'meat safe' (an ancient term) can be an effective solution in temperate to cold climates.

In 1984 Jón Kristinsson applied this concept in Minimum-Energy dwellings in Schiedam. The north façade meat safe had a small fridge, using far less energy than a traditional appliance.

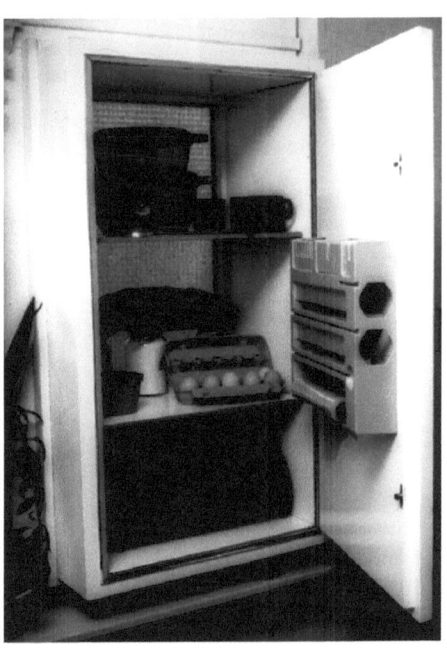

Fig. 10.06:   *Realisation of a new-fashioned meat safe in the north façade of the Minimum-Energy dwellings of Schiedam.*

Similar stories about improving the energy performance of modern households could be told about the efficient use of heat or warmth. Waste heat from electric or cooling devices could be used directly or indirectly – via storage – in heat-requiring functions, which occur nowadays by means of a heat pump boiler connected to the exhaust of a building. This internal heat loss could also often be reduced, as Kristinsson's drawing of an energy-saving bath demonstrates.

Fig. 10.07:   *Idea for a well-insulated bath tub, preserving the hot water for a longer period and simultaneously providing a table for other relaxing activities.*

10.04 The 'sund-pit' (early 1970s)

Fig. 10.08: The sund-pit, simple and effective.

Entertaining children in cold weather can be a challenge to every parent. In response Jón Kristinsson designed a simple hatch for his children's sand-pit, with a heat reflecting steel plate, keeping the sand warmer with a bit of low sunshine, especially apt for spring and fall.

10.05 Integrated street lanterns, Leerdam (1974)

Fig. 10.09: Image of the former Sparta field housing plan, with integrated lanterns attached to the dwellings.

In Leerdam we developed 116 social dwellings for employees of the world famous glass factory, on the former site of the Sparta football club. The brief asked for the preservation of existing trees. As a consequence of the ground conditions storerooms were integrated into the homes, instead of separate sheds. Cars were removed from external public areas and parked on four concentrated spots where access roads terminated.

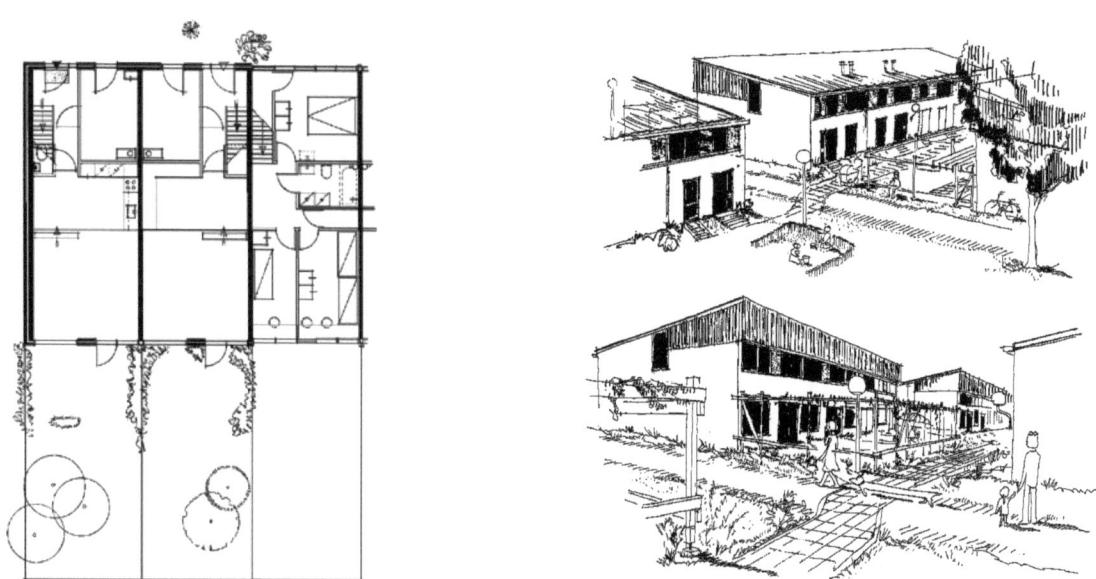

Fig. 10.10: Internal floor area of each house is 4.60 x 11.54 m, with minimum corridor space. With regard to the very long pile foundation needed in this area, storerooms are integrated into the dwellings.

The absence of a traditional street frontage, made for an unconventional solution for street lampposts. By attaching the street lighting, developed in cooperation with AEG, to the façade, less foundation piles had to be driven into the boggy ground.

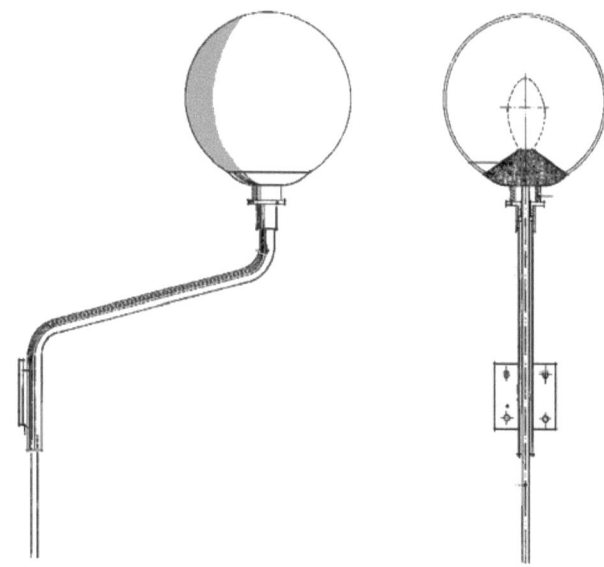

Fig. 10.11: Street lighting armatures, developed in cooperation with AEG.

10.06 Tidal mills (1991)

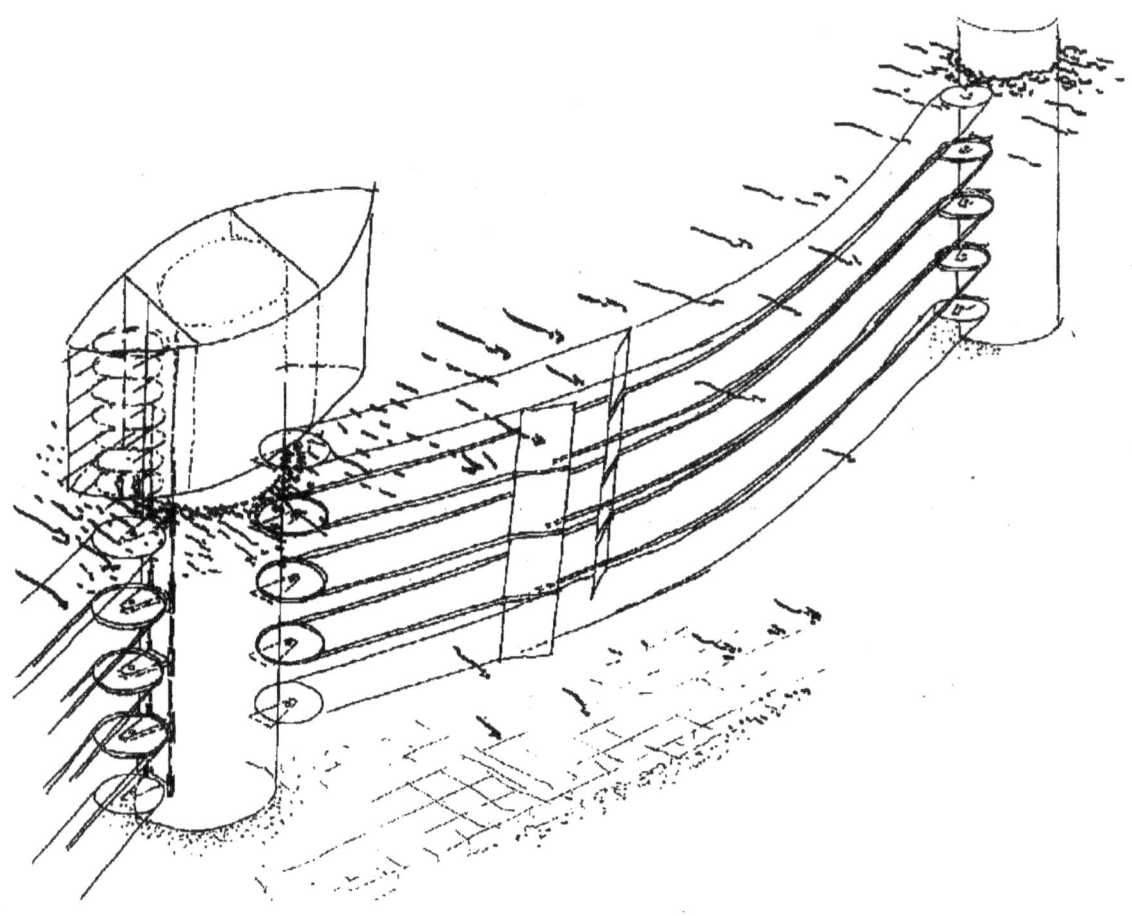

Fig. 10.12:   Sketch of a tidal mill at work in a sea or river currents.

The force of attraction of the moon and the sun on the earth causes tidal currents four times a day. Tidal power stations making use of the great height of fall between low and high tide and vice versa, are found at the river mouth of La Range in North-West France. Less well-known are tidal stations which only generate energy from the current without height of fall. Due to the low energy density an extensive collection area is of primary importance.

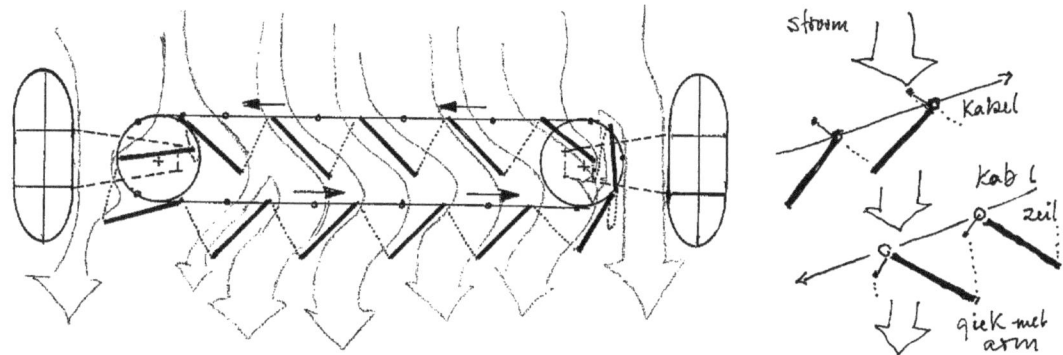

Fig. 10.13: Principle of the tidal mill: the sea or river current pushes sails along a conveyor like track, thereby setting the 'caterpillar' in motion. Both the upstream and downstream sails work to keep the movement going. Sails tack or jibe at the turning points.

"Slow is strong" we could say, because the rate of flow of tidal water is known, usually 5 km/hour. This invention belongs to a taxonomy of ecologically clean electricity generators all over the world.

Fig. 10.14: Jón Kristinsson demonstrating a scale model of his tidal mill (1991).[41]

---

[41] After twenty years Jón has started to think on tidal energy again, but this time in an integrated way: 'floating tidal power plants', wave energy, wind energy and algue protein harvest or fish ponds. You might find the lay-out and calculations of it in the next edition of this book.

10.07 North Sea atolls (1980)

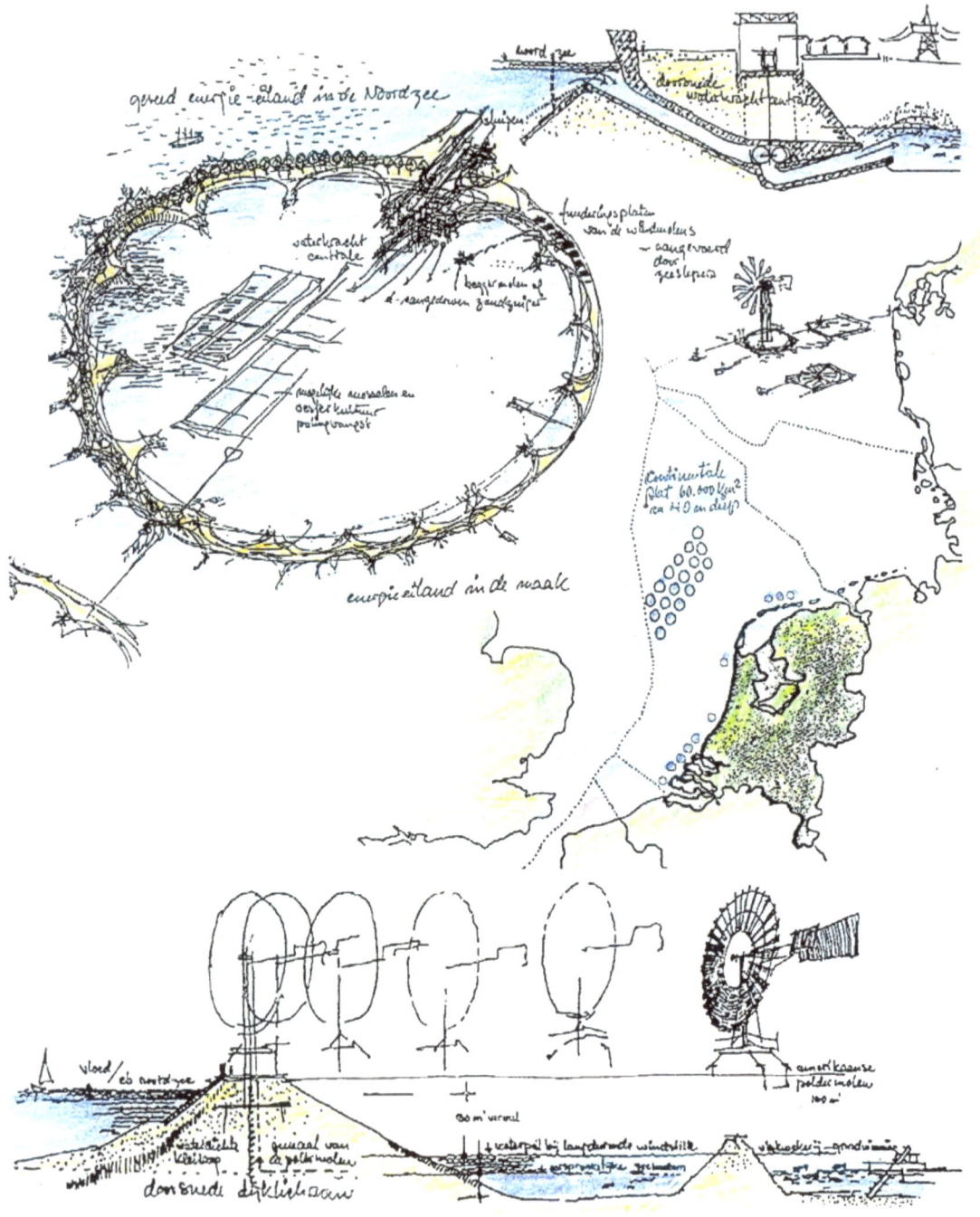

Fig. 10.15: Original drawings of the North Sea Atolls concept by Jón Kristinsson, presented on the Kristinsson's Christmas card in 1980.

In chapter 02 we discussed the threat of climate change, in particular to low-lying delta areas as the Netherlands. In this area the influence of the rise of the North Sea demands three solutions:

1. Tackle the problem at the source. The most adequate method would be taking away the cause of global climate change, for instance by halving the emission of carbon from fuel. For the time being this is still a dream.
2. The usual solution: raising the dikes. The sporadic convergence of extremely high tides (once every 200 years, although this figure may alter because of climate change) and a long-lasting north-western storm surge is a great threat currently resisted by high sea dikes and storm locks.
3. Development of new concepts? An analysis of the problem: the water table rises up to 5 m incidentally through wind and sea tide; the water table rises through global warming; great surges erode dikes and dunes. These problems can also be approached by abating the sporadic extreme springtide through a defence system in front of the coast. Thereby dikes need not be raised again and carbon production need not be reduced by force.

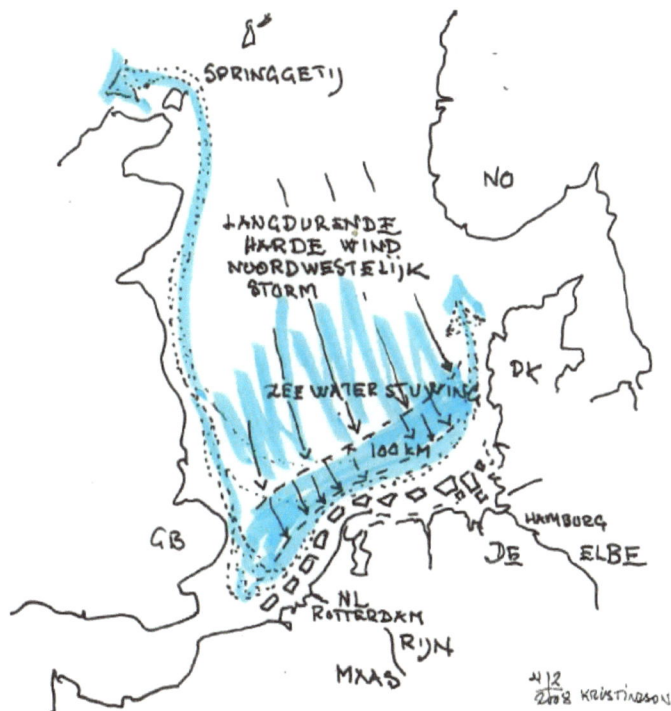

Fig. 10.16: An update sketch by Jón Kristinsson of the North Sea Atolls, acknowledging that all countries around the North Sea would benefit from this solution (2008).

An alternative solution would provide a buffer for seawater in case of a springtide once every 200 years. Therefore empty water basins need to be established in front of the Dutch coast. On average the North Sea is only 20 m deep in the seaway. An atoll island with a diameter of at least 10 km has a buffering capacity of about 4 km^3 (4 x 10^{12} litres) of seawater. The temporary storm surge level decrease will depend on the number of atolls.

The North Sea atolls could serve the following purposes:
- Coastal defence:
  - Storm surge water inlet into the depression inside the atolls.
  - Storm peak shaving so common defences can manage what comes through.
- Energy islands:
  - Peak hour electricity generated by inlet water turbines.
  - Large-capacity windmills for water drainage.
  - Kinetic energy storage through drained atolls.
- Productive islands:
  - Unlimited collection of sand and gravel in combination with water storage.
  - Storage of polluted dredging spoil from large rivers.
  - Fish ponds – green algae as fish food.
  - A working island that can be minimally manned.

Feasibility
On the basis of Jón Kristinsson's ideas of a 'necklace' of atolls along the coast of the Netherlands, in 2008 Noor van Andel calculated the investment costs and benefits of the endeavor. It turned out that the investment would amount to approximately € 43.2 billion. The yield of the wind turbines along the atoll ring would produce electricity of a value of € 11.7 billion. Algae production would lead to gains (capitalised to 10 years) of € 40.5 billion, thus leaving a profit of € 9.0 billion. So the greatest merit was to be achieved by produce from the inner grounds of the atolls. Fish farming was not taken into account.

Water wizard
The North Sea atolls concept was originally described and illustrated on the 1981 official Christmas card of Kristinsson Architects & Engineers. It was later presented as a chapter in the book issued at the 150th anniversary of the Dutch national department of Water Management, called 'Watertovenaars' ('water wizards') [d'Angremond, 1998].

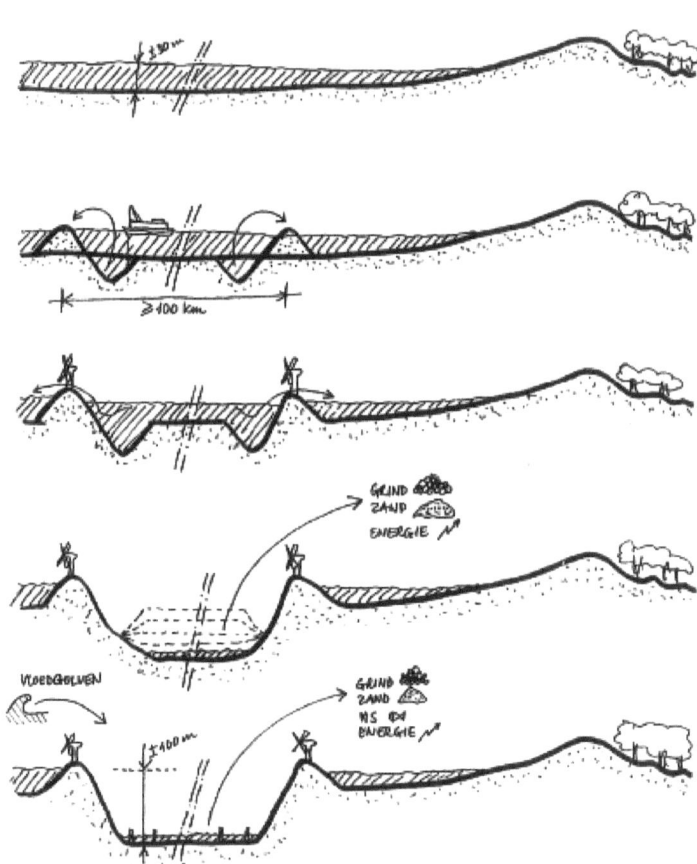

Fig. 10.17: *Construction sequence of a North Sea atoll (d'Angremond, 1998).*

10.08 Respect the tree

Fig. 10.18:   Need we say more? The Kristinssons' garden wall.

The citizens of Deventer perhaps know Jón Kristinssons better for his achievements in the city, rather than from his architecture. Ever since Jón and Riet became inhabitants of the old hanseatic city, they have been proactive members of the community. In an successful attempt to avoid unnecessary cutting of old trees in their street, Jón became chair to the Deventer Bomenstichting (Deventer tree foundation), which after their first successes remained an important party for municipal decisions regarding green spaces and trees. In 2006 the foundation presented a book on their work. In 2011 the old Hanseatic town of Deventer was awarded 'the greenest town in Europe'.
The most beautiful instance of the Kristinssons' respect to nature and trees is their garden wall.

10.09 Dying sustainably

The only certainty for every living creature is death. The process of dying is a personal experience, but the treatment of the dead body is worth some attention when we want to include the issue of sustainability (which is an odd connection to death…).

Fig. 10.19: Pyramid of Saqqara and the City of the Dead in Cairo, Egypt.

Time, people and religion each have their own extremes: from vultures to the Egyptian pyramids. Cairo's 'City of the Dead', with burial temples, sarcophagi and tombs.

Fig. 10.20: Piled graves in Arezzo, Italy (left); The crowded cemetery of Prague (right)

Limited space
Many European cities have beautiful cemeteries, but often an over-accumulation of tombstones such as in the old Jewish cemetery in Prague. Among others in Italy and Spain you see coffins piled up in mausoleums. In Japan you can find special abortion temples. The cemetery of Père

Lachaise, with its many celebrities is neglected. In contrast, in Cuban Havana the cemeteries are better taken care of than the city itself.

Fig. 10.21:   Abortion temple in Japan, with clothed puppets, and a cemetery in Havana.

The rich saved money for the afterlife, but often the available 'storeroom' was limited. In ancient times in Christian countries it was fashionable and expensive to be buried in the church. However, in the Netherlands was also troublesome with a limited depth and high ground water level. The Dutch expression of 'rich stinker' results from church masses where odours emanated from the decaying underground.

Durable but not sustainable
Graves that are not privately owned are cleared after a period of time. The remaining bones are collected in a common grave to make place for new graves. A few decades ago synthetic materials made their entry in the burial industry. Without the influence of ultraviolet sunlight synthetics do not decay underground. When a cemetery needs to be cleared away today, to make way for the construction of a road, for instance, it is amazing what one gets to see. The coffins that used to consist of wood are now usually made of synthetically glued chipboard with wood veneer. It does not decay. The grips, as well as the made-made lining, stay intact. The body has decayed almost completely, but in case the person was buried with synthetic clothing, the shoes can be taken out, the tie, shirt and other clothing sent to the dry cleaners and reused – perhaps!

Corpses that have been exposed to chemotherapy or excessive medication appear not to decay: they have been mummified. This all can be logically explained, but at the point of body bags this story becomes repulsive. Corpses of traffic victims, unidentified people in an extreme state of decomposition, as well as waste from hospitals such as amputated arms and legs, are often buried in zipped-up synthetic bags. Of these waste products foetuses, in all stages of development, are the most remarkable. In these closed body bags an anaerobic metabolism takes place instead of decay.

Fig. 10.22: The 1926 columbarium by W. M. Dudok [42].

Cremation

Cremation was already commonplace in ancient Greece. In the Netherlands it became legal in 1915. It was first possible in the Westerveld cemetery (Driehuis, near Haarlem) with the construction of an columbarium in 1926 by the architect W.M. Dudok. It was only in 1968 that burial and cremation became equal within the law. Cremation is often disapproved of culturally and religiously, but environmentally, as we have discovered here, can be seen from a whole different perspective.

Conclusion

- During the cremation process it is sensible to use an inner coffin made of cardboard, and an external decorative and reusable outer shell. Clothing will have to be environmentally friendly. In this way gas emissions will cause minimal pollution in the air.
- If burial is the preferred option, do so in a timber coffin with timber handles. A shroud made of linen, without pockets for money and credit cards, would be appropriate attire for the afterlife.

Fig. 10.23: Even in paradise, death is imminent.

---

[42] source: W.M. Dudok 1884-1974 architecture museum foundation

10.10 Lustrum books and Christmas cards

Amongst their pentannual lustrum books and conferences, the Kristinssons' have numerous other traditions, of which the Christmas cards are very well known amongst colleagues, commissioners and other contacts. To many of them, the upcoming Christmas card is always something exciting, as new ideas from Jón Kristinsson often appear for the first time on these cards. As discussed in the previous section, the idea of the North Sea atolls was such a revelation that came through the post, before it was disseminated to a larger audience.

Fig. 10.24:   The nine lustrum books issued by the Kristinsson Architects & Engineers: everytime an exciting and inspiring read.

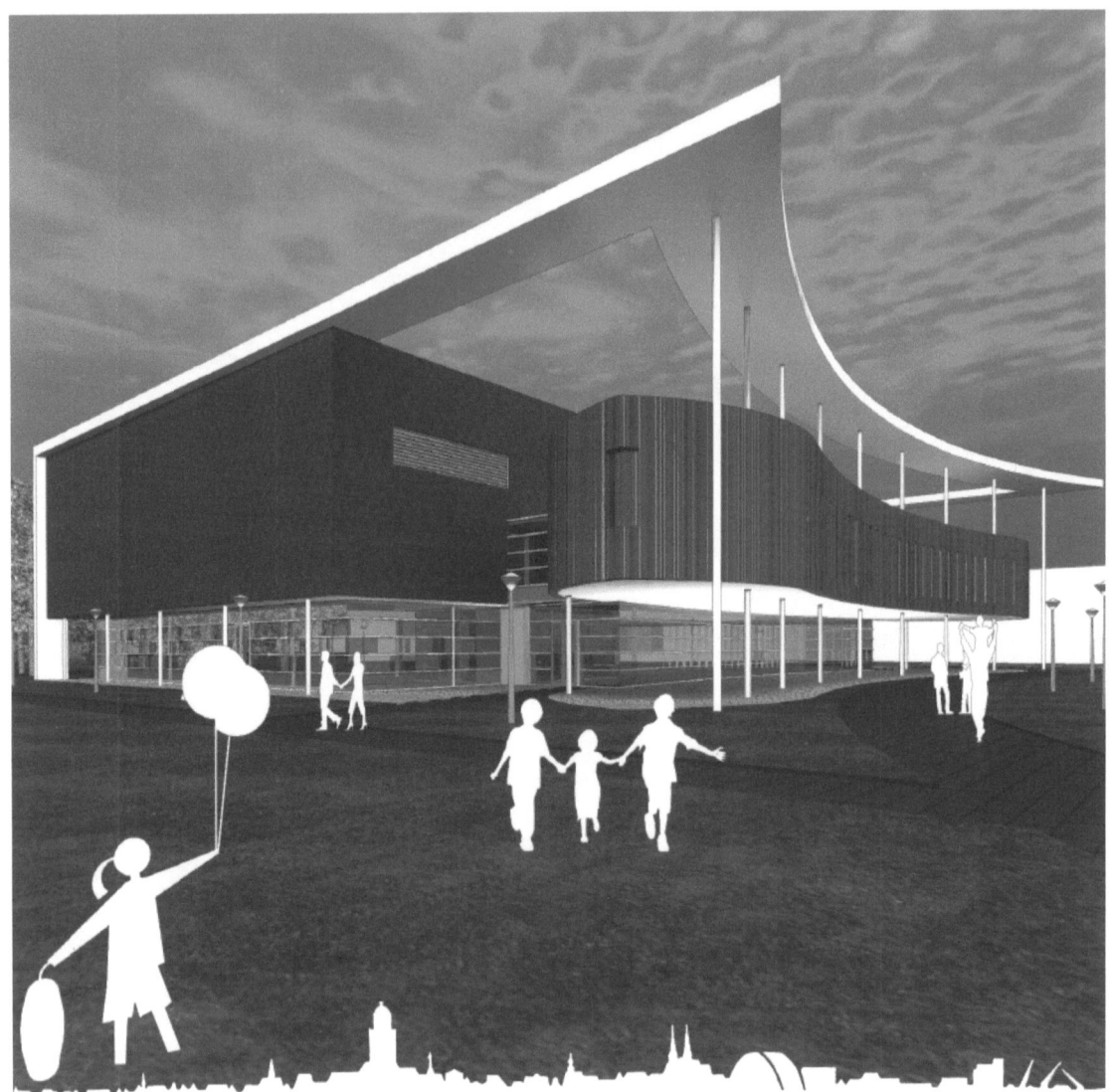

Fig. 10.25: The Kristinsson Architectural Engineers' Christmas card of 2010.

11
EPILOGUE

Significance

The Kristinssons' work is too vast to present in a book less than a thousand pages. All lustrum books of Kristinsson Architects & Engineers combined could perhaps give an impression. This book was intended to give an essential synopsis of the vision, theory and projects of Jón Kristinsson, conceived and realised. And more often: not realised. For, it is the fate and yoke of a pioneer that most of his ideas are not understood, that their meaning is lost with lesser souls, hence not put through or – even worse – neglected. In this sense, Jón has experienced many disappointments and resistance, up to this day. It is witness to his remarkable energy and positivity that throughout the 46 years of his career he has continued and persevered, for which homage needs to be paid also to his wife, Riet Kristinsson-Reitsema, for her inspiring and continued support.

Can we grasp the significance of Jón Kristinsson's ideas, inventions and designs? I think not. The way he preceded present-day's construction already in the late 1970s and early 1980s might give an impression of the catching up we will experience in the years to come. A lot of the master's ideas have still not been realised or died a premature death due to economical reasons. And economy is a sign of the times: unfeasible once may become feasible under altered conditions. Therefore, I hope and also expect that this book, finished in the year 2012, will be recognised for its newly applied techniques and design approaches for decades to come. And, mind, Jón Kristinsson is still active and productive – to the extent that this now published book cannot keep pace - I hope he will remain so for a very long time.

The book has presented and discussed technology, architecture and urbanism projects that have always appealed to me and taught me a way of thinking. More than this, together with a limited group of colleagues at Kristinsson's office and at the Delft University of Technology, I have had the indescribable pleasure to be taught much more about life than just integrated sustainable design. I am not referring to Jón's lessons on how to hang and store a suit in a rocking ship, or how to lay your pencil on a table for the fastest kick-start to writing, or how a domestic fly lands onto a ceiling upside down, or how books on elephants perfectly describe national peculiarities, or how one can make soup from a two-inch nail. I am not referring to these and many more useful and useless artefacts of Kristinsson's humorous mind. No, more than that, Jón Kristinsson is a master of life, who, if you are open-minded, can inspire you to a better, nicer, healthier, more meaningful way of life.

Once, at his professional farewell speech at TU Delft, I joked that his self-appraised 'management by exception' to us as employees was rather 'acceptance of no management'. It is only since I've had to manage a group of my own, I now understand the incredible value of being able to limit management to the essential interventions and let emerging talents grow (stimulated by the mental food of fresh ideas every single working day) and become more independent [43]. I will always be grateful for this and I am sure many others will too.

Thinking back, Jón's remark once that at his office no improper word could ever be heard, has proven to be true. Based on his principle to never do things for which you can be 'caught' later, Jón Kristinsson is a person of incredible friendliness, hospitality and decency, which – as all of his contacts can confirm – is something completely different from boring.
I cannot imagine a better teacher, on all aspects of life.

---

[43] Now, I must mention that Jón's wife Riet was his stronghold at home and at the office, whereas his two 'right arms' (Kristinsson's own words) Arjan van Timmeren and I could preserve the structure at the university.

On this three-years enterprise, the book was overtaken by a 48 minutes documentary 'between Sun and Magma' (Dutch with English subtitles) about Jón Kristinsson's vision on sustainable building. The intriguing documentary was filmed and edited by his son Kris, produced by his wife Riet, sponsored by a number of companies and especially by few hundred friends of Jón. This film is available on DVD, for instance at: www.boekhandelpraamstra.nl. I was happy to be witness to the process towards this other great product.

I sincerely hope that this book brings to you inspiration, imagination and understanding of an holistic approach to the built environment. And I hope that you will – as in the spirit of Jón and Riet Kristinsson themselves – make extra leaps forward in this area, be it as a politician, manager, commissioner, project developer, urban planner, architect, engineer, consultant, contractor, student, or at least as a user of that built environment. It is what a sustainable world for our children and grandchildren still dearly needs.

Acknowledgements
The translation, editing and writing of this book was unsponsored, in private time, and with love and pleasure.
Of course I want to thank Jón and Riet Kristinsson themselves for providing me with so much information on projects they achieved. Especially Riet, for the numerous hours spent on supplying me with images. I thank them also for the progress meetings: Jón, for the fine wine; Riet, for the tasty fish and seafood; both, for the immense pleasure of staying at their home and sharing with me a myriad of ideas on all kinds of societal, social and cultural subjects. You are truly homini universalis.
I also would like to specially thank Laura Kleerekoper for supporting me in translating a vast part of the original text from Jón Kristinsson's 2002 book. And special thanks to Craig Martin, who in the end spent a lot of time doing a thorough check on the English (rather Dunglish I'm afraid…), transforming into a second, neutral editor of the book. Michiel Fremouw, thanks for help on earlier versions of the sleeve. And thanks to Jim Voet, for his support on getting this actual paper stack published.
To my home front, Sandra, Noé and Isha: thank you for showing great patience and awarding me the private time to spend on this book. I hope you agree it was worth it.

Andy van den Dobbelsteen

References

- Andel E. van; Fine wire heat exchanger; available on-line: www.fiwihex.com
- Andel E. van & Oei P.T.; 'Verwarming van huizen, straks niet meer nodig' (first publication), in: Financieel Dagblad, 18 januari 2008
- d'Angremont K. (ed.); Watertovenaars; Bèta Imaginations publisher, 1998 (ISBN 90-75961-01-4)
- Architecten- en Ingenieursbureau Kristinsson; Een c.v.-loze woning voor de sociale woningbouw; in: 1st, 2nd, 3rd, 4th, 5th, 6th, 7th and 8th lustre book; Deventer 1971, 1976, 1981, 1986, 1991, 1996, 2001, 2006
- Barnett S.A.; The science of life - From cells to survival; Allen & Unwin, 1998 (ISBN 1 86448 610 4)
- Beukel A. van de; Pleidooi voor meer nutteloosheid (exit speech); TU Delft, 1997
- Björkholm Y. & Lindqvist M.; Ekologi som inspirerar, 12 miljöanpassade hus; AB Svensk Byggtjänst och för fattarna, 1996 (ISBN 91.7332.779.4)
- Blauw K.; Duurzame woningbouw in perspectief; DUP Satellite, 2001 (ISSN 1384-1173; 80, ISBN 90-407-2245-5, NUGI 655)
- Bono E. de; Lateral Thinking – Creativity Step by Step; Harper, 1973
- Boon H. den; Bouwen met zonne-energie; Ekologische Uitgeverij, 1979 (ISBN 90 6224 0275)
- Bouwfonds; Het energiezuinige woningtype van Kristinsson; Bouwfonds, 1994
- Brouwers R.; Lelystad wil het niet van de zonzijde bekijken; in: Wonen, TA/BK 21, 1977
- CBS (Centraal Bureau voor de Statistiek); Statistisch zakboek; SDU uitgeverij, The Hague, 1996
- Colborn Th. et al.; Our stolen future; Abacus, 1997 (ISBN: 0 349 10878 1)
- Commoner B.; The closing circle: nature, man and technology; Random House, USA, 1971
- Commoner, B.; The poverty of power; A. Knopf, New York, 1976
- DHV; Evaluatie minimum-energiewoning - Evaluatie van een praktijkexperiment van 76 eengezinswoningen; ; DHV Raadgevend Ingenieursbureau Amersfoort, 1985
- DHV; Evaluatie minimum-energiewoningen gestapelde bouw; DHV Raadgevend Ingenieursbureau Amersfoort, 1987
- Dobbelsteen A. van den (ed.), Integraal ontwerpen; MTO, Bouwkunde, TU Delft, 1995
- Dobbelsteen A. van den & Linden K. van der; 'Self-directing learning - Getting students to learn effectively about smart en bioclimatic design', in: PLEA 2007 - Sun, Wind and Architecture (816-821); NUS, Singapore, 2007
- Dobbelsteen A. van den, Roggema R., Stegenga K., Slabbers S.; 'Using the Full Potential - Regional planning based on local potentials and exergy', in: Brebbia C.A. (ed.), Management of Natural Resources, Sustainable Development and Ecological Issues (177-186); WIT Press, Southampton, 2006
- Dobbelsteen A. van den, Timmeren A. van & Kristinsson J.; Van blokkades naar potenties; Bouwkunde, TU Delft, 1995
- Dorling D., Newman M. & Barford A.; The Atlas of the Real World - Mapping the way we live; Thomas & Hudson, 2009
- Dubbelboer B.; Leer mij ze kennen de Drenten; A.W. Sijthoff, Leiden, 1968
- Duijvestein C.; Ecologisch bouwen (8th edition); SOM, Bouwkunde, TU Delft, 1993
- Duijvestein C.; Hoe duurzaam/durable is duurzaam/sustainable?, in: Jaarboek 2000; DIOC De Ecologische Stad, Æneas, 2000
- Duijvestein C.; Drie stappen strategie - Milieu Maximalisatie Methode - de drie lijnen van Duurzaam Bouwen, in: Praktijkhandboek Duurzaam bouwen; WEKA Uitgeverij Amsterdam, 2001
- Dyring A. & Dyring E.; Jorden-globala förändringar, Moderna Museet / Spårvagnshallarna; Trelleborg, Skogs Bockryker1 AB, 1994
- Ehrlich P. & Ehrlich A.; The population explosion; Hutchinson, London, 1990
- Eijk P. van; Water in de stedelijke vernieuwing, een participatiestrategie; Æneas, uitgeverij van vakinformatie, 2002 (ISBN 90 75365 48 9)
- Emoto M.; De kwaliteit van water, in: Vruchtbare Aarde no. 4 / 01
- Fussler C. & James P.; Driving Eco-innovation; Pitman publishing, 1996 (ISBN: 0 273 62207 2)
- Geurts H. & Kuiper J.; Weergaloos Nederland; Kosmos-Z&K Uitgevers/KNMI (ISBN: 90 215 94986)
- Gore A.; An Inconvenient Truth - The Planetary Emergency of Global Warming and What We Can Do About It; Rodale, New York, 2006
- Haas M. & Schmid P.; Bio-logisch bouwen en wonen - Gezond voor mens en milieu; Uitgeverij Ankh-Hermes bv-Deventer, 1990 (ISBN 90 202 2500 6)
- Hasselaar E.; How healthy is the Dutch dwelling; OBT-research, Delft University of Technology, 2001 (ISBN 90 4072257 9)
- Heel H.P. van & Jansen J.L.A.; Met zoeken en leren duurzaam op weg (Dies speech); TU Delft, 8 januari 1993
- Hendriks Ch.F. & Duijvestein C.A.J. (eds.); The Ecological City; Æneas Technical Publishers, 2002
- Hoogakker J.; 'Energie – de grote urgentie'; lecture at the postacademic course 'Op naar energieproducerende gebouwen' (Towards energy-rpoducing buildings), TU Delft, 2010

- Hough M.; Cities and Nature Process; Routledge L+NY, 1995 (ISBN: 0 415 12198 1)
- Husslage W. et al.; Stedelijke Ontwikkeling en Milieu (scriptieprijs); Ministerie van VROM, 1996 (ISBN 90 422 0052 9)
- Huynen M.M., Martens P., Schram D., Weijenberg M.P. & A E Kunst A.E.; 'The impact of heat waves and cold spells on mortality rates in the Dutch population', in: Environmental Health Perspectives, Vol. 109, No. 5, 2001 (463-470)
- IPCC (Intergovernmental Panel on Climate Change); Climate Change 2007: Fourth Assessment Report; IPCC, Switzerland, 1 February, 2007
- Jacobs A.B.; Great Streets; MIT Press, Cambridge MA, 1995 (ISBN: 0 262 10048 7)
- Jansen J.L.A. & Vergragt Ph.J.; Sustainable Technological Development (Accepted Proposal); TU Delft, 1992
- Jong T.M. de; Technische milieuplanning & ecologie; Bouwkunde, TU Delft, 1992
- Jong T.M. de & Dobbelsteen A. van den; Milieu-effecten van het energiegebruik, TU Delft, Faculty of Architecture, 1998
- Kasteren J. van; Duurzame Technologie; De Wetenschappelijke Bibliotheek, 2002 (ISBN 90 76988 021)
- Keeffe G.P., Means, Means - adventures in the Technoscape vol. 1; MSA Press, Manchester, 2008
- KNMI; Klimaatatlas 1970-2000; KNMI, De Bilt, 2006
- KNMI; Bosatlas van het klimaat; Wolters Noordhoff, Groningen, 2009
- Kristinsson J. et al.; Integraal ontwerpen - zonnewoningen te Leiderdorp; Bouwkunde, TH Delft, 1982
- Kristinsson J.; Architectural design for local conditions - Innovative low-energy concepts for the year 2025; IEA Workshop Future Buildings, Helsinki, 1-3 September 1992
- Kristinsson J.; Integraal Ontwerpen ofwel De Nieuwe NoodZakelijkheid (inaugural speech); TU Delft, 14 mei 1993 (ISBN 90 5269 131 2)
- Kristinsson J.; Permanent individual / collective transport; IFHP lecture, Gotenburg, 1 October 1997
- Kristinsson J.; Integraal Ontwerpen / Vitale Architectuur; Kristinsson-Reitsema BV, Deventer & Aeneas, Boxtel, 2002 (ISBN 90 75365 58 6)
- Kristinsson J.; Breathing Window; Proceedings International Conference Smart and Sustainable Building (SASBE 2003); QUT, Brisbane, 2003
- Kristinsson J.; Integraal Ontwerpen - van zon tot magma (exit speech); TU Delft, 7 June 2002 (ISBN 90 5269 3021)
- Kristinsson J. & Dobbelsteen A. van den; 'Breathing Window - The Next Step: First test Results of the Smart Room Ventilation System Prototype', in: Proceedings SASBE 2006 (49-56 (CD-rom)): CIB / SRIBS, Shanghai, 2006
- Kristinsson J. & Dobbelsteen A. van den; The Greenest Building in the Netherlands, in: Proceedings SB08 (World Sustainable Building Conference), Melbourne, 2008
- Kristinsson J. & Timmeren, A. van; Fine-Wire Heat Exchanger can effectively heat and cool houses, in: Proceedings PLEA 2008, Dublin
- Kristinsson J., Dobbelsteen A. van den & Timmeren A. van; 'Fine-Wire Heat Exchanger Works at Very Low Temperature', in: Proceedings PLEA2009 - Architecture Energy and the Occupant's Perspective; PLEA, Quebec City, 2009
- Kuiper Compagnons et al.; Aanzet Stadrandvisie Drachten (KC - 326.112.000); Gemeente Smallingerland, 1994
- Kuppan T.; Heat exchanger design handbook - Compact heat exchangers; M. Dekker Inc., New York, Basel, 2000 (ISBN: 0 8247 9787 6)
- Lawson B.; How designers think; Butterworth Architecture, Oxford, 1991
- Limperg K.; Naar warmere woningen; Van Holkema, Amsterdam, 1936 (TNO, 1960)
- Linden A.C. van der; Bouwfysica; Uitgeverij Waltman Delft, 1985 (ISBN 90 212 3095 X)
- Lomborg B.; The Sceptical Environmentalist; Cambridge University Press, 2001 (ISBN 0 521 01068 3)
- Luising A.; Integrated façade system with algae for waste water purification (master thesis); TU Delft, 1998
- Madge J.; Tomorrow's houses; London Pilot Press Ltd, 1946
- Mennink B.D. et al.; Kunstijsbanen en Energiebesparing (TNO-rapport no. 86060)
- Mollison B.; Permaculture; Island Press, 1990 (ISBN: 1 55963 048 5)
- Mulder A.; Levende systemen - Reis naar het einde van het informatietijdperk; Van Gennep, 2002 (ISBN 90 5515 310 9/ NUGI 1661)
- Nederlands Normalisatie-instituut; NEN 1087 (nl); NEN, Delft, 2001
- Nederlands Normalisatie-instituut; NEN 5077 (nl); NEN, Delft, 2001
- Nederlands Normalisatie-instituut; NPR 1088 (nl); NEN, Delft, 1999
- Newman P.W.G. & Kenworthy J.R.; Gasoline consumption and cities - A comparison of U.S. cities with a global survey and some implications; Murdoch University, Murdoch, W.A., USA, 1987
- Newton P.; 'Urban Form and Environmental Performance', in: Williams K., Burton E. & Jenks M. (eds.), Achieving Sustainable Urban Form (46-53); Spon Press, London/New York, 2001

- NOVEM; Regionaal Energiegebruik Gebouwde, Omgeving Minimum-Energiewoning (NOVEM publ. no.1); NOVEM, Sittard, 1983
- NOVEM/BNA; De EPN in het woningbouwontwerp – vuistregels; NOVEM/BNA, 2002
- Paulos J.A.; Ongecijferdheid; Bert Bakker, Amsterdam, 1991
- Rgd/Linden A.C. van der; Evaluatie van zes praktijkexperimenten; VROM, Den Haag, 1993
- Samsom/Tjeenk Willink; Handboek Ruimtelijke Ordening en Milieu (1st edition), Samsom H.D. Tjeenk Willink bv, 1997 (ISBN 90 422 01169)
- Saelens D. & Hens H.; The future for low-energy office design?, in: Proceedings International Building Physics Conference (339); FAGO, Eindhoven University of Technology, 2002 (ISBN 90 6814 112 0)
- Schuringa W.; Adviesbureau Jongen te Vlaardingen; Explanation press conference, 15 Januari 1981
- Silvester S.; Demonstratieprojecten en energiezuinige woningbouw; Erasmus Studiecentrum voor Milieukunde, 1996 (ISBN 90 71756 30 0)
- Sjoerdsma E.; Perspectieven voor lagere woonlasten; Haarlem, in: PBE, N.H. 1993
- Soest J.P. van; Integratieproject milieu en economie; Centrum voor Energiebesparing Delft, 1990
- Speth J.G.; Can the world be saved?, in: Ecological economics Vol. 1 (289-302)
- Sunikka M.; Policies and regulations for sustainable building - A comparative study of five European countries; DUP Science, 2001 (ISSN 0926 6240:19, ISBN 90 407 2266 8, NUGI 655)
- Timmeren A. van; Autonomie & Heteronomie; Eburon, Delft, 2006
- Tjallingi S.P.; De Strategie van de Twee Netwerken; RPD, The Hague, 1996
- Todd N.J. & Todd J.; From Eco-Cities to Living Machines; North Atlantic Books Berkley, California, 1993 (ISBN 1 55643 150 3)
- United Nations Population Division; World Urbanization Prospects - The 2007 Revision Population Database; UN, 2007
- Vakgroep Bouwfysica; Bouwfysica 1; Delftse Uitgevers Maatschappij, 1990 (ISBN 90 6562 048 6)
- Vale B. & Vale R.; Green Architecture: Design for an energy-conscious future; Thames and Hudson, 1991 (ISBN 0 500 27883 0)
- Vale B. & Vale R.; The New Autonomous House; Thames and Hudson, 2000 (ISBN 0 500 34176 1
- Verhoeven A.C.; Bouwfysica lecture notes; Civiele Techniek en Bouwkunde, TU Delft
- VROM; 60 dingen die u voor het milieu kunt doen (91367/a/9-91, 2991/062); Ministerie van VROM, The Hague
- VROM; Nederland 2030 – discussienota (97352/h/6-97, 15308/179), Ministerie van VROM, The Hague
- VROM; 40x intensief, innovatief, inspirerend ruimtegebruik (nominaties 2000); Ministerie van VROM, 2000 (ISBN 90 5239 170 x)
- Waard F. de; Tuinen van Overvloed; Spectrum, 1996 (ISBN 90 27 447551)
- Wackernagel & Rees W.; Our ecological footprint – Reducing Human Impact on the Earth; New Society Publishers, 1996 (ISBN 0 86571 312 x)
- Wageningen Universiteit, Het Morra Park, water als lust of last (Rapport 84); Sectie waterhuishouding, Wageningen Universiteit, 1999 (ISSN 0926 230X)
- Waterschap Salland; Waterschapshuis van Salland; waterschap Salland, 1980
- Weizsäcker E.V. von, Lovins A.B. & Lovins L.; Factor four: doubling wealth–halving resource use; Earthscan, London, 1997
- Weterings R.A.P.M. & Opschoor J.B.; De milieugebruiksruimte als uitdaging voor technologie-ontwikkeling; RMNO, Rijswijk, 1992
- Wiggers J.B.M.; Riolering wel en wee, in: Natuur en Techniek 1959, January 1991
- Wortmann E.J.S.A.; De zonneterp – een grootschalig zonproject; Innovatienetwerk, 2005

Abbreviations

BIEB	bouwen in eigen beheer ('building under one's personal control')
BNA	Bond van Nederlandse Architecten ('association of Dutch architects')
BW	Breathing Window
C-carrier	collective carrier
CDW	construction and demolition waste
CFC	chlorine-fluorine-carbonhydrade
CHP	combined heat and power
DESAR	Decentralised Sanitation and Reuse
DOSIS	Duurzame Ontwikkeling van Stad en Infrastructuur ('sustainable development of city and infrastructure')
DOSS	Duurzame Ontwikkeling van Stad en Stedenbouw ('sustainable development of city and urban planning')
DTO	Duurzame Technologische Ontwikkeling ('sustainable technological development')
EEC	European Economic Community
EPC	Energy Performance Code
EPS	Energy Performance Score
Fiwihex	fine-wire heat exchanger
GIW	Garantie Instituut Woningbouw ('warranty institute for housing')
I-car	individual car
ICT	information and communication technology
IEP	Innovation Engineering and Products
IFD	industrial, flexible, demountable
KNMI	Koninklijk Nederlands Meteorologisch Instituut ('royal Dutch meteorological institute')
MEMO	mens- en milieuvriendelijk ondernemen ('human and environment friendly enterpreneurship')
MEP	Milieu-, Energie- en Procesinnovatie ('environmental, energy and process innovation')
MTO	MilieuTechnisch Ontwerpen ('environmental design')
NAP	Nieuw Amsterdams Peil ('new Amsterdam level')
NOVEM	Nederlandse Organisatie voor Energie en Milieu ('Dutch organisation for energy and the environment')
NRC	Nieuwe Rotterdamse Courant ('new Rotterdam courier')
OPEC	Organization of the Petroleum Exporting Countries
PBE	ProjectBeheersbureau Energieonderzoek ('energy research project control office')
PPC	polypropylene copolymer
PREGO	Proefprojecten Rationeel Energiegebruik Gebouwde Omgeving ('experimental projects rational energy usage built environment')
PV	photovoltaic
PVC	polyvinyl chlorine
Rgd	Rijksgebouwendienst ('state government buildings authority')
RIVM	Rijksinstituut voor Volksgezondheid en Milieu ('state institute for public health and the environment')
SEP	Samenwerkende EnergieProductiebedrijven ('collaborating energy-producing companies')
STEG	steam engine on gas
STIC	Station for Transfer between Individual and Collective
StIR	Stimulering Intensief Ruimtegebruik ('stimulating intensive use of space')
TH Delft	Technische Hogeschool Delft, former name for the Delft University of Technology (TU Delft)
TNO	Toegepast Natuurwetenschappelijk Onderzoek ('applied physical scientific research')
TU Delft	Delft University of Technology
UN	United Nations
V4E	Vision for Energy, the producers of the Fiwihex
VIBA	Vereniging voor Integrale Bio-logische Architectuur ('society for integrated bio-logical architecture')
VINEX	Vierde Nota Ruimtelijke Ordening Extra ('fourth policy document on spatial planning extra')
VPRO	Vrijzinnig Protestantse Radio Omroep ('liberal protestant radio broadcasting company')
VROM	ministry of Volkshuisvesting, Ruimtelijke Ordening en Milieu ('housing, spatial planning and the environment')

Synopsis: events, projects and awards

1966	Founding of architects office Kristinsson, Deventer
1967	*Founding year of the Club of Rome*
1968	Dwelling Mr. and Mrs. Koster-Jongejan, Epse, using uncommon thermal insulation in the facade
1972	*"Limits to Growth", report of the Club of Rome*
1973	*First energy crisis*
1976	Competition of the Lelystad town hall design
1978	Realisation of the environmentally sound office for Twynstra Gudde management consultants, Deventer
1979	Realisation of the environmentally sound office for the Salland Water Board, Raalte
1979	*Second energy crisis*
1979	Idea sketch of energy-saving means for new dwellings, MEMO fair, Deventer
1979-1984	Solar cavity dwellings for the Stichting Zonnewoningen Leiderdorp
1980	"What will we do with fl. 10,000 extra in the housing sector?", Symposium Spijkenisse
1980	Design of the Dwelling without Central Heating, for the social housing sector
1980	Christmas card: energy atolls in the North Sea to lower the sea level in case of calamity
1981-1983	Minimum-Energy Dwellings, PREGO project, Schiedam
1981-1986	Research and product development – great influence on the building practice
1982	Project lectures on integrated design, TH Delft
1982	Commendation at the Second European Passive Solar Competition
1983	Realisation of energy storage in the underground, based on the principle of Lelystad
1984	Jón Kristinsson receives the Gulden Adelaar ('golden eagle'), Deventer award for culture and science
1987-1989	Energetic renovation of 32 tenement flats, Schiedam
1988	*Decline of the gas price: from Hfl. 2.85 to 2.01.*
1989	Nomination for the national renovation prize, for the 32 tenement flats in Schiedam
1989	Innovative design 'De Scheg' sports centre with semi-covered ice-skating rink, Deventer
1990	Realisation of the Deventer fire station with 'soil energy'
1990	Morra Park, Drachten, interdisciplinary elaboration as an exemplary plan according to to the VINEX
1990	*National Environmental Policy Plan, with an appendix on Sustainable Building*
1990	Consultants of BOOM develop the DCBA system for environmental assessment
1992	Realisation of 22 solar cavity dwellings in Morra Park, Drachten
1992	Jón Kristinsson part-time professor of Environmental Design, TU Delft
1994	DTO Workshop 'Economical Hague Office' for 2040
1994	DOSIS research TU Delft: the sustainable city backcasted from 2048
1994	Initiative for the urban edge vision of Drachten
1995	"Van blokkades naar potenties", sustainable development in three dimensions: Drachten, DOSS and DOSIS
1995	Two graduate students on future individual/collective commuter transport, TU Delft

1995		50/50 Manifestation Rotterdam, contrast propositions for a sustainable IJsselmonde
1995		*Introduction of the Dutch Energy Performance Code*
1995		*National approach plan for sustainable building by the Ministry of VROM*
1997		Winner of the national Exergy Dwelling competition
1998		Jón Kristinsson receives the Koninklijke/Shell Prize for 'sustainable development and architecture
1998		Vitruvius Prize awarded to Jón and Riet Kristinsson for sustainable and humane architecture
1999		Realisation of the sustainable fire station of Soest, with soil energy – European Glulam Award (for glued an laminated timber connections)
1999		StIR and IFD premium for Eco-living initiative 'De Kersentuin', Leidsche Rijn district, Utrecht
1999		Building trophy of the GGZ ('mental health service') for Kristinsson's work-living building for autistic personalities, Deventer
2001-2010		Development of the Breathing Window
2001		*New Energy Performance Code*
2001		Riet Kristinsson-Reitsema receives the Deventer Stadspenning ('city medal') for her special merits to the city's cultural climate and fine arts
2001		Riet Kristinsson-Reitsema withdraws from the board of Kristinsson Architects and Engineers; Daan Josée and Wim Welmer become leading in the board
2002		Exit speech of Jón Kristinsson: "Integrated design, from sun to magma"
2002		Building the ecological neighbourhood of 'De Kersentuin', Utrecht: design for life, adaptable, sustainable, water purification on personal ground, parking in parking garage, project house
2002		Realisation of sustainable houses for life, Doetinchem
2002		Realisation of 38 sustainable houses for life with various advanced heating and ventilation systems, Marrse-West, Nunspeet
2002		Development of water-filled hollow foundation piles
2002		First prize National school building competition 2002, for De Lingeborgh, Geldermalsen
2004		PLEA (Passive and Low Energy Architecture) Award presented to Riet en Jón Kristinsson at PLEA2004, Eindhoven
2006		By her Majesty's decision Jón Kristinsson becomes Ridder in de Orde van de Nederlandse Leeuw (Knight in the Order of the Dutch Lion)
2006-2012		Villa Flora, the greenest office in Europe, Venlo
2009		Andy van den Dobbelsteen becomes professor of Climate Design & Sustainability, the delayed successor of Jón Kristinsson
2009		Invited speech by Jón Kristinsson at SASBE2009 (Smart and Sustainable Built Environments), Delft
2009-2010		'Het Kievitsei' ('the Lapwing's Egg'), Sustainable World Campus, information centre at the Afsluitdijk, together with Witteveen + Bos and West 8
2009-2011		Staatsbosbeheer Boskantoor (forest office), Ugchelen. Very low temperature heating system.
2010		Jón Kristinsson is listed among the 100 most sustainable people of the Netherlands, position 61
2011		Inspired by Jón Kristinsson's work, the Stichting Integraal Duurzaam Ontwerpen (StIDO, foundation for integrated sustainable design) is founded, with as chair Dr. Jan Terlouw, successful author, former Dutch minister and ambassador for sustainable building
2011-2012		Kris Kristinsson, Jón's son, makes a trailer, promotion film and documentary (From Sun to Magma) on the vision, work and life of Jón Kristinsson – this work is supported by the StIDO and co-funded by business partners and the approximately 200 'Vrienden van Jón' (friends of Jón)

Biography of Jón Kristinsson

Jón Kristinsson was born in Reykjavík, Iceland, 6th of May 1936.

Academic career:
Jón studied architecture at the Delft University of Technology and was closely involved in establishing the Department of Industrial Design. Later he was a part-time staff member in the Building Construction Department and until 1978 a senior lecturer in the Building Physics Department. From 1992-2001 he was professor of Environmental Technology and Design at the TU Delft Faculty of Architecture.

Praxis in architecture and innovation:
Since 1966 Jón Kristinsson and his wife/colleague Riet Reitsema have headed a medium-sized architectural and engineering firm in Deventer, the Netherlands. Jón developed the concept of Integrated Design of Buildings. In 1976 he designed the integral, autarkic Municipal Office for Lelystad (not built), with the world's first season-related heat storage in wet clay soil, solar collectors in the focus of parabolic roof saucers, natural air humidification, self-regulation day lighting and controlling of the interior climate.
From 1979 to 1983 their office developed and delivered Minimum-Energy Dwellings and houses without central heating for the social sector in Schiedam, with the use of, amongst other things, passive solar energy, new thermal insulation techniques, heat recovery in small, balanced air heating units.
Over the years at TU Delft, Jón developed new concepts for the reduction of visible and invisible infrastructure of roads, transport, sewerage, drainage, gas, water, waste disposal, dismantling technology and means of communication. The ecological and financial advantages were evident.

For a long period Jón has been working on innovative high-tech decentralised ventilation in buildings, the 'Breathing Window'. The product was introduced to the market in the year 2010, but commercial obstructions have until today led to few examples of application. Jón is working on a new, further enhanced ventilation device based on the Breathing Window.

Awards:
Jón Kristinsson was the winner of the Dutch National Exergy competition in 1997 and received the Royal Dutch/Shell Award for sustainable architecture in 1998, the biennial European Glulam Award in 1999 and the PLEA Award (Passive and Low Energy Architecture) in 2004.

www.kristinsson.nl
www.breathingwindow.org

Biography of Riet Reitsema

Frederika Luidina (Riet) Reitsema was born in Beverwijk, the Netherlands, 21st of May 1936.
She studied at the Department of Architecture of the Delft University of Technology, the Netherland, from 1955 to 1965. Riet has worked at various architect's offices: Sterenberg, Ter Apel (1960), Sainsaulieu (1961) and Ducharm, Laras, Minost in Paris (1962).
Her final master's project was the design of a theatre in Groningen (1965).
After that she married Jón Kristinsson. They had four children, born in 1967, 1969, and twins in 1972.

In 1966 Riet started a medium-sized architectural and engineering firm in Deventer with her husband/colleague. They were touched by the 'Limits to Growth' report of the Club of Rome. Riet and Jón insulated their family homes far before the energy crises and designed the integral, autarkic Municipal Office for Lelystad 1976 (not built). Together they received the Vitruvius Award in 1998 for sustainable development and humane architecture, and the PLEA Award (Passive and Low Energy Architecture) in 2004.

Over the years and with Riet as editor, the Kristinsson's office published eight anniversary books, from 1971 to 2006. Based on the lectures given by her husband at Delft University of Technology, Riet also edited the Dutch book Vitale Architectuur - Integraal Ontwerpen (Vital Architecture - Integrated Design) in the year 2002.

Riet Reitsema retired in 2001 and received the Deventer Stadspenning (city medal) for her cultural merits to the city. In 2010 she established a foundation to support a movie of her husband's vision and projects of integrated sustainable design.

Biography of Andy van den Dobbelsteen

Andrew Adrianus Joannes Franciscus (Andy) van den Dobbelsteen was born in Tilburg, the Netherlands, 11th of April 1968. Andy studied at the Faculty of Civil Engineering of TU Delft, receiving his MSc degree in 1993, Jón Kristinsson being one of his supervisors. Later he completed a year of civil service at the Faculty of Architecture, with Kristinsson's chair, and continued working at TU Delft part-time until 2001. Between 1994-1996 he worked part-time with environmental architects opMAAT (Delft); 1996-2001 with NIBE (Naarden), as sustainable building consultant, head of division and quality manager.

In 2000 Andy commenced his PhD research into The Sustainable Office. Andy defended his thesis in 2004. In the period 2005-2009 he worked as assistant professor, specialising in smart & bioclimatic design and sustainable energy systems on various scales. In this period he developed, for instance, the method of Energy Potential Mapping, the New Stepped Strategy and the Rotterdam Energy Approach and Planning (REAP).

In 2009 Andy was appointed full professor of Climate Design & Sustainability, which in fact was the continuation of Jón Kristinsson's chair. He was chair to the 3rd CIB international conference on Smart and Sustainable Built Environments (SASBE2009), for which he received a commendation at the CIB World Building Congress 2010.

At the Faculty of Architecture of TU Delft Andy is currently section leader and coordinator of the faculty's Green Building Innovation research programme, as well as various interdisciplinary research projects. From 2007-2011 he also was external examiner to the MA Architecture + Urbanism course at the Manchester Metropolitan University.

Since 2001 Andy has undertaken freelance consultancy work in the area of sustainability. From 2005-2008 he was editor-in-chief of the Nieuwsbrief Duurzaam Bouwen ('sustainable building newsletter') and has since been an expert author for the twice prize-winning website www.duurzaamgebouwd.nl ('sustainably built'). He was chair to the Nationale Dubodag conference ('national day for sustainable building') and participates in research committees and competition juries. Andy continues to deliver lectures internationally.

www.ingramcontent.com/pod-product-compliance
Lightning Source LLC
Chambersburg PA
CBHW041829300426
44111CB00002B/27